Commercial Liability Risk Management and Insurance

Volume II

Commercial Liability Risk Management and Insurance

Volume II

DONALD S. MALECKI, CPCU
Editor, Property and Casualty Publications
The National Underwriter Company

JAMES H. DONALDSON, LL.B., LL.M.
of the New York and New Jersey Bar

RONALD C. HORN, Ph.D., CPCU, CLU
Professor of Insurance and Chairholder of Insurance Studies
Eastern Kentucky University

First Edition • 1978

AMERICAN INSTITUTE FOR
PROPERTY AND LIABILITY UNDERWRITERS
Providence and Sugartown Roads, Malvern, Pennsylvania 19355

Third Printing ● December 1981

Library of Congress Catalog Number   78-67497
International Standard Book Number   0-89463-006-7

Printed in the United States of America

Table of Contents

v

CHAPTER 8

Motor Vehicle Exposures

INTRODUCTION

Virtually all business firms own, lease, borrow, operate, or otherwise make use of motor vehicles that are designated for operation on the land. As a consequence, firms may suffer financial losses of great magnitude. They may be held legally liable to others, and there may also be physical damage to the vehicles themselves. This chapter will analyze the nature and scope of motor vehicle liability and physical damage loss exposures. Chapter 9 will focus on the insurance coverages and other methods by which a firm may handle the exposures it faces.

To avoid awkward repetition and grammatically questionable contrivances like "land-driven," the generic phrase "motor vehicle" will be used in this chapter to mean a vehicle that is designed for operation on the land. Other types of motor vehicles, such as aircraft and watercraft, will be discussed elsewhere.

The types of motor vehicles involved in this discussion will be those usually covered under the insurance policies issued to commercial operators of motor vehicles. Such vehicles include passenger vehicles, trucks of all kinds, buses, taxicabs, and motorcycles. In general, this chapter will deal with vehicles normally used on a highway, although a business organization can be exposed to loss through the use of motor vehicles in a variety of other ways. For example, in recent years business organizations have used various kinds of forklift trucks and other material-handling vehicles for a variety of indoor and outdoor uses, and they frequently incur losses as a result of such use. There are also many types of earthmoving and other construction equipment, such as shovels, backhoes, cranes, bulldozers, graders, rollers, and other mobile, motor-driven equipment which sometimes are operated inciden-

1

tally on a highway and which frequently are the source of losses. The liability of users of such equipment differs little, in general, from that of users of vehicles ordinarily operated on the highways. There is some difference in the types of accidents giving rise to liability, and, in many states, in the statutory regulations applicable when such vehicles are operated on a highway.

MOTOR VEHICLE LIABILITY EXPOSURES

Commercial motor vehicle liability exposures consist of the liabilities for bodily injury and property damage to which a person, corporation, partnership, joint venture, or other entity is exposed by reason of the ownership, maintenance, operation, or use of motor vehicles for commercial or business purposes. Note that this definition does not limit itself to a certain type of vehicle. Private passenger automobiles, for example, are frequently used for commercial purposes and would then fall within this definition.

It is not always easy to distinguish "motor vehicle" liability exposures from others which may overlap. True, there is an identifiable body of applicable law. It is likewise true that the insurance industry, for understandable reasons, has customarily treated motor vehicle liability insurance as a separate category. Nonetheless, the dividing lines are not always clear, especially from the viewpoint of a business firm facing a variety of overlapping exposures to loss.

Consider, for example, the firm that simultaneously faces motor vehicle, products, workers' compensation, and employers' liability exposures. For the purposes of this chapter, suffice it to say that the motor vehicle liability exposure involves the duties associated with the ownership, maintenance, or use of such vehicles for commercial purposes; it does not necessarily arise out of any business or social relationship which the firm may have with the person injured. The products liability exposure arises from the firm's duties as a seller of products, and the workers' compensation and employers' liability exposures arise from the firm's statutory and common-law duties, respectively, as an employer. Yet, it is well worth noting that motor vehicles and their component parts are themselves products, and that many motor vehicle accidents do meet the previously discussed tests of "arising out of and in the course of employment."

This portion of the chapter deals first with sources of commercial motor vehicle liability—the various legal theories that give rise to such liability, the nature and extent of activities that can create liability, the manner in which a party may be held liable for the acts or conduct of others in the use of a commercial motor vehicle, and the nature and extent of defenses available to the party against whom liability is sought. Subsequent sections deal with the liability of various members of corporations or partnerships, the rights of indemnity or contribution that one who is held liable might have against a third party or parties, liability of common carriers, exposures under no-fault laws, and the types of damages that may result from motor vehicle liability exposures.

Sources of Liability

Legal Basis Liability in tort is based upon a breach by the defendant of a duty owed to the plaintiff, which breach directly and proximately results in damage to the plaintiff. It should be pointed out that while many common-law principles, statutes, and other types of governmental regulations are applicable throughout the country, each state has a body of common law established by its court of last resort. Each state also has a body of legislative enactments which involve the various aspects of motor vehicle liability. All municipalities of significant size have ordinances controlling traffic, as well as other aspects of use of commercial vehicles, such as special ordinances dealing with cabs, buses, or trucks. There are also regulations of the Interstate Commerce Commission, as well as regulations of public utility commissions of the various states. Liability of a commercial user of motor vehicles is therefore affected by different rules or standards in different geographical areas. In a given situation, it is necessary to know and understand the applicable law.

In general, traffic laws of the jurisdiction where an accident or occurrence takes place will be applicable. There may be circumstances, however, where this will not be the case. When a claim arises as a result of a breach of an obligation created by contract, a court might well hold that the applicable law is that of the state where the contract was entered into. Interstate Commerce Commission regulations may also apply, irrespective of the state where an accident occurred. It should be understood that an accident may occur in one state and a lawsuit be instituted in another state. Under these circumstances, the court might apply the law of the state where the accident occurred, with respect to the operation or use of the motor vehicle, while applying the procedural law of the state in which the action was brought. Procedural law can frequently be a decisive factor. For example, the statute of limitations in the state where the action is brought might provide for a longer time than the statute in other states. Rules might be broader or narrower in terms of discovery permitted. Also, rules of evidence might permit or exclude testimony that is determinative of the issues in the case.

Many cases are brought in federal court. The usual basis of

jurisdiction for the federal court is "diversity of citizenship"; that is, where the plaintiff and the defendant(s) are residents of different states. Federal court rules of pleading, discovery, and evidence differ from rules applicable in many state courts (although the trend in recent years is for states to adopt rules based on the federal rules), and the differences between the federal rules and state rules can be decisive in many instances.

It is necessary in handling claims to understand and give consideration to these various different rules. However, it is not the purpose of this chapter to deal in detail with the specific rules applicable in different jurisdictions, but rather, to identify those basic principles that are common to most or all of the various jurisdictions, and to explain how and why liability can arise.

To repeat, legal liability in tort rests on breach of a duty owed by one party to another. In the absence of a duty, there can ordinarily be no liability. Even though an innocent party may be injured as a result of an accident involving a motor vehicle, there usually will be no liability if the injury was not the direct and proximate result of the breach of some duty owed to the injured party. For example, a pedestrian might be injured as a result of the operator of a truck losing control of the truck because of a defective steering mechanism, faulty brakes, or worn tires. If there were no breach of a common-law duty owed to the pedestrian, no breach of any contractual obligation assumed, and no breach of any duty created by statute or governmental regulation, there would be no liability.

Normally, the duties respecting the operation of motor vehicles arise from common law, statutes, regulations of various government boards or agencies, ordinances of municipalities, contract, or custom and usage, as described in the following subsections.

Common Law. The common law of any given state is based on prior decisions of the courts of the state. Rules change or evolve through new decisions. Seemingly inconsistent decisions in the same jurisdiction can make it difficult at times to state clearly or understand such rules. Frequently there is an occurrence which the court of last resort of the state has never had prior occasion to deal with. There are likewise some circumstances where it is necessary to attempt to predict what the court will do, and this requires an analysis of the decisions in other states and of decisions made in analogous or closely related circumstances in the state involved.

Common law is not merely what the courts have announced, then, but rather is that which a court can be reasonably expected to apply. Determination of a specific rule of common law requires retrospective study, though the task is essentially prospective in that it constitutes a prediction of how the court will rule.

The principle of negligence as the basis for liability is well established in our legal system. The basis of such liability is the duty every person owes to every other member of society to act in an ordinarily prudent manner. When a person fails to use ordinary care or prudence and injury results, liability for damages may follow. However, it is necessary that negligence, or failure to use ordinary care, be the direct and proximate cause of damages to the injured party for liability to exist. Thus, in most jurisdictions a party witnessing an accident might suffer a heart attack from stress and excitement without being permitted recovery from the party responsible for the accident, since negligence in the operation of the motor vehicle is only a remote cause of the heart attack.

In some cases it has been held that a party who has negligently loaded a truck will not be responsible for injuries and damages resulting from the improper load if another party had the opportunity and the duty to correct the improper loading and failed to do so. Under such circumstances, it has been said that the negligence of the conscious intervening agency acted to break the chain of causation between the party originally negligent and the ultimate injury.

The principle of proximate cause has traditionally been troublesome to law students, lawyers, legal writers, and courts. Decisions on issues of proximate cause show considerable inconsistency among the various jurisdictions, and frequently show inconsistency within a jurisdiction. However, the basic rule is universally recognized—negligence must be the direct and proximate cause of an injury before liability can accrue. Although the application of the rule to a given set of facts can be difficult, the fundamental rule holds true.

Statutes. A duty, the breach of which can be the basis for liability, can also be created by state or federal statute. All states have statutes controlling the operation of motor vehicles. These may include rules relating to speed, right of way, the erection and observance of traffic control signs and signals, as well as the regulation of all other aspects of the operation of motor vehicles on the highways and streets. Statutes also control parking or stopping on highways or streets. The violation of such a statute can give rise to liability.

Statutes may also create duties in other aspects of the maintenance and use of motor vehicles. For example, most states have some statutes dealing with the equipment on motor vehicles such as brakes, headlights, and taillights. Many states have statutes dealing with the size and weight of trucks. A breach of these obligations can give rise to liability. For instance, if the overloading of a truck results in injury to another because of failure of brakes, drive shaft, tires, or transmission of the truck, the violation of the statute respecting weight can be the basis for holding the operator liable.

Many states hold that the violation of a statute that provides for a specific rule of conduct is "negligence per se." This means that if such a statute is violated, the party violating the statute is legally negligent, and it is not necessary to inquire into the question of whether or not that party exercised ordinary care. This rule does not pertain when the statute merely provides a general rule, rather than a specific rule of conduct. If a statute prohibits entering an intersection when faced with a red light, the failure to obey that statute is negligence as a matter of law. When a statute provides that one may enter an intersection on an amber light if caution is used, a violation of such a statute will not be negligence per se. Likewise, a statute prohibiting the operator of a motor vehicle from changing lanes, except when the change can be made with safety to other users of the highway, is a general, rather than a specific provision; hence, a violation of such a statute is not negligence as a matter of law.

The same motor vehicle accident can raise issues respecting both common-law obligations and statutory obligations. The operator of a vehicle might be charged simultaneously (by a plaintiff) with exceeding the speed limit (a statutory violation) and failure to keep a proper lookout (a common-law violation).

While the statutes governing motor vehicles may be similar in many states, there are significant differences. In a given circumstance, it is necessary to know and apply the statutes of the state in which the incident that gave rise to the claim of liability arose.

Regulations. In recent years, administrative law has become one of the most rapidly developing fields of law. Such administrative rules and regulations result from decisions by legislative bodies to create administrative boards or agencies and empower such boards or agencies to establish, publish, and enforce rules and regulations. When such a board or agency does establish rules and regulations without exceeding the authority delegated to it by the legislature, such rules and regulations have the force of law. With respect to the operators of commercial motor vehicles, the most significant regulatory bodies are the Interstate Commerce Commission (ICC) and the public utility commissions of the various states.

Trucking firms operating in interstate commerce are licensed by the ICC. Many of the requirements of the ICC, such as those requiring filing of proof of insurance, are not those which can give rise to liability to injured parties. However, ICC rules extend to such things as the number of hours a driver may drive in any twenty-four-hour period, the amount of rest the driver must have between trips, physical requirements for driving trucks in interstate commerce, and various regulations respecting equipment. Violations of such regulations can be negligence. If the violations directly and proximately result in injury, liability can be incurred.

State public utility commissions similarly regulate the operation of commercial vehicles with a strong emphasis on the equipment. Width, height, length, weight, and load are usually controlled. Again, when violations of such regulations directly and proximately result in injuries, liability can be incurred.

The duties of business organizations operating commercial motor vehicles can also be affected significantly by rules and regulations of agencies other than the Interstate Commerce Commission and the public utilities commissions. Trucking companies, in loading and unloading, can be subjected to the application of a number of rules and regulations established by boards, both state and federal, which control safety in factories, workshops, and other places of employment. In order to transport certain types of goods, a trucking company might also be required to obtain special permits and subject itself to further rules and regulations. Rapidly developing are agencies devoted to environmental protection, with rules and regulations which, while primarily designed to protect the environment, can conceivably be the basis for a claim of liability.

A complete exposition of administrative law affecting the operation of commercial motor vehicles is not practical here, but its significance and increasing importance should be understood.

Ordinances. An ordinance is a legislative enactment by a municipality, and it may create a duty that forms the basis for liability. Generally, a municipality will pass ordinances controlling traffic and parking. Many such ordinances merely adopt the provisions of statutes of the state in which the municipality is located. Frequently there will be additional ordinances covering parking or other problems unique to the municipality involved.

Quite commonly, municipalities will control by ordinance the loading and unloading of trucks. The typical ordinance applies to the place(s) and time(s) when loading and unloading will be permitted. Local regulations may reduce speed limits in certain areas, prohibit left turns, prohibit commercial vehicles from operating on certain designated streets or roadways, or control the size, weight, and load of equipment using the city streets. Municipalities may also require vehicles using city streets to undergo periodic safety inspections.

There are usually licensing requirements for car rental agencies, taxicabs and taxicab drivers, and buses and bus drivers. A license to operate a taxicab or bus may require the periodic physical examination of the driver. Commonly, bus stops are designated by the municipality, and buses are forbidden to take on or discharge passengers at other locations. Bus routes and scheduling are frequently provided for and/or approved.

Frequently, a private bus company has a franchise negotiated with the city, which franchise has been approved by ordinance and has the force and effect of law. It may provide for the location of bus stops, routes, schedules, intersections where certain turns are required or prohibited, and many other details which must be rigidly adhered to by the bus company.

Contracts. Tort liability requires the breach of a duty. As discussed in Chapter 5, duties may arise out of a contract or agreement, and breach of such contractual obligations may constitute a tort. This becomes important, because a plaintiff's road to recovery in tort is often easier if it is possible to show a breach of an obligation assumed by express or implied contract; this relieves the plaintiff of the burden of proving breach of a statute, regulation, or ordinance.

Contractual relationships are frequently found in connection with motor vehicle operations. For instance, the basis of the relationship between a common carrier and passengers is primarily contractual, and obligations upon which tort liability is based are often found to be expressed or implied in the contract of carriage.

A trucking company may also undertake contractual obligations, which might be the basis for liability in tort, for injury occasioned at or near premises where cargo is to be loaded or unloaded. A trucking company might contract to furnish a "clean" tank truck and be held liable for injuries if an explosion occurs as a result of the presence of explosive vapors in the tank truck. If a trucking company agrees to spot a trailer on the premises of a customer, the terms of that agreement create obligations that expose the trucking company to liability to the customer's employees who may be injured while loading or working on or in the trailer.

A lessor of a truck and driver who relinquishes complete control to the lessee and who would not normally be liable for the operation of the truck might nevertheless be held liable if contractual liability is involved. For example, suppose a lessor contracted to furnish a skilled driver and roadworthy equipment, and suppose the driver was actually unskilled or the equipment unroadworthy. The lessor might be held liable even in the absence of any evidence of negligence on the part of the lessor.

Customs and Usage. Perhaps it would not be technically correct to state that the following of a particular custom or usage can, in itself, create duties, the breach of which will give rise to liability. However, evidence of custom and usage is frequently of decisive importance in assessing liability.

The following of a particular custom or usage can be considered evidence of an implied contract giving rise to certain duties or obligations. Thus, a worker injured while unloading plate glass in a manner differing from long-established custom might recover from the trucking company even if the new and different method of loading was in no way less safe.

Deviation from the path customarily used by trucks operating on a construction site can also form the basis of liability. In fact, evidence of the usual and customary method of doing a particular thing in any industry, including the operation of trucks, buses, and taxicabs, is frequently used to establish the standard of care followed by the ordinarily prudent operator. A deviation from that custom or standard can be held to constitute negligence.

Firms operating commercial motor vehicles frequently promulgate written safety rules for the guidance of drivers. If there is a violation of such a safety code and injury to another results, the safety code will normally be admitted in evidence as a recognition by the company of the standard which ought to be followed by the ordinarily careful and prudent driver.

It has been said that custom and usage is never controlling. A defendant is not immune from liability upon proof that his or her conduct was that which was usually and customarily followed in the industry or trade, nor is a defendant always liable to respond in damages upon proof that his or her conduct deviated from that usually and customarily followed. Custom and usage is normally evidentiary, constituting some evidence of the appropriate or proper standard of care. A jury might accept or reject the evidence. Nonetheless, deviation from a well-established custom or practice will generally result in a finding of negligence.

Activity Involved Four types of activity that might give rise to motor vehicle liability exposures have been identified—ownership, operation, maintenance, and use. Liability arising out of these types of activity will be discussed in the following subsections.

Ownership. Mere legal ownership of a motor vehicle is generally not sufficient in and of itself to create liability on the part of the owner for the negligent operation of the vehicle. When the owner of a truck lends it to another to be used for the other's own purposes, with no control over the operation of the truck retained by the owner, the truck's negligent operation will not normally create liability on the part of the owner.

Except where modified by legislation or administrative rules or regulations, the principles applicable to the liability of the owner of a motor vehicle are those applicable to the use of any other instrumentality not inherently dangerous.

Motor vehicles are not considered inherently dangerous; that is, they are not such dangerous instrumentalities as to render their owners liable for injury resulting from their operation unless they are negligently operated by the owner (or by some person for whose actions the owner is legally responsible under statute or common law). Thus, the rules requiring extra care in the use and control of instrumentalities that are dangerous per se are not applicable to motor vehicles.

While there are a number of ways in which the owner of a vehicle might be held responsible for its operation by another, it is important to understand that such liability is not based on bare legal title or ownership, at least under common law. Some states have, however, modified this rule by statute.

Operation. The negligent operation of a motor vehicle will, of course, give rise to liability to one injured as a result of such negligence. Liability in such cases arises not from the ownership but by reason of the negligent operation. The parties liable are the negligent operator and all others who may be legally responsible for his or her conduct.

Maintenance. Negligent maintenance of a commercial motor vehicle is frequently the basis of liability. The party whose negligence created the danger from which injury resulted is liable, along with those responsible for the conduct of such person. Again, ownership is not the controlling factor. Indeed, a firm using commercial vehicles may well have an entire fleet of vehicles all of which are leased and none of which is owned, but if the firm is negligent in failing to maintain a vehicle properly, it may be held liable. Thus, if the operator of a fleet of leased vehicles causes injury to another because of the operator's failure to properly maintain brakes, steering apparatus, tires, or wheels, the liability will be that of the firm operating the vehicles rather than the vehicle owner's.

Since liability in tort arises from a breach of a legally recognized duty, the person breaching such duty and also those responsible for his or her conduct will be held liable. The duty to maintain motor vehicles in safe operating condition can be found in common-law principles of negligence and ordinary care or can be created by legislative enactment, administrative rules and regulations, or contract.

Some legislative enactments impose upon the owner a nondelegable duty to maintain the vehicle. Under this kind of statute, the owner of a vehicle can be held liable even in the absence of any negligence on his or her part and even if he or she was not operating the vehicle. However, the basis of liability in such a case would not be mere legal ownership, but, rather, failure to fulfill the maintenance duty created by statute.

Use Other Than Operation on Streets or Highways. "Use" of a commercial motor vehicle includes more than its operation on the public streets or highways. As pointed out earlier, trucking companies might spot trailers to be loaded or unloaded by employees of the customer on the premises of the customer, and this use can create liability in a variety of ways. Furthermore, trucks operated on construction sites are frequently involved in accidents that give rise to liability.

Even a parked vehicle can be involved in occurrences that may create liability. Those states that recognize the so-called "attractive nuisance doctrine" may hold the owner and operator of a parked commercial motor vehicle liable if young children injure themselves or others by tampering with the vehicle and the person leaving the unattended vehicle should have anticipated this possibility.

When a thief negligently operates a stolen vehicle and injures another, some states will hold the owner of the stolen vehicle liable because he or she did not take proper measures to prevent or avoid theft. Other jurisdictions will hold that the owner's negligence under such circumstances is not the proximate cause of the ultimate injury.

In identifying loss exposures, it is important to remember that a motor vehicle can perform a number of functions other than transportation over public roads. It can be a portable warehouse, a display room to which the public is invited, or a cage for animals or livestock. It can serve any purpose for which a movable building is suitable. It can have mounted on it a variety of equipment such as winches, lifts, hoists, booms, or blades. Liability may arise out of any of these uses.

Liability for Operation by Others It is obvious that an individual may become liable for damages caused by a motor vehicle being operated by that individual. Less obvious are various other relationships that may give rise to liability arising out of the use of a motor vehicle, as discussed in the following subsections.

Employer-Employee. An employer may be held liable for injuries and damages that result from the negligence of its employee while acting within the scope of employment. To review this principle, which has obvious application to the operation and use of commercial motor vehicles, the liability of the employer does not arise by reason of the employer's ownership of a vehicle but, rather, by reason of the employer's responsibility for the employee as long as that employee is acting within the scope of employment. However, for tort liability purposes, it is important to distinguish between the employer-employee relationship (historically referred to in the common law as the "master-servant" relationship) and the relationship that results from the hiring of an independent contractor.

The employer's liability for employees' conduct arises from the control that the employer has the right and duty to exercise over employees. The employer has the right to hire or fire employees and to tell them when, where, and how to perform their employment obligations.

The relationship between an employer and an independent contractor arises, on the other hand, when there is a contract that merely provides for the accomplishment of a certain end or objective. An independent contractor has control over the method employed to achieve the desired end. One who contracts with an independent contractor is generally not responsible for the negligence of the independent contractor.

It is not always easy to distinguish between an employee and an independent contractor. Various evidentiary factors, such as method of payment, right to select tools and equipment, and right to employ others or control of hours of work, may be considered. The ultimate test, however, is the right of the employer to control the conduct of the other.

The aforementioned issues can arise with respect to commercial motor vehicles in many ways. For example, taxicab companies often contract with drivers who own their own taxicabs and whose income is derived from a division of the fares. A taxicab company will normally hire a dispatcher who will direct the drivers to at least a portion of the customers they serve, and all of the drivers will normally operate under the name of the taxicab company.

Trucking companies frequently contract with drivers who own their own rigs and who are paid on the basis of trips and loads they handle. The driver may hire his or her own backup driver. The driver will be instructed only as to where to pick up a load and where and when to make delivery. Such an arrangement can exist in long-distance trips, interstate trucking, or in local hauling. It is also common for a newspaper publisher to have contractual relations with persons who deliver newspapers with their own trucks.

In cases like these, many decisions hold the relationship of the driver to be that of an employee, whereas many others say he or she is an independent contractor. The unique facts of each case will control. Determination as to whether a driver will be considered an employee or an independent contractor requires not only an analysis of all of the facts and details involved in the case but also other decisions of the courts of the state involved.

Assuming that the driver of a vehicle is deemed to be an employee, his or her employer will still not be liable unless the employee was acting within the scope of employment at the time of negligent conduct.

However, the fact that an employee violated an employer's instructions to operate a vehicle carefully and in observance of all traffic laws will not prevent the employer from being liable if there is an accident.

When an employee deviates from the scope of employment, the employer will not normally be liable. Thus, if a truck driver deviates from a prescribed route in order to drive home for lunch, the employer will not be responsible for an accident that occurs while the driver is on the way home. There is a division of authority as to whether or not the employer might be liable after the employee has finished lunch and is heading back toward the ordinary route.

The mere fact that an employer consents to an employee's use of the employer's motor vehicle does not necessarily render the employer responsible for the employee's negligence. A salesperson or truck driver may be permitted to take a vehicle home overnight and use the vehicle for personal errands, but the employer will normally not be responsible for the negligence of the employee during such personal use.

However, in some cases an employee may take the vehicle home to serve the purposes of the employer because the employer does not have garage facilities. In such cases the employer may be held liable for an accident that occurs while the employee is either driving home or to work. The same rule has been applied in some cases where the employee is permitted to take the vehicle home in order to serve some other purpose of the employer. For example, it might be applied to a situation in which a sales representative does not report to the office in the morning but goes immediately from his or her home to a customer's place of business. The rule might also be applied to a construction worker who drives home a truck loaded with tools and on the following morning drives the truck to a construction site.

The question of the employer's liability can also arise when an employee unlawfully assaults someone. In some cases, where the assault arose in some manner directly and intimately involved with the employer's business, such as the enforcement of the employer's rules, the employer has been found to be liable. Generally, however, the employer will not be liable for an employee's act of assault. It should be kept in mind that, if an employer directs an employee to commit a wrongful act, the employer will be liable for the results of such act. If an employer instructs his truck driver to drive over someone's premises or instructs his employee to eject another person from the employer's premises, the employer will be liable for damages resulting from the employee's wrongful act.

Loaned Employee. Commercial motor vehicle owners frequently furnish drivers for vehicles they lease to others. If complete control over the conduct of the driver is relinquished by the driver's general employer, the lessee, rather than the owner, will be liable for the negligence of the driver.

Questions involving loaned employees can arise in a variety of circumstances. A person who owns a fleet of dump trucks and employs drivers may lease trucks and drivers to a contractor involved in construction. The lease may be on an hourly basis, a day-to-day basis, or a week-to-week basis. Normally, the lessee pays a stipulated sum to the owner, without any breakdown as to an amount for the vehicle and an amount for the driver. The driver's wages are paid by the owner.

In such cases, courts will look to various factors. In some cases, it has been held that the test is whether the lessee has the right to reject the driver if found to be unsuitable, or whether the lessee is required to accept the driver and the equipment as a unit. Some decisions have emphasized the question of whether or not the lessee merely advises the driver where and when to pick up and deliver loads, or has the right to control every aspect of the driver's performance, including the route taken, speed driven, and other aspects of operating the equipment.

As in the situation where the issue is whether a driver is an employee or an independent contractor, the facts of each case must be fully analyzed in view of the pertinent decisions of the courts of the state involved. In general, liability will result from control, and the party having control of the driver will be called on to respond for damages.

It might seem that these decisions regarding loaned employees could be used to establish a defense on the part of the lessor. Actually, these principles have more often been used to find liability on the part of the lessee than to find the lessor free of liability. In practice, a plaintiff will normally recover against either party on proof of any significant degree of control. A showing of substantial or even greater control on the part of the other will not necessarily constitute a defense. For instance, a dump truck owner who leases a truck with a driver may be held to have retained sufficient control to be liable for injuries resulting from negligent operation by the driver, even when there might be sufficient evidence of control by the lessee to support liability on the part of the lessee.

Statute, Regulation, or Ordinance. In some states the owner of a motor vehicle is, by statute, liable for injuries resulting from the negligent use of the motor vehicle, whether or not the owner would be liable under principles of common law. In states having such a statute, of course, mere legal ownership of a vehicle is sufficient to fasten liability on the owner.

It should be noted, however, that such liability does not replace other liabilities. The negligent operator of a vehicle personally will be liable to an injured party, as will the other persons responsible for the conduct of the operator (such as the operator's employer).

It should also be noted that the statutes creating liability on the part of an owner ordinarily create such liability only when the vehicle is used with permission of the owner. However, it is not necessary that there be express permission. Permission may be implied in some circumstances, such as a situation where it is common practice for employees to borrow an employer's vehicle to go to lunch or run personal errands. The fact that the employer had knowledge of the practice, and failed to put a stop to it, can constitute an implied permission.

While there are decisions holding an owner liable for the negligent operation of a vehicle by a thief, when the owner left the keys in a vehicle, such liability is based upon the negligence of the owner in leaving the keys in the automobile, rather than on the fact of ownership.

Commercial Name on Vehicle. When a commercial vehicle is negligently operated so as to cause injury, the business organization whose name appears on the vehicle may be held liable even in the absence of any other evidence that the operator of the vehicle was an employee of the business organization and was acting within the scope of his or her employment. Some courts have adopted the reasoning that the name on the truck constitutes some evidence that the truck was being operated in the employment of the business organization, while other decisions have been based on considerations of public policy. Still other courts have restricted the application of the rule to situations where the accident occurred at a location along a regularly established route of the company whose name was on the vehicle or to situations where it could be shown that vehicles of the company whose name was on the vehicle often traveled near the location of the accident.

It is not uncommon for holders of ICC and public utilities commission permits to enter into contractual arrangements with owner-operators of trucks for the regular and/or exclusive use of the truck and owner-operator. The driver of the truck operates under the permit of the trucking company and frequently has the trucking company's name painted on the truck. Under such circumstances, a number of cases have held that the trucking company is liable for the negligent operation of the vehicle even though in every other respect the owner-operator is an independent contractor, not an employee of the trucking company.

Furnishing Defective Vehicles. One who negligently furnishes a defective vehicle to another may be held liable to a person injured as a direct and proximate result of the defect. Liability under such circumstances does not stem from ownership of the vehicle. Neither does it make any substantial difference whether the negligent party sold the vehicle, leased it, bailed it, or simply loaned it for no consideration.

Liability in such circumstances stems from negligence in placing a dangerously defective motor vehicle in the hands of another under circumstances where, even in the exercise of ordinary care, the use of the vehicle with resulting injury is foreseeable. Sales agencies and leasing agencies can be subjected to liability in this fashion.

Some decisions have recognized a distinction in the case of used vehicles sold "as is," on the theory that the buyer understands (or can be expected to understand) that the used vehicle has not been inspected for defects and should be so inspected by the buyer before being put into use. In such cases, the courts have sometimes held that the chain of causation between any negligence on the part of the seller and the ultimate injury was broken by the negligence of the purchaser, who had an obligation to inspect and repair.

Negligent Entrustment. The owner or any other party having control of a motor vehicle may be liable when he or she entrusts the motor vehicle to one who is either unskilled in its operation or otherwise incompetent to operate it. Liability does not arise out of the relationship of the parties but from the act of entrustment of the motor vehicle with permission to operate it to one whose incompetency, inexperience, or recklessness is known or should have been known to the party entrusting the motor vehicle. The driver need not be an employee of the owner acting within the scope of the owner's employment.

It has also been held that the negligence of an incompetent driver to whom the vehicle is entrusted is not an intervening cause that will break the chain of causation between the negligence in entrusting the vehicle and the injury. Also, the responsibility of the party entrusting the vehicle may follow the continued operation of the vehicle even when it is operated beyond the scope of the permission granted. However, in order to establish liability, it is necessary that the party entrusting the vehicle to the incompetent driver have knowledge of the driver's incompetence, inexperience, or reckless tendency as an operator, or at least that the entrusting party should have, in exercising ordinary care, known of such fact. A leasing agency may be held liable under this theory. In fact, liability of a leasing agency might be established by the mere failure to inquire as to the qualifications, competency, or sobriety of the lessee.

In some areas there are legislative requirements that an automobile-leasing agency require proof of a driver's license before leasing a vehicle. Entrustment of a vehicle to an unlicensed driver has sometimes been held to be a proper basis for liability, although other jurisdictions have held that mere failure to own a valid driver's license is not, in itself, sufficient to establish that a person is not qualified to operate a motor vehicle properly and safely. On the other hand, it has been held that the entrustment of a motor vehicle to a minor under the age required by law to obtain a driver's license can be the basis of liability, although this circumstance will not normally occur with respect to commercial motor vehicles. It should also be pointed out that an injured party might seek to establish liability on the basis of negligent entrustment, while at the same time pursuing the theory that the driver was an employee of the defendant acting within the scope of the defendant's employment. This can be a device through which a plaintiff may attempt to put before the jury inflammatory evidence which otherwise might not be admissible, such as other accidents in which the driver was involved, driver's record of traffic convictions, or sobriety on occasions other than at the time of the accident in question.

Contract. A party may contractually assume liability for the negligent operation of a motor vehicle by others. A typical situation arises in the "hold harmless" agreement, by which one contracting party agrees to protect the other from liability. Such contracts generally have been held valid, and not against public policy, even when they protect the contracting party from personal negligence.

Thus, if a customer of a trucking company agrees to hold the trucking company harmless from liability incurred in carrying out the contract, the customer may be held liable for injuries resulting from negligent operation by a truck driver. Conversely, the trucking company might be held liable for negligence on the part of the customer's employees in loading the truck, if the contract so provides. A trucking company might also be held liable for negligent operation by a driver where otherwise the loaned employee situation might furnish a defense, if the terms of the contract so provide, or where the contract calls for providing a competent driver, and the driver is not qualified to operate the equipment.

Ordinarily, a contract expressly assuming the liability of another must be in writing. But an agreement to furnish a competent driver may be oral, or even may be implied from the circumstances surrounding the transaction.

Leased Vehicles. As previously discussed, the owner of a leased vehicle is not normally liable for the negligence of the lessee or the lessee's employees in the operation of the vehicle. There are, however, other ways in which liability can accrue to the owner. If the owner leases a vehicle that is defective at the time of the lease, either as a result of negligent repair of the vehicle or negligent failure to inspect the vehicle, and if an innocent third party is injured as a direct and proximate result of such defect, the owner can be liable even though he or she exercises no control over the vehicle at the time the accident occurs. This liability does not arise from the operation of the vehicle.

Even the question of whether or not the vehicle was negligently operated has no bearing on the owner's liability. The liability to the injured party accrues as the result of the prior negligence of the owner in maintenance of the vehicle.

It has also been noted that the owner of a leased vehicle who also leases an operator with the vehicle may be held responsible to a third party for injuries that occur while a vehicle is being operated on behalf of the lessee. The owner of a leased commercial motor vehicle might also be held liable for injury occurring as a result of the negligent operation of the vehicle during the period of the lease, where the lessor's name is prominently displayed on the vehicle. The effect of displaying the name of a business organization on a commercial motor vehicle has been discussed earlier.

The situation can also arise where taxicab companies own their vehicles, but lease the vehicles to drivers who are in fact independent contractors. Even when the drivers are in fact independent contractors, rather than employees, and they function independent of effective control by the company, the company will ordinarily be held liable for their negligent operation of the vehicle when they act under the name of the company.

Agency by Estoppel or Apparent Agency. It is a well-established rule of the law of agency that when a party by his or her conduct leads another to rely upon the apparent authority of an agent to act in his or her behalf, that party is estopped or prohibited by law from denying the authority of the agent to so act. While this rule has its principal application in the field of contracts, it has been applied to liability arising from tort. For example, suppose a customer is injured in a department store as a result of the negligent maintenance of a particular department. Ordinarily the store cannot successfully defend itself by showing that the department involved was operated by an independent contractor who, under the terms of a contract not known to or disclosed to the customer, assumed the exclusive obligation to maintain the department.

This principle can also be applied to circumstances involving commercial motor vehicles, such as a taxicab company leasing taxicabs to independent contractor drivers. Another illustrative situation is the bus company that accepts a charter which it is not equipped or staffed to handle itself and then subcontracts with another bus company to handle the charter. When an accident occurs as a result of the negligence of the bus operator, the passengers who relied upon the fact that they were dealing with the original bus company might well recover from the original bus company. Other persons injured in the accident in other vehicles might not be able to establish such liability, since they did not rely in any manner on the bus company that originally accepted the charter.

Normally, for liability to be established on the basis of agency by estoppel or apparent agency, it is necessary that the defendant-employer lead the injured party to believe, and to rely on the belief, that the person negligently causing injury is an agent or employee acting within the scope of his or her agency or employment. The same principle applies when the negligent person is in fact an employee but at the time of negligent conduct is exceeding his or her actual authority. If the employer has led the injured party to act on the belief that the employee was within his or her authority, the employer may be held liable.

Defenses

Despite the many factors that lead to legal liability for motor vehicle occurrences, there are many defenses that may serve to relieve a party of liability. The defenses of contributory negligence or comparative negligence, assumption of risk, intervening agencies, governmental and family immunity, and other statutory defenses will be discussed in the following subsections.

Contributory Negligence or Comparative Negligence The common-law rule is that there can be no recovery for injuries when it appears that the person injured was guilty of *contributory negligence* (i.e., when the injury was the result of the united, mutual, concurring, and contemporaneous negligence of the parties to the transaction). This rule is fully applicable to commercial motor vehicle cases. Thus, in an action founded upon a collision between a commercial motor vehicle and another vehicle, no recovery can be had for injuries sustained as a result of the defendant's negligence if the plaintiff's own negligence directly contributed to the injuries, except in jurisdictions where the contributory negligence defense has been abolished or modified by statute or judicial revision.

The early common law, in determining responsibility for an injury, took no account of the degree to which either of the parties could be shown to have been responsible for the injury. A plaintiff who could be said to have been at fault in any degree would be barred from recovery. Many jurisdictions approved this principle, and charged the jury to the effect that the plaintiff was barred from recovery if his or her own negligence directly contributed in the "slightest degree." The modern trend has been to disapprove of so stringent a rule. Further, some jurisdictions have, by legislation, adopted a rule of *comparative negligence*.

Comparative negligence requires the jury to determine the *degree* to which the plaintiff's negligence contributed to the injury. In some jurisdictions, the plaintiff will be permitted to recover that portion of damages that are proportionate to the defendant's negligence, even where his or her own negligence is greater than that of the defendant. In other jurisdictions, the plaintiff is denied recovery if his or her negligence is greater than the defendant's, and in still others, he or she is denied recovery if his or her negligence is equal to that of the defendant.

Typical of a situation where the comparative negligence rule might come into play is one in which a defendant turns left in front of an oncoming vehicle which is being operated at a high rate of speed. Under the common-law rule (contributory negligence), if the speed contributed to the cause of the accident, the operator of the speeding automobile could not recover any portion of damages. Under a comparative negligence rule, a jury might determine that his or her negligence contributed to the accident to the extent of 25 percent, and he or she would therefore be entitled to recover 75 percent of the damages from the operator of the vehicle which turned left in front of him or her.

It should also be noted that, even in jurisdictions which do not have a comparative negligence rule, it is not uncommon for juries to render a verdict in favor of a negligent plaintiff; however, the award for damages will be somewhat smaller than if they felt that the plaintiff had been blameless. This is especially true in the case of commercial motor vehicles in which a wealthy defendant is involved.

It is also important to understand that the defense of contributory negligence is not so absolute as to apply in every case where the plaintiff is negligent. In general, contributory negligence does not constitute a defense when it can be shown that the defendant acted willfully, wantonly, or recklessly, and this principle has been applied to motor vehicle cases. It has been held, for instance, that when the operator of a large truck leaves it parked upon a high-speed, limited-access highway at night for a substantial period of time with no lights or flares, and when the operator makes no effort to either remove the truck or give warning to motorists, such conduct might constitute willful or wanton misconduct. Thus, the negligence of the operator of a motor vehicle which collides with the stopped truck does not bar recovery for the motorist's injuries. However, even when the defendant is chargeable with willful or wanton misconduct, an injured party might be barred from recovery if his or her own conduct constituted willful or wanton misconduct.

The rule of contributory negligence also might not be applicable in the case of an emergency faced by a plaintiff when the emergency was not one of the plaintiff's own making. The emergency and the apparent danger associated with it must be taken into consideration in determining the question of contributory negligence. A simple error in judgment under emergency circumstances does not necessarily constitute contributory negligence.

It should be pointed out that the requirement of proximate cause also applies to contributory negligence. In order for the contributory negligence of a plaintiff to bar his or her recovery, the plaintiff's negligence must be a direct and proximate cause. This principle is illustrated by the difficulty that has been experienced in successfully defending cases where an injured plaintiff failed to utilize a seatbelt installed in his or her vehicle. While some jurisdictions have recognized that there can be contributory negligence under such circumstances, proof is nonetheless required that, but for the plaintiff's negligence in failing to wear the seatbelt, the injury would not have occurred. It is difficult to establish that a fracture of a foot or leg, or an injury to an arm or hand, or even a facial injury occasioned by striking a steering wheel would have been prevented by the use of a seatbelt.

When applicable, the so-called *last clear chance doctrine* will also prevent the negligence of a plaintiff from barring the plaintiff's recovery. Suppose a plaintiff negligently gets into an inextricable position of peril. That plaintiff's own negligence will not bar recovery if the proximate cause of his or her injury was the failure of the defendant to reasonably exercise his or her last clear chance to avoid injury after he or she became aware or should have become aware of the plaintiff's perilous position. This doctrine applies when both parties are negligent but the plaintiff has ceased to be negligent. The rule presupposes antecedent fault or negligence on the part of the plaintiff. It does not apply when the negligence of the plaintiff continues so as to be concurring negligence with that of the defendant. Continuing or concurring negligence on the part of the plaintiff or contemporaneous negligence by both parties will prevent the application of the doctrine.

For the plaintiff to bring himself or herself within the operation of the last clear chance rule, he or she must establish that, while personal negligence may have placed him or her in a position of danger, all negligence on his or her part ceased for a sufficient time prior to the accident to have enabled the defendant, in the exercise of ordinary care, to avoid the accident.

The application of the last clear chance doctrine could arise in a situation where the driver of an automobile disobeys a stop sign and collides with another automobile, as a result of which the driver is thrown from his or her own vehicle onto the roadway. If injured so as to prevent getting out of the roadway, he or she might recover from the operator of a third vehicle which negligently strikes him or her. Although negligence placed the driver in the position of peril, his or her negligence had come to a stop, and he or she was unable to become extricated from the position of peril.

Some jurisdictions have further limited the application of the doctrine of last clear chance to situations in which the defendant had actual knowledge of the presence of the plaintiff in a position of peril. They have refused to apply the doctrine under circumstances in which the defendant merely failed to use ordinary care to discover the dangerous position of the plaintiff.

With respect to the defense of contributory negligence, it should finally be noted that different rules apply to an injured minor. Different states recognize different ages as preventing the application of the rule of contributory negligence. Normally there will be one age below which a child cannot be contributorily negligent (usually seven), and another age limit (usually fourteen) below which a child is required to use only that degree of care that is normally exercised by children of his or her own age. Care owed by a minor is only that normally used by a reasonably intelligent minor of the same age, education, and training.

Assumption of Risk Under the assumption of risk defense, a person is precluded from recovery, if with knowledge of a danger, he or she nonetheless voluntarily exposes himself or herself to the risk of injury. This rule does have application to cases involving commercial motor vehicles. Thus, suppose a truck driver negligently parks a truck at a loading dock and leaves a space between the rear of the truck and the loading dock. A worker loading the truck is aware of the space, attempts to step over it, and misjudges the space, thereby falling. Since the injured party will be held to have assumed the risk, recovery will be precluded.

Although the defenses of contributory negligence and assumption of risk differ, they may be applicable to the same set of facts. Contributory negligence is based upon the failure of a plaintiff to exercise ordinary care to avoid injury; it is directed toward the plaintiff's conduct. The defense of assumption of risk is based upon the plaintiff's voluntary and conscious assumption of a known risk; it is therefore directed toward his or her mental state. A passenger who steps off a bus into a hole in the roadway might be considered to have been contributorily negligent if he or she failed to look before stepping down. Yet, the passenger might be held to have assumed the risk if he or she saw the hole and attempted to step over it.

In some jurisdictions, it has been held that the defense of assumption of risk will not be applicable, even though a plaintiff voluntarily exposes himself or herself to a known danger, where the conduct of the defendant has placed the plaintiff in a position where he or she has no practical choice but to become exposed to the risk. This principle can have application to a passenger in a bus who is faced with no method of leaving the bus other than by stepping on a surface, either on a portion of the bus or on the ground outside, which is dangerous by reason of moisture, ice or snow, or foreign substances.

Intervening Agencies Many jurisdictions recognize the principle that a defendant will not be liable for negligence when it creates a dangerous condition if it can be shown that the dangerous condition could or should have been corrected by a conscious, intervening agency that had knowledge of the dangerous condition and a duty to correct it. One illustrative case involved a truck which had been negligently loaded. A part of the load fell off of the truck and caused injury. The party who was negligent in loading the truck was not held liable to the injured party because the truck driver, after learning of the improper loading, failed to take steps to correct it, and instead drove the truck with the improper and dangerous load.

It has also been held, in the case of a trucking company that furnished a tank truck containing explosive vapors, that the trucking company was not liable for injuries occasioned by reason of an explosion. The company to whom the truck was delivered took full charge and control of the truck, with knowledge of the presence of the vapors, and the explosion occurred while company employees were attempting to clean the truck.

In the examples noted above, the party originally chargeable with negligence escaped liability because there was an intervening agency which had full knowledge of the dangerous condition and which assumed control of the vehicle. Such assumption of control, with full knowledge, broke the chain of causation between the original negligence and the eventual injury. This rule is essentially an application of the rule that negligence alone will not create liability unless the negligence is the proximate cause of the injury.

Governmental and Family Immunity The defense of immunity is seldom applicable in cases involving commercial motor vehicles, but in a limited number of cases it might have application. For example, a significant but decreasing number of jurisdictions recognize immunity for tort liability among members of a family. It has thus been held that one spouse may not sue another, nor may a child sue his or her parent. However, even when immunity is recognized, it is normally not applied to circumstances in which the injury arose out of a business relationship that existed between the members of the family involved. Thus, while a father might not otherwise be liable for negligently injuring his son in the operation of a motor vehicle, the fact that the son was a paying passenger, or that father and son were on a business trip involving them both, might avoid immunity.

A state is normally immune from suit in the absence of statutes specifically permitting the bringing of suit against the state. Municipal corporations often have immunities provided by statute, particularly for such functions as police and fire protection. Some states also recognize a common-law immunity on the part of municipal corporations, so long as they are engaged in functions that might be considered purely governmental, as opposed to such functions as selling water or power.

However, even when the governmental body itself is immune from liability, an employee or contractor operating a motor vehicle on behalf of the governmental agency will not share in the immunity in the absence of a statute so providing. Therefore, when an employee of the state negligently operates a state-owned vehicle, the state might be immune from liability, but the driver will not be. For this reason, it is not uncommon for states to provide liability insurance to protect the drivers of its vehicles. The situation is the same with respect to other governmental entities having immunity, such as municipal corporations, counties, townships, or boards of education.

There are a limited number of cases in which the immunity of the governmental entity might protect the operator of a vehicle. If an employee of the state, or a contractor doing work for the state, is acting within the scope of employment or contract, that fact will not normally provide the immunity enjoyed by the state if he or she is negligent in performing the work or the contract. However, when the act causing injury is done in exact conformance with instructions by the state, there will be no liability, even though the decision to so act could be considered negligent. Thus, when a contract with a state requires a contractor to drive heavily loaded trucks over a private roadway or a city street, the contractor might not be held liable for the ensuing damage.

Other Statutory Considerations Immunity from liability might be created by statute. To the extent they are applicable, workers' compensation statutes render the employer immune from common-law liability for injuries to employees. Guest statutes restrict the liability for injured gratuitous guests to injuries resulting from conduct more culpable than mere negligence, such as "wanton or willful misconduct, " "gross negligence," or "willful negligence." The guest statute is of decreasing significance. In recent years, a number of guest statutes have been declared unconstitutional, although in some states they have withstood constitutional attacks. Different results have not been grounded on differences in the statutes but rather stem from different views on constitutionality by the courts involved.

Some states by statute render police and fire fighters immune from liability for injuries caused while they are responding to emergencies.

Such statutes create issues as to what constitutes an "emergency" or when the emergency begins or ends.

Liability of Members of Business Organizations

Because the liability of a commercial firm often involves the relationship of various parties, it is desirable to relate the relationships among the parties in various types of business organizations specifically to motor vehicle liability exposures.

Corporations Corporations usually involve stockholders, officers and directors, and employees. Stockholders as such are not liable for torts of employees of the corporation. And, while the corporation itself may be responsible for the torts of employees who are acting within the scope of their employment, officers and directors are not, by virtue of their position alone, personally liable for the torts of employees of the corporation. This means that officers and directors are not personally liable for an employee's negligence in the operation of a motor vehicle.

Co-Employees Although a corporation is liable for the torts of its employees acting within the scope of their employment, the negligent employee is primarily liable. Any co-employee who participates in the negligent act or omission may also be held liable. Thus, when two or more employees negligently load a truck, all such employees who actually were negligent might be held liable.

However, such liability arises as to each employee only because of that employee's negligence. The negligence of the co-employees is never imputed to them simply by reason of the fact that they are co-employees, or by reason of the fact they they were both involved in the same operation. If one employee negligently loads the truck, whereas another negligently operates the truck, they may be jointly liable, each for individual acts of negligence. Normally, the commercial motor vehicle exposure will not involve serious issues concerning the liability of anyone other than the corporation itself and the operator of the vehicle. The standard liability insurance policy protects the driver, and the limits of the policy are therefore available to the plaintiff upon establishing liability against the driver. The corporation itself is almost always included as a defendant, sometimes in order to reach assets beyond policy limits, but more often to have a better "target" for the jury.

Partnerships One criterion of a partnership is mutual agency: each member of a partnership acting within the scope of the business of the partnership acts for all and is bound by the acts of all. Each partner will be responsible for liabilities incurred by the acts or omissions of other partners, so long as such acts or omissions are within the scope of the business of the partnership. Therefore, when two or more persons create a partnership for the operation of a trucking business, each partner will be individually responsible for injuries resulting from the operation of the equipment by other partners.

From the earliest times, the sharing of profits and losses has been regarded as a factor essential to a partnership existence. A partner not only shares in the profits, but must share in the losses, and is liable to third parties for any obligation owed by the partnership. This includes liability incurred in tort. A partnership is liable for the results of the negligence of its employees who are acting within the scope of their employment. When a truck driver employed by a partnership injures another, the injured party may recover not only from the partnership as an entity, but has a right of recovery against all partners. In order to satisfy the claim, he or she may reach not only the partnership assets, but may reach all assets individually owned by any of the partners.

A general partner, then, may be held individually liable for injuries incurred as the result of the negligent operation of commercial motor vehicles, whether the negligence was that of a partner or an employee of the partnership. The same is true when the partnership has incurred liability as the result of the negligent operation by others, as through contract or negligence on the part of a loaned employee.

A limited partner who does not actively participate in the operation beyond his or her investment in the partnership business will not be liable to third parties. However, the partner might still be liable for negligence insofar as he or she does participate. For instance, if a trucking business is formed as a limited partnership, the limited partner will not be liable for injuries sustained by third parties as the result of negligence in the operation of the trucks by other partners or by employees. The mere fact that one is a partner will not create liability so long as one is a limited partner. However, if a partner operates the equipment and negligence results in injuries to another, he or she will then be liable to such injured party, not because of his or her status as a partner, but as a direct result of negligent conduct.

With respect to liability to third parties arising from injuries through the operation of a commercial motor vehicle, a partnership, as an entity, will be liable in the same fashion as a corporation. The principal difference is in the individual liability on the part of partners which does not exist in the case of stockholders in a corporation.

The liability of the general partner will normally be unlimited, while the liability of the limited partner is similar to that of a stockholder in a corporation, in that the limited partner risks no more than his or her contribution to the business enterprise. As noted, however, contribution in a partnership may not consist entirely of limited partners. It is necessary that there be at least one general partner who will have unlimited personal liability with respect to obligations of the partnership, including those arising in tort.

Indemnity or Contribution

Indemnity, in general, is the right of a party who has been required to pay the debt of another to be reimbursed by the party owing the primary obligation. *Contribution* is the legal principle that requires equalization among a number of parties of an obligation incurred or owed by all of the parties.

Contribution differs from indemnity. Indemnity is the right to reimbursement that a person has by virtue of having been compelled to pay what another should pay in *full*. Contribution, on the other hand, is the right to *equitable or partial* reimbursement which a person has by virtue of having been compelled to pay what another should pay in *part*.

These two concepts will be explored in greater detail in the following subsections.

Indemnity

Employer—Employee. An employer may be held liable for damages resulting from the negligence of an employee when such negligence arises during and out of the scope of the employee's employment. This liability on the part of the employer is unrelated to fault. It arises by operation of law through the employer-employee relationship.

The liability of the employer to the injured party, however, is secondary to the primary liability of the employee whose negligence actually caused injury. When a party secondarily liable, such as an employer, is required to pay as a result of the negligence of the primarily liable employee, he or she is entitled to reimbursement from the employee whose negligence exposed the faultless employer to liability.

Primary-secondary liability arises, however, only in those circumstances where the employer is free from fault and is held liable only because of the negligence of the employee. If the employer is chargeable with negligence separate from that of the employee, with the negligence of both concurring to produce injury to another, then the liability to the injured party is joint and several, rather than primary and secondary, and no right of indemnity arises.

Thus, if a truck driver injures a third party as a result of the violation of a traffic rule, the trucking company will be liable to the injured party; but if the trucking company is called upon to pay, it has the legal right to seek reimbursement from the truck driver.

On the other hand, if the negligence of the truck driver in the operation of the truck concurs with negligence on the part of the trucking company in maintaining the truck, then the liability of the driver and the trucking company is joint and several. No right to indemnity exists.

When tortfeasors are jointly and severally liable, the injured party normally has the right to seek recovery from any or all of the joint tortfeasors. The injured party may bring action against all of the joint tortfeasors, and if a joint judgment is rendered against all of the joint tortfeasors, he or she can collect any or all of the judgment from any of the joint tortfeasors at his or her discretion. When one of the joint tortfeasors was required to pay more than a proportionate share of the damages, the common law gave no right of indemnity against the other joint tortfeasors. (At common law, no rights to contribution were recognized. As will be discussed later, the trend has been toward establishing rights of contribution in such circumstances.)

Because of the way insurance policies are written, questions of indemnity and contribution do not frequently arise with respect to commercial motor vehicles. The omnibus clause of the owner's liability insurance policy invariably insures a driver who is using the vehicle with the permission of the owner. Under those circumstances, when an employee is not using the vehicle with permission, the employee will not be insured, but there will also be no liability on the part of the owner. Therefore, the owner will have no need to seek indemnity from the driver.

The full range of situations that can arise with respect to applicable liability insurance coverages are not within the scope of this chapter, but it should be kept in mind that one who is rendered liable to an injured party as the result of the negligence of another in the operation of a vehicle, and whose liability arises only because of the relationship between the one rendered liable and the actual tortfeasor, has a legal right to be indemnified by the actual tortfeasor.

Passive Versus Active Negligence. Most circumstances where indemnity has been held to be available involve situations in which the relative fault of the tortfeasors is not a critical issue. Indemnity generally depends upon the existence of a certain relationship between the parties, contractual or otherwise. However, a number of jurisdictions have recognized a rule of indemnity providing that, even though more than one party is chargeable with actual negligence, and the multiple acts or omissions constituting negligence concurred to produce a single indivisible injury, the party guilty of *passive* negligence may have a right to be indemnified by the party chargeable with *active* negligence. This rule has been expressed in different ways in different jurisdictions and in different decisions, and the concept is one that is quite difficult to apply to a given set of circumstances.

For instance, when a vehicle is negligently operated so as to collide with a negligently parked vehicle, it can be argued that the parked vehicle was only passively involved; or, conversely, it can be argued that the act of parking negligently constituted active negligence. The rule is normally applied so as to hold one merely passively negligent when one's liability arises from the failure to do something that should have been done. Thus, when a beer truck driver delivers barrels to the basement of a customer, utilizing trap doors on the public sidewalk in front of the customer's place of business, and negligently injures a passerby, either in the movement of the trap doors or in negligently leaving them open or partially open, the owner of the premises might be held liable to the injured party by reason of a nondelegable duty not to create a dangerous condition on a public sidewalk. However, the owner's passive negligence in failing to prevent the creation of the dangerous condition by the truck driver, or failure to prevent the negligent act by the truck driver, will not prevent the owner from enforcing indemnity against the truck driver who was actively negligent. The same sort of situation might arise when an overloaded truck, in making a delivery, cracks a sidewalk, or when the operator of a truck-mounted crane, in attempting to hoist a sign into place, drops it on a sidewalk. An injured party might be able to recover from the owner of the premises, but such owner, being liable only as a result of passive failure to prevent injury, will normally have rights of indemnity against the active tortfeasor. The question can also arise in railroad crossing accidents when there is a claim of negligence on the part of the railroad which fails to erect required signs or to utilize other required signals.

Similar issues can arise in injuries occurring during loading or unloading. Suppose a truck is negligently loaded, causing injury. The trucking company might be held liable even in the absence of any participation in, or knowledge of, the improper loading. Under such circumstances, the trucking company, merely passively negligent in failing to inspect the load, might be entitled to indemnity. It depends upon whether the particular jurisdiction recognizes the indemnity-for-passive-negligence rule, as well as upon the applicable definition of "passive." The same can be said of the other situations described.

Contract. A contract is perhaps the most frequent basis for the creation of rights of indemnity. In fact, some courts have considered indemnity rights to arise solely from contracts, though they have given effect to rights of indemnity in those circumstances where there has been no express contract, by implying a contract of indemnity.

By express agreement, one may undertake to protect, or hold harmless, another party from liability. For example, a party contracting with a trucking company might require the trucking company to protect it from any liability arising from the negligence of the trucking company.

In any given case, the exact language of the hold harmless clause in question will control. Contract law, rather than tort law, is basically applicable, and the clear intention of the parties will normally be given effect unless the contract is held to be contrary to public policy. (Contractual liability exposures were discussed extensively in Chapter 5.)

Enforcement of the Right of Indemnity. At common law, a cause of action for indemnity does not arise unless and until the party seeking indemnity actually pays the injured or damaged party. *Third-party procedure,* provided for in the Federal Rules of Civil Procedure and in those states that have adopted rules of procedure similar to or patterned after the federal rules, has added a new dimension to the enforcement of rights of indemnity. Through this procedure, a defendant in a lawsuit may file a third-party complaint against another party who the defendant claims is liable to the defendant for all or any part of any judgment that might be rendered in favor of the plaintiff and against the defendant. Technically, the cause of action still does not arise until the indemnitee has actually made payment, but the indemnitee's right to bring the indemnitor into the litigation is accelerated. If the indemnitee does not utilize third-party procedures, for instance, the statute of limitations will not start to run against the indemnitee's right of indemnity until he or she has made payment.

Unless there are jurisdictional obstacles, moreover, a defendant who has rights of indemnity against another will almost invariably utilize third-party procedures to bring the indemnitor into the litigation if such procedures are available in the court in which the action is brought. By doing so, the necessity of making formal demands at various stages is eliminated.

At common law, a problem of proof also arose, even after an indemnitee was subjected to and paid a judgment. There is a division of authority as to whether or not the indemnitor is bound by the judgment in the prior action to which he or she was not a party, or whether it was necessary for the indemnitee to re-litigate the case which was successfully litigated against him or her, including proof not only of liability but of damages. This problem can also be avoided through the use of third-party procedures. When an indemnitor is brought into litigation by third-party procedures, it is discretionary with the court whether all issues will be resolved in one trial, or whether there should be separate trials of the original plaintiff's claim against the defendant and the defendant's claim for indemnity against the third-party defendant. Normally, this discretion will be exercised, where practicable, in favor of a single trial. Even when separate trials are ordered, the case will usually proceed on other matters, such as discovery and pre-trial conferences, as a single case. This can be particularly significant with respect to pre-trial conferences, when settlement is commonly discussed, and when recommendations with respect to settlement are not infrequently made by the court. Such recommendations by the court, while not always accepted and followed, are seldom ignored; at times they are decisive factors in producing settlement.

Third-party procedures have, therefore, provided a method by which an indemnitor can be required to enter the litigation, participate in and be subjected to discovery procedures, attend pre-trial settlement conferences, and participate in the trial of the issues involving the indemnitee. Because the indemnitor is required to come to grips with the problem at an earlier stage, pre-trial settlements are frequently made in cases that might otherwise have resulted in at least one trial.

Third-party procedures are not unique to commercial motor vehicle litigation, of course, but they do have widespread application to such litigation. Relationships between different trucking companies or between trucking companies and customers, landlords, or independent contractors, as well as various contracts, can give rise to rights of indemnity.

Similar to a third-party complaint is the use of a crossclaim for indemnity. A *third-party complaint* is utilized when a defendant seeks indemnity from a party who was not also made a defendant in the original action, a party who is a stranger to the litigation until the third-party complaint is filed.

A *crossclaim* is a claim of one defendant against another party who is already a defendant. Such crossclaims can be utilized to enforce rights of indemnity. For instance, if the plaintiff sues a truck driver as well as the driver's employer, the employer can assert a claim for indemnity through the use of a crossclaim against the driver. Similarly, if a plaintiff sues two separate truck lines, or a bus company and another defendant who chartered a bus, or a taxicab company and an independent contractor driver, a defendant who claims a right of indemnity against the other may assert such right by crossclaim. The case proceeds essentially as it would when such claims of indemnity are asserted by third-party procedures, with the court having a discretion as to whether all issues are to be tried in a single trial or in separate trials.

Contribution The doctrine of contribution is founded upon principles of equity that require that those who voluntarily assume a common burden should bear it in equal proportions. One party should not normally be subjected to bear more than a just share of the obligation to the advantage of other parties who share the obligation.

The doctrine of contribution developed at common law. Modern trend, however, has modified the common-law doctrine, and this trend affects the enforceability of the doctrine.

Traditional Common-Law Rule Versus Modern Trend. Starting with early English decisions, the common law recognized the rule that the law would not enforce contribution between joint tortfeasors. This exception to the allowance of contribution was based on the principle that the law would not aid persons who were participants in wrongful acts but would leave them where their wrongful action placed them. Accordingly, there was no right of contribution between persons whose concurrent negligence made them liable for damages. Nor was there a right of contribution between defendants against whom a joint judgment had been rendered when the judgment was recovered on the basis of concurrent negligence on the part of the defendants. The common law traditionally left tortfeasors where their wrongful act placed them, and contribution was not permitted. However, the modern trend is very clearly toward permitting contributions among joint tortfeasors, either through judicial reinterpretation of the common law or through the enactment of statutes providing for such contributions. More than half of the states have adopted legislation providing for some form of contribution between joint tortfeasors, while others have recognized a common-law right to contribution, particularly those jurisdictions that have established, by statute or by judicial decision, the rule of comparative negligence.

Contribution, where permitted, may take several forms. It may provide for proportionate liability among joint tortfeasors according to the percentage of the total fault chargeable to each; it may provide for equal contribution among all joint tortfeasors, irrespective of the degree or percentage of fault; or it may provide for equal division in the absence of such a disproportionate fault among the joint tortfeasors as to render inequitable the equal distribution among them of the common liability.

The adoption of a rule permitting contribution between joint tortfeasors has coincided, in general, with the negligence and personal injury law explosion of the past years. The expansion of theories of liability available to plaintiffs and the increasing number of parties who might be held liable for a single injury, along with changes in procedural law providing for more liberal joinder and addition of party defendants, have combined to make the common-law rule prohibiting contribution between those participating in a wrongful act appear unjust and inequitable. Where once it could be said that a wrongdoer should suffer the consequences of wrongdoing and not be aided by the court, modern trends in the law exposed to liability many defendants whose conduct did not appear to be so outrageous that in good conscience they should be required to pay more than their fair share of the cost of satisfying a successful plaintiff's claim. Perhaps the modern tortfeasor may be looked on less as the culpable perpetrator of a wrongful act injuring a victim than as a victim who has stumbled into trouble. In any event, most jurisdictions now permit contribution in some form between joint tortfeasors.

Quite complex procedural and substantive problems can arise from contribution. Where, in an action involving multiple defendants, one defendant has a personal defense against the plaintiff that is not available to the other defendants, he or she normally cannot be held liable for contribution. Thus, a guest in a private passenger car that collides with a truck or other vehicle might bring action against the trucking company, which would not be entitled to contribution from the operator of a car in which the plaintiff was riding, even if that operator were negligent, in jurisdictions that have a guest statute which bars liability for simple negligence on the part of the driver of an automobile to his guest-passenger.

A co-employee of a truck driver might be injured in a collision between the truck and another vehicle, where both drivers were negligent. If the injured employee brings action against the other driver, the other driver would normally not be permitted contribution from the trucking company, which would have no liability to its employee under the workers' compensation laws. This is because workers' compensation laws normally provide that an employer who complies with the law is immune from any further liability arising from injury to the employee. While the decisions are not uniform, it has generally been held that the statute grants immunity from liability to the employer not only from a direct action against the employer by the employee but also from claims of indemnity or contribution from tortfeasors who are held liable to the employee.

The same kind of situation can arise in those jurisdictions that recognize family immunities. For instance, a son riding in his father's automobile is injured because of the joint negligence of his father and the operator of another automobile. The son might bring action against the operator of the other automobile, who would not have any right to contribution from the plaintiff's father because of the father's immunity from suit by his son.

Problems can also arise as the result of differing obligations. The operator of a common carrier, such as a taxicab driver or a bus driver, normally owes the highest degree of care to passengers that is consistent with the practical operation of the vehicle, whereas the operators of other vehicles owe only ordinary care. Special relationships or obligations can also be created by contract, which can complicate the nature and extent of obligations owed to an injured party by different tortfeasors.

Even more so than in other situations, it is necessary to look to the statutes and decisions of the jurisdictions involved, the particular facts of a given case, and the decisions of the jurisdiction in similar factual situations in order to determine what rights of contribution, if any, may exist.

Enforcement of Right. Enforcement of the right of contribution is quite similar, in most respects, to enforcement of the right of indemnity. Third-party procedures normally can be utilized for contributions as well as for indemnity. Decisions of some jurisdictions have also recognized the right of a defendant sued alone to bring joint tortfeasors into the action as defendants, rather than as third-party defendants.

A cause of action for contribution normally does not accrue until the party seeking contribution has either actually made payment to an injured party in an amount greater than his proportionate share, or has been subjected to a judgment for more than his proportionate share. The statute of limitations for contribution will not start to run until one of these events occurs. It is therefore not necessary for a party seeking contribution to utilize third-party procedures. He or she may simply litigate the case to a conclusion and, following an adverse judgment, seek contribution from the other tortfeasors.

Common Carriers

A carrier is a business organization that transports goods or passengers. In order for a carrier to be regarded as a *common* carrier, it must dedicate its property to public use in such a manner that its services are available to the public generally and indiscriminately, and the carrier must hold itself ready to serve the public impartially to the limit of its capacity. If the carrier is employed by one or more definite parties by special contract, or for a special undertaking, it is a *private* carrier.

A common carrier has also been defined as a carrier that holds itself out to the public as engaged in the business of transporting persons or property from place to place, for compensation, offering its services to the public generally. The transportation must be provided for compensation as a business activity and not as a casual occupation, and it must be offered indiscriminately to the public generally.

The principal distinguishing characteristic of a common carrier is its public profession, by words or course of conduct, as to the service offered. A common carrier is normally required to carry all that is offered to it, provided a reasonable compensation is tendered; if it refuses when it has the capacity available, it may be liable for such refusal.

Railroads, express companies, bus companies, taxicab companies, amusement rides known as scenic railways, shipping lines, barge lines, airlines, ferries, and even passenger elevators have been deemed to be common carriers. However, the following discussion will be confined to common carriers that utilize motor vehicles to carry passengers.

Applicable Law The duties, obligations, and liabilities of common carriers may be effected or determined by principles of common law which may well vary from state to state. Statutes controlling the conduct and operations of common carriers also will vary among different jurisdictions. Regulatory agencies such as public utilities commissions may also provide different rules in different jurisdictions. Municipalities, including most large cities, will normally have ordinances that affect or control common carriers, particularly bus companies and taxicab companies. When a common carrier is involved in interstate activities, federal statutes or Interstate Commerce Commission regulations may well be involved.

No attempt will be made here to cover all of the various statutes, ordinances, regulations, and common-law rules that might apply to the liability exposures of common carriers. Instead, an effort will be made to acquaint the student with some general principles of common law that affect the liabilities of common carriers utilizing motor vehicles, and the general effect of legislation and regulatory rules and regulations on such common carriers. Obviously these may differ sharply from one jurisdiction to another.

Powers and Duties of a Common Carrier A common carrier has the right to adopt and enforce reasonable rules and regulations for the conduct of its business so that it can (1) perform its duties in a systematic and efficient manner, and (2) secure the safety and promote the comfort and convenience of its passengers. It is an implied term of the contract of carriage that the passenger will obey the reasonable rules and regulations of the carrier, if he or she has or reasonably should have knowledge of such rules and regulations.

The common carrier may prescribe rules dealing with regular places for taking on or discharging passengers; prohibiting passengers from standing in certain areas of the vehicle during operation; prohibiting passengers from smoking; limiting the size or number of packages or baggage; and prohibiting passengers from extending any portion of their bodies out of windows, as well as any other rule reasonably designed to promote the safety, comfort, or convenience of all passengers.

A common carrier of passengers is under a public duty to accept all who offer themselves as passengers and are ready to pay the fare and abide by reasonable rules and regulations of the carrier. The common carrier may decline to carry persons after its vehicles are filled, and it also may refuse to accept passengers or continue to transport passengers who, by improper behavior, such as drunkenness, obscene language, or vulgar conduct, are an annoyance or a danger to other passengers.

Frequently, applicable statutes or regulations may affect the obligations of a common carrier with respect to accepting passengers. For instance, while a common carrier of passengers might normally enforce a rule prohibiting passengers from bringing pets or animals onto the conveyance, a statute or ordinance might require a common carrier to accept a seeing-eye dog accompanying a blind person. A common carrier of passengers also has a duty to the public to exercise reasonable care to keep its vehicles running on an established schedule and prevent unreasonable delay, although it cannot guarantee the precise time its vehicles will arrive or depart.

Relationship of Carrier and Passenger In general, the relationship between a common carrier and a passenger begins once an individual becomes a passenger and terminates when the passenger has been discharged. There are, however, many variables involved in determining exactly when this relationship is created, and when it terminates, and liability for any accident may depend on whether it occurred during the course of such a carrier-passenger relationship.

Creation of Relationship. The basis of the relation of carrier and passenger is primarily contractual, although the obligations and liabilities with which a common carrier of passengers is charged are also based upon considerations of public policy and arise by implication of law. Apart from the contractual relationship between carrier and passenger, the law plainly imposes certain duties upon the carrier, the basis for which is found in the inherent regard with which the law views human life and safety. The contract between carrier and passenger may be expressed in a ticket or otherwise, or it may be implied from the conduct of the parties.

The relationship is generally created by the passenger's offer to become a passenger and the acceptance by the carrier of the passenger after he or she has come under the control of the carrier. The passenger must present himself or herself to use the transportation at the time and place and in the manner provided by the carrier for that purpose. Usually, there must be the intention of taking passage on a particular vehicle, along with some physical contact with the vehicle, or with the designated place of boarding, before the relationship of passenger-carrier is created. Physical contact, however, is not always the deciding factor. The ultimate question is generally whether or not the person intending to take passage has actually placed himself or herself under the care of the common carrier. For instance, if a bus is not ready to receive passengers, the mere act of entering the bus, without the knowledge of the bus company, will not establish the relationship of passenger and carrier. Even though there is physical contact with the bus, the person entering the bus has not become a passenger, since he or she has not actually placed himself or herself under the care of the common carrier.

The purchase of a ticket will not alone create the relationship of passenger and carrier, nor is the purchase of a ticket essential to the creation of the relationship, except where the rules of the bus company require such purchase as a condition precedent to the right to be transported on the bus.

It has been held, for instance, that a person entering the terminal of a bus company with the intention of purchasing a ticket and embarking on a bus might become a passenger of the bus company even before purchasing the ticket. However, it has also been held that when the rules and regulations of a bus company require the purchase of a ticket as a condition precedent and a bus driver is not authorized to receive cash fares, a person does not become a passenger even by boarding the bus and offering a cash fare to the driver.

Local bus companies (and occasionally taxicab companies) have designated places where passengers may be picked up. The mere presence of a person at such a location, with the intention of taking transportation on a bus or a taxicab, will normally not be sufficient to create the passenger-carrier relationship, nor will the mere signaling of such person to the driver of a bus or a taxicab be sufficient. However, it has been held that when such person has signaled and the vehicle has stopped, he or she has virtually become a passenger.

When a bus does stop at a usual place to take on and discharge passengers and a person is in the act of stepping onto the bus, he or she normally is regarded as a passenger and is entitled to protection as such, although the bus driver may not be aware of the fact that he or she is boarding the bus.

The question as to whether or not a person has yet become a passenger can be of critical significance in determining the liability of the common carrier. Until the person actually becomes a passenger, the carrier normally owes only the duty to exercise ordinary care to avoid injury, this duty being the same that the carrier or any other person owes to all members of society. For instance, if a person is running across the street in order to catch a bus and is struck by the bus, the liability or nonliability of the bus company will normally be determined on the basis of rules applicable to any other pedestrian. However, once the relationship of passenger-carrier has been established and the passenger has placed himself or herself under the control and protection of the common carrier, other duties and liabilities arise. These will be dealt with later.

Termination of Relationship. The carrier-passenger relationship normally continues until the passenger has been discharged in safety from the vehicle and has had a reasonable opportunity to depart safely from the place of discharge. If the passenger is not discharged in a safe place, the carrier's responsibility may continue until the passenger has had a reasonable opportunity to reach a place of safety.

Usually, the relationship of carrier and passenger is terminated when a passenger on a bus alights in a place of safety, whether or not the place is a regular stopping place. However, the relationship might not terminate if the passenger is discharged at a place made dangerous by ice and snow, or by other hazards, such as moving traffic. When a taxicab driver discharges a passenger in the middle of a street, for instance, and the passenger is required to cross moving lanes of traffic in order to reach the safety of the curb, he or she might remain a passenger until reaching the curb.

Normally, where one has ridden beyond one's destination, he or she still remains a passenger and is entitled to protection as such, until actually being discharged in a place of safety. When a person boards a bus with the intention of riding to a certain destination, then changes his or her mind and tries to leave the bus before it starts to move, he or she remains a passenger until leaving the bus. In the same manner that a person becomes a passenger when intentionally placing himself or herself under the control and protection of the carrier, the relationship is terminated when the passenger intends to and does remove himself or herself from the control and protection of the carrier.

Liability for Injuries to Passengers In general, the right of a passenger to recover for injuries depends upon the showing of negligence or willfulness on the part of the carrier or the carrier's employee. The mere fact that an injury occurred to a passenger while on a bus or in a taxicab, or while boarding or alighting from such a conveyance, will not alone be sufficient to fasten liability upon the carrier. If a bus or taxicab collides with another vehicle, injuring the passenger, or in suddenly stopping or swerving to avoid such collision a passenger is injured, the carrier will not be liable for the resulting injuries if the occurrence was caused solely as the result of the negligence of the operator of the other vehicle. Also, if injury occurs as the result of defective equipment or weather conditions under circumstances where there is no negligence on the part of the carrier or its employer, no recovery may be had against the carrier.

It is generally recognized that a common carrier of passengers has a higher duty toward its passengers than that ordinarily owed by operators of motor vehicles. Generally, that duty is to exercise the highest degree of care for the safety of passengers that is consistent with the practical operation of the business of operating as a common carrier. It has also been stated that a carrier is liable for injury or death that results from "the slightest negligence" on the part of the operator, or "the least degree of imprudence" or "the least degree of want of care" on the part of the operator. Different decisions in different jurisdictions might state the duty in different terms, but it is generally recognized that the duty of a common carrier to its passengers is greater than the duty owed by the operator of a motor vehicle to operators of other vehicles, pedestrians, or any other third persons.

Common carriers are liable for the acts of their employees to the same extent as other employers, as covered in a preceding section. The carrier will be liable when the act of the employee giving rise to liability is done within the scope of employment. The applicability of this rule is not affected if the act exceeded the authority given by the employer or was in disobedience of the employer's orders (as when a bus driver violates a safety rule promulgated by the bus company).

In the operation of a bus, the driver is the *alter ego* of the company. In performing any act associated with the duties of a bus driver, he or she is clothed with the authority of the company, and the company is responsible for his or her acts. If a bus driver accepts baggage, intoxicated passengers, or materials, in violation of company rules and in excess of the driver's authority, the company may still be liable for any injuries occasioned by such acts, since such acts are within the scope of the driver's duties as such.

In accordance with the general rule that negligence will not create liability unless the negligence is the proximate cause of the injury for which recovery is sought, a common carrier will not be liable for every injury to its passengers, even when there was contemporaneous or coincidental negligence on the part of the passenger, unless the negligence on the part of the carrier directly and proximately contributed to the injury. Thus, when a bus or a taxicab is overcrowded and a passenger is injured in a collision with another vehicle, negligence in permitting the overcrowding will not be the basis of liability unless it can be shown that without such overcrowding the injury would not have occurred.

However, a carrier that does fail in its duty to a passenger is responsible for the consequences of its negligence, without regard to the fact that the negligence of a third party may have contributed to, or may even have been the principal cause of, the injury. In order to justify recovery against a carrier it is not necessary to show that the carrier's negligence was the sole cause of the injury. Therefore, when a passenger is injured as a result of the concurrent negligence of the driver of a bus or taxicab and another vehicle, the passenger may recover from the carrier.

Further, although the carrier will not be liable for the sole negligence of another party, the law does impose upon a carrier, under some circumstances, the duty to take appropriate precautions from dangers of which the carrier is or should be aware. Thus, when a strike of its employees is in progress, a carrier that continues to operate its transportation system is under the duty to exercise the highest degree of care to protect its passengers from strike-related injuries.

Except when special statutes, ordinances, or regulations apply to common carriers, the basic principles of law applicable to operators of other motor vehicles determine the liability of a carrier to its passengers, with the exception of the greater degree of care owed by a carrier to its passengers. These principles include the defenses of contributory negligence and assumption of risk, as well as the principles of negligence and proximate cause. In the case of carriers, these principles will be applied to different factual situations unique to carriers, but the basic rules of law apply.

Particular Circumstances. When one enters an area for the purpose of becoming a passenger on a carrier, the carrier may be liable for injury to the passenger caused by the negligence of the carrier. Thus, the condition of a bus depot, bus stop on the street, taxicab office, or a designated pickup point for taxicab passengers on the street may be the basis for liability. There are conflicting decisions as to whether the carrier's duty to prospective passengers at such places is that of exercising ordinary care or the highest degree of care. Those decisions recognizing a lesser duty are based on the reasoning that the danger of injury is not as great under such circumstances as it is on a moving vehicle since a passenger has greater control over his or her own movements before actually entering the vehicle; hence, one is better able to protect himself or herself from danger. However, whether a finding of negligence requires the showing of lack of ordinary care or lack of the highest degree of care, negligence under such circumstances can be the basis of liability for resulting injury.

Therefore, it is the obligation of the carrier to furnish proper light in places where it picks up and discharges passengers. If a prospective passenger falls and is injured as a result of inadequate or defective lighting, the carrier may be liable. So also may a carrier be liable for overcrowding or slippery conditions in such places.

BOARDING AND ALIGHTING. In considering the question of the liability of a carrier for injuries to one who is about to board a conveyance, it is necessary first to determine whether the relationship of carrier and passenger has been created. The determination as to whether at the time of injury the injured party was a passenger will determine whether the carrier owed ordinary care or the highest degree of care to prevent injury.

The duty of a common carrier of passengers to provide a safe and convenient means of entering and leaving its vehicles includes the exercise of due care in the construction of reasonably safe steps upon its vehicles. A bus company may be held liable when a passenger slips on a step which has been made unusually slippery when wet as the result of wear. A bus company may also be liable for the accumulation of ice and snow on the step of a bus, when the driver makes no effort either to prevent such accumulation or warn passengers of it.

Normally, a carrier owes a duty not only to exercise the highest degree of care for the safety of its passengers while on the vehicle, but also to exercise the highest degree of care in providing a safe place for the passengers to leave the vehicle. When the operator of a vehicle discharges passengers, appropriate care must be exercised at the place where the passenger is discharged. The operator must also give consideration to the age, sex, and health of the passenger. What might be the exercise of proper care for one passenger might well be negligence for another. Thus, while a taxicab driver might be justified in stopping his or her taxicab some distance from the curb to discharge an adult passenger who is young and healthy, the exercise of proper care in the case of a passenger who is aged or blind might well require pulling up to the curb and assisting the passenger from the taxicab. So long as the relationship of carrier and passenger exists, the passenger is under the protection of the carrier, and the duty of the carrier includes taking proper precautions to protect the passenger from dangers which may be anticipated from exterior events or circumstances or from the unique condition or character of the passenger.

The operator of a bus may be negligent in closing the door as a passenger is entering a bus. It is not normally negligent for the driver to start the vehicle before all passengers have had the opportunity to be seated, although this might give rise to liability to an aged or physically handicapped passenger.

A bus driver should also use due care in watching for persons intending to board the bus. The carrier will be liable for an injury to a prospective passenger who is knocked down if the bus starts up prematurely. However, there is no liability if the operator is not chargeable with knowledge that the person was attempting to board it. When a prospective passenger raps on the door of a bus or a taxicab and then is knocked down by the moving vehicle, there will be no liability unless it can be shown that the driver did or should have observed the prospective passenger.

While normally a person who attempts to board a moving vehicle might be held to have assumed the risk of injury in doing so, there are circumstances in which the carrier will be liable. Thus, when a bus driver slows down, but does not stop, and the slow rate of speed is such as to be an invitation to a passenger to board, it is the duty of the driver to retain the slow speed long enough to permit the passenger to get safely aboard.

The duty of a carrier of passengers to bring its passengers safely to their destination necessarily implies that the carrier will afford sufficient time and opportunity for the passengers to leave the vehicle. It has been held that when a bus comes to a full stop, for any purpose, and a passenger is in the act of alighting, it is negligent for the driver to start the vehicle before the passenger has had a reasonable opportunity to get off safely. It has further been held that merely affording the passenger a reasonable time to alight will not be sufficient. The carrier must not only provide a reasonable time for the passenger to leave the vehicle safely. It also has a duty to see that the passenger has actually been safely discharged before starting the vehicle in motion. However, the carrier may not be liable if the operator starts the vehicle in motion and the passenger has not actually started to leave the vehicle but has merely changed position in preparing to leave.

A carrier is not normally liable for injuries sustained by a passenger who attempts to leave the vehicle while it is in motion. Also, when a bus has stopped and opened its doors prior to crossing a railroad track, in keeping with statutory requirements, and the driver has no knowledge that anyone is attempting to leave the bus, it will not be negligent for the driver to close the door or start the bus while the passenger is attempting to leave.

While it has been held that what constitutes a reasonable time for a passenger to enter or leave a conveyance is not to be determined by the age or decrepitude of a passenger, the more general rule is that regard must be shown for the passenger's age, sex, and physical condition. If a passenger is known to the operator to be blind, sick, aged, infirm, or of tender years, the carrier is charged with the duty of allowing such person sufficient time to enter or leave in safety, regardless of whether that time is longer than is normally allowed to or required by other passengers.

When a carrier has discharged a passenger safely into the street, the relationship of carrier and passenger ceases, since the carrier is not normally liable for injuries received by the passenger after leaving the vehicle. Normally, the operator of the vehicle has no duty to warn a departing passenger of dangers of street traffic which are as obvious to the passenger as to the operator. The passenger has the duty of exercising ordinary care for his or her own safety after alighting. As stated, there may be exceptions to this principle in the case of a young child or an aged or infirm person.

There also may be an exception to this principle under circumstances in which the operator of a bus or a taxicab is aware of dangers of passing traffic which are not known to, or might not be reasonably anticipated by, the passenger. Under such circumstances, the driver may have the obligation to warn the departing passenger.

However, under any circumstances, once the passenger has left the conveyance and has reached a place of safety, the relationship of carrier and passenger has fully terminated. The carrier will no longer be liable for injuries resulting from passing traffic. Conversely, when a prospective passenger is crossing a street to board a bus or a taxicab, the relationship of carrier and passenger has not yet been created. The driver thus has no duty to warn the prospective passenger of the dangers of approaching traffic.

EQUIPMENT. Because a common carrier of passengers has the duty of providing adequate, safe, and serviceable vehicles and equipment for the safe conveyance of its passengers, it will be liable for injuries resulting from its negligent failure to do so. Those travelers who ordinarily entrust themselves to common carriers have limited means of knowing the adequacy or safety of the vehicles and equipment. However, while the common carrier owes to its passengers the highest degree of care in this respect, it owes only the highest degree of care consistent with the practical operation of the transportation system by the carrier, in view of dangers that may be reasonably anticipated. Thus, the mere fact that a passenger is injured by reason of the manner of construction of a motor vehicle is not of itself necessarily sufficient to fasten liability on the carrier. Factors to be considered include: whether the equipment is obviously dangerous; whether the nature and manner of the injury could have been reasonably anticipated; whether similar injuries have occurred in similar fashion from the same equipment; whether the equipment is widely and safely used; the nature, extent, and frequency of safety inspections; the availability of better and safer equipment; and any other factor relevant to the question of whether or not the carrier has exercised the highest degree of care consistent with the practical operation of the transportation system.

Recent developments in the field of products liability open up new avenues of potential liability against common carriers. Thus, where the manufacturers of passenger cars may be required to make their product crashworthy so that an occupant will not be injured in an accident or so that a collision will not cause fire, a common carrier will probably be required to acquire and operate the most modern and "crashworthy" equipment. Accordingly, even when an accident is not the result of negligence in the operation of a vehicle by a bus driver or taxicab driver, the carrier might nonetheless be held liable for resulting injuries if it can be shown that the passenger would not have sustained injury if the carrier had utilized an available vehicle of different design.

Apart from selection and acquisition of equipment that is safe, a carrier has the obligation to exercise the appropriate degree of care in the maintenance of its equipment. This obligation includes not only the repair of defects that become apparent but also periodic inspections of all parts of the equipment. The nature, extent, and frequency of such inspections will depend upon the nature of the equipment or the portion of the equipment involved, but the inspections must meet the requirement that they constitute the highest degree of care consistent with the practical operation of the transportation system.

However, it should be kept in mind that even when a carrier fails to make any inspection of its equipment and injury results from a defect in or the disrepair of the equipment, the carrier will not be liable unless it can be established that its failure to inspect was the proximate cause of injury. If the defect or the disrepair was not of such a nature that proper inspection would have resulted in discovery and correction of the condition, it cannot be said that the failure to inspect was the direct and proximate cause of the injury, and the carrier will not be liable. Therefore, if injury results from a steering defect which could not have been discovered by any practicable method of inspection, a carrier will not be liable even if it made no inspection at all.

Apart from defects in the equipment itself, a common carrier can be liable for injuries resulting from dangerous or unsafe conditions occurring in its vehicles. The duty to exercise the highest degree of care practicable for the safety of passengers includes reasonable inspection of the floors of the vehicles. When a bus company has knowledge of foreign substances on the floor of the bus, it is required to make reasonable efforts to remove the foreign matter or warn passengers. If, as a result of its failure either to remove the material or warn the passengers, a passenger slips and falls, the bus company may be liable. The same may be true if a bus operator permits passengers to obstruct the aisles of the bus with packages, handbags, or other articles.

OPERATION OF VEHICLE.   In general, a common carrier is required to comply with the statutes and ordinances controlling the operation of motor vehicles. A common carrier must obey traffic signals, stop signs, speed limitations, and other regulations controlling the movement of motor vehicles on the public highways. Except when different provisions are made for common carriers such as buses and taxicabs, vehicles operated by common carriers are required to observe the same rules as other vehicles. In determining whether a collision between a bus or taxicab and another vehicle was the result of the negligence of the driver of the bus or taxicab, statutes and ordinances applicable to all motor vehicles will be considered. A violation of such statutes on the part of the bus driver or taxicab driver will normally constitute negligence. However, when injury to a passenger occurs, the common-law duty to exercise the highest degree of care for the safety of passengers is also pertinent.

It should be kept in mind that in many jurisdictions there are statutes and ordinances that have special application to common carriers such as buses and taxicabs. Such special provisions must also be considered in determining the liability of a common carrier under a given set of circumstances.

One frequent source of litigation involving bus companies is the claim of injury from sudden jerking, jolting, or stopping of the bus. In general, a carrier is not liable for injuries to a passenger resulting from application of the brakes in order to prevent a collision which could reasonably be considered more dangerous than the consequences of a sudden stop. Thus, if a child darts into the street immediatly in front of a moving bus and the operator of the bus immediately applies the brakes to avoid striking the child, the bus company will not be liable to a passenger who falls and is injured.

However, when the driver of the bus is personally negligent in creating the emergency situation, such negligence might be the proximate cause of the injuries. The bus company might be liable to the passenger even though he or she is injured in falling when the bus driver applies the brakes to avoid collision. Thus, if the bus is exceeding the speed limit or going through a red light or a stop sign, thereby creating a situation in which a collision could be avoided only by the immediate application of the brakes, the bus company would be liable to a passenger who falls and is injured when the brakes are applied, even though the driver is successful in avoiding a collision. Negligence in such cases consists not of applying the brakes, but of creating the situation in which the sudden application of brakes is the only means of avoiding a more serious consequence.

Some cases have held that while a bus company is not liable for the results of an emergency stop when the emergency is not created by the negligence of the bus driver, the burden is on the bus company to explain any such sudden stops.

Liability for injuries resulting from sudden stops has been discussed in terms of buses, since standing passengers are the most frequent source of injuries from such circumstances. However, the same rules apply with respect to taxicabs.

In considering the liability of common carriers to their passengers for injury, the principal factor is the requirement that the common carrier must exercise the highest degree of care for the safety of its passengers consistent with the practicable operation of the transportation system. However injury occurs, whether as the result of operation of the vehicle, maintenance of the vehicle, or otherwise, if the carrier fails to meet this standard, it will be liable.

CONDITION OF DRIVER. Common carriers may incur liability to injured passengers as the result of the physical or mental condition of the operator. Some jurisdictions require medical examinations of bus and taxicab drivers. Eye examinations are often required before licenses to operate buses or taxicabs will be granted. Even in the absence of such requirements, a common carrier is required to make reasonable efforts to make sure that the operators of its vehicles are mentally and physically qualified to be entrusted with the care of their passengers. In general, the courts have not required common carriers to investigate exhaustively the backgrounds of their drivers, nor must they require periodic medical examinations of all drivers. Nonetheless, it has been held that a carrier will be liable if a passenger is injured as the result of a physical or mental defect of a driver, and the carrier either knew or should have known of the mental or physical defect but nonetheless hired the driver and entrusted the passenger to his or her care.

When a mental or physical defect results in negligent operation of a vehicle, it is sufficient merely to show the negligent operation of the vehicle. It is not necessary for the passenger to show further negligence on the part of the company in hiring or retaining the operator. However, the issue may become important in cases in which the negligent operation on the part of the driver is not clear, but it can be shown that the accident might have been prevented by a better or healthier driver.

It should also be pointed out that the condition of a driver might expose a carrier to liability even in the absence of negligence on the part of the driver or on the part of the carrier in employing the driver. There is at least one decision applying a theory of contract liability to such a situation. In that case, the driver passed out, and the passenger was injured when the bus ran into a pole on the side of the street. It was undisputed that the driver had never suffered such an attack before and had passed several physical examinations wherein nothing was found wrong. Although it was conceded that there was no evidence to support a finding of negligence on the part of the carrier in employing the driver, the court stated that the case was essentially one for breach of contract of carriage.

It is also true that the defense of contributory negligence might well be available if the condition of the driver is a factor. One case involved a passenger in a taxicab who became intoxicated together with the driver. The passenger stayed in the taxicab, without protest, in spite of erratic and dangerous driving on the part of the driver. The passenger was held to be contributorily negligent. The same rule has been applied where a passenger entered a taxicab carrying liquor and gave the driver several drinks.

Under circumstances in which the condition of the driver is an issue, the basic principles applicable to the liability of a carrier control. The carrier owes the highest degree of care for the safety of its passengers consistent with the practicable operation of the system, and this includes furnishing appropriate employees and equipment. This requirement is founded on principles of public policy, on a contract of carriage, or both. The passenger owes a duty of ordinary care to avoid becoming injured.

ASSAULT BY A CARRIER'S EMPLOYEE. In general, a carrier will be liable for injuries to a passenger resulting from assault by the carrier's employee. This is an exception to the general rule that an employer will normally be liable only for acts of an employee committed within the scope of employment. Some decisions involving injuries to passengers of common carriers have found liability based upon the reasoning that anything done by the vehicle's operator which is in any way connected with the operation of the vehicle or the handling of passengers is within the scope of employment. An assault on the passenger is therefore within the scope of employment. This approach, however, requires a finding of some connection between the driver's employment and the assault, which in some situations might be difficult.

The view generally taken is that the common carrier's liability for an assault by one of its employees on a passenger is not dependent on the question of whether the employee was acting within the scope of authority or in the line of duty but is based upon the broad duty of the common carrier to protect its passengers from assault. Under this view, even though the employee of the carrier goes far outside his regular duties and assaults the passenger under circumstances having no relationship to the carriage, the carrier is nonetheless liable for the resulting injuries.

However, it should be noted that the liability thus fastened on the carrier arises from its duty to protect the passenger. It is therefore based upon the relationship of carrier and passenger. After that relationship has terminated, the carrier will not necessarily be liable for an assault on a passenger by its employee. Yet, the mere fact that the assault took place outside the conveyance does not necessarily establish that the carrier is not liable. The relationship of carrier and passenger continues until the passenger has been deposited in a place of safety, so if a bus driver or taxicab driver immediately follows a departing passenger out of the conveyance and assaults the passenger, the carrier may yet be liable.

The authorities are in conflict as to whether or not abusive or insulting language or provocative conduct on the part of a passenger, which in turn results in assault by the carrier's employee, will relieve the carrier from liability for the assault. Carriers have been held liable for injuries to a passenger assaulted by an employee of the carrier even when the passenger clearly provoked the employee by previously striking him.

A carrier may also be liable for injuries inflicted on one of its passengers through the negligence or willfulness of a fellow passenger or other third party when, by the exercise of proper care on the carrier's part, the danger might have been foreseen and prevented. The liability of a carrier for injuries under such circumstances arises from the failure of the carrier to afford the passenger proper protection if the carrier knew or should have known that the danger existed and could be prevented by proper care.

The same rule is applicable if a passenger is assaulted by another passenger. The duty of the carrier to protect its passengers includes the duty to protect them from assault. Under circumstances in which the carrier had the opportunity to know of the danger of assault and prevent it, the carrier might be liable for injuries resulting from the assault by one passenger on another.

CONTRIBUTORY NEGLIGENCE. The defense of contributory negligence has been discussed in previous sections, including the effects of the comparative negligence rule. Contributory negligence will not defeat recovery unless the passenger's negligence directly and proximately contributed to his or her injury. Neither will the negligence of a passenger necessarily defeat recovery when, through the negligence of the carrier, the passenger is placed in a hazardous situation and attempts to escape the danger by pursuing a dangerous course of action which might otherwise be considered negligent. Thus, when a passenger, in an attempt to avoid danger resulting from the carrier's negligence, attempts to leave the vehicle while it is moving, believing, upon reasonable grounds, that this is the best chance to escape injury, he or she is not contributorily negligent.

Young children are not expected to exercise the same degree of care for their own safety as adults. Cases are in conflict, however, respecting the liability of a carrier to children who are in the care of their parents or other adults. Some decisions have held that the carrier is entitled to expect the parents to protect the child. When the parents are negligent in failing to do so, such negligence will bar recovery against the carrier by the child. Other decisions have held to the contrary, holding the carrier liable even though the child's parents were negligent. It should be noted, however, that the contributory negligence on the part of the parents will nonetheless bar recovery by the parents for any claim they might have for medical expenses or loss of services resulting from injury to the child.

Contributory negligence on the part of a passenger has been held to bar recovery under a wide variety of circumstances. It has been held that a passenger who slips and falls on snow, ice, or a foreign substance on the floor of a bus, with full knowledge of the condition, may not recover damages. Attempting to board or alight from a moving vehicle has also been held to be contributory negligence.

On the other hand, it has been held that it is not necessarily contributory negligence for a passenger to step off a vehicle in the nighttime without looking. The passenger is entitled to assume that the driver will not deposit him or her in an unsafe place. If a passenger falls into an excavation, without first looking, the question of whether he or she exercised ordinary care for his or her own safety is one for the determination of a jury.

A passenger does have the obligation to exercise ordinary care for his or her own safety. When there is reason to anticipate the possibility of danger, he or she may not necessarily rely upon the obligation of the operator to deposit him or her in a place of safety. Therefore, when a passenger departs from a conveyance into a moving lane of traffic without looking, he or she will be contributorily negligent.

A passenger may also be contributorily negligent in permitting an arm, or some other portion of the body, to protrude through the window of the moving conveyance, when this act results in injury. A passenger may be negligent in standing, when seats are available, in distracting the driver, in falling over packages of which he has knowledge, or by any other act or omission that constitutes a failure to exercise ordinary care for personal safety.

While the issue of contributory negligence frequently arises under factual situations that are unique to the carrier-passenger relationship, the basic principles applicable are those applicable in negligence law in general.

Limitations of Liability.   Efforts to limit the liability of a common carrier to passengers, whether by exculpatory agreement or otherwise, generally have been held to be invalid, even when consented to by the passenger. Two considerations are involved: (1) public policy, in particular the importance the law attaches to human life and safety, which consideration forbids the relaxation of care on the part of a common carrier; (2) the position of advantage which the common carrier has, in that the carrier and the passenger do not normally deal on an equal footing, the passenger desiring to go from one place to another, and the carrier frequently providing the only available means of transportation.

Such agreements may be applicable in the case of a private carrier. Some cases have even held such agreements applicable to companies that are common carriers, but which in the particular circumstance are functioning as private carriers.

There is also some authority to the effect that a carrier and passenger may validly agree to a limitation of liability when the limitation of liability is accompanied by a reduction in fare. Courts that have upheld such agreements do so on the basis that the considerations of public policy that normally prohibit such agreements do not apply when the passenger is given the choice either to pay full fare or agree to a limitation of liability in return for a reduced fare.

With respect to gratuitous passengers, as opposed to passengers who are paying fares, the authorities are split. The federal rule recognizes the validity of agreements limiting liability in the case of gratuitous passengers, while the various states are divided on the issue. Some states hold such agreements invalid, while others give them effect. Even in those jurisdictions which do give effect to such agreements, it is frequently held that, in the case of a limitation of liability printed on a free pass, the limitation is effective only if the passenger has expressly assented to the limitation. Furthermore, even in those jurisdictions that do give effect to agreements limiting liability, such agreements are not given effect in the case of wanton or willful misconduct or gross negligence on the part of the carrier.

Common carriers often give their employees free passes which may be utilized by the employee or the employee's family. Generally, a limitation of liability contained on such passes will be given effect if the pass is really a gratuity. However, if the granting of such a pass is a part of the contract of employment, it is not truly a gratuity, and a limitation of liability may not be given effect.

A common carrier cannot escape liability to its passengers by leasing its equipment to another to operate. Under such circumstances, the common carrier will still be liable to the passenger for injuries occasioned by the negligence of the lessee. A lessee of equipment will also be liable for injury to the passenger, including liability arising from a defect in the leased equipment.

The same rule is applicable in the case of an independent contractor. In an earlier section, rights and liabilities that arise from the independent contractor relationship were discussed. In general, since one who employs an independent contractor does not control the operation of the contractor, he or she is not liable for the negligence of the independent contractor. It has been held that the duty a common carrier owes to its passengers is a nondelegable duty, and the obligation to the passenger cannot be circumvented by contracting with another to fulfill that obligation. Therefore, the carrier will be liable to the passenger for injuries occasioned by the negligence of an independent contractor or the employees of an independent contractor.

Law Applicable Although the authorities are not unanimous, generally the law applicable will be the law of the jurisdiction in which the contract of carriage was entered into. This will normally be the location where a ticket was bought, the fare paid, or the trip commenced. There are some jurisdictions, however, which have held that the law of the jurisdiction where the accident causing injury occurred will be applied.

The federal courts will, as in other circumstances, apply the appropriate state law. However, if interstate commerce is involved and there is a federal rule applicable, the federal rule will apply. If interstate commerce is not involved or there is no federal rule applicable, no problem will arise if the contract of carriage and the accident causing injury occurred in the same state. Under those circumstances, the law of that state will apply. If the contract of carriage and the place where the accident occurred are in different states, it will be necessary to determine the conflict of law rule recognized by the state in which the action is brought. Such rule will determine whether the law to apply is the law of the place where the contract of carriage was entered into or the law of the place where the accident occurred.

It can be seen that in many circumstances the selection of a court in which to bring an action by a plaintiff's counsel may be of critical importance. When a defendant has a presence in more than one state, it may normally be sued in any state in which it is present. When there is a diversity of citizenship between a plaintiff and a defendant, a plaintiff may bring the action in federal court; or, if a plaintiff brings the action in state court, a defendant may have it removed to the federal court. Such "shopping" for a court or jurisdiction favorable to one party or the other is common. Normally an astute plaintiff's counsel will attempt to have a case litigated, where possible, in a court and jurisdiction in which the most favorable substantive and/or procedural law for a particular case will be applied. Astute defense counsel will do the same. The possibilities of such "shopping" are prevalent, of course, in the case of common carriers who operate in a number of different states.

No-Fault

Historically, liability insurance was just that. The insurer undertook to protect the insured from liability asserted against the insured by third parties. The person protected by automobile insurance was the insured, not the injured third party, and the existence of insurance in no way affected the basic law relating to the liability of one person to another for injury in tort. Liability insurance merely protected the insured from a loss occasioned by recovery against the insured through the existing system for establishing liability.

Development of No-Fault In the past three-quarters of a century, the automobile has become one of the important factors in contemporary American life. Increasing use of the automobile, along with other factors, resulted in increasing injuries and increasing liability claims. The automobile operator who was faced with such a claim and did not have sufficient personal assets to meet such a claim became the rule rather than the exception. Liability insurance eventually became looked upon as something protecting the injured party as well as the insured. Over the years, to protect from the impecunious defendant persons injured in an automobile accident, various schemes were devised and instituted—compulsory liability insurance, unsatisfied judgment funds, and finally, in the 1950s, uninsured motorist coverage. These plans had little to do with attempting to change the underlying legal system or concepts of liability. They merely attempted to provide ways to satisfy claims that were legally valid and meritorious under the existing system.

However, since the early years of the automobile, plans have also been advanced to replace the existing tort system with a system based upon the same principles as workers' compensation so as to provide stated benefits for all persons injured in automobile accidents without a need to prove fault. It is said that the first such scheme was proposed in 1914. Many other such plans have been advanced through the years. It remained for a Harvard professor, Robert E. Keeton, and a University of Illinois professor, Jeffrey O'Connell, to propose a system that seemed to add something in the way of benefits, take little away, and, probably most important, cost less to the insurance buyer. A constituency was now found among other vocal advocates of reform.

The Keeton-O'Connell plan was proposed in 1964. It would have provided basic protection from economic loss without respect to fault, while preserving the right to sue in tort if damages for pain and suffering were in excess of $5,000 (or all other items of damages were in excess of $10,000). The plan promised a considerable reduction in premium, a large part of which was claimed to be possible by the elimination of expenses to the company and to injured parties in the investigation and litigation of injury claims.

Since then, a wide variety of similar schemes have been proposed under the general designation of "no-fault." The only thing in common among these systems is the expansion of first-party benefits payable without respect to fault.

Present No-Fault Plans The no-fault concept, for a variety of reasons, has won widespread political support. As of early 1977, twenty-four states and Puerto Rico had enacted some no-fault system. Four of these systems were optional, while the rest were compulsory. In 1974, a national plan passed in the Senate.

Provisions of the no-fault plans varied widely. Some preserved the tort system intact, merely adding first-party benefits, and some preserved the tort system with the exception of a deduction for payments made under a no-fault provision. The rest partially abrogated the negligence system in motor vehicle cases, retaining the right to sue in tort for injuries of a certain type or severity, where a "threshold" of a certain amount of expenses or damages was exceeded, or for intentional torts. A great variety of thresholds were used. Some plans also provided for reductions of recovery for amounts received from collateral sources such as workers' compensation, disability income insurance, and medical expense insurance.

Some plans provided subrogation rights for the insurer making no-fault payments. Where subrogation was possible, many systems provided for arbitration among insurance carriers on such subrogation claims. Some states retaining tort recovery provided that an insurer paying no-fault payments would have a lien to such extent on any recovery made by its insured against a culpable third party.

Of the plans enacted, nineteen provide for some or all commercial motor vehicles to be affected by the no-fault law. Each statute contains a definition of motor vehicles affected by the act, and the statute of any given state must be looked to to determine whether a specific kind of commercial motor vehicle will be affected and, if so, the extent to which it will be affected. Generalizations are difficult with respect to no-fault insurance because of the wide variety of systems. Moreover, many inconsistencies and ambiguities in the various acts have not yet been clarified by judicial construction or interpretation.

No-Fault Litigation As might be expected, the earliest litigation dealing with any of the no-fault plans often attacked their constitutionality. Decisions regarding constitutionality have ranged from complete approval of the plans, to partial approval, to complete disapproval. Of those receiving partial approval, the portions held to be unconstitutional have included certain arbitration requirements, or provisions held to be discriminatory, such as a provision limiting access to the tort system to cases involving a fracture of a weight-bearing bone. A number of existing no-fault laws have not yet been tested on constitutional grounds in the courts of last resort of their states, and, of course, it can be anticipated that there may be more states which will enact no-fault laws. The constitutionality of provisions either including or excluding commercial motor vehicles, or certain kinds of commercial motor vehicles, will be determined on a state-by-state basis. Efforts are being made to enact a national no-fault plan that might either establish national standards or provide certain minimum standards which all states must meet by appropriate legislation.

Issues in No-Fault It is difficult at this point to predict all of the problems which might arise or how the courts will resolve them. They will necessarily by resolved on the basis of the specific provisions of each applicable no-fault law.

Use. Problems have arisen and will continue to arise respecting what might constitute "use" of a commercial motor vehicle under applicable no-fault laws. Some such laws include a provision for extension of "use" of the vehicle to include loading and unloading. Some do not. A New York case held that a woman who slipped and fell carrying groceries to her car which was parked one block away, was not entitled to benefits because she was not yet loading her car. A body of case law will have to be established in New York and in other states having similar provisions in order to determine when the process of loading begins and ends in various circumstances.

In another case, a New York court held that a pedestrian who tripped over a fuel hose extended from a fuel truck across a public sidewalk was entitled to no-fault benefits since the vehicle was in "use" at the time. On the other hand, another New York case held that when the operator of a snowmobile collided with a parked car, there could be no recovery since the parked automobile was not in "operation or use."

Maintenance. Questions might arise as to whether or not use and operation of a vehicle includes maintenance—so as to protect a mechanic injured while repairing a vehicle—or whether a fire fighter or other person attempting to put out a fire in a vehicle is protected. Circumstances giving rise to such questions are unlimited.

Passenger. Another problem which will arise involves the question of the term "passenger" as it is used in some no-fault laws. In New Jersey it has been held that a passenger who left an automobile and was burned in a sudden explosion while watching a service station attendant put water into the car was still considered an occupant or passenger and was entitled to no-fault benefits. Again, the question of when an occupant or passenger becomes or ceases to be such will necessarily be resolved only after a sufficient passage of time to permit the creation of a body of case law construing the provisions of the various no-fault laws.

Which Insurer Should Pay Benefits. The issue of which insurer is responsible for paying benefits arises more frequently than that of whether or not a party is entitled to benefits at all. Some laws provide that an injured party will collect no-fault benefits from his or her own insurer, unless he or she is not the owner of a motor vehicle or covered by personal insurance, in which case he or she will receive benefits from the insurer of the striking car. When there is a "chain reaction" accident, the question may arise as to whether the striking car is the vehicle that actually made contact with the injured party, or whether the vehicle that initiated the chain reaction is the striking car. Problems may also develop with respect to tractor-trailer combinations with divergent ownership and insurance coverage. An accident involving a tow truck pulling a disabled vehicle can raise such an issue, particularly when the actual contact involved the towed vehicle.

Extraterritoriality. The fact that many states do not have no-fault laws and that existing laws vary widely will also create a number of problems when accidents occur in states other than the state of residence of the injured party or the state where the insurance was written. It is anticipated that a considerable amount of jurisdictional "shopping" will result. This may well be made more prevalent by the fact that most insurers operate in more than one state, with the result that they are amenable to service of summons in many jurisdictions other than that where the accident occurred or where the policy was written.

The Impact of No-Fault It is apparent that many more questions can be raised than can be answered. The first no-fault law was enacted in Massachusetts in 1971. This has been followed by twenty-four more, varying widely with respect to their provisions and including provisions dealing with the types of motor vehicles that will be affected. The acts are not only inconsistent with each other but frequently contain internal inconsistencies and ambiguities. Typically, they are characterized by poor legal draftsmanship. A reading of almost any no-fault law reveals numerous instances in which the drafters obviously did not anticipate the types of situations which might arise or the legal effect of certain provisions.

While one of the claimed virtues of no-fault legislation was the elimination of litigation in automobile accident cases, there already has been a considerable amount of litigation directly arising from no-fault legislation. This litigation has barely scratched the surface in clarifying and construing no-fault legislation and in testing the constitutional validity of the various provisions of such legislation. Hence, no present publication could hope to give any definitive answers to the various questions that might arise involving commercial motor vehicles. Any such work could become obsolete within months.

The existence of no-fault coverage itself may alter the evidence respecting the nature and extent of injury. Typically, when there are threshold requirements before a tort recovery may be had, an injured party may shop for a physician who will render sufficient treatment to exceed a monetary threshold for medical expenses, or who will render an opinion that an injury is permanent, where permanency of injury is required for tort recovery.

As no-fault legislation develops, it may involve a profound change in commercial motor vehicle exposures. The nature and basis of liability, as well as the procedures for establishing and enforcing rights, may be completely altered.

Damages

Damages may be categorized as compensatory or punitive damages. The subject of damages will be reviewed here only as it affects motor vehicle exposures.

Compensatory Damages

Bodily Injury. A person sustaining bodily injury as a direct and proximate result of negligence in the operation, maintenance, or use of a commercial motor vehicle is entitled to recover such amount as will fairly and justly compensate for the injuries sustained. It is a recognized and established principle that the compensation awarded to one who is injured shall be equivalent to, or commensurate with, the loss or injury sustained. The injured person may recover for all damages proximately resulting from the injury.

By the same token, the negligent party is liable only for the damages that are the direct and proximate result of the negligence. Such loss may include all medical expenses reasonably necessary in the treatment of the injury, cost of transportation to and from a doctor's office or hospital, as well as all loss of income directly and proximately resulting from the injury. A further sum may be included to compensate the injured party reasonably and fairly for the pain and suffering experienced as a result of the injury. The injured party may also recover for *anticipated* future medical expenses, loss of income, and pain and suffering. While these general principles are almost universally recognized, jurisdictions differ in applying these principles to specific aspects of damages.

For instance, many states have adopted the so-called *collateral source rule*. This provides that the injured party's damages may not be reduced by payments from collateral sources, such as workers' compensation benefits, medical payment insurance, group insurance, social security benefits, veterans' benefits, sick leave benefits, or any other source not provided by the negligent party. Some jurisdictions apply the collateral source rule rather rigidly, while others apply it to benefits from some sources but not to others.

Decisions also differ with respect to the effect of federal income tax on an award for bodily injury damages for lost income. Such an award is not taxable, but many jurisdictions have held that the injured party may still recover for the gross amount of income lost as a result of inability to work, without deduction for the income tax savings.

Evidentiary rules in a given jurisdiction may also have a significant impact on the damages which may be recoverable. For instance, some jurisdictions permit only evidence of probabilities. They require expert medical testimony to establish that a given injury was probably the result of the accident in question, or that future medical expenses, disability, loss of income, or pain and suffering are probably going to occur. Other jurisdictions will permit evidence relating to possibilities to be considered by the jury.

Certain persons other than the injured party may have a right to recover for losses sustained as a result of the injury. Parents who have incurred medical expenses as a result of injury to their child may have the right to recover such expenses from the negligent party, as well as the value of the loss of services which they might have sustained as a result of the child's injury. One spouse may also have a similar derivative action as a result of injury to the other spouse; and this may include, along with recovery of economic loss, the right to recover for loss of consortium.

Specific rules of evidence applicable in different jurisdictions perhaps have more impact on questions of damages than on questions of liability. As pointed out, rules respecting testimony of expert witnesses can be of critical importance on questions of the nature and extent of injuries as well as lost income. Rules respecting the admissibility of various kinds of documents and records can also be of considerable significance, either by way of establishing damages or in mitigating them, such as records showing such things as previous injuries, previous claims, and poor work record.

Death. At common law there was no recovery for wrongfully caused death. However, every jurisdiction has enacted a wrongful death statute. The typical statute provides for a right of recovery on the part of the decedent's next of kin. The nature of recoverable damages may differ. Many statutes limit recovery to financial loss which occurs as a direct and proximate result of the death. Some statutes permit jurors to consider more intangible factors such as loss of companionship or mental anguish in assessing damages. In fact, the trend is very definitely toward liberalization of the strict rule limiting recovery to pecuniary loss, both by way of legislative action amending the statutes, and by judicial reinterpretation of existing statutes.

Generally, the wrongful death action is different from the action by a decedent's estate for damages owing to the decedent. When a person is injured, sustaining medical expenses, loss of income, and pain and suffering, the right to recover for such items of damages survives death, and the decedent's estate may bring action to recover such damages. The wrongful death action normally is brought on behalf of the next of kin for their benefit and is usually restricted to damages resulting from the death.

Expert testimony from economists is frequently utilized in bodily injury actions and wrongful death actions, to establish the present value of the income the decedent would have made had he or she lived a normally expected life span, and also to establish the percentage or porportion of projected income that would probably have been spent for the benefit of the next of kin seeking damages. The economist may also make projections or calculations relating not only to projected income but also to pension or other benefits that might have accrued to the decedent or the decedent's spouse, or differences in such benefits resulting from early death.

Life expectancy tables are often used as a basis for such projections. Life expectancy tables merely show an average life expectancy, and any individual may, by reason of poor health, have a greatly reduced life expectancy.

Property Damage. The general principles governing the amounts allowable for property damage have been discussed in previous chapters. Beyond such general principles, the specific means of measurement depends largely on the type of property that has been damaged or destroyed as well as the factual question of whether there has been any economic loss from the deprivation of the property's use. The measures of loss which flow from the damage, destruction, or abstraction of commercial motor vehicles will be discussed under a subsequent heading in this chapter. Hence, to avoid unnecessary repetition, no further elaboration will be attempted here, except to note the rather obvious fact that trucks and other large commercial motor vehicles are instruments through which millions of dollars of property damage can easily occur in a single mishap.

Punitive Damages Exemplary or punitive damages are those that are given in addition to ordinary compensatory damages on account of the wanton, reckless, malicious, or oppressive character of the act complained of. While the basic principles of law are essentially the same in assessing punitive damages in cases involving commercial motor vehicles as they are in other situations, there are some practical differences. In some jurisdictions, where the purpose of punitive damages is solely to punish the offender, evidence of the financial status of the defendant is permitted to go to the jury on the theory that it is necessary for the jury to have a full understanding of the defendant's ability to pay in order to determine what amount of punitive damages is appropriate as a punishment.

Punitive damages are more frequently sought in actions in which there is a "deep pocket," such as a corporate defendant, because juries are more likely to assess punitive damages against well-to-do defendants. However, while an employer is liable for damages resulting from the negligence of an employee acting within the scope of employment, he or she is not necessarily required to respond in punitive damages for every act of an employee which might be the basis for the assessment of such damages against the employee.

When the employer has authorized, ratified, acquiesced in, or participated in the employee's conduct that gives rise to the right to recover punitive damages, the employer might be held liable. The employer might also be held liable in punitive damages if he or she has failed to exercise reasonable care in selecting or retaining an employee who maliciously or willfully injures another.

There are circumstances in which the employer might be called upon to respond in punitive damages as a result of the act of an employee, where the act was a necessary or integral part of employment or was clearly in furtherance of some purpose on behalf of the employer. Thus, if a truck driver assaults another person in an argument over priority in loading or unloading the truck, the employer might be held liable.

In cases in which punitive damages may be recovered, or in which a plaintiff is seeking such recovery, frequently there are issues respecting insurance coverage. Some jurisdictions do not permit insurance coverage for punitive damages as a matter of public policy. The acts that give rise to punitive damages are frequently of a type that may fall under an exclusion in a liability policy. However, there is an increasing incidence of claims for punitive damages and an increasing willingness on the part of courts to submit such issues to juries.

MOTOR VEHICLE PHYSICAL DAMAGE EXPOSURES

The phrase "motor vehicle physical damage exposures" customarily refers to loss exposures faced by owners and bailees of motor vehicles and to potential losses which may result in *direct loss*—a decrease in intrinsic value—and/or an *indirect loss*— a loss of use due to damage, destruction, breakdown, or disappearance of the vehicle itself. Fundamentally, there are a number of similarities between motor vehicle physical damage exposures and the exposures which owners and bailees of other kinds of real and personal property face.

Factors Affecting Physical Damage Exposures

The loss potential for motor vehicles, as with virtually all kinds of property, is affected by its location, management and maintenance, purpose of use, and intensity of usage.

Location or Garaging Location or "garaging" of motor vehicles is especially important with respect to certain kinds of perils. Vehicles that are garaged in deteriorating neighborhoods or in areas of high crime rates are demonstrably more susceptible to acts of vandalism and theft. Vehicles in certain locations also may be unduly exposed to damage by the elements of nature. Moreover, congested areas are as much a threat to vehicles as they are to surrounding structures.

Indoor storage of motor vehicles does not always reduce exposures. The construction, location, occupancy, protection, and exposure of buildings are important in considering this alternative. So will the catastrophic loss potential be increased when there is a high concentration of valuable vehicles and related equipment in one structure.

Maintenance The manner in which motor vehicles are maintained and managed has a significant effect on physical damage loss potential. Those who are indifferent about servicing their vehicles regularly or those who lack programs of preventive maintenance can eventually expect mechanical breakdowns and other costly problems. Such abuses can be the proximate cause of accidents involving physical damage of a larger magnitude (and of injuries and damages to others). Worn tires and brake linings are the cause of many mishaps. Proper maintenance of vehicles, therefore, can go a long way in reducing loss frequency, just as it can for buildings, machinery, and boilers.

Use Carefully used for their intended purpose, many commercial vehicles can survive several hundred thousand miles of use. Misuse of vehicles can shorten their useful life. For example, a dump truck that is constantly used to haul gravel in loads beyond its rated capacity will more likely sustain damage than a similar vehicle that is properly used.

Operator Experience and Training Collision losses may be minimized if discretion is exercised in selecting vehicle operators who are experienced, responsible, and relatively free of traffic violations and accidents. The degree of sophistication required of operators will obviously depend upon the size of operation and the type, size, and usage of vehicles, but the condition of the labor market also may have an effect on the requirements that can actually be imposed at any given time. Many owners of commercial fleets which utilize large, costly trucks or buses often require prospective employees to undergo rigorous physical examinations and to take road tests. Then, following their employment, the employees may be required to attend periodic training sessions. Other employers are less demanding. They may simply require prospective employees to complete applications and to show proof that they hold valid licenses to operate the vehicles in question.

A program of hiring and training qualified help is as important a factor in reducing motor vehicle physical damage loss exposures as is a program of preventive maintenance. Both are essential. An irresponsible driver who abuses a vehicle that is regularly serviced and maintained can cause as many problems as a poorly maintained vehicle that is operated by a qualified person.

Purpose and Intensity of Use Both purpose and intensity of use can have adverse effects upon the physical conditions of motor vehicles. For example, an ambulance or a fire truck is more likely to be involved in an accident than a limousine that is used only for weddings and funerals.

Intensity of usage refers to vehicle activity in terms of the amount of time a vehicle is exposed to street traffic or in terms of the distance a vehicle must continuously travel in fulfilling its purpose. It stands to reason that the more intense the usage, the greater the exposure to loss. For example, a truck that is used for retail and wholesale delivery of lumber is more likely to be subject to physical loss than the same type of vehicle that is used by a carpenter to travel to and from job sites. On the other hand, a taxicab that is used day and night will usually be faced with more conditions that can physically affect it than the same type of vehicle owned by a corporation and furnished to one of its salespersons.

Entities Exposed

Commercial, charitable, and public entities are among those exposed to motor vehicle physical damage losses. They may be owners or bailees of vehicles. The latter can consist of users under rental or lease agreements, borrowers, or those that maintain temporary control over the vehicles of others, such as automobile dealers, repair shops, service stations, operators of parking lots, and storage garages. Such a bailee may be legally liable to the owner of a vehicle damaged while in the bailee's care, custody, and control.

Owners Over 142 million privately and publicly owned motor vehicles were registered in the United States in 1976.[1] Table 8-1 illustrates the percentage of these vehicles that were commercial vehicles, as well as their chances of loss.

There are a variety of buses in use. Their sizes, particularly in terms of passenger capacity, differ widely depending upon usage. However, those owned and operated by commercial transportation companies generally are the larger and more sophisticated models. A wide variety of trucks also are in use. These include pickup, panel, delivery vans, platform, cattlerack, refrigerated, furniture vans, open-top vans, beverage trucks, utility trucks, garbage and refuse collectors, winch and cranes, wreckers, pole and logging, auto transports, tank trucks for liquids or dry bulk, and concrete mixers. These range in weight size from a ton and a half pickup to diesel-operated trucks with five axles and a gross vehicle weight of 76,000 pounds.[2]

Owners of commercial vehicles face costly outlays in purchasing and maintaining them. Depending upon the type, size, and number of such vehicles owned, losses can range from $5,000 to $50,000 or more if one of these vehicles is physically damaged or destroyed. Furthermore, in view of the continuing increases in the prices of materials, parts, and labor, the cost of vehicles, and thus the dollar loss potentials, obviously will continue to rise sharply in the foreseeable future.

Renters or Lessees Entities which cannot afford to purchase and maintain their own motor vehicles often rent them, for a day, a week, a month, or a year or more, as needed. Even for those who can afford to buy, leasing often offers a number of advantages. First, a renter or a lessee may be able to use its working capital to produce a better rate of return. Secondly, a leasing arrangement is a form of financing that does not appear as a liability on a financial statement and, as such, tends to affect a lessee's line of credit less than alternative means of financing. Likewise, renters and lessees may have newer vehicles than an owner

Table 8-1

Types of Motor Vehicles Involved In Accidents—1976*

Type of Vehicle	In Fatal Accidents		In All Accidents		Percent of Total Vehicle Registration[1]	Number of Occupant Fatalities
	Number	Percent	Number	Percent		
All Types	59,000	100.0%	28,400,000	100.0%	100.0%	[5]
Passenger cars	41,200	69.8	23,100,000	81.3	76.9	27,400
Trucks	12,400	21.0	4,100,000	14.5	19.0	5,350
Truck or truck tractor	7,800	13.2	3,290,000	11.6	18.2	[4]
Truck tractor and semi-trailer	3,600	6.1	530,000	1.9 ⎱	0.8	[4]
Other truck combinations	1,000	1.7	280,000	1.0 ⎰		[4]
Farm tractors, equipment	140	0.3	23,000	0.1	[2]	120
Taxicabs	410	0.7	180,000	0.6	0.2	270
Buses, commercial	310	0.5	180,000	0.6	0.1	100
Buses, school	190	0.3	55,000	0.2	0.2	60
Motorcycles	3,000	5.1	385,000	1.4 ⎱	3.6	2,850
Motor scooters, motor bikes	150	0.3	17,000	0.1 ⎰		150
Other [3]	1,200	2.0	360,000	1.2	[4]	1,100

1. Percentage figures are based on numbers of vehicles and do not reflect miles traveled or place of travel, both of which affect accident experience.
2. These vehicles are not included in total vehicle registrations; estimated number—5,000,000.
3. Includes fire equipment, ambulances, special vehicles, other.
4. Data not available.
5. In addition to these occupant fatalities, there were 8,300 pedestrian, 900 pedalcyclist, and 100 other deaths.

Note: Emergency vehicles—Sample data for "Other" vehicles shows that while emergency vehicles represented only 6 percent of the "Other" vehicles involved in all accidents, they were involved in 16 percent of the fatal accidents suffered by "Other" vehicles in 1976. Based on these percentages, about 20,000 emergency vehicles were involved in motor-vehicle accidents in 1976; approximately 190 were in fatal accidents.

*Reprinted with permission from *Accident Facts* (Chicago: National Safety Council, 1977), p. 56.

that has to use and depreciate its vehicles over a period of years. Leasing may offer tax advantages as well.

Yet, if special care is not exercised, renting and leasing arrangements can produce certain disadvantages. As bailees, renters and lessees generally are held liable for any loss or damage to vehicles in their care, custody, or control, and attributable to their negligence.

However, the standard of care imposed upon bailees can be limited or broadened through contractual agreement of the parties. For example, rental or lease agreements may contain provisions restricting the operation of vehicles to certain persons or to certain areas. They may also contain the stipulation that the vehicles be returned to the owner in as good a condition as they were received. If any of these provisions is violated, renters or lessees can be held liable for resulting loss or damage to those vehicles regardless of fault.[3]

What all of this means is that there may be times when users of motor vehicles, particularly those under long-term contracts, will have to exercise the same degree of care with motor vehicles as they would if they were the actual owners. In fact, many of the same physical damage loss exposures that face owners also confront lessees, especially under long-term leases.

Borrowers or Users Entities that borrow or use motor vehicles of others also are considered bailees. But, because borrowing results in a gratuitous bailment, the standard of care required of a borrower may differ from that of a renter or lessee. If the vehicle is borrowed for the mutual benefit of the owner and the user, the latter generally is liable for any loss or damage attributable to negligence. However, if the borrower derives sole benefit from the use of a nonowned motor vehicle, the borrower generally will be charged with a higher standard of care. These situations must be handled with caution, therefore, particularly when the vehicles are very expensive or are specialized units.

Furthermore, in the absence of some form of agreement between the parties, borrowing arrangements can work to the disadvantage of the owner. The borrower, for example, may not feel obligated to exercise caution with the property of others. In any case, if the borrower is unable to make good for any loss or damage, the owner may be forced to retain the damages as a practical matter. Owners of vehicles, therefore, must view such arrangements with care.

Garages, Storage Places, and Parking Lots Owners and operators of service stations, repair shops, storage garages, and parking lots normally maintain temporary custody of automobiles and other motor vehicles belonging to others. In that capacity, they are considered "bailees for hire," and generally they are held liable for loss or damage caused by their failure to exercise ordinary care. Ordinary care, of course, depends upon the circumstances. Regardless of what these businesses may do or try to do in absolving themselves of claims, they are seldom, if ever, immune from liability.

There may be occasions, however, when some of these businesses will exercise more caution than is necessary in protecting the vehicles of others simply to maintain their customers' goodwill. There may even be occasions when some of these entities will pay for certain damages to customers' vehicles even though the bailee is not really at fault.

Claims against such bailees for physical loss or damage to vehicles of others originate predominantly from conditions on the premises. Although the conditions will vary with the type and the size of facility, conditions and practices that foster claims include buildings and premises that are not suited for the type of operation involved, unsupervised accommodations that tend to become congested, such as often occurs with multi-level parking stations, the requirement that keys be left in vehicles and the policy of some businesses of permitting overnight parking without adequate security. The location of the business premises in relation to the character of the neighborhood and surrounding structures is also a factor, just as it is for other entities that own or lease motor vehicles.

Sources of Loss

Physical damage losses to motor vehicles can be either direct losses or indirect losses.

Direct Losses A direct loss, simply stated, is one wherein property itself is damaged, destroyed, or lost due to some peril. Direct losses can come about in a variety of ways, depending upon the exposure and the peril. Regardless of existing conditions, some losses are accidental in the sense that they are unexpected or unforeseen (such as some acts of God). Other losses are not accidental or fortuitous, such as loss by wear and tear or gradual deterioration. Some losses are intentional.

Obviously, motor vehicles can sustain considerable damage through collision. Tractors often collide with semitrailers by jackknifing. Vehicles can be damaged or destroyed by collision with other vehicles, animals, trains, bridge abutments, or other objects. Losses can stem from such hazards as bad weather conditions, negligence of the driver, carelessness of other motorists, faulty brakes, worn tires, and other conditions enhanced by failure to maintain vehicles properly.

Many motor vehicle physical damage losses result from conditions on premises or within buildings. Conditions that may damage a building may also damage vehicles in or near the building. Congested or unsupervised areas for parking vehicles can result in scratches and dents by collision between vehicles or objects on the premises. On the other hand, carelessness in servicing or in repairing vehicles can result in mechanical or electrical breakdowns. Automobile hoists and elevators that are not maintained or operated properly also can bring about damage to vehicles.

Furthermore, keys left in parked vehicles increase the likelihood of vehicle thefts. Vehicles parked overnight on premises that are not provided with safeguards, such as sufficient lighting or watch patrol services, are susceptible to loss by tire slashing, windshield breakage, and other forms of vandalism and malicious mischief, as well as theft of vehicles or their parts.

Windstorms, tornadoes, hurricanes, ice, hailstorms, dust, sandstorms, extremes of temperature, floods, rising waters, and earthquakes are among the common elements of nature that can take their toll in physical damage losses. The elements cause direct loss by upset, by wind-blown objects, or by pitting, among others. It sometimes does not matter, as previously mentioned, whether the vehicles are in the open or within structures. It really depends upon the peril involved or upon the severity of the peril.

The way in which vehicles are used, maintained, and serviced also has a great deal to do with the frequency and severity of direct losses. Only a few conditions are conducive to vehicle theft losses. Some of these were mentioned earlier. The conveyance of valuable cargo is another condition conducive to theft of vehicles. In addition, many vehicles are stolen when they are left idling while their operators are at truck stops, at highway rest stations, or while they are attending to business at various establishments, such as at stores and restaurants.

Indirect Losses An indirect loss is one that occurs as a consequence of a direct loss. Loss of use of a vehicle following its damage or destruction by the peril of fire, theft, or collision is one such example.

Depending upon the circumstances, loss of use of vehicles can be costly to a business—sometimes costlier than any physical damage losses. Consider the service station, for example, that derives a substantial portion of its income from providing towing services with an old but well-kept tow truck. Any physical damage to that truck may not amount to much. But if that truck becomes unusable for any period, the owner may lose a substantial part of its income until the vehicle can be restored to service. It may be necessary to incur extra expense in renting another vehicle. This loss of income and additional expense also can come about when a vehicle is stolen. Before it is returned or replaced, a substantial loss can result.

Entities that have fleets of vehicles may have replacements readily available in the event of contingencies, which may reduce indirect loss exposures; but if a large number of fleet vehicles are damaged by a tornado or act of vandalism, the number of replacements needed may not be readily available. Indirect losses may then be substantial.

Measures of Loss Motor vehicles are usually costly. Furthermore, everything that is used in making motor vehicles—steel, rubber, glass, plastics—continues to rise in price as do labor costs. Add to the purchase price the costs of proper maintenance and servicing, parts and labor, gas and oil, and license fees and other taxes, and one has a costly investment in each vehicle.

Losses also occur. And, when they do, it sometimes becomes complicated to measure the damages. Entities sometimes value their vehicles with some degree of partiality, especially when their vehicles perform well. However, motor vehicle physical damage losses generally are valued on the basis of the cost of repair, actual cash value, or fair market value. (The latter two valuations sometimes are used synonymously, although some argue that they mean different things.) In any event, actual cash value essentially means the replacement cost of vehicles less any depreciation.

The dollar size of a loss to any one vehicle depends largely upon the type, size, age, condition of vehicle, and whether it is custom-built or foreign-made. Also important are the availability of parts and their costs, along with the cost of labor time in repairing them, and any sales taxes that may apply.

The measure of a loss also depends upon the extent of damages. Motor vehicles can be (1) partially damaged, (2) totally destroyed, or (3) damaged to such an extent that they are considered to be "constructive total losses," as explained below.

Partial Losses. Vehicles that are partially damaged may be repaired with new, rebuilt, or used parts. Because trucks, buses, and special equipment are often made in limited quantities or have custom-made features, the cost of parts or sections may be higher than those for mass-produced private passenger automobiles because the parts may not be readily available. Labor costs also may be higher when specialized work is involved.

Total Losses. Generally, when vehicles are damaged beyond repair, the measure of their damages is based upon their actual cash values at the time of loss. A vehicle with an actual cash value of $10,000 before a loss and no salvage value following a loss would represent a total loss of $10,000.

Constructive Total Losses. Often, depending upon the extent of damage and the age, condition, and value of a vehicle, the cost of repairs will exceed the difference between the vehicle value immediately before the loss and the value immediately after the loss. In these situations, vehicles are normally considered "constructive total losses." They are deemed total losses because it would cost more to repair them than to replace them with like kind, age, and quality.

For purposes of illustration, suppose a truck's actual cash value just before an accident was $15,000. Following that accident, it is estimated that repairs will cost approximately $12,000. However, there may be certain hidden costs that could amount to as much as $500. The salvage value of that vehicle (its remaining value based upon reusable parts, equipment, tires, etc.) is determined to be $3,000. Since the total amount of repairs ($12,500) and the salvage amount ($3,000) exceeds the actual cash value of $15,000, the vehicle is considered to be a constructive total loss.

Loss of use and the extra expenditures following damage are other important factors that cannot be overlooked in determining whether a constructive total loss is involved.

Finally, it is important to note that determining component part and other equipment values sometimes is as much a problem as determining vehicle damages. One common method in determining values is comparison with vehicle prices in the market. Many guidebooks ("Red Books" or "Blue Books") are available to provide the average values on various makes and models of vehicles as well as their wholesale, retail, and finance values.

Combined Loss Exposures

Although this chapter has separately analyzed liability and physical damage loss exposures, it is important to recognize that many motor vehicle accidents involve losses in both categories. A negligent driver causing a collision between two motor vehicles may incur physical damage losses in getting an owned vehicle repaired, as well as liability losses for physical damage to the other vehicle and bodily injury to injured persons. Although two types of loss exposures are involved, they are by no means independent, and any program to identify loss exposures should recognize the probability of both types of loss in a single occurrence, or multiple losses within a single fiscal period. Both liability and physical damage loss exposures are usually insured against in the same insurance policy, as discussed in the following chapter.

Chapter Notes

---

1. *Accident Facts* (Chicago: National Safety Council, 1977), p. 40.
2. *1975 Motor Truck Facts* (Detroit: Motor Vehicle Manufacturers Association, 1975), pp. 10 and 56.
3. 43 A.L.R. 3d 1283.

CHAPTER 9

Treatment of Motor Vehicle Exposures

INTRODUCTION

The motor vehicle liability and physical damage exposures analyzed in the previous chapter can be treated by both insurance and noninsurance techniques. Most of this chapter will deal with insurance against motor vehicle exposures. Noninsurance techniques will, however, be analyzed at the end of the chapter.

Since insurance is designed to provide protection against insurable loss exposures, it will be obvious to the student that motor vehicle insurance tracks closely with the motor vehicle loss exposures analyzed in Chapter 8. However, there are some ways in which insurance policies provide coverage beyond that required to protect the interests of the named insured. And, in other cases, there are loss exposures that are not insured by the basic forms in use. Many of these additional exposures can be insured by the use of appropriate endorsements, provided the exposure is recognized and the insured requests the coverage.

Chapter 8 uses the term "motor vehicle" with respect to the subject of the discussion. Many of the legal decisions discussed there can be applied to a variety of types of land motor vehicles. The situation is different with respect to insurance, because the language of the policies attempts to carefully define the subject of insurance. So, where legal terminology is used in Chapter 8, insurance terminology will be used in this chapter, and words like "automobile" and "mobile equipment" will be considered to have their insurance meanings as defined in the policy. These terms will be specifically analyzed later in this chapter.

The insurance section of this chapter is divided into three

subsections. The first and largest subsection relates to motor vehicle liability insurance. Most of the discussion in this section will center on the 1973 edition of the commercial automobile liability (CAL) policy. The second subsection will analyze various forms providing motor vehicle physical damage insurance. (Inland marine forms, which may be used for various types of mobile equipment, are not the subject of this chapter. Inland marine insurance is treated in CPCU 3.)

A new automobile insurance form is slated for introduction in 1978 and should be in common use by the time this text is introduced. Therefore, a third subsection of the insurance discussion will briefly compare the business auto policy (BAP) with the CAL and auto physical damage forms previously discussed. The discussion at that point is based on information available at the time this chapter was prepared.

COMPREHENSIVE AUTOMOBILE LIABILITY INSURANCE

Some insurance companies that specialize in certain types of commercial automobile liability insurance—such as insurance on long-haul trucks, buses, or taxicabs—draft their own nonstandard policies. While the provisions of these policies sometimes vary significantly from those of standard forms, most tend to resemble the commercial automobile liability policy provisions of the Insurance Services Office (ISO). Since a large portion of commercial automobile liability insurance is written under the standard provisions of the ISO, it is ISO's comprehensive automobile liability forms that will be analyzed here. The coverage descriptions in this chapter are based on 1973 and 1974 editions of these forms—the editions in use as this is written.

Another form, the basic automobile liability coverage part, is used somewhat less commonly than the CAL discussed here. The basic automobile liability coverage part differs from the CAL in that it provides coverage only for owned automobiles specifically named in the declarations, although hired automobiles and nonowned automobiles can be added by separate endorsements. Coverage for newly acquired automobiles is also very limited, but it can be broadened by endorsement.

Commercial entities that insure their motor vehicle liability exposures usually purchase either a comprehensive automobile liability policy (CAL), or a comprehensive general-automobile liability policy (CGAL). Both policies provide identical basic coverages for commercial automobile liability exposures. The only difference between the two is that the latter also includes CGL coverage for nonautomobile liability exposures.

A complete CAL policy for basic coverages is formed by combining two forms—the standard policy jacket, which contains general definitions and conditions common to standard general liability policy provisions, and the comprehensive automobile liability coverage part, which contains the insuring agreements, exclusions, and special provisions applicable to motor vehicle coverages. A CGAL policy, in addition to these two forms, requires the CGL coverage part.

Because we are analyzing auto insurance as a separate topic, the subject matter of these pages deals primarily with the provisions of the CAL policy. However, there is a lot to be said for combining automobile and general liability insurance under one policy rather than having a CAL policy with one insurer and a CGL policy with another. Such a combination avoids many disputes concerning which insurer must protect an insured in a given claim. Considerable argument can be generated when two insurers handle these exposures, particularly when a claim falls within the "gray areas" between the provisions of these two policies.

A classic example of a gray area involves claims stemming from the loading and unloading of motor vehicles. Whether coverage in a given instance applies under automobile insurance or under general liability insurance is often a difficult question. There is little uniformity among the courts when it comes to determining which of the two insurers is obligated to protect its insured in such cases. When a CGAL policy is written, only one insurer is involved, and it makes little difference whether a covered claim is the subject of automobile liability insurance or general liability insurance.

In spite of the obvious advantages of combining coverages with one insurer, there are times when liability coverage must be split due to marketing, underwriting, or other considerations beyond the control of the producer or the insured. For example, a firm with an unusual automobile liability or general liability exposure may have to obtain one of its coverages on the specialty market; or a firm that desires to maintain good business relations in the community may place its insurance among several producers. Whatever the reason, this practice of splitting coverages among different insurers can cause problems when a claim develops.

Nature and Scope of Coverage

The basic provisions of the CAL policy are few. However, additional provisions may be required by law and/or may be needed in tailoring coverages to the needs of certain entities. The basic coverage of this policy includes only one peril—the legal liability of insureds for two coverages—bodily injury liability and property damage liability caused by an occurrence and arising out of the ownership, maintenance, use, loading, or unloading of any automobile. (The definitions of bodily injury, property damage, occurrence, and automobile are in the policy jacket because they also apply to other liability contracts that may be enclosed in the same jacket.)

Only six exclusions apply to this basic contract. Most other provisions relate to the peculiarities of this insurance, such as persons insured, limits of liability, territorial scope of coverage, and additional definitions and conditions.

Influence of Statutes The coverage of the CAL policy is not prescribed by law in the same sense as is the coverage of a workers' compensation policy. Nevertheless, this policy usually must be amended, in part, with provisions prescribed by state or federal laws that control an insured's automobile liability exposures. In some instances, however, the provisions that apply in the basic contract are automatically controlled to some extent by law. This means that the provisions of laws are read into the terms of these policy provisions. The following are illustrations of how laws can sometimes significantly alter the coverage of this policy.

Cancellation. The standard policy jacket contains a cancellation provision specifying the obligations of the named insured and the insurer when coverage is to be discontinued. Although the named insured can usually cancel coverage at any time by written notice to the insurer, the insurer is required to provide the named insured with at least ten days' notice if the insurer wishes to cancel. Whether that ten days' notice is legal really depends upon the state law in question. Some state laws require longer periods of notice. When the cancellation provisions of a given state law differ from those stated in the policy jacket, the insurer must conform to the legal requirements. If a policy is not amended under such circumstances, the state law is nevertheless in effect.

Out-of-State Insurance. One provision of the CAL coverage part that is heavily influenced by law deals with out-of-state insurance. Out-of-state situations need to be considered because of the mobility of automobiles, and because of the varying financial responsibility laws of different states illustrated in Table 9-1. Financial responsibility laws provide that a person involved in an automobile accident may be required to furnish proof of financial responsibility—usually furnished in the form of automobile liability insurance—in at least certain minimum limits. It can be seen that a vehicle insured in Louisiana for the minimum limits to meet Louisiana financial responsibility requirements would not seem to have sufficient insurance to meet the financial responsibility limits of Virginia, if involved in an accident there. However, this potential problem is addressed in the CAL policy.

The CAL provides that when an insured is operating a motor vehicle in any state or province where insurance requirements under financial responsibility laws are greater than the limits provided by the policy, the limits of liability and the coverages specified in those other jurisdictions automatically apply to the policy for as long as the vehicle remains there.

Entities whose trucks and buses operate on an interstate basis, or operate intrastate but form a part of an interstate organization, are subject to the Motor Carrier Act of 1935 and to the control of the Interstate Commerce Commission (ICC). Those entities that elect to insure—under a CAL or a CGAL policy, for example—rather than to retain their automobile liability exposures, not only must purchase a policy from an insurer approved by the ICC, but also must obtain at least the minimum limits specified by that federal agency. The minimum liability limits for truckers (common or contract carriers) are currently $100/300/50. Limits for buses range from $100/300/50 to $100/500/50, depending upon their seating capacity. An endorsement prescribed by the ICC must also be attached to the CAL or CGAL policies. Among its requirements is the stipulation that the insurer is liable for *any* loss caused by the insured's negligence—even though the circumstances giving rise to loss are otherwise excluded by the policy. An insurer, in other words, must pay any loss for which an entity, as a carrier subject to that law, is liable; but if the loss that is paid is one that the insurer would not have been required to pay in absence of the ICC endorsement, the motor carrier is obligated to reimburse the insurer to the extent of any payment that was made.

Automobile Liability Exposures Covered The comprehensive auto liability policy is so named because it *automatically* covers an entity for its liability arising out of the ownership, maintenance, use, loading, or unloading of *any* automobile from three principal exposures: (1) automobiles owned by an entity, (2) automobiles hired by or for an entity, and (3) nonowned automobiles. The definitions are important here.

Owned Automobiles. An owned automobile is one that an entity legally owns. The entity either has full title to it or partial title to it pending the payment of any encumbrance. However, automobiles leased for periods of twelve months or more are also treated as owned automobiles according to the rules of the ISO Commercial Automobile Manual.

Hired Automobiles. A hired automobile is an automobile that is not owned but is loaned to the insured or is used under contract on

Table 9-1
Automobile Financial Responsibility Laws in the
United States, Canada, and Mexico*

United States State	Liability[1] Limits	State	Liability[1] Limits
Alabama	10/20/5	South Carolina	15/30/5
Alaska	25/50/10	South Dakota	15/30/5
Arizona	15/30/10	Tennessee	10/20/5
Arkansas	10/20/5	Texas	10/20/5
California	15/30/5	Utah	15/30/5[3]
Colorado	15/30/5	Vermont	10/20/5
Connecticut	20/40/5	Virginia	25/50/5
Delaware	10/20/5	Washington	15/30/5
District of Columbia	10/20/5	West Virginia	10/20/5
Florida	10/20/5	Wisconsin	15/30/5
Georgia	10/20/5	Wyoming	10/20/5
Hawaii	25/unlimited/10		
Idaho	10/20/5	Canada	
Illinois	10/20/5	Alberta	$50,000
Indiana	15/30/10		inclusive[2]
Iowa	10/20/5	British Columbia	$75,000
Kansas	15/30/5		inclusive
Kentucky	10/20/5	Manitoba	$50,000
Louisiana	5/10/1		inclusive
Maine	20/40/10	New Brunswick	$50,000
Maryland	20/40/5		inclusive
Massachusetts	5/10/5	Newfoundland	$75,000
Michigan	20/40/10		inclusive
Minnesota	25/50/10	Northwest Territories	$50,000
Mississippi	10/20/5		inclusive
Missouri	10/20/2	Nova Scotia	$35,000
Montana	25/50/5		inclusive
Nebraska	15/30/5	Ontario	$100,000
Nevada	15/30/5		inclusive
New Hampshire	20/40/5	Prince Edward Island	$35,000
New Jersey	15/30/5		inclusive
New Mexico	15/30/5	Quebec	$35,000
New York	10/20/5		inclusive
North Carolina	15/30/5	Saskatchewan	$35,000
North Dakota	10/20/5		inclusive
Ohio	12.5/25/7.5	Yukon	$50,000
Oklahoma	5/10/5		inclusive
Oregon	15/30/5		
Pennsylvania	15/30/5	Mexico	
Rhode Island	25/50/10	Entire country	30/60/10

1. The first two figures refer to bodily injury liability limits and the third figure to property damage liability. For example, 10/20/5 means coverage up to $20,000 for all persons injured in an accident, subject to a limit of $10,000 for one individual; and $5,000 coverage for property damage.
2. The "inclusive" limit means there is $50,000 of liability insurance available to settle either bodily injury or property damage claims—or both—up to that amount.
3. May be $25,000 single limit.

*Reprinted with permission from *Insurance Facts* (New York: Insurance Information Institute, 1977), p. 66.

behalf of the named insured entity with or without the use of a hired operator. Note that this definition includes a borrowed automobile, a point which is often overlooked. This category also includes automobiles rented for periods of less than twelve months. Not included within this category, however, are those automobiles owned or registered in the name of any executive officer, partner, employee, or agent of a firm, whether such person is given an operating allowance or not.

One example of a hired automobile with an operator would involve a funeral director who hires a hearse and its driver for services as needed. An example of an automobile hired without an operator would involve any firm that rents, leases, or borrows a truck when moving its operations from one location to another. Note that these hired automobile arrangements involve bailments. The entity hiring a vehicle, with or without an operator, expects to derive a certain benefit from its usage. The one supplying such vehicle also expects something of value in return, whether it is money or an exchange of services.

Nonowned Automobiles. A nonowned automobile, as defined in the policy, is one that is neither "owned" nor "hired." An example would be an employee's personal automobile which occasionally is used on business activities of a firm or the car of a salesperson who receives an operating allowance for using his or her personal automobile on company business.

Automobiles Versus Mobile Equipment. Owned, hired, and non-owned automobiles are the subject of coverage under the CAL policy in many different situations. This is as it should be since this policy is intended to encompass the automobile liability exposures of many different types of businesses. But there nevertheless are certain limitations. To determine the types of vehicles that may or may not be covered, one must refer to the definition of automobile in the policy jacket:

> ...a land motor vehicle, trailer or semi-trailer designed for travel on public roads (including any machinery or apparatus attached thereto), but does not include mobile equipment.

Note that no attempt is made here to limit the term "automobile" to four-wheel vehicles propelled by motors. (In this respect, commercial auto policies differ from many personal automobile policies that are designed to cover private passenger automobiles.) Because "automobiles" are described as "land motor vehicles," this rules out aircraft and watercraft. Whatever else is included or excluded within the meaning of the term "land motor vehicle" is less certain because that term is not defined in the CAL policy.

A land motor vehicle is generally understood to be any driven motor vehicle that conveys people or property on land whether it travels on wheels, treads, or rails; but because of the qualification "designed for travel on public roads," this rules out most motor vehicles operated on rails. Land motor vehicles operated on treads are not necessarily ruled out, although "mobile equipment" is specifically outside the meaning of the term "automobile" insofar as the CAL policy is concerned. Because "mobile equipment" is excluded from automobile coverage, an understanding of that term is essential to an understanding of the term "automobile."

The term "mobile equipment" is defined in the policy jacket as:

> A land vehicle (including any machinery or apparatus attached thereto), whether or not self-propelled, (1) not subject to motor vehicle registration, or (2) maintained for use exclusively on premises owned by or rented to the named insured, including the ways immediately adjoining, or (3) designed for use principally off public roads, or (4) designed or maintained for the sole purpose of affording mobility to equipment of the following types forming an integral part of or permanently attached to such vehicle: power cranes, shovels, loaders, diggers and drills; concrete mixers (other than the mix-in-transit type); graders, scrapers, rollers and other road construction or repair equipment; air-compressors, pumps and generators, including spraying, welding and building cleaning equipment; and geophysical exploration and well servicing equipment.

Remember that any land vehicle or equipment that does not come within the definition of "mobile equipment" is considered to be an "automobile" and therefore subject to coverage by the CAL policy. Otherwise, such a vehicle is "mobile equipment" and is automatically covered under CGL policy provisions—if an entity has such insurance. It will be noted later that mobile equipment if it is used beyond its intended scope, can acquire the status of an automobile. This is another reason both automobile and general liability exposures should ideally be handled under one policy or at least by one insurer.

Note that because "or" rather than "and" separates each of the four numbered groups within the definition of "mobile equipment," it is necessary that the vehicle or equipment in question meet only *one* of the four categories. Yet even this lengthy definition sometimes requires judicial interpretation. As a result, it is often difficult for insurers and insureds to state without qualification that a vehicle is either an "automobile" or "mobile equipment."

For example, in one case the court held that a general liability policy rather than an automobile policy applied when a hoist attached to a truck injured an employee of the truck's hirer.[1] This accident arose from the operation of the hoist, which had nothing to do with the truck or its motor. Such truck and hoist, therefore, were determined to be mobile equipment under item (4) of the mobile equipment definition in the policy jacket. However, in another case, a dump truck used to carry blacktop for highway repair came within the definition of "automobile" and was deemed to be covered under a CAL policy rather than as "mobile equipment" under the CGL policy.[2] The court ruled that the truck's primary and intended use was for the transportation of material. But the truck's mechanical use as an inclined plane to facilitate and expedite the unloading process was subordinate to the primary use.

It might be particularly difficult to determine whether or not a snowmobile qualifies as mobile equipment in many common circumstances. However, since the CGL policy specifically excludes bodily injury or property damage arising out of snowmobiles, this is a moot point. Where there is a snowmobile exposure, specific liability insurance must be arranged, either under an automobile liability policy or under a policy specially designed for the snowmobile exposure.

There are two important considerations in this whole area of automobiles versus mobile equipment and their respective insurance coverages. First, general liability insurance excludes bodily injury or property damage due to *transporting* any mobile equipment by an automobile that is owned, operated, rented, or loaned to any insured. The effect of that exclusion is to make any mobile equipment—while being transported—a part of the automobile and therefore subject to automobile liability insurance. However, the problem is that the definition of "automobile" in the CAL policy does not include mobile equipment, whether the latter is transported or not. So, there is a coverage gap between the two policies when mobile equipment is transported by an automobile—a problem which is not easily resolved. A firm undoubtedly would have to make some special arrangement with its insurer to cover that exposure.

The second consideration is applicable only in those situations when an entity retains its general liability exposures. Here, mobile equipment which normally would be the subject of general liability insurance should be covered under automobile liability insurance if the liability exposures of mobile equipment are greater than any entity wants to retain. To reduce costs, however, an entity has the choice of obtaining full or partial coverage against the liability exposures of such equipment. Under full coverage, an entity receives protection against the locomotion and the operations exposures.

Locomotion exposures are those that arise while mobile equipment is operated or transported upon public roads. *Operations exposures* are those that stem from the use of mobile equipment at work sites. Under partial coverage an entity receives protection only against the locomotion exposures of mobile equipment. In either case, a special endorsement must be attached to the policy signifying such coverage. Of course, if an entity retains both its automobile and general liability exposures, this second point need not be considered.

From the preceding discussion it becomes apparent that whether an owned, hired, or nonowned vehicle is the subject of coverage by the CAL policy is not always easily determinable. Much depends upon the type and usage of such vehicles, upon any statutory provisions that apply and, of course, upon the definitions of "automobile" and "mobile equipment." All of these factors, therefore, should be kept in mind by an entity when it desires to obtain proper insurance protection.

Persons and Entities Insured As important as determining which vehicles are covered under a CAL policy (or under the automobile section of a CGAL policy) is the extent to which any persons or entities are insured. The fact that an owned, hired, or nonowned automobile is covered by a CAL policy means little if the person owning, maintaining, using, or loading or unloading it, or the entity responsible for its operation or usage, is not insured.

Those who are insured and the extent of their protection hinges upon the severability of interests provision and the omnibus clause of the CAL policy. Both are extremely complex provisions, not because of their wording, but because of the ways their provisions are interpreted by those seeking protection following loss, as well as by the courts. Underlying circumstances of losses, moreover, are so varied and court decisions are so diverse that it often is difficult to ascertain with any certainty the actual scope of these provisions, particularly the omnibus clause. Court decisions nevertheless do provide food for thought and a wealth of jurisdictional precedents which can go a long way in determining how best to handle troublesome exposures.

Severability of Interests Provision. The severability of interests provision forms a part of the definitions section of the policy jacket within the definition of "insured." The provision states:

> The insurance afforded applies separately to each insured against whom claim is made or suit is brought, except with respect to the limits of the company's liability.

This provision treats each person or organization seeking protection as if each of them has separate coverage by that policy. So, if one insured is determined to be without coverage, this has no effect on other insureds seeking coverage. However, the limits of liability stated in the policy are not cumulative, regardless of how many claims or suits are brought. It is therefore possible to have a claim involving several persons who are considered insureds only to find that the limits of liability are insufficient to cover the judgment(s) rendered against all of them.

To illustrate the effect of the severability of interests provision, suppose an employee is operating a company-owned automobile with two of the company's customers riding as passengers. The employee loses control of the automobile, and it goes down an embankment, injuring all three occupants. Suit is brought by the two customers against the employee and her employer. The insurer of the employer must defend the employer—the named insured, and the employee—as an additional insured, against the suit brought by the two customers. If the policy is written for limits of $100/300/100, that is the maximum which will apply to both suits. Those limits, in other words, do not apply separately to those against whom suit or claim is made.

Omnibus Clause (Persons Insured). The omnibus clause is within the CAL coverage part itself because it identifies those who are considered as insureds for purposes of automobile liability exposures. The label "omnibus clause" does not appear in the policy—the policy section under analysis here is captioned "Persons Insured." However, this section is usually referred to as the omnibus clause because an omnibus is a vehicle that is designed to carry many passengers.[3] Likewise, the omnibus clause extends the CAL policy to insure any person using, or any organization responsible for the use of, an insured automobile.

The first section of the omnibus clause lists those who are insureds. The second section of the omnibus clause describes situations when a person or an organization is not considered to be an insured. In order to understand the nature and scope of protection provided to insureds in a given instance, it is sometimes necessary to make reference to both sections of the omnibus clause.

ENTITIES THAT ARE INSUREDS. The named insured, partners and executive officers, and any other person or organization may be insureds under the basic provisions of the CAL policy.

Named Insured. The named insured is the person or organization listed in the policy declarations. The named insured can be an individual, a partnership, a corporation, or an unincorporated association. It could also include two or more partnerships that are involved in a joint venture, a parent corporation and its subsidiaries, or a corporation and those individuals who have controlling interest.

Partners and Executive Officers. When the named insured is a partnership or a joint venture, partners are included as insureds. Executive officers are considered to be insureds when the named insured is a corporation or an unincorporated association. Either partners or executive officers are insureds while using an automobile owned or hired by the *named insured*. However, both are subject to limitations dealing with nonowned automobile exposures.

A partner or an executive officer using a nonowned automobile is insured only when the automobile is being used in the business of the named insured. The important point here is that the automobile in question must be nonowned from the standpoint of the named insured *and* of any partner or executive officer. This requirement dealing with partners and executive officers is not readily obvious because, as noted earlier, a nonowned automobile is defined as one that is neither owned nor hired. One could assume from that definition that an automobile owned by a partner or an executive officer is as much a nonowned automobile from the standpoint of the partnership or the corporation as a personal automobile of an employee. This assumption is basically true. But the second section of the omnibus clause rules out protection for "any executive officer with respect to an automobile owned by him or a member of his household," and later, "an automobile owned by or registered in the name of a partner." So, while partners or executive officers are considered insureds when using an owned or a hired automobile of the named insured, their status as insureds concerning the use of any nonowned automobile requires that the vehicle be one that is neither owned nor registered by them—for example, a car that either may borrow from a neighbor or from an employee for use during the course of the named insured's business.

Since automobiles belonging to partners in a partnership are being discussed here, this is an appropriate place to call attention to the very last paragraph of the omnibus clause. Nobody is insured under the policy for accidents involving a vehicle owned by *one* of the partners, or a nonowned vehicle used in another partnership or joint venture in which the insured is involved.

Any Other Persons.   Protection of the CAL policy is extended to persons other than the named insured, its partners, or executive officers; but the protection to other persons, though not necessarily limited in scope, is conditional in two ways: (1) such other persons must meet certain prerequisites as to usage of a named insured's owned or hired automobiles, or (2) they must be within the capacity of a lessee or a borrower of the automobile, an employee of either, or an employee of the named insured when any loss arises from the loading or unloading of such automobiles. As the policy puts it, the following are insureds:

   (c) any other person while using an owned automobile or a hired automobile with the permission of the named insured, provided his actual operation or (if he is not operating) his other actual use thereof is within the scope of such permission, but with respect to bodily injury or property damage arising out of the loading or unloading thereof, such other person shall be an insured only if he is:
       (1) a lessee or borrower of the automobile, or
       (2) an employee of the named insured or of such lessee or borrower;

Several points are important here:

1. *The automobile involved must be one that is owned or hired by the named insured.* When an automobile is hired by the named insured, the owner of that hired automobile (or its agents and employees) is (are) not considered insured under any circumstances. Such parties should buy their own insurance. However, when the named insured is a sublessee of a hired automobile, the lessee of such automobile is an insured, under the sublessee's CAL policy, for losses involving the loading or the unloading of such hired automobile. The scope of this provision is handled more fully later.

2. *The word "using" has a broader meaning than the word "operating."* The former connotes the employment of an automobile for a particular purpose, whereas the latter refers to the actual control or to the actual driving of an automobile.[4] Furthermore, when a vehicle is being unloaded, it is being used to the same extent as if it were being driven, and the person doing the unloading is entitled to the same protection as the owner or the operator of such vehicle.[5]

   Arguments concerning the use of automobiles are common, particularly with respect to accidents arising from their loading or unloading. Also, most such cases are extremely complex because they often encompass the omnibus clause, the severability of interests clause, and the fellow-employee exclusion which precludes the protection of a negligent employee who injures a fellow employee.

3. *Use of an automobile can include a situation when a person (original permittee) has permission to use an automobile of the named insured and, in some cases, even when the original permittee permits another person (second permittee) to operate or to use that automobile.*[6]

Whether the original permittee is considered to be an insured depends on whether his or her actual operation or actual use is within the scope of permission granted by the named insured. Little problem exists when the original permittee is obviously within the scope of permission granted by the named insured or when the original permittee is granted express authority to allow others to use or to operate the automobile; but when the named insured specifically prohibits the permittee to delegate use to another or when the named insured is silent as to permission, it may be extremely troublesome to determine whether the original permittee is an insured. Space prevents a comprehensive discussion of all the problem areas. However, it would appear that an original permittee who does not have express permission to allow another to use an automobile or whose permission is silent has a better opportunity for protection when he or she is at least a passenger in an automobile being used within the scope of permission by the named insured. Much really depends upon the circumstances of each case and sometimes upon the law of a state.

When the original permittee allows still another party to use the automobile, the question arises as to whether that second permittee is an insured. Protection is usually extended to a second permittee while using or operating an automobile with consent of the original permittee who has the permission of the named insured to allow others to use it. There are, however, instances when the courts have held that the right to designate additional insureds is personal to the named insured and cannot be delegated by others. A second permittee, furthermore, has been denied protection while using an automobile for personal purposes when a named insured specifically prohibited an original permittee from allowing others to use it. The courts, moreover, are divided concerning protection of a second permittee even when the original permittee is a passenger in the vehicle and the automobile is being used within the permission granted to the original permittee by the named insured. A great deal here seems to depend on the latitude of permission given by the named insured.

When loading or unloading is involved, lessees and borrowers of an automobile are insured against bodily injury or property damage as are employees of either the lessee, the borrower, or the named insured. Based on some of the court cases that have involved this clause, it would appear that to be considered a lessee or a borrower of an automobile, some form of contractual or possessory right of the automobile must exist. Another complicated area related to situations involving the loading and the unloading of vehicles deals with employees who seek protection under the omnibus clause because they have caused injury to other employees, particularly fellow employees.

The final group that may qualify as insureds under the omnibus clause of the CAL policy includes any person or organization whose liability is of a vicarious nature—that is, it arises from the acts or omissions of another who is an insured in any one of the previous categories of insureds: named insured, partner, executive officer, or any other person using an owned or hired automobile with the permission of the named insured. As an example, consider an employer whose employee negligently causes an accident while operating a truck of another firm with permission of its owner. The employer would be insured by the truck owner's CAL policy.

ENTITIES THAT ARE NOT INSUREDS. The omnibus clause appears to be very broad in covering a variety of persons and organizations as insureds. However, the second section of the omnibus clause does have several limitations which prevent covering certain exposures that should be covered under other policies of the named insured or of others.

Fellow-Employee Exclusion.   The policy states that:

(i) any person while engaged in the business of his employer with respect to bodily injury to any fellow employee of such person injured in the course of his employment...[is not an insured.]

This limitation, sometimes referred to as the fellow-employee or cross-employee exclusion, serves a twofold purpose. One is to make workers' compensation insurance, rather than automobile liability insurance, the exclusive remedy of an employee who is injured by the negligence of a fellow employee while both are working within the scope of their employment. The other purpose, somewhat related to the first one, is to distinguish an employer's liability to its employees from that of an employer's liability to the general public. By making that distinction, an employer is relieved from having to cover its employees under automobile insurance when they are already protected under workers' compensation laws.[7]

In spite of its apparent clarity, this provision dealing with fellow-employee suits is the subject of many troublesome questions, depending upon the circumstances of losses. The following are among the more common questions raised about the meaning of the cross-employee exclusion.

1. What is meant by the phrase "while engaged in the business of his employer"?
2. Are partners or executive officers considered to be employees within the terms of the cross-employee exclusion?
3. Is a loaned or a borrowed employee considered to be a fellow employee of the named insured's regular employees?
4. Must the negligent worker and the injured worker be employees of a common employer?[8]

Although a number of court decisions have been made regarding these questions, it is obvious that the decisions often depend on the circumstances of each individual case.

Owners of Nonowned or Hired Cars.   The policy states that:

(ii) the owner or lessee (of whom the named insured is a sub-lessee) of a hired automobile or the owner of a non-owned automobile, or any agent or employee of any such owner or lessee...[is also not an insured.]

The purpose of this provision is to keep the CAL policy of the named insured from providing primary coverage for others. As noted previously, a lessee of a hired automobile is considered an insured under the omnibus clause only in losses arising out of the loading or unloading of automobiles. Owners of nonowned automobiles should have their own insurance and are not considered insureds under this policy, except when they become vicariously liable because of acts or omissions of those who are insureds under this policy.

Executive Officers' Own Cars.   Another category of persons not insured is "(iii) an executive officer with respect to an automobile owned by him or by a member of his household." Automobiles of such persons should be insured under individual automobile liability policies (discussed in CPCU 2). The executive officer's employer would also be protected on a primary basis under the omnibus clause of the executive's individual automobile policy.

Trailers.   Any person or organization, other than the named insured, is outside the scope of coverage with respect to:

(1) a motor vehicle while used with any trailer owned or hired by such person or organization and not covered by like insurance in the company (except a trailer designed for use with a private passenger automobile and not being used for business purposes with another type motor vehicle), or

(2) a trailer while used with any motor vehicle owned or hired by such person or organization and not covered by like insurance in the company.

Trailers designed for use with private passenger automobiles are not particularly hazardous, even when they are used in business. But since the CAL policy is designed for trucks, buses, and other conveyances, any trailer used with these vehicles is considered to be an extrahazardous exposure requiring additional insurance. The purpose of the above limitation, referred to as the cross-trailer exclusion, is to avoid covering a person or organization that should have purchased from the same insurer primary insurance on both trailers and trucks pulling those trailers.

Automobile Business.   Another category of persons not insured is

(v) any person while employed in or otherwise engaged in duties in connection with an automobile business, other than an automobile business operated by the named insured.

As defined in the CAL coverage part, the term "automobile business" would include automobile dealerships, service stations, and parking garages, among others. The purpose of this provision is to prevent the CAL policy of the named insured from covering any person who really should be covered as an insured under the policy of another entity that is in the automobile business.

Partners.   The final provision of the omnibus clause dealing with exposures of partnerships, joint ventures, and individual partners of either is more in the form of an exclusion. It rules out coverage entirely for

> ... bodily injury or property damage arising out of (1) a non-owned automobile used in the conduct of any partnership or joint venture of which the insured is a partner or member and which is not designated in this policy as a named insured, or (2) if the named insured is a partnership, an automobile owned by or registered in the name of a partner thereof.

Few people realize the significance of this entire provision and yet its existence appears to be quite readily justified. As mentioned earlier, the omnibus clause includes a partner as an insured while he or she is using a nonowned automobile in the business of the named insured. However, a person conceivably could be a partner of more than one partnership, or a member of a joint venture which is formed by some or all partners of a partnership. Were it not for section (1) of this exclusion, the CAL policy would encompass the coverage of more exposures than are anticipated by the premium charge. The exclusion, therefore, requires that the partnership or the joint venture for which a nonowned automobile is being used be specifically declared in this policy.

Section (2) of this exclusion also is often misunderstood. Its purpose is to keep the CAL policy of the named insured partnership from covering exposures that should be handled under the personal insurance portfolios of the partners.

An especially important point about section (2) of this exclusion is its effect on the partnership and the other partners if one of the partners uses his or her personal automobile for business purposes. If a claim results from the use of a personal automobile, neither the partnership nor the other partners will be protected as insureds under the CAL policy, not even when such policy is written in the name of the partnership. However, there may be some degree of protection available to the partnership if the partner who is involved in a claim has an individual automobile liability policy, because the omnibus clause of most personal automobile policies includes as an additional insured any other person or organization legally responsible for the use of the insured automobile. Whether this protection will suffice depends upon the size of claim and the limits of liability of the personal automobile policy.

Until 1974, strange as it may seem, no standard insurance was available to protect partnerships in these situations. Now, extra coverage is available. It is commonly referred to as "broad form employers non-ownership liability coverage for partnerships." This coverage, in effect, provides a partnership with excess protection over that which may be available to the firm under the individual automobile policies of its partners.

Modifications of Coverages and Other Provisions Features of the CAL policy mentioned thus far are merely those basic, standard provisions that automatically apply regardless of the entity that purchases this policy. Because characteristics of entities vary, and state statutes sometimes require special contract provisions, the basic provisions of the CAL policy usually have to be amended by forms and endorsements to reflect those needs or requirements.

For example, when an entity desires automobile medical payments or uninsured motorists insurance, the appropriate coverage form must be attached to this policy. What forms may be appropriate depend on the state in which coverage is written. While countrywide forms of those two coverages are available for use in a number of states, special state endorsements sometimes have to be used in order to reflect the statutory provisions of a given territory. Also, special state forms commonly are required in lieu of countrywide forms when certain mandatory deductibles apply in a given state, when cancellation provisions require special state conditions concerning notices, and when personal injury protection (no-fault automobile insurance) applies to users of commercial vehicles in certain states.

Countrywide and special state forms and endorsements are also available when an entity's exposures call for amendment to the CAL policy to limit or broaden coverage or other policy provisions. When a firm is a fuel oil dealer, for example, an "erroneous delivery of liquid products" endorsement is always required on the CAL policy to exclude from the automobile policy coverage such things as delivering the wrong fuel or delivering the right fuel to the wrong address if the injury or damage occurs after the delivery is completed.

Because there are several hundred forms and endorsements available for use with the CAL policy, it would be impractical to even list each of them here. What we will do, however, is select *examples* of entities whose operations require the addition of forms or endorsements in order to limit or broaden coverage provisions beyond those provided by the basic provisions of the CAL policy. The nature, scope, and purpose of such extra coverages as medical payments and uninsured motorists insurance will also be noted.

Truckmen. Entities that haul or transport goods, materials, or commodities for others are commonly referred to as "truckmen." These entities may have one, several, or large fleets of vehicles consisting of single-unit trucks such as vans, panel delivery trucks, straight body units having gross vehicle loaded weights (GVW) from under 10,000 pounds to over 45,000 pounds, as well as truck-tractors equipped for pulling semitrailers with gross combined weights (GCW) of 45,000 or more pounds. These trucks may operate intrastate or interstate within a radius ranging from under 50 miles to over 200 miles, and may be used for hauling goods as a contract carrier—operating exclusively for one firm or as a common carrier—hauling for whoever may require the services of a trucking firm.

TRUCKMEN SPECIFIED VEHICLES FORM. A trucking firm that has only a few automobiles to haul goods of another intrastate or interstate, and that does not often add or change automobiles, is best covered under a CAL policy with the truckmen specified vehicles form. This form requires a description of the vehicles to be covered and also bases the costs of insurance on the usage and weight of the vehicles and the radius within which the described automobiles operate.

When the truckmen form is attached to the CAL policy, it also affects the omnibus clause of the policy in a number of significant ways.

First, the *loading and unloading* provision of the omnibus clause is further amended to limit the scope of protection to others. The effect of this amendment is to preclude a person or an organization, along with its agents and employees, from obtaining primary protection as additional insureds under the truckmen's CAL policy simply because they are hired to transport property by automobile for the named insured. The intent of this limitation is to compel any other carrier hired by a trucker to look to its own primary insurance for protection.

Second, the omnibus clause is further redefined so that it does not encompass as insureds any person or organization, including its agents and employees, that may be engaged in the business of transporting property for others, including property of the named insured in any of the circumstances discussed as follows.

When bodily injury or property damage occurs while the automobile of another—a lessee or an owner of a hired vehicle for example—is not being used exclusively in the business of the named insured *and* is not being used over a route the named insured is authorized to use by federal or public authority—such as the Interstate Commerce Commission, coverage is precluded. The reason for this limitation, as illustrated in Figure 9-1, is to prevent an insurer of the named insured, motor carrier A, from having to protect motor carrier B simply because the latter is conveying part of A's cargo as an accommodation made possible when both carriers are authorized to travel on the same routes. If an accident occurs while motor carrier B is carrying part of A's load and part of another firm's load, this limitation requires B's insurer to handle the claim because B would not be considered as an insured under A's CAL policy. Although named insured A also should be protected under B's policy, this truckmen form does give the named insured A excess protection over any other valid and collectible insurance of others. This policy limitation indirectly benefits the named insured A

Figure 9-1

Truckmen Form Example

because it prevents a motor carrier with a poor accident record who is otherwise considered to be an insured, without restriction, under the omnibus clause, from adversely affecting the named insured's insurance experience. Thus, in the example, any accidents *B* would have would not normally affect *A* 's insurable loss history. Note, however, that if motor carrier *B* in Figure 9-1 is transporting property exclusively for the named insured *A* over an authorized route when an accident occurs, motor carrier *B* would be considered an omnibus insured under the truckmen form of the named insured's CAL policy if *B* is not using a retention program in lieu of insurance. Furthermore, any such person or organization operating as an insured motor carrier is considered as an insured while its automobile is en route, at the request of the named insured, to engage in the exclusive transportation of the named insured's goods.

When a person or an organization is engaged in transporting property of the named insured on an exclusive basis over an authorized route, it still is not considered as an omnibus insured if it uses retention rather than insurance to meet the security requirements of any motor carrier law. Such motor carrier, in other words, must have automobile liability insurance to otherwise qualify. This limitation is viewed as a protective measure from the insured's standpoint because firms retaining their losses usually are thought of as being somewhat less cooperative in claim situations than other insurers.

When a person or an organization is engaged in the exclusive transportation of property for the named insured over an authorized route and uses hired automobiles, such person or organization may still be disqualified as an omnibus insured if its policy does not cover the owner or lessee of a hired automobile on a direct primary basis. The intent of this provision is to place the obligation of protecting an owner of a hired automobile—on a primary basis at least—on the hirer of such automobile. This is as it should be since motor carrier regulatory authorities make carriers responsible to the public for the use of all vehicles operated by them under their permits whether such vehicles are owned, hired, leased, or borrowed. Most insurers likewise agree to protect all such interests to some extent while owned, hired, leased, or borrowed vehicles are being used in furthering the business ventures of their named insureds, although some independent insurers of truckers refuse to be responsible to owners of hired vehicles. This policy limitation, therefore, protects against covering here the obligations that rightfully are those of the insurers of carriers that lease, hire, or borrow vehicles.

When an independent contractor is engaged by the named insured to handle local pickup and delivery for the named insured, it is not an insured under the form even though such person or firm is authorized to serve in a territory by federal or public authority. The purpose of this limitation is to prevent the independent contractor from relying upon the named insured's policy for primary protection. As a nonowned automobile from the named insured's standpoint, coverage does apply to the named insured on an excess basis over any other valid and collectible insurance that may apply on the independent contractor's behalf.

This truckmen form also contains the following additional restrictions and conditions.

- Drivers and other persons furnished with an automobile hired by the named insured are not considered to be employees of the named insured. (However, if employers of such other persons are without workers' compensation insurance for some reason, the named insured in all likelihood will be responsible to such persons for whatever benefits may be due.)
- Any rail, water, or air carrier is not considered to be an insured under this policy if bodily injury or property damage occurs while a trailer, being transported, loaded, or unloaded by any such carrier is detached from the named insured's automobile.
- Insurance under this form is considered to be excess over any other valid and collectible insurance with respect to (1) any automobile of the commercial type while it is leased or loaned to any person or organization, other than the named insured, and is used in the business of transporting property for others, (2) any hired private passenger automobile, or (3) any nonowned automobile.

Based upon the provisions of this truckmen form, named insureds receive substantial protection on a primary basis when they use owned, described automobiles to transport goods for others. However, when the services of other truckers are enlisted by the named insured, problems can develop. To avoid problems, the other truckers must be insured for automobile liability insurance, and at the time of loss these truckers must be using their vehicles exclusively for the named insured's benefit over authorized routes of the named insured if they expect protection as omnibus insureds under the named insured's CAL policy.

TRUCKMEN GROSS RECEIPTS OR MILEAGE FORMS. A trucking firm that utilizes a large number of automobiles to haul goods for others, hires the services of others, or hires out its automobiles to others to transport property, is best suited to the truckmen gross receipts or mileage forms rather than the truckmen specified vehicles form, because the truckmen gross receipts or mileage forms do not require specific identification of vehicles. Numerous endorsements for deletions or additions of vehicles and other transactions therefore can be avoided. These forms base premium charges either on the total gross receipts (as that term is defined in the forms) which the firm receives for its business transactions during the year, or on the basis of total mileage (as defined in the forms) that such vehicles are used during the year. While the premium charged at policy inception is based upon the estimated gross receipts or mileage that is expected during the year, the final premium is determined at year end by audit.

Two such truckmen gross receipts or mileage forms are available. The first one, Form A, applies to any owned, hired, or nonowned automobile, including private passenger automobiles. Form B, on the other hand, applies to any owned or hired automobile of the *commercial type*. This form does not apply to private passenger automobiles.

While the omnibus clause under Forms A and B, dealing with persons insured, corresponds closely to the omnibus clause within the basic provisions of the CAL policy, most other provisions, dealing with persons who are not insured, correspond to those same restrictions and exceptions that form a part of the truckmen specified vehicles form.

However, there are two notable additions within Forms A and B that are not found in the basic omnibus clause of the CAL policy or in the omnibus clause of the truckmen specified vehicles form.

The first of these omnibus clause provisions covers an independent trucking firm—an owner or lessee of a hired automobile—as an insured, if bodily injury or property damage occurs (1) while the hired automobile is being used exclusively in the business of the named insured *and* (2) while the hired automobile is being used over a route the named insured is authorized to serve by federal or public authority. Note that both conditions (1) and (2) are "while" clauses. This means that if an accident should occur *while* those two conditions are not being met— a trucker is carrying part of another's load over an authorized route, or a trucker is carrying all of the named insured's cargo over a deviated route—such owner or lessee of a hired automobile cannot qualify for protection as an insured under these forms which are attached to the named insured's CAL policy.

Forms A and B also contain a provision that a trucking firm, as owner or lessee of a hired automobile, is not covered as an insured after arrival of the hired automobile at its destination under a single trip contract which does not provide in writing for the return trip of such automobile. This specification that requires the terms of a return trip to be in writing is aimed at preventing coverage of truckers who claim they are returning from a trip at the time an accident occurs when in reality they are seeking another hauling job, carrying a partial load of another, or using their vehicle for purely personal purposes.

TRUCKMEN—INSURANCE FOR NONTRUCKING USE FORM. It is common for an owner or lessee of a truck-tractor to haul goods of another firm using that firm's semitrailer on a one-way trip. The trucker carrying the goods of another exclusively and over an authorized route of such other firm is covered under the automobile liability insurance of the firm that hires the trucker. However, once the truck-tractor is unhooked from the semitrailer at its destination, the trucker is without insurance. What the trucker needs for protection while the truck-tractor is unhooked is the "truckmen—insurance for nontrucking use form" on its CAL policy. As the name of that form denotes, a trucker is given protection only during the time the truck-tractor is being used for nontrucking purposes. This form is also commonly referred to as *bobtail* liability insurance. A truck-tractor is said to be bobtailed when the semitrailer is disconnected from the truck-tractor and is being used by the trucker in circumstances not covered in any lease agreement.

It is also common for a trucking firm to lease out its combined truck-tractor and trailer to haul goods exclusively for another concern. When the complete unit is thus used, the automobile liability insurance of a concern whose goods are being transported will also protect the trucker to point of destination or for a round trip if the hirer requires such services and so agrees in writing. However, when the lease agreement between the trucker and the hirer ends with the unloading of the trailer at point of destination, and the trucker must return without a load, this empty travel is commonly referred to as *deadheading*. A truck-tractor and its trailer is said to be deadheading when the combined unit is heading back to its point of origin with a dead load (an empty trailer), as opposed to a live load (a trailer containing some cargo).

The essential difference between deadheading and bobtailing is that in the former the trucker is returning an unloaded trailer, while in the latter the trucker is returning only with the truck-tractor. A trucker who is deadheading is in need of the same protection following the completion of a hauling contract as the trucker who is bobtailing. Some insurers will not provide deadhead or bobtail coverage, so insurance must often be sought in the specialty lines market.

OTHER TRUCKING FORMS. A variety of other forms exist for trucking firms that require special tailoring of coverages under their CAL policy. Such forms include those used when hauling is done exclusively for one concern on a long-term contract basis, gross receipts and mileage forms that are used only when truckers are not common carriers or petroleum carriers that travel over irregular routes, and a number of special state endorsements which amend certain provisions of truckmen forms to correspond with state statutory provisions.

Repossessed Automobiles of Finance Companies and Banks. Finance companies and banks often repossess automobiles of persons who are unable to continue the payments of their automobile loans. Since these repossessed automobiles are technically owned by the finance companies and banks, the CAL policies covering such organizations automatically cover the maintenance, operation, and use of such repossessed automobiles, as owned vehicles, until they are ultimately disposed of. When such organizations handle many repossessed automobiles during the year, insurance for such automobiles can be expensive since they are treated like other owned vehicles.

To cut insurance costs, and to more accurately reflect loss exposures, CAL policies of these lending organizations can be amended with a repossessed automobile form. This form, in effect, protects the organization with respect to any automobile while it is being repossessed and while any such automobile is being maintained or used in connection with resale. Coverage under this form, however, does not include as an insured any person or organization from whom an automobile is repossessed, and coverage does not apply to any such repossessed automobile while it is being used for other business purposes of the organization or for personal, pleasure, or family purposes by anyone associated with the named insured organization.

Advance premiums for this coverage are based upon the estimated number of such automobiles expected to be repossessed during the policy period. The final premium is then determined upon audit.

Public and Private Liveries. Entities operating as public or private liveries by conveying passengers for hire must have their CAL policies amended by appropriate forms that coincide with the nature of their operations. Livery conveyances can include airport buses, chartered buses, club sedans serving only members of an organization under contract, school buses, general passenger buses, taxicabs, and automobiles used for funerals.

PRIVATE LIVERY AUTOMOBILE. When an individual or a firm is in the private livery business—transporting persons for social functions, funerals, touring, or other similar purposes rather than being available for hire to the public at large—an endorsement must be attached to the

CAL policy. This endorsement contains certain exclusions which limit coverage to private livery situations. First, the automobile may have no more than an eight-passenger seating capacity. If it exceeds that capacity, it will be subject to classification as a bus. Second, the automobiles must be rented from the named insured's own residence or business location. This requirement keeps such entity from stationing itself for hire at various public establishments and hence operating as a public taxi. The automobiles must be operated by the named insured or its employees. This is to avoid the additional exposure that can be created when such vehicles are leased or rented to others.

PUBLIC LIVERY—TAXIS. A person or firm that owns or leases automobiles that have seating capacities of no more than eight persons (excluding the driver) and are used for conveying the public at large for certain fares determined by zone or by meter, are classified as public liveries—taxis. When such automobiles are insured under a CAL policy, an endorsement must be attached to alter certain coverage provisions.

Such automobiles, first of all, must be operated by the named insured or its employees. If they are rented without drivers, coverage is excluded because the exposure is a hazardous one which the insurer does not want to unknowingly cover. Second, the exclusion under basic provisions of the CAL policy dealing with damage to property in the insured's care, custody, or control is amended to provide coverage for damage to property of passengers while such automobiles are being used for hire. Third, coverage does not extend to other persons or organizations for whom passengers or property is being transported for the named insured when such other person or organization is required to carry automobile liability insurance under any motor carrier law. If a taxi operator, for example, delivers property of another to a bus depot or accommodates passengers by transferring them to an interstate bus line, no one connected with those other carriers is considered to be an omnibus insured under the livery owner's CAL policy. Finally, no coverage applies while the automobile is being operated as a bus or operated on a schedule along a regular route. The purpose of these restrictions is to keep an insurer from providing coverage on exposures that require different classifications and higher insurance charges.

Automobile Medical Payments Coverage. Automobile medical payments coverage is a form of accident insurance that is limited to land motor vehicle incidents without regard to fault. Its purpose, in general, is to provide a prompt source of medical expense reimbursement for pedestrians or persons injured while occupying an automobile. This type of coverage is also considered a means of eliminating or at least reducing the size of a bodily injury liability claim which might otherwise arise in absence of prompt medical coverage. In many ways, automobile medical payments coverage is similar to medical payments coverage written in connection with premises and operations insurance. There is a distinct difference, however, in that the latter is not intended to provide coverage for injuries to the insured.

Usually included under automobile medical payments coverage are reasonable expenses necessarily incurred within one year from the date of accident for medical, surgical, x-ray, dental services, prosthetic devices, and necessary ambulance, hospital, professional nursing, and funeral services. This coverage is restricted by the limits applying to each person. Only a few exclusions apply. These, for the most part, are meant to prevent overlapping coverage that may be available under workers' compensation insurance, and to prevent catastrophic losses stemming from such perils as war, insurrection, and rebellion.

The automobile medical payments coverage part for use on a countrywide basis with the CAL policy is flexible as to the persons and the automobiles it covers. If a firm furnishes owned or leased automobiles to its executive officers or partners for business and pleasure purposes, such persons and their families can be covered under this policy simply by designating them as insureds and designating the automobiles furnished to them in the schedule of that coverage part. Such persons are insured not only while occupying such automobile, but also as pedestrians. Employees, of course, are not covered for injuries arising out of and during the course of their employment because they normally are subject to workers' compensation insurance. This is one reason an employer often will not buy medical payments coverage on those of its automobiles expected to be occupied exclusively by employees in the course of their employment. A firm, moreover, can be more selective with the protection it desires to provide to persons other than those considered as insureds. A firm may decide to provide medical payments coverage only to persons who are customers or permissive users of automobiles. To provide these persons with proper protection, the firm must designate to which types of automobiles this coverage is to apply. It can select among owned or hired automobiles, licensed owned private passenger automobiles, any automobiles specifically designated in the schedule, or any nonowned automobile.

Except with respect to owned automobiles designated in the schedule to which medical payments coverage applies, coverage is always on an excess basis over any other valid and collectible insurance available to an injured person.

Uninsured Motorists Coverage. Uninsured motorists protection basically amounts to insurance against being injured in an accident with an at-fault motorist who is not protected by bodily injury liability insurance. (Some of the state special coverage parts dealing with uninsured motorists coverage also provide property damage liability insurance on an optional basis.) Subject to the policy limits, the insurer providing this coverage puts its insured in the same position as the insured would be in if the motorist responsible for the accident had carried bodily injury liability insurance. Uninsured motorists coverage applies only if the uninsured motorist is *liable* for the resulting injury. This coverage, therefore, is not automobile accident insurance in the same sense as is automobile medical payments insurance.

While a countrywide uninsured motorists coverage part is available for use with the CAL policy, a variety of state special uninsured motorists coverage parts are also available to cope with the peculiarities of state laws.

The countrywide coverage part—which is practically a separate insurance contract because it has a declarations page, insuring agreements, exclusions, and conditions—is flexible insofar as the persons it protects besides the named insured are concerned. Those persons who also are protected as insureds are discussed in the following paragraphs.

The coverage part covers any individual named in the schedule as a designated insured, including—while resident of the same household— his or her spouse and relatives of either. Who may be considered a designated insured is strictly open to the discretion of the named insured. A firm, for example, may decide to limit designated insureds to executive officers, partners, and key employees, or it may even extend protection to certain other employees who have considerable outside exposures, such as salespersons.

Any other person, a customer for example, is covered while in or upon, entering into or alighting from an insured highway vehicle or a temporary substitute for such vehicle. An insured highway vehicle is one that is described in the schedule as such and to which bodily injury liability coverage of this policy applies. Here again, there is considerable latitude with respect to the automobiles that may be covered. The named insured can limit coverage to any automobile owned by it, such as trucks or a private passenger automobile; any highway vehicle specifically designated in the schedule, such as contractor's road equipment, including newly acquired vehicles; any mobile equipment owned, leased, and registered by the named insured; or any other automobile the insured desires to cover. The important point is that for coverage to apply, the proper automobiles must be designated in the schedule of the coverage part.

Also covered is any person entitled to recover for damages because of bodily injury to which this insurance applies, as mentioned above. Such person could be the surviving spouse of an employee, a guardian, or a parent.

Exposures Excluded, Rationale

Only six exclusions appear in the basic provisions of the CAL policy, and a nuclear energy liability exclusion is usually added by endorsement. At least one of these exclusions—the contamination or pollution exclusion—is subject to modification in some states, as noted later. Furthermore, coverage parts and endorsements added to this policy in order to tailor coverage to particular businesses sometimes modify other basic exclusions, but more commonly add exclusions or limitations to this policy.

Basic Policy Exclusions The basic policy excludes assumption of liability under contract; liability payable under workers' compensation or similar laws; bodily injury to any employee; damage to property owned, being transported, or in the care, custody, or control of the insured; war and allied perils concerning immediate medical expense; contamination or pollution; and nuclear energy liability.

Assumption of Liability Under Contract. No coverage applies under the CAL policy for any assumption of liability under contract or agreement, written or otherwise, by the insured (named insured and others who are insureds under this policy). The purpose of that exclusion is to make contractual liability insurance the primary method for handling contractual assumptions of the insured other than so-called incidental contracts—lease of premises, sidetrack agreements, and so forth—which are automatically covered by CGL policy provisions.

Entities rent or lease automobiles for a variety of reasons.[9] Rental and leasing firms often require contracts containing various hold harmless agreements. The combined effect of the contractual liability exclusion and such rental or leasing agreements on coverage depends on exactly what liability is being assumed.

As a matter of law, persons are responsible for their own negligence if it results in injury or damage to third parties. Liability incurred through the insured's negligence as a driver cannot be liability assumed by contract. Therefore, entities that have a CAL policy are protected against liability arising out of their own negligent use of such rented or leased automobiles.

Nevertheless, problems may arise when a lessee contractually agrees to release a lessor from liability arising out of the operation of an automobile, even though some of the fault lies with the *lessor*. Thus, a contract with such an agreement could conceivably hold the *lessee* accountable for liability beyond the scope of coverage of the CAL policy—for example, an accident caused by a mechanical defect that is either known or should have been known to exist by the lessor. This means that even when the lessee is free of any negligence, it may still be obligated to protect the lessor against its liability to others resulting from that defective automobile. Since the CAL policy covers the insured against legal liability imposed by the tort of negligence, this contractual assumption by the lessee would not be covered. In order to handle this exposure, a lessee may be required to add the lessor as an additional insured under the lessee's CAL policy, to delete the contractual assumption exclusion, to purchase contractual liability insurance, or to exercise some noninsurance technique.

Responsibility of a lessee for the assumption of damage to property in its care, custody, or control is not the subject of general liability or contractual liability insurance. The proper method is first-party coverage (property insurance). However, a contract that holds the lessee responsible for all loss costs and damages to the leased automobile can also be a source of many hardships to a lessee. Since a contract for the lease of an automobile is essentially a bailment for the mutual benefit of both parties—lessor and lessee, a lessee normally is liable only for loss or damage to an automobile attributable to the lessee's negligence. However, this obligation, imposed by law, can be expanded by contract to hold the lessee liable for damage to an automobile even in the absence of negligence.[10] An actual case that illustrates the effect of an assumption of liability by a lessee for loss or damage to a leased vehicle is Morrow, Inc. v. Paugh, 91 N.E. (2nd.) 858. The lessee agreed to restore the automobile, upon expiration of the lease, in as good condition as when it was received. Despite the fact that the automobile was destroyed in a collision and fire without fault of the lessee, the court held the lessee liable for those damages because of the lessee's unqualified undertaking to perform such a contract.[11]

Liability Payable Under Workers' Compensation or Similar Laws. The CAL policy excludes any obligation for which the insured or its insurer may be held liable under workers' compensation, unemployment compensation, disability benefits, or similar laws. The purpose of this exclusion is to avoid duplicating, under the CAL policy, what properly is the subject of statutory employee protection.

This exclusion, as clear-cut as it may appear, sometimes causes arguments. The criterion for the use of this exclusion under the CAL policy is that an insured's loss be subject to payment under one of the laws mentioned above. The fact that the insured is without proper coverage, as required by those laws, is of no significance. For example, in Bruggeman v. Maryland Casualty Co., 73 Fed. (2nd.) 587, the exclusion was held to apply against the insured employer even though the insured did not have workers' compensation insurance to cover a compensable work-related injury. However, in Sumrall v. Aetna Casualty & Surety

Co., 124 So. (2nd.) 168, this same exclusion was held to be inapplicable to a partnership that elected not to come within the provisions of its state workers' compensation law. Not being subject or liable under an elective law, the partnership was protected under its automobile liability policy in a suit brought against it by a widow of a partner who was killed while a passenger in a partner's automobile.

Bodily Injury to an Employee. No coverage applies under the CAL policy for bodily injury sustained by any employee of the insured arising out of and in the course of the employee's work. Neither does coverage apply to any obligation of the insured to indemnify another because of damages arising out of such injury. This exclusion, however, does not apply to a work-related injury of an insured's domestic employee, unless benefits either are payable or are required to be provided under a workers' compensation law.

The purpose of the first part of the exclusion is to make workers' compensation or employers' liability insurance, rather than the CAL policy, the exclusive remedy for an employee's injury.[12] The net effect of the exclusion, therefore, is to avoid duplicating coverage under the CAL policy. In spite of its apparent clarity, the exclusion is often the source of argument. Most arguments center on the question of whether the first part of the exclusion is meant to apply only to the insured who is the employer of an injured employee or to all insureds seeking protection under the CAL policy as well. This question commonly arises following incidents stemming from the loading and unloading of vehicles. A lessee of a truck or an employee of such lessee, for example, may be so careless in unloading the vehicle as to injure an employee of the firm receiving the goods. Since lessees and their employees are considered to be omnibus insureds under the CAL policy of another—during the course of loading or unloading vehicles—these persons normally seek protection under a firm's CAL policy if suit is brought against them by an injured employee of the firm. Whether these omnibus insureds will be protected in the event of such suits in spite of the exclusion of "bodily injury sustained by any employee of the insured" is uncertain. Courts have decided for and against the protection of such omnibus insureds.

The second part of this exclusion deals with an obligation of the insured to indemnify another because of damages stemming from an employee injury. Its purpose is to avoid involving an insured and its insurer of automobile liability insurance in third-party-over actions. Such actions can arise following an employee's injury caused by the negligence of both an insured employer and some third party in the use of an automobile. The employee may collect workers' compensation benefits and may then institute a suit against the negligent third party.

If the injured employee is awarded a judgment against the third party, that third party, or its insurer which pays such award, may then proceed in subrogation against the negligent employer for at least part of those damages.

Because of the latter exclusion, the CAL policy will not respond to such third-party-over actions against an insured. Workers' compensation insurance is the exclusive remedy against the employer. However, if this loss involves a noncompensable employee injury, the insured should have protection against a third-party-over action under its employers' liability insurance, or under its contractual liability coverage—if the insured assumes liability of another for such loss under a contract or agreement.[13] The purpose of this exclusion, therefore, is not only to prevent the duplication of coverage under the CAL policy but also to require that third-party-over actions be handled under more appropriate coverages.

This entire exclusion of bodily injury to an employee does not apply to the insured's domestic employee because the workers' compensation and employers' liability policy does not apply to a domestic unless benefits are payable or required to be provided under a workers' compensation law. With the advent of broader workers' compensation laws encompassing even domestic employees on a mandatory basis, this exception is becoming less significant than it once was.

Care, Custody, or Control. The so-called care, custody, or control exclusion of the CAL policy (and other liability policies) excludes a number of exposures that are either more appropriately handled under other forms of insurance or involve too much of a moral hazard to cover under the CAL policy.

Property subject to the care, custody, or control exclusion includes owned automobiles, including those leased for periods in excess of one year; nonowned, hired, and loaned automobiles; and mobile equipment and cargo being transported, loaded, or unloaded by or on behalf of an insured.

It stands to reason that since an entity cannot be liable to itself for damage to its own property, a CAL policy—which is a contract covering the legal liability of an insured imposed by law—is not the method of covering damage to property owned by an insured. The care, custody, or control exclusion, therefore, requires insureds who own property or who possess property of others to take other means to protect such property. Insureds can exercise several noninsurance techniques, which are discussed later in this chapter, or they can obtain various first-party insurance policies covering a variety of perils. Physical damage insurance on automobiles and mobile equipment, and motor truck cargo coverage, which is a form of inland marine insurance, are some means of treating this excluded exposure.[14]

The only exception to this exclusion is a residence or a private garage, not owned but rented or used by an insured, and damaged by a private passenger automobile covered under the CAL policy. The reason for this somewhat insignificant exception is that an exposure of this nature is not likely to produce a moral hazard. An insured who negligently damages a private garage of another, for example, should receive protection against any claim for damages to the structure, but the insured is not likely to benefit, monetarily, from such loss to the same extent as when the garage is owned by the insured.[15]

War and Allied Perils Concerning First Aid Expenses. The standard policy jacket, which forms an integral part of the CAL policy, contains a supplementary payments provision dealing, in part, with coverage for immediate medical expenses. Under that coverage, the insurer agrees to reimburse an insured for first aid expenses incurred by the insured for the benefit of others at the time of an accident. The only condition of such coverage is that the first aid expenses be incurred for bodily injury to which this policy applies. This coverage, futhermore, is in addition to the applicable limits of liability of the CAL policy. The coverage extension is aimed at promptly assisting injured persons and at reducing the severity of any claim or suit that eventually may arise.

However, the CAL policy and other automobile liability policies contain a restriction on the immediate medical expense provision. No coverage applies when bodily injury or property damage results from an incident involving an automobile in war, whether declared or not, civil war, insurrection, rebellion, revolution, or to any act or condition incident to any of the foregoing. The rationale for this restriction is that any one of these perils can cause catastrophic results, particularly since coverage is provided without limitation as to amount and without regard to liability. Were it not for the restriction, insurers could find themselves providing coverage beyond all expectations due to a minor supplementary payments provision.

Contamination or Pollution. The policy excludes any bodily injury or property damage arising from contamination or pollution by automobiles on land, in the atmosphere, or in any body of water.[16] A similar exclusion also applies to most other forms of liability insurance. The only exception is when the contamination or pollution is sudden *and* accidental.

This exclusion applies for many reasons.[17] Losses usually are attributable to prolonged exposures. It is an almost impossible task to determine what damages are caused by automobiles of any one entity.

Contaminants and pollutants are also capable of producing catastrophic results. In addition, this exclusion is viewed as a means to encourage entities to take whatever steps are necessary to prevent or to at least control this exposure within acceptable limits.

Nuclear Energy Liability Exclusion. The CAL policy is also subject to a nuclear energy liability (broad form) exclusion. Because of its lengthy provisions, this exclusion usually is attached to the policy by endorsement. The primary purpose of the exclusion is to preclude coverage under the CAL policy (1) when an entity is covered under a separate nuclear energy liability policy, (2) when an entity would have been protected under a nuclear energy liability policy were it not for its termination because the limits were exhausted, or (3) when an entity is subject to protection under any govermental indemnity. Otherwise, an entity under the CAL policy is protected against its liability from this exposure.

Other Exclusions, Limitations   When the basic, standard provisions of the CAL policy are amended in order to tailor coverage of an entity to a particular type of operation or to extend protection to other forms of coverages, such as medical payments and uninsured motorist insurance, additional exclusions or limitations commonly accompany the amending forms and endorsements. One example of a limitation, mentioned earlier, is the redefinition of the omnibus clause that is necessary when the truckmen specified vehicles form is attached to the CAL policy. Another example is the public livery endorsement that excludes losses when automobiles are rented without drivers. Countless numbers of other coverage parts and endorsements for use with the CAL policy exclude or limit the scope of the basic CAL policy provisions. The principal reasons for most such exclusions or limitations are to require additional premiums against extraordinary exposures or to require coverage under other policies. The following are additional examples.

Explosives Exclusion. Firms whose automobiles are used for the transportation of explosives are subject to an explosives exclusion endorsement. The effect of the endorsement is to exclude automobile insurance with respect to the explosion of explosives that are manufactured, sold, transported, handled, or distributed by the firm. The purpose of the exclusion is obvious. It attempts to prevent the coverage of a transportation exposure which requires an additional premium.

Erroneous Delivery of Liquid Products Exclusion. A CAL policy covering an entity whose automobiles are used for the bulk transportation of liquid products must be amended by an erroneous delivery of liquid products endorsement, briefly mentioned earlier. This endorsement excludes bodily injury or property damage arising (1) out of the delivery of any liquid product into a wrong receptacle or to a wrong address, or (2) out of the erroneous delivery of one liquid product for another. This exclusion applies only when bodily injury or property damage occurs after such operations are completed or abandoned at the site of delivery. The purpose of this exclusion is to make completed operations insurance the subject of the exposure. Note, however, that bodily injury or property damage arising before any such operations are completed or abandoned is covered under the CAL policy as an element of loading or unloading coverage.

Rolling Stores, Showrooms, or Salesrooms—Automobile Type. A firm that has automobiles equipped as rolling stores is subject to a rolling stores endorsement. It is the purpose of this endorsement to exclude bodily injury or property damage arising out of the products liability hazard. Coverage for this exposure is available under products liability insurance for an additional premium.

MOTOR VEHICLE PHYSICAL DAMAGE INSURANCE

Motor vehicle physical damage insurance is one of several risk management techniques available to business concerns exposed to potential losses of intrinsic and/or use values from the damage, destruction, breakdown, or disappearance of their owned, nonowned, or leased vehicles. As explained in Chapter 8, perils such as fire, theft, falling objects, windstorm, vandalism, flood, earthquake, collision, and upset are the proximate causes of loss. Hazardous conditions, on the other hand, tend to increase the frequency and/or severity of loss.

Business concerns that select insurance transfer as their primary risk management technique for handling all or part of their motor vehicle physical damage loss exposures do so for several reasons. One is that a firm may not be financially capable of retaining losses much over the usual deductibles normally required with automobile physical damage insurance. Another reason may be that such insurance is available at an affordable price. Also, insurance companies often provide valuable loss control advice and assistance which is important to firms regardless of their size. Whatever the reason, automobile physical damage insurance can be a valuable asset to businesses, so long as it is used for loss exposures that cannot be retained or cannot be better handled by some other technique.

Nature, Scope, and Rationale of Coverages Under the Basic Contract

Motor vehicle physical damage insurance for commercial firms, as well as for charitable and public entities, is usually written in combination with the CAL policy, although the coverage can also be obtained separately from the CAL policy. The two automobile physical damage insurance contracts available under standard ISO provisions for all firms other than automobile dealerships are the nonfleet and fleet automatic forms.

Differences Between Nonfleet and Fleet Automatic Forms While the nonfleet and fleet automatic forms are virtually identical in most respects, the forms differ on points of (1) eligibility, (2) method of covering automobiles of the private passenger and commercial-type, and (3) automatic coverage for newly-acquired additional and replacement vehicles.

Nonfleet Form. Briefly, the nonfleet form is designed for firms that have *fewer* than five motor vehicles of any type owned and specifically described in the schedule attached to the form. A newly acquired automobile that replaces an owned automobile specifically described in the schedule of the nonfleet form is also covered to the same extent as the vehicle being replaced, provided the firm notifies its insurer of such replacement vehicle within thirty days of its delivery date. Unless a firm reports the replacement vehicle within that thirty-day period, the firm will be without further coverage. On the other hand, a newly acquired additional vehicle is covered only when the nonfleet form covers *all* owned vehicles of the firm *and* its insurer is notified of such vehicle acquisition within thirty days of the delivery date. If a nonfleet form does not cover all owned vehicles of a firm, a newly acquired additional vehicle is not covered until the insurer is notified of the acquisition. In other words, a firm does not receive the thirty days' automatic coverage.

Fleet Automatic Form. The fleet automatic form is designed for firms that have five or more vehicles of any type owned and/or leased for periods of not less than one year. This form's major advantages are that (1) it eliminates the necessity of having to report newly acquired additional and/or replacement vehicles of the type already covered by the form, and (2) it permits a firm to insure its motor vehicles on a blanket basis (without description) subject to audit at policy expiration or on a scheduled basis whereby each vehicle must be described.

The following six categories represent the choices a firm must make to insure its "covered" automobiles. The first five categories are considered blanket coverage of the fleet automatic form, while the sixth is nothing more than scheduled coverage of the nonfleet form.

1. "All covered automobiles" regardless of type, e.g., owned and/or leased private passenger automobiles, commercial vehicles of the pickup, express, sedan or panel delivery-type, including truck-tractors, trailers, semitrailers and mobile equipment whether or not registered for public road use.
2. "All registered covered automobiles" (which include all of the aforementioned vehicles, except mobile equipment, which are not registered for road use.[18]
3. "All covered automobiles of the private passenger-type."
4. "All covered automobiles of the commercial-type."
5. All covered automobiles as designated in any of the above four categories, excluding leased vehicles, or, under collision coverage, any vehicle not having an actual cash value of at least a certain dollar amount as specified in the schedule.
6. The covered automobiles described in the schedule.

The extent of automatic coverage on a firm's fleet depends upon its selection of the above categories. For example, if a firm selects (1) above for comprehensive and collision insurance, coverage automatically applies to that firm's owned and leased automobiles, regardless of type, as well as to any of its newly acquired additional and replacement vehicles during the policy period. But if a firm selects (3) above, coverage automatically applies only to that firm's owned and leased private passenger automobiles and any newly acquired additional and replacement private passenger automobiles. All other types of vehicles which are acquired must be reported to the insurer if coverage is desired. If a firm desires only physical damage insurance on a selected number of its commercial-type vehicles, (6) above, those vehicles must be described in the schedule. Furthermore, coverage of newly-acquired additional and replacement commercial-type vehicles corresponds to the nonfleet form. Thus, if any one of the described commercial vehicles is replaced during the policy period, coverage automatically applies to the replacement vehicle for thirty days from its delivery date. After that period, the replacement vehicle must be reported to the insurer if coverage is to continue. On the other hand, coverage on a newly-acquired additional commercial vehicle must be reported to the insurer as soon as the firm obtains ownership, because the thirty-day automatic coverage period is inapplicable to newly-acquired additional vehicles unless a firm insures all of its owned and leased commercial vehicles.

With an understanding of how "covered" automobiles can be selected under each of the two automobile physical damage insurance forms, one can gain a better insight into the provisions of the forms and their rationale. While the fleet automatic form is the broader form from the standpoint of coverage on leased vehicles and automatic coverage on newly acquired additional and replacement vehicles, the basic characteristics, other coverage provisions and exclusions are identical for both forms. The following discussion therefore applies to both the fleet automatic and nonfleet forms.

Basic Characteristics of the Fleet and Nonfleet Forms Both the fleet and nonfleet forms contain the following provisions: coverage agreements, consisting of six types of coverages (perils) from which an insured may choose; supplementary payments, which are payable in addition to the applicable limits of liability; exclusions; a limit of liability provision explaining the amount of loss payable to any one covered automobile; territorial scope of coverage; additional definitions of bold face terms, which appear in the forms; and a set of conditions which apply in addition to the conditions of the standard policy jacket.

Coverage Agreements. Under the coverage agreements of the fleet and nonfleet forms, the insurer agrees to pay for loss to covered automobiles resulting from any of the following groups of perils: comprehensive; collision; fire, lightning or transportation; theft; windstorm, hail, earthquake or explosion; or combined additional coverage.

COMPREHENSIVE. Comprehensive coverage is considered to be the broadest available form of automobile physical damage insurance, because it provides a firm with "all-risks" protection on its covered automobiles from any direct and accidental causes, except collision. While the meaning of "collision" is important in understanding the full scope of comprehensive coverage, it is important to note for the moment that the comprehensive insuring agreement states that "breakage of glass and loss caused by missiles, falling objects, fire, theft or larceny, windstorm, hail, earthquake, explosion, riot or civil commotion, malicious mischief or vandalism, water, flood, or . . . colliding with a bird or animal, shall not be deemed loss caused by collision." While the above enumerated perils may appear at first glance to be limitations on comprehensive coverage, they merely serve to distinguish between comprehensive and collision losses.

For example, if part of an aircraft falls and collides with a firm's covered automobile, the resulting damage to the vehicle is treated as a comprehensive loss rather than a collision loss. If an operator of a covered automobile accidentally strikes a deer which is crossing a highway, damage to the vehicle is handled as a comprehensive loss.

While this distinguishing phrase may give the appearance that comprehensive is a clear and all-encompassing coverage, disputes nonetheless are quite common. Most such disputes center on distinguishing between comprehensive and collision losses, even though an insured has both coverages, because collision coverage usually is written with a deductible, whereas comprehensive coverage often is written without a deductible, or with a lower deductible.

Space does not permit an in-depth treatment of all problem areas in distinguishing between comprehensive and collision losses, but the following actual cases will help to illustrate just how complicated matters can become.

Windstorm Losses. The problem with windstorm losses is in establishing whether the force of the wind is actually the proximate cause of loss. For example, an insured maintained that, because of wind, his automobile rolled out of his carport, down a hill, and struck a tree. Since it was established that the wind during the time of loss was merely a moderate breeze, the court held the loss to be one of collision, rather than windstorm.[19] On the other hand, damage to a truck which overturned while rounding a curve in a windstorm was held to be covered as a comprehensive loss.[20]

Vandalism Losses. When a child released the brakes on an automobile parked on a hill, the resulting damage following its collision with another vehicle was held to be caused by vandalism and covered by comprehensive physical damage insurance.[21] But in similar cases, where the loss was only *suspected* of having been caused by children, courts have ruled the loss was covered by collision insurance.

Animals. While comprehensive coverage clearly encompasses loss by collision with birds and animals, there is some question whether damage by collision with a pedestrian is considered to be a comprehensive loss. Although no court cases are known to exist on this point, damage to a vehicle following collision with a pedestrian more than likely would be handled as a collision loss, because there is sufficient evidence in legal texts to support the view that the term "animal," as used in insurance contracts at least, is not meant to include human beings.[22]

It is not always a simple matter to categorize a loss as one of comprehensive coverage. The same holds true of collision and upset losses, which are the subject of the second coverage agreement of fleet and nonfleet forms.

COLLISION. Collision coverage expressly encompasses losses involving (1) collision of a covered automobile with another object or with a vehicle to which it is attached, e.g., jackknifing of a truck-tractor with its trailer, and (2) upset. Note that collision or upset is not contingent upon the happening of a peril, as is the case with comprehensive coverage, but is itself a peril. Collision coverage concerns itself with losses for which collision or upset is the proximate cause, because, when a comprehensive peril causes a collision, the resulting collision loss is usually considered to be the subject of comprehensive coverage.

While the absence of definitions for "collision" and "upset" in automobile physical damage forms sometimes causes problems of interpretation, the former term is generally taken to mean a striking together with violent impact. Taking this meaning of the term "collision" into perspective, there is a collision loss when a covered automobile strikes another object with violent impact, such as when a vehicle collides with another automobile, with an overhead bridge abutment, with a tree or pole, or when a parked covered automobile is struck by a moving vehicle.

However, difficulties are presented by losses involving automobiles which plunge off bridges or swerve off highways and come into contact with bodies of water, because water damage is usually thought of as a comprehensive loss. Based on the court decisions involving vehicles which come into contact with water, the distinguishing factor between a comprehensive and collision loss lies with the proximate cause. If a flood were to damage a vehicle, loss is covered by comprehensive, because flood is the proximate cause and is a peril of comprehensive coverage. But if a vehicle collides or comes into contact with water for no other reason than negligence of the vehicle operator, loss is considered to be one of collision coverage. The following actual cases have been upheld as collision losses: an automobile went through a bridge guardrail and plunged into a river;[23] a vehicle went off the highway and fell over a riverbank;[24] an automobile went over an embankment and into a water-filled ditch.[25]

Another problem area of collision losses involves vehicles which are damaged when they come into contact with roadbeds and soft shoulders of highways. Whether such losses are considered to be collisions depends upon the circumstances. For example, one court ruled against collision coverage when a roadbed gave way under a vehicle, causing the vehicle to sink in soft soil, because the vehicle, while being operated, was in contact with the roadbed and, hence, did not collide or strike against the roadbed. However, impact with a roadbed when one of the wheels of an automobile fell off was considered to be a collision in another case.

What constitutes an "upset" of a vehicle can also be troublesome. Generally, a vehicle does not necessarily have to completely overturn for the incident to be considered an upset. The real test of an upset seems to be whether the vehicle preserves its equilibrium.

Despite the problems just described, the combination of comprehensive and collision coverage is regarded as the broadest form of vehicle protection available. However, not all firms require such broad vehicle protection. Some firms are able to retain many of their losses and may require coverage only against certain perils which are capable of producing large, financially unmanageable losses. A firm that has a high concentration of vehicle values at one terminal or parking lot may require insurance only against certain perils, such as fire, windstorm, hail, earthquake, or flood; or a firm may consider the broad and more expensive protection of comprehensive coverage to be unnecessary. In circumstances such as these, other coverages or coverage combinations may be selected under fleet and nonfleet forms—fire, lightning, and transportation coverage; theft coverage; windstorm, hail, earthquake, and explosion coverage; or combined additional coverage.

FIRE, LIGHTNING, AND TRANSPORTATION COVERAGE. When a firm selects fire, lightning, and transportation coverage, it receives protection for direct and accidental loss or damage to its covered automobiles by (1) fire or lightning, (2) smoke or smudge damage stemming from the sudden, unusual, and faulty operation of any fixed heating equipment on premises, where covered automobiles are located, and (3) transportation losses encompassing the stranding, sinking, burning, collision, or derailment of any conveyance that is transporting a firm's covered automobiles.

THEFT COVERAGE. Although theft coverage applying to loss by theft and larceny is available as a separate coverage item, it usually is written in conjunction with fire, lightning, and transportation coverage or with one of the subsequent groups of coverages.

WINDSTORM, HAIL, EARTHQUAKE, AND EXPLOSION COVERAGE. The coverage combination of windstorm, hail, earthquake, and explosion is self-explanatory. However, any loss resulting from rain, snow, or sleet, whether wind driven or not, is excluded.

COMBINED ADDITIONAL COVERAGE (CAC). To reduce physical damage insurance costs, some firms can purchase combined additional coverage which pays for loss caused by windstorm, hail, earthquake, and explosion; riot and civil commotion; the forced landing or falling of aircraft, including its parts or equipment; vandalism and malicious mischief; flood or rising waters; and external discharge or leakage of water.

It is difficult to make a comparison between losses covered by combined additional coverage—which is on a specified or named perils basis—and comprehensive coverage, because the latter gives "all-risks" protection for loss by fire, lightning, transportation, theft, falling objects other than aircraft, and breakage of glass. However, if necessary, a firm can purchase theft coverage and/or fire, lightning, and transportation coverage along with its combined additional coverage ("fire, theft, and CAC"). Coverage for glass breakage still cannot be obtained without purchasing comprehensive coverage, but there may be circumstances when the glass breakage exposure is slight or nonexistent, particularly when a firm is insuring only commercial-type vehicles, including trailers and semitrailers. Trailers do not usually have glass. A firm therefore may be able to forgo the purchase of comprehensive coverage and instead obtain combined additional coverage along with coverage for one or two other perils, usually for less than the cost of comprehensive coverage.

TOWING COVERAGE. The fleet and nonfleet forms also offer optional towing coverage in most states. This coverage, which is identical to that coverage provided by the physical damage coverage forms of personal automobile policies, pays for towing and labor costs because of a covered automobile's disablement, regardless of cause, provided the labor is performed at the place of disablement. The limit is $25 per disablement for towing and labor costs. However, if a vehicle has to be towed to a garage before work can be performed on the vehicle, only the towing charges are covered up to the $25 limit.

In addition to the preceding optional physical damage coverages from which a firm may choose, a certain amount of protection is provided automatically for certain consequential losses under a provision entitled, supplementary payments.

SUPPLEMENTARY PAYMENTS. The supplementary payments provision of fleet and nonfleet forms, like the physical damage portions of personal automobile policies, provides consequential loss coverage in connection with transportation and theft losses, in addition to the applicable limit of an insurer's liability.

Transportation Losses. When a firm has comprehensive or transportation coverage, the insurer will pay any general average and salvage charges the firm becomes legally obligated to pay as the result of loss while its vehicle(s) is being transported on a conveyance. General average is a concept of ocean marine insurance involving the voluntary sacrifice of property on a vessel in order to save the remaining cargo and the vessel. When property is sacrificed, all those who have an interest in the cargo as well as the vessel must contribute to the loss of property that was sacrificed, in proportion to what each party's value of property bears to the total value of property before the loss. Whatever amount of general average costs are assessed against the insured, the insurer will pay them. Salvage charges, also an ocean marine concept, are the costs incurred by salvors for their services in attempting to save, for example, a vessel stranded at sea, including the vessel's cargo. Any such salvage charges assessed against a firm that has automobiles on such a vessel are paid by the insurer under this supplementary payments provision.

Theft Losses. In the event of theft of an entire covered private passenger automobile that is not used as a public or livery conveyance and is not up for sale by a dealer, the insurer will reimburse the insured for the expenses incurred in renting a substitute automobile. Coverage for rental reimbursement of a substitute automobile commences forty-eight hours after the theft has been reported to the insurer and police, and coverage terminates when the automobile is returned to the insured or when the insurer pays for the loss of the entire automobile. However, the insurer is obligated to pay no more than $10 a day for rental costs and no more than $300 in the aggregate. This supplementary payment for loss of use applies only when a firm has comprehensive coverage or separate theft coverage.

Exclusions in Fleet and Nonfleet Forms. Aside from the exclusion of losses of a catastrophic nature, such as war, and losses of a nonaccidental nature, such as wear and tear, most exclusions in fleet and nonfleet forms are directed toward certain automobile uses and/or automobile equipment. The following subsections analyze the exclusions and their rationale.

PUBLIC OR LIVERY CONVEYANCES. No automobile physical damage coverage of any kind applies to a covered automobile while it is being used as a public or livery conveyance *unless* such use of a vehicle is declared to the insurer and the exposure is described in the schedule of the appropriate form. This exclusion serves to keep the insurer informed of such uses because public or livery conveyances, ranging from taxicabs to large buses, have a high intensity of usage. And, as explained in Chapter 8, the high intensity of usage usually correlates with greater exposure to loss.

LOSSES OF A NONACCIDENTAL NATURE—EXCEPTIONS. Insurance does not apply to a covered automobile for damage due to and confined to (1) wear and tear, (2) freezing, or (3) mechanical or electrical breakdown or failure unless the damage results from another loss that is insured. Such losses can eventually be expected to happen and are particularly intensified through an insured's neglect in maintaining automobiles. However, the above losses are covered when they result from other covered losses. For example, if an automobile is stolen and abandoned, and when it is found its radiator is frozen and its motor block is cracked because of insufficient antifreeze, the entire loss is covered by comprehensive coverage (or separate theft coverage). If an automobile sustains mechanical failure because someone puts a harmful substance in the gas tank, the entire loss is covered under comprehensive or combined additional coverage as a vandalism or malicious mischief loss.

TIRES. Loss or damage to tires is not covered under the fleet and nonfleet forms, with two exceptions.

Coverage applies when loss to tires is *coincident* with and from the same cause as other loss covered by the form. For example, if an insured has comprehensive coverage and a tornado damages his or her automobile and tires, the entire loss is covered, because loss to the tires is coincident with the same cause (tornado) as other covered loss to the automobile. However, if a piece of metal hurtles from a passing truck and strikes the insured's automobile tire without damaging any other part of the automobile, loss to the tire is not covered.

Coverage also applies when damage to tires is caused by fire, vandalism, malicious mischief, or theft, even if no other part of the automobile is damaged, provided, of course, theft or the peril that causes damage is covered by the form. For example, if vandals slash an insured's tires, loss is covered if the insured has comprehensive or combined additional coverage. If the insured has only fire, lightning, and transportation coverage, loss to the tires would not be covered.

CATASTROPHIC LOSSES. Neither automobile physical damage form covers loss or damage to the covered automobile caused by war, whether declared or not, civil war, insurrection, rebellion, revolution, or any act or condition incident to any of the foregoing, as well as radioactive contamination however caused.

SOUND REPRODUCING OR RECORDING EQUIPMENT. Because tape players, tapes, citizen's band radios, two-way mobile radio and telephones, scanning receivers, and accessory equipment are susceptible to loss or damage, particularly by theft, most automobile physical damage forms exclude loss or damage to such equipment, although some coverage is available for an additional cost.

CAMPER BODIES. Loss to a camper body (a unit mounted upon a covered vehicle and equipped as sleeping or living quarters) is excluded if the camper body is not designated in the policy declarations and it was owned by the named insured at the inception of the policy period or renewal period. However, a camper body acquired during the policy period is automatically covered until policy expiration. It must then be declared if coverage is to continue. This exclusion serves (1) to prevent a camper body being automatically covered as part of an automobile's equipment, and (2) to give the insurer the proper rate reflected by the insurable value of a camper body.

VEHICLE ENCUMBRANCES. Since a designated loss payee's interest in insured vehicles is protected in the policy, no policy provision thus far discussed would preclude coverage for the loss payee if the owner in some way cheats the loss payee out of payments on the car. Such business perils which come about because of the loss payee's bad judgment in issuing credit are beyond the scope of coverage intended by auto physical damage insurers issuing a policy on the vehicle owner. Therefore, the policy excludes loss under comprehensive and theft coverages stemming from conversion, embezzlement, or secretion by any person in possession of the covered automobile under a bailment lease, conditional sale, purchase agreement, mortgage, or other encumbrance. This exclusion prevents the insurer from having to pay the remaining debt owed on such automobile to any loss payee or other creditor when the automobile is stolen or sold with the intent to defraud the creditor.

BREAKAGE OF GLASS IN A COLLISION LOSS. Collision coverage is seldom if ever purchased without comprehensive coverage or coverage against some other group of perils. Nonetheless, an exclusion—really more of a clarification—states that breakage of glass is not considered an item of coverage under collision if glass coverage is otherwise provided under comprehensive coverage. But if comprehensive coverage does not apply, breakage of glass in a collision is treated as part of collision coverage, and recovery for glass breakage and other damage to the automobile is subject to the collision deductible.

LOSS RESULTING FROM RAIN, SNOW, OR SLEET. Combined additional coverage, like the separate coverage combination of windstorm, hail, earthquake, and explosion, does not cover loss to an automobile resulting from rain, snow, or sleet.

OTHER EXCLUSIONS The preceding exclusions are those which apply to the basic provisions of the fleet and nonfleet forms. When endorsements are attached to either form in order to tailor coverage to particular needs, additional exclusions commonly apply.

Valuation Since automobile physical damage insurance is a first-party coverage, the amount of loss payable to a firm for damage, destruction, breakdown, or disappearance of its automobiles will depend upon the values of such automobiles at the time of loss. Depending upon the coverage, valuations may be based upon actual cash value or stated amount.

Actual Cash Value Versus Stated Amount. Collision coverage under the fleet and nonfleet forms is almost always written on an actual cash value basis, while comprehensive, combined additional coverage, and other named perils may be written either on an actual cash value or a stated amount basis.

When automobile physical damage coverage is written on an actual cash value basis, the letters "ACV" are indicated in the schedule of the fleet or nonfleet form as the limit of liability for each vehicle to be covered on that basis. Although the amount of loss payable is prescribed in the limit of liability provision of the fleet and nonfleet forms (discussed later), the insurer's obligation for loss is limited to the replacement cost of the automobile or the automobile part, less any depreciation. Consider, for example, a truck that was purchased new in 1970 for $20,000 and which is totally destroyed by fire in 1981. If the cost of a comparable new truck at the time of loss is $45,000, the insurer is neither liable for an amount of $20,000 or $45,000. Instead, the insurer is liable only for an amount sufficient to replace the truck with one of like condition at the time of loss. Thus, the insured will receive an amount comparable to the value of a $45,000 truck which is eleven years old, less any deductible.

When automobile physical damage insurance other than collision coverage is written on a *stated amount* basis rather than an actual cash value basis, a dollar amount is designated in the schedule of the fleet or nonfleet form opposite the automobile to be covered in that manner. Despite the stated amount, however, the insurer's liability in the event of loss is still limited to the actual cash value of the automobile. The only advantage for using stated amounts, therefore, is when a firm's automobiles (1) have expensive specialized equipment which reflects higher than normal values, (2) are subject to rapid depreciation through prolonged usage, or (3) are amortized (written off) over shorter periods than the normal use expectancies of the automobiles.

For example, consider a $50,000 truck that has a normal use expectancy of ten years. If a firm decides to amortize the vehicle over a five-year period so that it may be sold or put in trade for a new vehicle at the expiration of that period, the stated amount of each successive annual policy period will decrease by an amount of $10,000. Since the rate for physical damage insurance will be based upon the stated amount, the insured will be paying less for its insurance than if the vehicle were to be insured on an actual cash value basis, assuming that the stated amount is always less than the actual cash value of the vehicle. If the stated amount at the time of a loss is less than the actual cash value of the vehicle, the insured will receive no more than the stated amount. On the other hand, if the stated amount is higher than the actual cash value of the vehicle, the insured will receive a loss settlement based only on the actual cash value of the vehicle at the time of loss.

In spite of the uses for stated amounts, one authority advocates that the actual cash value basis is more advantageous for the following reasons:

1. It avoids the problem of over and under insurance. It is not necessary for the insurer to inspect each car prior to insuring or, as an alternative, to guess at its precise value at the inception of coverage. And it avoids the problem posed by declining values over the policy period.
2. It provides better coverage for the insured. If market values should happen to rise or if the insured adds new equipment or tires to his car, has a new motor installed, or has the car repainted, his insurance protection can rise automatically with the enhanced value of the car.

3. It simplifies handling. There is no problem in arriving at the amount of insurance to be stated. It is not necessary to multiply amounts of insurance by rates in order to compute premiums.
4. It minimizes moral hazard. The insurer is not tempted to make a valued contract out of a contract of indemnity. Nor can the insurer use the stated amount as an instrument of unfair competition.
5. It reconciles the treatment of comprehensive claims with that accorded collision claims, which are nearly always paid on an actual cash value basis. Consider, for example, the case of an automobile destroyed in a collision that occurs during the course of a theft. Does it not seem illogical for the insurer to effect settlement under its collision coverage on an actual cash value basis and (alternatively) under its comprehensive (theft) coverage on a stated amount basis?[26]

Whatever form of valuation is ultimately selected by a firm for its automobile physical damage insurance (a firm, of course, may have some of its automobiles on a stated amount basis and some on an actual cash value basis), the amount payable is dictated by the limits of liability provision of the fleet and nonfleet forms.

Limit of Liability. The limit of liability provisions of the fleet and nonfleet forms specify that the maximum limit of an insurer's liability for loss to any one covered automobile does not exceed the *least* of the following three amounts:

1. the actual cash value of the covered automobile or any part of such automobile at the time of loss; or
2. the cost to repair or replace the covered automobile or part with other of like kind or quality, with deduction for depreciation; or
3. the limit of liability that is stated to apply to a covered automobile, provided that when coverage is written on a stated amount basis, a newly acquired automobile that is not described in the declarations will be adjusted on the basis of actual cash value.

In the event of any covered loss, furthermore, the insurer has the option of paying for the loss in money or it may (1) repair or replace the damaged or stolen property, (2) return at its own expense any stolen property to the named insured with payment for any damage, or (3) take all or any part of the damaged or stolen property at the agreed-upon or appraised value. However, abandonment of property to the insurer is not permitted under any circumstances.

Policy Period—Territory—Purposes of Use Both the fleet and nonfleet forms specify that physical damage insurance applies only to loss—that is, direct and accidental loss or damage—that occurs (1) during the policy period, (2) while the covered automobile is within the United States, its territories, possessions, or in Canada, or is being transported between ports, and (3) if a covered automobile described in the schedule is maintained and used for the purpose stated in the form. Thus, for example, if a firm leases one of its trucks to another firm and that truck is stated by the insured to be used solely by the insured for the transportation of its own cargo, the insurer has the right to deny coverage if the truck should become damaged by a covered peril within the policy period and territory. Note, however, that this restriction does not apply to a newly-acquired covered automobile, because such vehicle will not be described in the schedule of the form until policy renewal.

Supplemental Coverages

Many different commercial automobile physical damage insurance forms and endorsements are available for tailoring coverages to the particular needs of businesses. Although space limitations preclude discussions or even brief descriptions of all such forms and endorsements, the following supplemental coverages of common interest to many business concerns will be noted: physical damage insurance for nonowned automobiles (primary and excess coverage), garagekeepers' coverage, and physical damage insurance for automobile dealers.

Physical Damage Coverage for Nonowned Automobiles As noted earlier, the fleet and nonfleet forms provide physical damage insurance on only those nonowned automobiles that are leased by a firm for periods of twelve months or more. Any other type of nonowned automobile maintained or used by a firm, even if covered for liability, is not covered against physical damage loss unless additional insurance is obtained. For example, if a firm borrows or rents a truck as a temporary substitute for one of its own trucks which is in need of repair, and that borrowed or rented truck is damaged while in the care, custody, or control of the borrower or renter, the insurer of the fleet or nonfleet form is under no obligation to pay for those damages. To overcome this coverage gap, two physical damage forms for nonowned automobiles are available for an additional cost. One provides coverage on a primary basis and the other provides coverage on an excess basis.

Primary Coverage. When primary coverage on nonowned automobiles is obtained, the insured has the choice of purchasing collision coverage subject to a deductible, along with comprehensive, combined additional coverage, or fire and/or theft. In addition, the insured must specify the maximum limit of liability which is to apply to (1) any one nonowned automobile, (2) all nonowned automobiles at any one location, and (3) all nonowned automobiles.

For purposes of this primary coverage, a nonowned automobile means a land motor vehicle, trailer, or semitrailer which is:

(a) not owned wholly or in part by the named insured or an employee of the named insured, or registered in the name of the named insured, and

(b) is being operated by or is in the custody of the named insured, or

(c) is being operated by or is in the custody of any employee or agent of the named insured, but only when such operation or custody is directly related to the business of the named insured.

Not covered under this form is the rental reimbursement expense incurred when a nonowned automobile is stolen. If a firm desires rental reimbursement coverage, it is available under the fleet form for an additional charge. When this primary coverage on nonowned automobiles is purchased, the insurer agrees to waive its right of subrogation against the owner of any nonowned automobile in the event any loss is paid under this form.

Excess Coverage. Excess coverage for nonowned automobiles is identical to primary coverage, with one exception. The excess coverage form does not apply to a loss when there is other insurance which would apply, whether the other insurance covers the interest of the named insured, the owner of the nonowned automobile, or any other person or organization that has rented or furnished the nonowned automobile to the named insured. This excess coverage is useful to the firm that occasionally borrows or rents an automobile for which no physical damage insurance applies, or when physical damage insurance applies over a large deductible. In the former circumstance, this excess coverage will provide full coverage for the nonowned automobile, whereas in the latter case the insurer of the excess coverage will cover only that part of the loss not covered by the insurer of the nonowned automobile. For example, if the nonowned automobile is covered subject to a $1,000 deductible and the excess coverage applies subject to a $500 deductible, the insurer of excess coverage will pay for the uninsured portion of the loss less the $500 deductible. The insured will have to retain the $500 deductible.

Garagekeepers' Insurance Garagekeepers' insurance is a form of bailee coverage available to automobile repair shops, service stations, and parking lot or storage garages. Garagekeepers' insurance provides coverage for damage to automobiles of others while in the custody of such businesses for purposes of repair, servicing, storage, or safekeeping. The need for garagekeepers' insurance arises from the fact that garage liability insurance, discussed in Chapter 2, does not cover property damage losses to automobiles in an insured's care, custody, or control.

Scope of Coverage. Under the ISO program of garagekeepers' insurance introduced in 1977, coverage is available for loss by (1) fire, explosion, theft of the entire automobile, riot, civil commotion, vandalism, and malicious mischief (with a mandatory deductible of $100 for each vehicle and a maximum deductible per occurrence of $500), or (2) comprehensive coverage, subject to the same deductibles as (1), and (3) collision coverage, subject to deductibles of $100, $250, or $500.

A business has the option of purchasing garagekeepers' insurance in one of the following three ways:

1. Direct coverage on a primary basis. This pays for all losses to customers' automobiles from an insured peril, subject to any deductible(s) that may apply.
2. Direct coverage on an excess basis. This pays for that part of a loss by an insured peril that is not otherwise covered under a customer's automobile insurance.
3. Legal liability insurance. This covers only loss to a customer's automobile from an insured peril for which the garagekeeper is legally liable. If the garagekeeper is not held to be *legally liable* for the resulting loss, the insurer is under no obligation to pay the loss, even though it results from an insured peril. However, under the supplementary payments provision of the form, the insurer still has the right and duty to defend its insured, even if the allegations are groundless, false, or fraudulent.

Subject to any applicable deductible, the amount actually payable under any one of the above three coverage options depends on the limit of liability stated for each location and on the maximum number of automobiles stated to be at any one location. If the limit of liability is adequate and the number of automobiles actually on the insured's premises at the time of the loss does not exceed the specified maximum, the insured is covered in full, subject to any applicable deductible. However, if the number of automobiles on premises exceeds the stated maximum at the time of loss, a provision similar to the coinsurance clause of property forms applies, and the insured will have to share part of the loss with the insurer. For example, suppose a repair shop purchases comprehensive coverage on a direct primary basis for a limit of $50,000 and indicates that there will be no more than ten customers' automobiles on the premises at any one time. At the time of an explosion loss, there are actually twenty automobiles on the premises and ten of them are totally destroyed for a total loss of $40,000. In this event, the maximum liability is limited to that proportion of the loss that the maximum number of automobiles stated in the policy bears to the actual number of automobiles at the location at the time of loss. The amount payable, therefore, is (5 automobiles/10 automobiles) × $40,000 loss = $20,000. Note that if there were only ten automobiles on the insured's premises at the time of loss, the insured would recover its loss in full up to the $50,000 limit.

Exclusions. The garagekeepers' form does not cover losses stemming from the following conditions or circumstances.

EMPLOYEE DISHONESTY. This exclusion encompasses theft stemming from any fraudulent, dishonest, or criminal act by the named insured, a partner, member, employee, trustee, or authorized representative, whether such person is acting alone or in collusion with others.

HOIST OR ELEVATOR LOSS. No customer's automobile is covered for loss or damage arising out of the use of an elevator or an automobile servicing hoist designed to raise an entire automobile.

DAMAGE TO PRODUCTS OR TO COMPLETED WORK. No coverage applies to defective parts, accessories, or materials furnished by the insured or for faulty work performed by the insured.

CONTRACTUAL LIABILITY. Any agreement made by the insured to be responsible for loss to a customer's automobile is not covered. (Note that coverage for damage to products or to completed work is optionally available with a mandatory deductible.)

RACING. No coverage applies to an automobile or other property while the automobile is being used in any prearranged or organized racing, speed, or demolition contest, any stunting activity, or in the practice or preparation for any such contest or activity.

OTHER EXCLUSIONS. Loss due to war is excluded, as is loss by civil war, insurrection, rebellion, revolution, or any act incident to the foregoing; and no coverage applies to loss caused by radioactive contamination. Neither is there coverage for *loss of use* of an automobile stemming from fire, explosion, vandalism, or malicious mischief.

Automobile Dealers' Physical Damage Insurance Automobile dealers' physical damage insurance is designed to provide dealers with coverage in the event of direct and accidental loss or damage to (1) their owned automobiles used in the sales agency business, including repair service, and (2) automobiles held for sale, held on consignment, or held by the dealer pending delivery after sale.

The automobile dealers' form, which can be written as a separate policy or in conjunction with the garage liability policy, comprehensive automobile liability policy, or comprehensive general-automobile liability policy, gives businesses the option of four coverages from which to choose: (1) collision coverage, (2) fire, lightning, and transportation coverage, (3) theft and larceny coverage, and (4) supplemental coverage which is the equivalent of the combined additional coverage provided by the fleet and nonfleet physical damage forms. Not available with the dealers' form are comprehensive coverage and coverage against the perils of windstorm, hail, earthquake, and explosion.

The territory of the dealers' form encompasses the United States, its territories, possessions, Canada, and the area between ports of that territory. However, coverage is contingent upon a specific listing of all named locations (owned, rented, or controlled places of business known to exist at policy inception), along with a limit of liability applying to each such location.

The dealers' form also requires the named insured to declare a limit of liability on each covered automobile in transit and on each unnamed location—additional locations and temporary locations used by the dealer during the policy period. However, a dealer who acquires an additional location must report such acquisition to the insurer within forty-five days, whereas a temporary location must be reported to the insurer within seven days. If a dealer fails to report an additional location or a temporary location following the expiration of these periods, it will be without coverage.

Coverage of the dealers' form can be written on a monthly or quarterly reporting basis, depending upon the fluctuation of values, or on a nonreporting form basis. Dealers' reporting forms operate the same as other property insurance reporting forms, discussed in CPCU 3, Chapter 3.

Two types of protection not provided under the basic provisions of the dealers' physical damage insurance form but available by endorsement for an additional cost are (1) driveaway collision coverage and (2) false pretense coverage.

Driveaway Collision Coverage. Under the basic coverage provisions of the dealers' form, no coverage applies to loss by collision to any covered automobile, while being driven, towed, or carried by the dealer's owned or hired motor vehicle, trailer, or semitrailer, from point of purchase or distribution to point of destination if such points are more than fifty miles apart. For example, if an automobile dealer has to pick up a car from the stock of another dealership sixty-five miles away, no collision coverage would be afforded to the car because of this exclusion. Since such interdealership transfers of automobiles are common, the exclusion can create an important gap in coverage. If coverage is desired against this limitation, driveaway collision coverage may be purchased.

False Pretense Coverage. The dealers' physical damage form does not apply to loss of title or possession of an automobile through any fraudulent scheme, trick, device, false pretense, embezzlement, conversion, secretion, theft, or larceny committed by any person who is entrusted with the custody or possession of a covered automobile. For example, if a prospective customer were to test-drive an automobile and abscond with it, the dealer would be without coverage for the loss of its automobile.

When false pretense coverage is added to the dealers' physical damage form, the dealership receives coverage for loss resulting from its voluntarily parting with the title or possession of a covered automobile if it is induced to do so by any fraudulent scheme, trick, device, or false pretense. As conditions precedent to false pretense coverage, the dealer (1) must have had full and valid title to such covered automobile before the loss, (2) must obtain a warrant for the arrest of the person(s) who took wrongful title or possession of the automobile, as soon as possible after such loss, and (3) maintain title and regain possession of the covered automobile if and when it is ultimately located. In the event the automobile is recovered, the insurer's limit of liability for loss is not to exceed the actual cost and expense of recovering and returning the automobile, plus the cost of any replacement or repairs necessitated by physical damage to the automobile subsequent to loss.

BUSINESS AUTO POLICY

The comprehensive automobile and basic automobile policies of the Insurance Services Office have been in use for more than two decades and are scheduled to be replaced during 1978. Replacing these two policies is a contract referred to as the business auto policy (BAP). The business auto policy reflects an effort toward simplification which should be an asset to buyers. However, the creation of a new policy also creates the opportunity for insurers to delete provisions of questionable value, broaden the scope of some coverages, and introduce restrictions of other coverages. Some such modifications are a reaction to court decisions which have interpreted policy coverage much more broadly than the policy designers ever intended.

In the pages that follow, readers will be given an insight into the characteristics and structure of the business auto policy as well as an opportunity to see how that policy compares on a provision-by-provision basis with the comprehensive automobile policy. A comparison is particularly valuable because some insurers may continue to use the CAL in lieu of the new policy, and it is necessary for buyers to identify the differences in the two forms.

Coverage Characteristics

To be more readable and less likely to be misunderstood, the business auto policy uses terms and language which are more personal than those of most other policies. Meeting the objective of clarity at the outset, the policy first lists and defines certain words and phases. Most of the terms and phrases need not be explained here, because they are similar to terms used with the comprehensive automobile liability and physical damage policy. In that category are "auto," "bodily injury," "insured," "loss," "mobile equipment," and "trailer." (The BAP uses the term "auto" rather than "automobile.")

Those terms which do require mention are defined as follows.

"You" and "your" mean the person or organization shown as the named insured in ITEM ONE of the declarations.

"We," "us" and "our" mean the company providing the insurance.

"Accident" includes continuous or repeated exposure to the same conditions resulting in bodily injury or property damage the insured neither expected nor intended.

"Property damage" means damage for or loss of use of tangible property.

Although the term "accident" is used in lieu of "occurrence," the former term still is defined as it once was under "occurrence." According to ISO's explanatory memorandum regarding the business auto policy, the term "accident" is better understood by the insuring public. "Property damage" also is defined differently here than in the comprehensive automobile policy, but it creates no change. The present definition merely reduces the verbiage to that essential to provide the intended coverage.

The business auto policy is a self-contained contract. It does not need to be attached to the standard policy jacket to form a complete contract, as has been the case with the comprehensive automobile policy. This new approach also prevents the issuance of a comprehensive general-automobile liability policy. However, insurers have the option of combining the business auto policy and the comprehensive general liability policy by using a common declarations page. Whether separate or combined policies are used, it is desirable for one insurer to provide both forms of protection in order to prevent problems within the so-called "gray areas" mentioned earlier in this chapter.

The new policy is written on a single-limit basis (dual limits are available by endorsement) and is structured in such a way as to provide a number of coverages from which insureds may choose.

Structure of Coverage

The business auto policy is designed to replace several policies

Figure 9-2
Declarations—Business Auto Policy

Item Two—Schedule of Coverages and Covered Autos
This policy provides only those coverages where a charge is shown in the premium column below. Each of these coverages will apply only to those autos shown as covered autos. Autos are shown as covered autos for a particular coverage by the entry of one or more of the symbols from item three next to the name of the coverage.

COVERAGES	COVERED AUTOS (Entry of one or more of the symbols from item three shows which autos are covered autos)	LIMIT The most we will pay for any one accident or loss	PREMIUM
LIABILITY INSURANCE	1		$
PERSONAL INJURY PROTECTION (or equivalent added No-fault coverage)		SEPARATELY STATED IN EACH P.I.P. ENDORSEMENT MINUS $ _____ Ded. APPLICABLE TO THE NAMED INSURED AND RELATIVES ONLY	
ADDED PERSONAL INJURY PROTECTION (or equivalent added No-fault coverage)		SEPARATELY STATED IN EACH ADDED P.I.P. ENDORSEMENT	
PROPERTY PROTECTION INSURANCE (Michigan only)		SEPARATELY STATED IN THE P.P.I. ENDORSEMENT MINUS $ _____ Ded. FOR EACH ACCIDENT	
AUTO. MEDICAL PAYMENTS INSURANCE	3		$
UNINSURED MOTORISTS INSURANCE			$
PHYSICAL DAMAGE INSURANCE COMPREHENSIVE COVERAGE	7	ACTUAL CASH VALUE OR COST OF REPAIR, WHICHEVER IS LESS MINUS $ _____ Ded. FOR EACH COVERED AUTO FOR ALL LOSS EXCEPT FIRE OR LIGHTNING	

PHYSICAL DAMAGE INSURANCE
SPECIFIED PERILS COVERAGE

ACTUAL CASH VALUE OR COST OF REPAIR, WHICHEVER IS LESS MINUS $25 Ded. FOR EACH COVERED AUTO FOR LOSS CAUSED BY MISCHIEF OR VANDALISM

PHYSICAL DAMAGE INSURANCE
COLLISION COVERAGE

ACTUAL CASH VALUE OR COST OF REPAIR, WHICHEVER IS LESS MINUS $_____ Ded. FOR EACH COVERED AUTO

PHYSICAL DAMAGE INSURANCE
TOWING AND LABOR
(Not Available in California)

$25 for each disablement of a private passenger auto

Item Three—Description of Covered Auto Designation Symbols

SYMBOL	DESCRIPTION
1	= **ANY AUTO.**
2	= **OWNED AUTOS ONLY.** Only those autos you own (and for liability coverage any trailers you don't own while attached to power units you own). This includes those autos you acquire ownership of after the policy begins.
3	= **OWNED PRIVATE PASSENGER AUTOS ONLY.** Only the private passenger autos you own. This includes those private passenger autos you acquire ownership of after the policy begins.
4	= **OWNED AUTOS OTHER THAN PRIVATE PASSENGER AUTOS ONLY.** Only those autos you own which are not of the private passenger type (and for liability coverage any trailers you don't own while attached to power units you own). This includes those autos, not of the private passenger type, you acquire ownership of after the policy begins.
5	= **OWNED AUTOS SUBJECT TO NO-FAULT.** Only those autos you own which are required to have No-Fault benefits in the state where they are licensed or principally garaged. This includes those autos you acquire ownership of after the policy begins provided they are required to have No-Fault benefits in the state where they are licensed or principally garaged.

SYMBOL	DESCRIPTION
6	= **OWNED AUTOS SUBJECT TO A COMPULSORY UNINSURED MOTORISTS LAW.** Only those autos you own which, because of the law in the state where they are licensed or principally garaged, are required to have and cannot reject uninsured motorists insurance. This includes those autos you acquire ownership of after the policy begins provided they are subject to the same state uninsured motorists requirement.
7	= **SPECIFICALLY DESCRIBED AUTOS.** Only those autos described in item four for which a premium charge is shown (and for liability coverage any trailers you don't own while attached to any power unit described in item four).
8	= **HIRED AUTOS ONLY.** Only those autos you lease, hire, rent or borrow. This does not include any auto you lease, hire, rent, or borrow from any of your employees or members of their households.
9	= **NONOWNED AUTOS ONLY.** Only those autos you do not own, lease, hire or borrow which are used in connection with your business. This includes autos owned by your employees or members of their households but only while used in your business or your personal affairs.
10	=

currently in use. Depending on which BAP coverages are activated in the declarations (and which endorsements are attached to the policy) the BAP can be set up to provide coverage similar to basic auto liability (coverage on owned autos only of the type specified), comprehensive auto liability (blanket coverage on owned, nonowned, and hired autos of all types or of certain specified types), fleet automatic physical damage, and/or nonfleet physical damage. The policy declarations are also set up to indicate the applicability of personal injury protection (no-fault coverage), medical payments coverage, uninsured motorists coverage, and/or towing and labor coverage.

Figure 9-2 contains excerpts from a typical declarations page to illustrate how the declarations are used to show what coverages apply. In item two, the coverages are listed and a space is provided for entry of one or more of the "symbols" (numbers from 1 to 10 described in item three) to indicate which vehicles are covered autos. (The term "covered auto" now replaces such terms as owned automobile, nonowned automobile, hired automobile, designated automobile, and insured and uninsured highway vehicle, which are common to the comprehensive automobile policy.)

If a firm desires liability insurance on all of its owned, nonowned, and hired autos, medical payments and uninsured motorists coverages on owned private passenger autos, and comprehensive physical damage coverage on specifically described autos, the numerical symbol "1" must be designated opposite liability insurance, the symbol "3" must appear opposite medical payments, as well as opposite uninsured motorists coverages, and the symbol "7" must be designated opposite comprehensive physical damage coverage, as shown in the figure.

When any one or more of the symbols "1" to "6" are selected, the insured receives automatic coverage on any owned autos acquired during the policy period. However, when symbol "7" is used, a newly acquired auto is covered only if (1) the company already insures all autos an insured owns for the coverage provided, or the auto replaces one which was previously owned and insured, and (2) the insured informs the company within thirty days after such acquisition that he or she wants the auto to be added for that coverage.

Although not readily obvious, the new method of selecting autos and coverages can present problems unless the system is understood and care is exercised when coverage is written. Even a seemingly minor error in entering symbols on an application or declarations page could produce problems in the event of a loss. Also, if anything less than comprehensive coverage (symbol "1") is purchased, it is important that the automobile exposures be identified and carefully monitored so that they can be handled properly with insurance or noninsurance techniques as the exposures arise.

Liberalizations and Limitations

Most of the differences, including additions and reductions of coverages, between the basic liability provisions of the business auto policy and the comprehensive automobile liability policy are mentioned later in the comparison chart of provisions. However, there are three liberalizations and one limitation in the business auto policy which deserve comment and will not be mentioned later. The liberalizations are that (1) trailers with a load capacity of 2,000 pounds or less are now automatically covered for liability without additional charge, (2) mobile equipment transported by covered autos is now covered by the business auto policy (the comprehensive automobile policy contained a "coverage gap" with respect to that exposure) and (3) the so-called "public or livery" exclusion has been withdrawn from use even with respect to basic auto coverage, symbol "7," written under the business auto policy. The limitation that is newly introduced with the business auto policy is that there no longer is automatic liability protection for temporary substitute autos unless an insured selects coverage for all autos, symbol "1," or includes hired autos only, symbol "8," on an "if any" basis along with its other selections. However, physical damage insurance on temporary substitute autos continues to be available by endorsement.

Coverage Comparison

Figure 9-3 compares the basic liability and physical damage provisions of the comprehensive automobile and business auto policies. The basic provisions are those elements, i.e., insuring agreement, exclusions, and conditions, that form a complete policy of minimum coverages. Thus, the comparison does not involve such other coverages as personal injury protection, medical payments and uninsured motorists, because each is available by endorsement. The physical damage provisions that are compared make no reference to fleet automatic or nonfleet forms, because the difference is one of mechanics rather than coverage. Thus, the fleet automatic form provides coverage on newly acquired autos of the type insured, whereas the nonfleet form does not. However, the choice of perils is the same under each form.

Figure 9-3
Comparison of Auto Liability Provisions

(1973) Comprehensive Automobile Policy	(1978) Business Auto Policy	Differences
	Insuring Agreement	
Pay on behalf of the insured all sums which the insured shall become legally obligated to pay as damages because of bodily injury or property damage to which this insurance applies, caused by an *occurrence* and arising out of the ownership, maintenance, use, *loading or unloading of any automobile.*	We will pay all sums the insured legally must pay as damages because of bodily injury or property damage to which this insurance applies, caused by an *accident* and resulting from the ownership, maintenance or use of a *covered auto.*	The new policy (1) uses the word "accident" in lieu of "occurrence," but the former term is defined just as it once was as an occurrence, (2) does not contain the phrase "loading or unloading," because the scope of that coverage is more restricted (see Exclusions), and (3) refers to a "covered auto" instead of "any automobile," because the policy is structured to cover specified autos or all autos depending upon the insured's choice.
The company shall have the right and duty to defend the insured on account of bodily injury or property damage, even if the allegations are groundless, false or fraudulent, and shall make an investigation and settlement of claim or suit as is deemed expedient; but the company is not obligated to pay any claim or judgment or to defend after the applicable limit of liability has been exhausted.	We have the right and duty to defend any suit asking for damages. However, *we have no duty to defend suits for bodily injury or property damage not covered by the policy.* We may investigate and settle any claim or suit, but the payment of liability insurance ends the company's duty to defend or settle.	Generally the same, except that the new policy states more affirmatively that the company has no obligation to defend or settle when the claim is excluded.
	Supplementary Payments	
The company will pay in addition to the limit of liability:		
1. All expenses incurred by the company and all costs taxed against the insured in any suit defended by the company.	1. Same.	

(1973) Comprehensive Automobile Policy	(1978) Business Auto Policy	Differences
2. All interest on any judgment which accrues after entry of the judgment but before the company pays or tenders that part of the judgment which does not exceed the limit of liability.	2. Same.	
3. Premiums on appeal bonds required in any suit.	3. Same.	
4. Premiums on bonds to release attachments not to exceed the limit of liability.	4. Same.	
5. Cost of bail bonds which are required of the insured because of an accident or traffic law violation arising out of the use of any vehicle covered by the policy, not to exceed $250 per bond and the company has no obligation to apply for or furnish any such bond.	5. Same.	
6. Reasonable expenses incurred by the insured at the company's request in assisting the company in the investigation or defense of any claim or suit, including actual loss of earnings not to exceed $25 *per day.*	6. Up to *$50 a day* for loss of earnings (but not other income) because of attendance at hearings or trials at the company's request.	The new policy pays $25 more per day than the old policy and makes it clear that no other income is covered other than loss of earnings; i.e., wages or salary. Reasonable expenses also are covered by the new policy under a separate provision.

Continued on next page

(1973) Comprehensive Automobile Policy	(1978) Business Auto Policy	Differences
7. Expenses incurred by the insured for first aid to others, at the time of accident, for bodily injury to which this policy applies.	7. No similar provision.	This provision was removed under the new policy because claims were infrequent. But if claims should arise under the new policy, they would not be covered.
	Exclusions	
This insurance does not apply to:		
1. Liability assumed under any contract or agreement.	1. Same.	
2. Any obligation for which the insured or any carrier as his insurer may be liable under any workmen's compensation, *unemployment compensation*, disability benefits law, or under any similar law.	2. Any obligation for which the insured or his or her insurer may be held liable under any workers' compensation or disability benefits law or under any similar law.	The new policy does not contain reference to unemployment compensation, because the exposure is remote, i. e., the policy excludes bodily injury to employees and fellow employees.
3. Bodily injury to any employee of the insured arising out of and in the course of his employment by the insured or any obligation of the insured to indemnify another because of damages arising out of such injury; but this exclusion does not apply to any injury arising out of and in the course of domestic employment by the insured, unless benefits are payable in whole or in part or required to be provided under any workmen's compensation law.	3. Any obligation of the insured to indemnify another for damages resulting from bodily injury to the insured's employee.	Exclusions (3) and (5) of the new policy are the same as exclusion (3) of the old policy. Two separate exclusions are used in the new policy for purposes of clarity.
	4. Bodily injury to any fellow employee of the insured arising out of and in the course of his or her employment.	Exclusion (4) of the new policy appears as part of the "persons insured" provision of the old policy. However, there is no difference between the subject matter which is excluded under both policies.
	5. Bodily injury to any employee of the insured arising out of and in the course of his or her employment by the insured. However, this exclusion does not apply to bodily injury to domestic employees who are not entitled to workers' compensation benefits.	

(1973) Comprehensive Automobile Policy	(1978) Business Auto Policy	Differences
4. Property damage to (1) property owned or being transported by the insured, or property rented to or in the care, custody or control of the insured, or to which the insured is for any purpose exercising physical control, *other than property damage to a residence or private garage by a private passenger automobile covered by this policy.*	6. Property damage to property owned or transported by the insured or in the insured's care, custody or control.	The exclusions of both policies are similar, except that the new policy does not contain the exception of (and therefore does not cover) damage to a residence or private garage by a private passenger automobile.
5. Bodily injury or property damage due to war, whether declared or not, civil war, insurrection, rebellion, revolution or any act incident to any of the foregoing with respect to expenses of first aid under the supplementary payments provision.	No similar exclusion.	The new policy does not require this exclusion, because it does not cover first aid expenses.
No similar exclusion.	7. Bodily injury or property damage resulting from the loading of property before it has been put in or on the covered auto or the unloading of property after it has been taken off or out of the covered auto. This exclusion does not apply to loading or unloading by means of a mechanical device that is permanently attached to the covered auto.	This exclusion of the new policy is designed to limit coverage of loading and unloading to the "immediate" operation of placing property onto, or removing it from, a covered auto, with the one exception as noted concerning mechanical devices. Thus, the operation of loading (and, hence, coverage) commences as soon as property is picked up or lifted and ends when the property is placed in or upon the covered auto. The operation of unloading begins as soon as the property is being removed from the covered auto and ends when the property comes to rest on the ground, on a pallet or dock.

Continued on next page

(1973) Comprehensive Automobile Policy	(1978) Business Auto Policy	Differences
6. Bodily injury or property damage caused by various contaminants or pollutants as described in the policy, except when the discharge is sudden and accidental.	8. Same.	The purpose of this exclusion is to prevent the comprehensive auto policy from covering exposures that are more appropriately the subject of coverage under various general liability forms.
The broad form nuclear energy liability exclusion endorsement also must be attached to this policy.	The same endorsement likewise must be attached to this policy.	
	Persons Insured	
Each of the following is an insured under this insurance to the extent set forth below:	Who Is Insured:	Note: The following comments are concerned with general changes between the persons insured provision or so-called "omnibus clause" of both policies. A comprehensive insight into the differences is impossible, because the old policy covers any automobile (owned, nonowned, or hired), whereas the new policy covers any covered auto, i.e., all owned, nonowned, or hired autos, or autos specified.
(a) Named insured;	1. You are an insured for any covered auto.	
(b) Any partner or executive officer, but with a nonowned automobile only while such automobile is being used in the business of the named insured;	2. Anyone else is an insured while using with your permission a covered auto you own, hire or borrow except:	The new policy does not contain the equivalent of paragraph (b) of the old policy, because a partner or executive is likely to have the named insured's permission to use a covered auto.
(c) Any other person while using an owned or hired automobile with the permission of the named insured, provided his operation or other actual use is within the scope of permission, but respect to bodily injury or property damage arising out of loading or unloading, such person shall be an insured only if he is (1) a lessee or borrower of the automobile, or (2) an employee of the named insured, lessee or borrower;	(a) Someone using a covered auto you hire or borrow from one of your employees or a member of his or her household. (b) Someone using a covered auto while he or she is working in a business of selling, servicing, repairing or parking autos. 3. Anyone liable for the conduct of an insured described above is an insured but only to the extent of that liability. However, the owner or anyone else	Paragraphs (2) and (2a) of the new policy replace (c) and (iii) of the old policy without change. The only exception is that the new policy does not contain the

(1973) Comprehensive Automobile Policy	(1978) Business Auto Policy	Differences
(d) Any other person or organization but only with respect to his or its liability because of acts or omissions of an insured under (a), (b) or (c) above. None of the following is an insured:	from whom you hire or borrow a covered auto is an insured only if that auto is a trailer connected to a covered auto you own.	restriction concerning permissive use, i.e., that the auto be operated or used within the scope of permission. The user is an insured if he or she has permission to use the named insured's owned or hired auto (but not a nonowned auto).
(i) Any person while engaged in the business of his employer with respect to bodily injury to a fellow employee;		Paragraph (2b) of the new policy serves the same purpose as paragraph (v) of the old policy.
(ii) An owner or lessee of a hired automobile, the owner of a nonowned automobile, or the agent or employee of such owner or lessee;		Paragraph (3) of the new policy replaces (d) and (ii) of the old policy without change.
(iii) An executive officer with respect to an automobile owned by him or by a member of his household;		The new policy does not contain the equivalent of paragraph (iv) of the old policy, referred to as the "cross trailer" exclusion. The new policy now protects a person or organization, on a primary basis, against its vicarious liability stemming from its owned or hired trailer while it is connected to the named insured's owned, covered auto.
(iv) Any person or organization, other than the named insured, with respect to:		
(1) a motor vehicle used with any trailer owned or hired by such person or organization and not covered by like insurance in the company (except a trailer designed for use with a private passenger auto and not being used for business purposes with any other type of auto), or		Paragraph (i) of the old policy concerning bodily injury to fellow employees is replaced with an exclusion under the new policy.

Continued on next page

(1973) Comprehensive Automobile Policy	(1978) Business Auto Policy	Differences
(2) a trailer used with any motor vehicle owned or hired by such person or organization and not covered by like insurance in the company; (v) Any person while employed or otherwise engaged in the automobile business, other than such business operated by the named insured. This insurance does not apply to bodily injury or property damage arising out of (1) a nonowned automobile used in the conduct of any partnership or joint venture of which the insured is a partner or member and which is not designated in the policy as a named insured, or (2) if the named insured is a partnership, an automobile owned by or registered in the name of such partner. Regardless of the number of (1) insureds under this policy, (2) persons or organizations who sustain bodily injury or property damage, (3) claims made or suits brought or (4) automobiles to which this policy applies, the company's liability is limited as follows: Coverage C—The limit of bodily injury stated as *"each person"* is the limit for all damages, including damages for loss of care and services because of bodily injury sustained by one person as the result of	**Limits of Liability** 1. Regardless of the number of covered autos, insureds, claims made or vehicles involved in the *accident*, the most we will pay for all damages resulting from any one accident is the liability insurance limit shown in the declarations. 2. All bodily injury and property damage resulting from continuous or repeated exposure to substantially the same conditions will be considered as resulting from one *accident*.	Finally, the new policy does not contain the equivalent of the last provision found in the persons insured section of the old policy concerning exposures of partnerships, joint ventures, and individual partners of either. Paragraph (1) of that provision is deemed not to be necessary, because the new policy only covers persons, e.g., partners or executive officers, with respect to the named insured's nonowned autos used with the latter's permission. Paragraph (2) of that provision dealing with autos owned by partners is handled by separate endorsement. The partnership would have primary protection under a partner's personal auto policy, but can purchase excess protection with the addition of partnership nonownership liability coverage. The limit of liability provision of the new business auto policy is considerably shorter, because coverage is provided on a single-limit basis. The only difference between the two policies is reference to the word accident in the new policy in lieu of occurrence. However, accident is defined identically to the definition of occurrence which forms a part of the old policy. Thus, there is no difference between the two policies, except for more concise language.

(1973) Comprehensive Automobile Policy	(1978) Business Auto Policy	Differences
any one *occurrence,* but the total liability for all damages sustained by two or more persons in any one occurrence shall not exceed the bodily injury limit applicable to *"each occurrence."* Coverage D—The limit of the company's liability for all damages because of all property damage sustained by one or more persons or organizations as the result of any one occurrence shall not exceed the limit of property damage liability stated as applying to *"each occurrence."* Coverage C and D—For purposes of determining the company's limit of liability, all bodily injury and property damage arising out of continuous or repeated exposure to substantially the same general conditions shall be considered as arising out of one *occurrence.* This insurance applies to bodily injury or property damage which occurs within the territory described in paragraph (1) or (2) of the definition of policy territory.	Policy Territory We cover accidents or losses which occur during the policy period: A. In the United States of America, its territories or possessions, Puerto Rico or Canada; or B. While the covered auto is being transported between any of these places.	The old policy relies on the definition of "policy territory" in the standard policy jacket to which all liability forms must be attached. The new policy, being a separate contract, has its own definition. In both policies, the territorial scope is the same, except that the new policy specifically lists Puerto Rico because it is neither a territory nor a possession. *Continued on next page*

(1973) Comprehensive Automobile Policy	(1978) Business Auto Policy	Differences
	Excess Insurance	
With respect to a hired or nonowned automobile, this insurance shall be excess over any other valid and collectible insurance available to the insured.	For any covered auto you don't own, the insurance provided by this policy is excess over any other collectible insurance.	No difference other than that the new policy combines this provision under one section. (See Other Insurance.)
	Out of State Insurance	
If, under the provisions of the motor vehicle financial responsibility law, compulsory insurance law or any similar law, a nonresident is required to maintain insurance with respect to a motor vehicle and the insurance requirements are greater than the insurance provided by the policy, the limits of the company's liability for the coverages provided shall be as required by such law; provided that the insurance shall be reduced to the extent that there is other valid and collectible insurance.	1. While a covered auto is away from the state where it is licensed we will: a. Increase this policy's limits to meet those specified by a compulsory or financial responsibility law in the jurisdiction where the covered auto is being used. b. Provide the minimum amounts and types of other coverages, such as "No-Fault," required of out of state vehicles by the jurisdiction where the covered auto is being used.	The new policy, unlike the old policy, automatically increases the limits, even though a state does not impose this requirement on nonresidents. However, this liberalization is limited to liability limits and not to limits under no-fault laws.
No person is entitled to receive duplicate payments for the same elements of loss.	2. We will not pay anyone more than once for the same elements of loss because of these extensions.	
	Insuring Agreements	
1. The company will pay for loss to automobiles, under:	1. We will pay for loss to a covered auto or its equipment under:	
Coverage O—Comprehensive—from any cause except collision. For purposes of this coverage, breakage of glass, loss caused by missiles, falling	a. Comprehensive Coverage. From any cause except the covered auto's collision with another object or its overturn.	Essentially the same scope of coverage, because the new policy has a separate provision stating that glass breakage, hitting a bird or animal, falling

(1973) Comprehensive Automobile Policy	(1978) Business Auto Policy	Differences
objects, fire, theft or larceny, windstorm, hail, earthquake, explosion, riot, vandalism, malicious mischief, water, flood, colliding with a bird or animal shall not be deemed loss by collision.		objects or missiles will be paid under comprehensive coverage if it is carried by the insured.
Coverage P—Collision—caused by collision.	c. Collision Coverage. Caused by the covered auto's collision with another object or its overturn.	The new policy is more limited because it covers loss by overturn, whereas the old policy covered loss by upset. There is a distinct difference between overturn and upset, with the latter being more liberal because a vehicle does not have to be completely overturned to have an upset.
Coverage Q—Fire, Lightning or Transportation—caused by (a) fire or lightning, (b) smoke or smudge due to faulty operation of heating equipment, (c) stranding, sinking, burning, collision or derailment of any conveyance on which the auto is being transported. Coverage R—Theft—caused by theft or larceny. Coverage S—Windstorm, Hail, Earthquake or Explosion—caused by windstorm, hail, earthquake or explosion. Coverage T—Combined Additional Coverage—caused by (a) windstorm, hail, earthquake or explosion, (b) riot or civil commotion, (c) forced landing or failing of any aircraft, (d) malicious mischief or vandalism, (e) flood or rising waters or (f) external discharge or leakage of water.	b. Specified Perils Coverage. Caused by: (1) Fire or explosion; (2) Theft; (3) Windstorm, hail or earthquake; (4) Flood; (5) Mischief or vandalism; (6) Sinking, burning, collision or derailment of any conveyance transporting the covered auto.	The new policy combines fire, theft, and combined additional coverages into one package referred to as "specified perils coverage." The rationale for the above is that all those perils usually are purchased if comprehensive coverage is not otherwise selected. To make coverage flexible, however, an endorsement is available with the new policy to provide coverage for fire only or fire and theft coverages.

Continued on next page

(1973) Comprehensive Automobile Policy	(1978) Business Auto Policy	Differences
2. The company will pay under:	2. Towing. We will pay up to $25 for towing and labor costs incurred each time a covered auto of the private passenger type is disabled. However, the labor must be performed at the place of disablement.	
Coverage V—Towing—for towing and labor costs necessitated by the disablement of covered automobiles, provided the labor is performed at the place of disablement. Coverage up to $25 per disablement on private passenger type automobiles.		
	Supplementary Payments	
In addition to the applicable limits of liability, the company will:	No similar provision.	This provision has been dropped with the new policy because of its infrequent use. Were it to arise, there would be no coverage.
(a) with respect to such transportation insurance as is afforded, pay general average and salvage charges for which the named insured becomes liable;		
(b) reimburse the named insured, in the event of theft of the entire covered automobile of the private passenger type, expenses incurred for the rental of a substitute automobile during the period commencing 48 hours after such theft has been reported to the company and the police and terminating when the covered automobile is returned to use or the company pays for loss; but the reimbursement shall not exceed $10 per day nor more than $300.	We will pay up to $10 per day to a maximum of $300 for transportation expense incurred by you because of the total theft of a covered auto of the private passenger type. We will pay only for those covered autos for which you carry either Comprehensive or Specified Perils Coverage. We will pay for transportation expenses incurred during the period beginning 48 hours after the theft and ending when the auto is returned or we pay for the loss.	The only difference between the two provisions is that the new policy permits the rental reimbursement to be used for other transportation expenses, such as taxi and bus fare. The old policy limits the reimbursement to the rental of a substitute private passenger automobile.

(1973) Comprehensive Automobile Policy	(1978) Business Auto Policy	Differences
	Exclusions	
This insurance does not apply:	This insurance does not apply to:	
(a) to any covered automobile while used as a public or livery conveyance, unless such use is specifically declared in the policy.	No similar exclusion.	The business auto policy is broader in scope from this standpoint.
(b) to damage which is due and confined to (i) wear and tear, or (ii) freezing, or (iii) mechanical or electrical breakdown or failure, unless damage is the result of other covered loss.	Wear and tear, freezing, mechanical breakdown, unless caused by other loss covered by this policy.	
(c) to tires unless (i) loss is coincident with and from the same cause as other covered loss, or (ii) damaged by fire, and if the automobile is of private passenger type by vandalism, malicious mischief or theft.	Blowouts, punctures or other road damage to tires unless caused by other covered loss by the policy.	The business auto policy now makes it clearer that blowouts, punctures, and other road damage to tires are not separately the subject of coverage. The old policy is not clear on this point, and, hence, a source of problems to insurers.
(d) to loss by war, whether declared or not, civil war, insurrection, rebellion, revolution or any act or condition coincident with the foregoing; and radioactive contamination.	Loss caused by declared or undeclared war or insurrection or any of their consequences. Loss caused by radioactive contamination.	
No similar exclusion.	Loss caused by the explosion of a nuclear weapon or its consequences.	Purpose of the exclusion is to avoid coverage for loss resulting from explosion of a nuclear weapon by a terrorist group.
(e) to loss to (i) any device or instrument designed for recording, reproduction of sound unless the device is permanently installed in the covered auto; any tape, wire, record disc or other medium for use with any device for recording or reproduction of sound.	Loss to tape decks or other sound sound reproducing equipment not permanently installed in a covered auto. Loss to tapes, records or other sound reproducing devices designed for use with sound reproducing equipment.	Two exclusions are used with the new policy instead of one as applies with the old policy for purposes of simplification.

Continued on next page

(1973) Comprehensive Automobile Policy	(1978) Business Auto Policy	Differences
(f) to loss to a camper body designed for use with a covered automobile if not designated in the policy and it was owned by the named insured at policy inception or renewal.	No similar exclusion.	Exclusion does not apply to new policy, because it has very little application to commercial firms.
(g) under comprehensive and theft coverages, loss or damage due to conversion, embezzlement or secretion by any person in possession of a covered automobile under any bailment lease, conditional sale or other encumbrance.	No similar exclusion.	
(h) under collision coverage, to breakage of glass if other insurance is otherwise provided.	We will pay for glass breakage, loss caused by hitting a bird or animal or by falling objects or missles under comprehensive coverage if you carry that coverage for the damaged covered auto.	
(i) under windstorm, hail, earthquake or explosion, or combined additional coverages, to loss resulting from rain, snow or sleet, whether wind-driven or not.	No similar exclusion.	
Under separate endorsement, loss to any sound receiving equipment which is designed for use as a citizens' band radio, two-way mobile radio or telephone and including accessories.	Same exclusion forming part of the basic policy provisions.	

(1973) Comprehensive Automobile Policy	(1978) Business Auto Policy	Differences
	Conditions	
1. Premium. All premiums shall be computed by using the company's rules, rates and rating plans. The "advance premium" is a deposit premium which is credited to the amount of earned premium due at policy expiration.	No similar provision. Same provision but it appears in the declarations page of policy.	
2. Inspection and Audit. The company shall be permitted but not obligated to inspect the named insured's property and operations. Such an undertaking shall not be construed as warranting that the property or operations are safe, healthful or in compliance with any law.	F. At our option we may inspect your property and operations at any time. These inspections are for our benefit. By our right to inspect, we make no representation that your property or operations are safe, not harmful to health or comply with any law, rule or regulation.	
3. Financial Responsibility Laws. When this policy is certified as proof of financial responsibility for the future, such insurance as afforded shall comply with the provisions of such law.	No similar condition, but essentially the same provisions apply under the Out of State Extensions section of the policy.	
4. Insured's Duty in the Event of Occurrence, Claim or Suit. (a) In the event of an occurrence, written notice shall be given to the company or its authorized agent, (b) If claim is made or suit is brought, the insured shall forward every demand, notice or summons and (c) The insured shall cooperate with the company in making settlements, attending trials and hearings.	A. Your Duties After Accident or Loss. Essentially the same requirements.	The new policy does not require sworn proof of loss within a specified time. But a proof must be provided if the company requests one.

Continued on next page

(1973) Comprehensive Automobile Policy	(1978) Business Auto Policy	Differences
5. Action Against Company. No action shall lie against the company, unless as a condition precedent, there has been full compliance with all terms of this policy nor until the amount of insured's obligation has been determined.	E. Legal Action Against Us. No legal action may be brought against us until there has been full compliance with all terms of this policy. In addition, under liability insurance, no legal action may be brought against us until we agree in writing that the insured has an obligation to pay.	
6. Other Insurance. The insurance provided by this policy is primary, except when stated to apply in excess of or contingent upon the absence of other insurance. When this policy and other insurance apply to loss on the same basis, the company is liable for a greater proportion of loss than that stated below: (a) Contribution by Equal Shares. If all other valid and collectible insurance provides for contribution by equal shares, the company shall not be liable for a greater proportion of such loss than would be payable if each insurer contributes an equal share until the share of each insurer equals the lowest applicable limit of liability under any one policy or the full amount of loss is paid. (b) Contribution by Limits. If any other insurance does not provide for contribution by equal shares, the company shall not be liable for a greater proportion of any loss than the applicable limit of	B. Other Insurance. For any covered auto you own this policy provides primary insurance. For any covered auto you don't own, the insurance provided by this policy is excess over any other collectible insurance. However, while a covered auto which is a trailer is connected to another vehicle the liability coverage this policy provides for the trailer: a. Is excess while it is connected to a motor vehicle you don't own. b. Is primary while it is connected to a covered auto you own. When two or more policies cover on the same basis, either excess or primary, we will pay only our share. Our share is the proportion that the limit of our policy bears to the total of the limits of all the policies covering on the same basis.	The new policy's "other insurance" provision follows that of other automobile insurance, i.e., primary on owned automobiles, excess on hired and nonowned automobiles. In addition, the new policy is not subject to contribution by equal shares; only contribution by limits or the so-called "pro-rata" clause. The new policy also contains special provisions for cross trailer coverage which now applies. A nonowned or hired trailer connected to a covered auto is covered on a primary basis, whereas a nonowned or hired trailer connected to a nonowned motor vehicle of the named insured is covered on an excess basis.

(1973) Comprehensive Automobile Policy	(1978) Business Auto Policy	Differences
liability for such loss bears to the total limit of liability of all valid and collectible insurance against such loss.		
7. Subrogation. In the event of any payment under this policy, the company shall be subrogated to all the insured's rights of recovery against any person.	C. Our Right To Recover From Others. If we make any payment, we are entitled to recover what we paid from other parties. Any person to or for whom we make payment must transfer to us his or her rights of recovery against any other party.	
8. Changes. Notice to or knowledge possessed by any agent shall not effect a waiver of any part of policy.	G. Changes. This policy contains all the agreements between you and us. Its terms may not be changed or waived except by endorsement.	The new policy also contains a liberalization clause which permits broadening coverage when no additional charge is involved.
9. Assignment. Assignment of interest shall not bind the company without its consent. If the named insured should die such insurance shall apply to the legal representative as named insured.	H. Transfer Of Your Interest. Your rights and duties under this policy may not be assigned without our written consent.	The subject matter concerning death of the named insured is available by endorsement with the new policy.
10. Cancellation. This policy may be cancelled by the named insured by mailing written notice to the company stating when cancellation is to be effective. This policy may be cancelled by the company by mailing written notice to the named insured stating when, not less than 10 days thereafter, such cancellation shall become effective.	D. Cancelling This Policy During the Policy Period. You may cancel the policy by returning it to us or by giving us advance notice of cancellation. We may cancel the policy by mailing you at least 10 days notice at your last address known to us. We may deliver any notice instead of mailing it. Proof of mailing will be sufficient proof of notice.	

Continued on next page

(1973) Comprehensive Automobile Policy	(1978) Business Auto Policy	Differences
11. No Benefit to Bailee. None of the provisions of this policy shall inure directly or indirectly to the benefit of any carrier or other bailee for hire.	I. No Benefit to Bailee—Physical Damage Insurance Only. We will not recognize any assignment or grant any coverage for the benefit of any person or organization holding, storing or transporting property for a fee.	
No similar separate provision.	J. Bankruptcy. Bankruptcy or insolvency of the insured shall not relieve us of any obligations under this policy.	The old policy's provision on bankruptcy appears under condition 5, Action Against the Company.
12. Appraisal—Physical Damage. If the named insured and the company shall fail to agree on the amount of loss, either may within 60 days after proof of loss demand an appraisal. Each shall select a competent appraiser, the appraisers will select a competent and disinterested umpire to whom differences will be submitted.	K. Appraisal For Physical Damage Losses. If you and we fail to agree on the amount of loss either may demand an appraisal of loss. You and we shall each select a competent appraiser and the appraisers shall select a competent and disinterested umpire to whom differences are submitted.	
13. Declarations. By acceptance of this policy the named insured agrees that the statements are his agreements and representations and that the policy is issued in reliance upon those representations.	No similar condition.	The new policy does not contain a Declarations condition, because it has not been effective in holding named insureds to their representations.

NONINSURANCE TECHNIQUES FOR HANDLING MOTOR VEHICLE EXPOSURES

As has been mentioned throughout this text, there are only four general kinds of noninsurance techniques from which a firm can choose in handling its loss exposures: (1) avoidance, (2) control, (3) retention, and (4) noninsurance transfer. Whatever technique or combination of techniques is ultimately chosen depends upon the nature of the business and its exposures, as well as on the loss-producing magnitude of these exposures and their potential impact upon the financial structure of the business.

Liability Exposures

By and large, motor vehicle liability exposures are difficult to treat with noninsurance techniques other than loss control for at least two reasons. First, there are many ways, as discussed in Chapter 8, in which a firm may be held liable because of the ownership, maintenance, and use of its owned, nonowned, and hired automobiles. And, second, the very nature of liability loss exposures creates uncertainties in terms of loss severity. Thus, no one knows for sure just what amount of damages will be sought by a claimant and what amount of damages ultimately will have to be paid by a firm that is held liable. Chances are, therefore, that firms either will finance loss exposures with insurance, as is often required by law, or will utilize funded retention programs. Some firms will also use noninsurance techniques whenever possible to avoid, transfer, or control their known exposures to loss.

Avoidance Although avoidance guarantees absolute safety from loss, few firms will find avoidance practical, because a business cannot be operated without being exposed to some losses. For example, a corporation that decides against the purchase of a subsidiary company whose operations utilize a large fleet of trucks operated on a competitive basis in a geographical area in which the corporation desires to expand avoids the chances of sustaining any losses as the owner of that subsidiary. However, that corporation also loses the opportunity to expand its operations and to obtain a better return on its investment.

Certain motor vehicle liability exposures nonetheless can be avoided in isolated cases. For example, a firm in the business of trucking goods of others on a local basis (within a fifty-mile radius of its principal place of business) may decide against the expansion of operations on a long-haul basis because of the stringent rules and regulations imposed by the Interstate Commerce Commission and the possibility of more serious losses. A firm in this situation may avoid certain hardships and losses stemming from accidents by not creating an interstate exposure in the first place, but this avoidance also reduces its chances for growth.

The foregoing examples are just some of the ways by which firms may be able to avoid certain losses. As a matter of practice, however, avoidance is usually the exception rather than the rule.

Control Control is the single most important technique for preventing and minimizing virtually all types of liability losses, for the following reasons. Controllable losses can *cause* serious injury to persons or damage to property of others and can *result* in increased insurance costs.

While there are many incentives for an effective loss control program, particularly the preservation of a firm's assets and productivity potential which otherwise may be lost to the payment of losses, the actual organization and administration of an ongoing loss control program is not always easy. Many of the obstacles in implementing these programs, especially from among management level people whose support is essential to the success of such programs, were discussed in earlier chapters. However, even when management gives its support to a program of loss control and delegates responsibility and authority toward the implementation and operation of these programs, a great deal of input, in terms of time, energy, and money, is still required before measures can be taken to control losses.

Of importance to a firm that embarks upon a loss control program for its motor vehicle liability loss exposures is the first stage wherein troublesome exposures are identified. Although poorly-maintained vehicles, severe weather conditions, road conditions, and faults of other motorists can contribute to a firm's adverse loss experience, the annual statistics of the National Safety Council repeatedly show that motor vehicle losses are largely attributable to the human element, i.e., to the driving habits and ages of drivers (over 50 percent of all accidents in 1976 being caused by drivers of age twenty-nine and under).[27] Thus, when a firm begins identifying its principal sources of motor vehicle liability exposures, the firm that has records and statistics on the frequency and severity of its past losses is at an advantage because it may be able to predict losses likely to recur and identify employees who are more likely to become involved in accidents.

Whether or not these records of accident loss histories are available, a firm still has to screen new employee-drivers from the standpoint of their driving experience, as well as their past loss experience and moving traffic convictions. Motor vehicle reports (MVRs) can usually be obtained from the state licensing authority. The information on driver experience should be obtained whether employees simply park customers' automobiles in storage garages or drive owned passenger buses coast-to-coast.

When appropriate measures are taken to identify sources of frequent and/or severe motor vehicle losses and violations, the management of a firm is in a position to determine what has to be done to prevent and control losses. When drivers have had a series of serious moving violations and/or accidents, it may be wise to replace those drivers. On the other hand, for drivers who have had few traffic violations and one or two minor accidents, it may be to the firm's advantage to require the drivers to attend special classes. It may even help if the firm requires its better drivers to attend driver safety classes merely as a preventive measure. Of course, when a firm is subject to ICC jurisdiction, the firm must comply with certain rules and regulations concerning qualifications of vehicles and operators. As mentioned in Chapter 8, the ICC requires that drivers meet certain physical requirements and that drivers not be permitted to drive their vehicles longer than a certain specified number of hours in any day.

If a firm does not take corrective measures with problem drivers and it does not monitor its program on a periodic basis to see if adjustments are necessary, the whole program of loss control may be in vain. Nothing better depicts what can happen when a firm fails to take corrective measures in controlling its motor vehicle liability losses than actual case histories. Two such cases described by Glass in a discussion of his company's Fleet Evaluation Program for enhancing loss control are worth repeating.

> In one case, a fleet of sixty trucks was plagued with losses considerably over the average. Investigation showed that 42 percent of their drivers had a history of four or more moving traffic violations in their Motor Vehicle Records. Although only 10 percent of the drivers were under age 25, they were involved in 33 percent of the reported accidents. Moreover, the turnover in drivers was high—40 percent each year. Here, effective driver selection and training would clearly remedy the situation. Yet, management chose otherwise. As a result, the loss experience continued at a rate three times the average for that geographic location.

> In the other case, a fleet of 20 trucks had high losses, also attributable to driver problems. Because of high turnover, 42 percent of the drivers were employed less than a year. A large number of drivers, 35 percent, were under age 25 and were involved in 50 percent of all the reported accidents. Accident repeaters with a record of two or more accidents a year were involved in 44 percent of these accidents. Even though these factors were brought to the attention of management and identified as the causes of the high loss experience, they were ignored. Without controls, the accident frequency and loss experience continued at twice the average, then worsened during a three year period.[28]

While this discussion of loss control as a technique for handling motor vehicle liability losses has dealt primarily with drivers, many of the points that have been made in these pages apply equally well to other employees who are in some way involved with motor vehicles. Thus, firms should formulate and enforce standard safe operating procedures for anyone who is in any way involved with motor vehicles. For example, material handlers who load and unload motor vehicles, and mechanics who have responsibility for maintaining vehicles are just as important to a company's loss control program as its vehicle operators. By implementing and enforcing workable standards and control measures, firms may be able to prevent and control some of their motor vehicle liability losses and hence lower their insurance costs and increase cash flow. In fact, some firms may be forced to implement control measures because of the high costs of primary and excess insurance.

Retention Aside from the very large firms that select funded retention as their primary technique for handling motor vehicle liability and other liability losses, the majority of businesses probably rely upon insurance. Furthermore, businesses that purchase insurance often receive valuable loss control and claim handling services from insurers.

Many large firms with motor vehicle liability insurance nonetheless might find it desirable to partially retain some of their losses through the use of deductibles if they can afford to retain large losses and can realize appropriate savings in their premium costs. Much depends upon the size of deductibles and corresponding premium savings. However, occasions may arise when firms will have no other choice but to partially retain some of their losses. These losses may stem from uninsured exposures known to exist (active retention), as well as from exposures not known to exist (passive retention). Since either circumstance can have an adverse effect upon the cash flow of firms when loss occurs, risk managers, producers, or risk management consultants should do everything possible to find ways to handle uninsured exposures that can present losses of an uncertain magnitude and to identify and treat as many of these exposures as possible in order to keep the unknown exposures of motor vehicles to an absolute minimum.

Noninsurance Transfer When the opportunity exists, businesses sometimes find noninsurance transfers to be advantageous in dealing with their motor vehicle liability exposures. In general, a noninsurance transfer is used to transfer an activity-producing exposure of motor vehicles or to transfer the financial consequences of a motor vehicle liability exposure, or sometimes both.

An example of a noninsurance transfer involving the transfer of at least part of the financial consequences of a motor vehicle liability exposure is the firm that requires its sales people to operate their own automobiles on company business, rather than purchasing a fleet of automobiles for use by its sales help. The firm is still exposed to liability of a vicarious nature—the employer is responsible for the acts or omissions of its employees during the course of business operations, but the automobile policies of employees are now primary in the event of an accident.[29] If the liability limits of an employee's personal automobile policy are insufficient to settle a large loss, the employer can rely upon the nonownership liability coverage of the CAL policy for excess coverage. However, to make sure that the employer's nonownership liability coverage will apply only as excess rather than as primary protection, an employer can insist that its employees maintain high primary liability limits and provide certificates of insurance as proof of these high limits, as well as proof that primary insurance does in fact apply. As a holder of certificates of insurance, the employer will be notified of any change in its employees' personal automobile policies, such as when an employee's policy is canceled by the insurer for some reason.

However, there are two problems with the above approach. The first is that if an employee's personal automobile liability insurance limits are found to be too low following an accident, the employer may be held accountable for suggesting the limits in the first place. The second problem is that maintaining insurance certificates can create more paperwork for an employer than is worth the effort. A more reasonable approach may be for the employer to make clear to its employees that the usual driving allowance is intended to cover insurance and automobile maintenance costs. While the limits purchased by employees may still be inadequate, there is a better chance that employees will carry some insurance than if no directive is issued explaining the purpose of the mileage allowance. In the end, the employer is still protected on an excess basis under its own insurance.

Firms in the business of leasing out automobiles on a long- or short-term basis can also utilize the technique of noninsurance transfer by requiring lessees to sign contracts agreeing to hold the leasing companies harmless in the event of motor vehicle liability losses caused by lessees.

The only conceivable way in which an activity-producing exposure involving motor vehicles can be transferred is when a firm decides to sell out to another firm. The buyer is then confronted with the exposures that were once the seller's alone. On the other hand, a firm that decides to sell its fleet of owned automobiles for some reason, such as high maintenance and insurance costs or poor loss record, probably will not effect a noninsurance transfer of an activity-producing exposure, because, in all likelihood, it may still be confronted with certain liability exposures stemming from the use of nonowned and/or hired motor vehicles.

Thus, while the technique of noninsurance transfer may not be totally suitable in a particular circumstance, that technique nonetheless may be used in conjunction with other techniques in handling the exposures confronting a firm. It is all a matter of how much importance a firm places on the identification and analysis of its motor vehicle liability exposures and on the decisions it makes in deciding upon the techniques to use. Also, there is always the possibility that a decision could turn out to be improper for the exposure. It is therefore of the utmost importance that a firm monitor its decisions from time to time and make adjustments whenever they are warranted. While the techniques ultimately chosen in handling motor vehicle liability loss exposures will depend upon the nature of the business and its financial structure, loss control is a necessity in any event.

Physical Damage Exposures

The same four noninsurance techniques available for handling motor vehicle liability loss exposures can be used to handle motor vehicle physical damage loss exposures. However, the latter exposures, unlike the former exposures, are calculable because the values of vehicles and the estimated probable maximum loss of each such vehicle can be determined on the basis of their market values. Thus, barring a concentration of vehicles in one place, a firm is not confronted with the uncertainties of loss severity as with motor vehicle liability exposures. The net result is that a firm faced with certain motor vehicle physical damage loss potentials will apply the noninsurance techniques differently from the way it applies them for its motor vehicle liability exposures.

Avoidance Avoidance is commonly viewed as a technique of last resort for most loss exposures, including physical damage exposures of motor vehicles, because its principal use is to avoid the creation of an exposure to loss which would present so great a loss potential that it could not be more appropriately handled by some other technique. And, while avoidance completely precludes the chance of loss, it also prevents a firm from obtaining a potential profit on its investment. So avoidance is generally an unrealistic approach, particularly from the standpoint of motor vehicle physical damage loss exposures, because (1) there are usually better ways of handling those exposures, and (2) physical damage exposures cannot be completely disassociated from motor vehicles owned or used by a firm. Since almost every vehicle has a certain value, a firm must look to the best alternative to protect that asset from loss. A firm can do this by using one or more of the other noninsurance techniques, or, if none is suitable, the firm can look to insurance as a solution.

Control Most sources of physical damage loss described in Chapter 8 can be prevented or controlled through the exercise of care. In fact, much of the discussion of motor vehicle damage exposures in Chapter 8 could just as well have been placed under the present heading, because simple loss control measures can eliminate or reduce many of the hazards that give rise to loss exposures.

Loss control is particularly important when a firm has a high concentration of values at one location exposed to loss from one or more perils, such as a trucking firm that garages a number of its vehicles at one terminal. Such an exposure is a source of concern to many firms, because protective measures against some perils do not necessarily guarantee the prevention of loss from other perils. For example, a firm may hire guards to protect the vehicles against loss by theft, vandalism, and fire, but that measure will not control the potentially catastrophic exposures to tornado, hurricane, or earthquake loss. To prevent and control major losses from the peril of tornado, for example, the only alternative may be to prevent the garaging of many vehicles at one location. However, that measure is not always feasible, and earthquakes and hurricanes cause damage over large areas. Complete control of the catastrophe exposure is often impossible, a factor that undoubtedly is a cause of concern to many firms.

Retention Full retention of automobile physical damage loss is usually worthwhile unless (1) the total loss of one or more vehicles amounts to more than a firm can safely stand to retain, (2) as a lessee of motor vehicles, the terms of the lease agreement require that physical damage insurance be purchased and a certificate of insurance (as proof of such coverage) be issued to the lessor, or (3) the firm is confronted with an uncontrollable catastrophe exposure, such as when many vehicles are garaged at one location.

Generally, when either of the circumstances in (1) and (2) above exists, firms can still retain at least part of their physical damage losses through the use of deductibles or the purchase of limited insurance, such as choosing fire, theft, and CAC coverage, rather than the more costly "all-risks" comprehensive insurance. It makes good sense to use deductibles if total retention of physical damage losses is not possible, because a firm usually can treat its smaller losses as a current operating expense and still realize some savings in its insurance costs. When the catastrophe circumstances in (3) above confront a firm, limited insurance undoubtedly will be the only practical solution.

The publication of one risk management consulting firm suggests three possible ways by which this catastrophe exposure, consisting of a high concentration of motor vehicles at one location, may be handled:

1. With a blanket property (fire and allied lines or "all-risk" coverage such as a difference-in-conditions) policy, delete the "licensed motor vehicle" exclusion. The deductible should be high enough to protect the insurer from routine claims.
2. Write a separate "all-risks" property policy or insuring agreement to a blanket property policy covering all *loss* in excess of a major deductible. Be sure that coverage is effected in excess of the deductible, on a per-loss basis, rather than covering all vehicles valued in excess of a predetermined figure. The latter would cover high-valued vehicles, but not large concentrations of low-valued vehicles.
3. Include under the auto physical damage coverage form attached to the CAL (or CAGL)and cover:
   a. Fire and other major perils subject to an annual aggregate (stop loss) deductible, or
   b. Noncollision (comprehensive) coverage with a high deductible only for garaging locations.[30]

The aforementioned solutions merely suggest possible approaches. The ultimate choice will depend upon the characteristics of loss exposures that confront firms.

Noninsurance Transfer The opportunities for using the technique of noninsurance transfer in handling automobile physical damage loss exposures are not as diverse as for other types of exposures. Unless a firm sells out and hence transfers its activity-producing exposure of automobile physical damage to the buying firm, the only other form of noninsurance transfer is that which concerns itself with the financial consequences of loss, and, with respect to the latter technique, there are not too many alternatives wherein it can be used.

As noted earlier with repect to the uses of noninsurance transfers with automobile liability loss exposures, the two common approaches for using the technique of noninsurance transfer for handling physical damage exposures are when a firm leases out its automobiles to others and when a firm requires employees to use their own automobiles for company business and provides the employees with a mileage allowance to handle insurance costs. Another common approach is when a firm purchases the automobiles for its employees and requires the employees to maintain proper insurance against liability and physical damage insurance.

All told, the automobile exposure is usually one of the most severe loss exposures facing commercial enterprises. Because of the potential for third-party claims for sizable damages as a result of bodily injury or property damage, even the firm with occasional use of a nonowned vehicle faces a severe loss exposure. In addition, firms with few vehicles are faced with a frequency exposure. When high-valued vehicles are involved, the physical damage exposure can also be quite severe. Because of the overall frequency and severity of motor vehicle loss exposures, it is important for virtually any commercial enterprise to identify and analyze this exposure carefully and select an appropriate mix of risk management techniques for its treatment.

Chapter Notes

1. Schmidt v. Luchterhand et al., 214 N.W. (2nd.) 393.
2. Truck Insurance Exchange v. Transamerica Insurance Co., 104 Cal. Rptr. 893.
3. Maurice E. Gosnell, "Omnibus Clauses in Automobile Insurance Policies," *Insurance Law Journal*, p. 237.
4. 4 A.L.R. 3d 10.
5. Travelers Ins. Co. v. Employers Casualty Co., 380 S.W. (2nd.) 610. Although this case dealt with the unloading of an automobile, the loading of an automobile conceivably would be considered as use of such vehicle as well.
6. 4 A.L.R. 3d 10.
7. 45 A.L.R. 3d 288.
8. Ibid.
9. An automobile rental agreement generally is understood to mean a contract of hire by hour, week, month, or any period less than a year. An automobile lease agreement, on the other hand, usually signifies a contract of hire extending over a period of one year.
10. 43 A.L.R. 3d 1283.
11. Ibid.
12. If an insured assumes a liability of another in situations dealing with employee injuries, the subject of coverage is then contractual liability insurance rather than workers' compensation or employers' liability insurance.
13. The subject of third-party-over actions and the assumption of liability under contract dealing with employee injuries is treated more fully in Chapter 7.
14. Motor truck cargo insurance and other inland marine coverages are analyzed in CPCU 3, Chapters 9 and 10.
15. Calvin H. Brainard, *Automobile Insurance* (Homewood, IL: Richard D. Irwin, 1961), pp. 182-183.
16. This exclusion does not apply with respect to automobiles that are registered or principally garaged in Maryland, New Hampshire, North Carolina, and Vermont. A CAL policy issued in these states must either contain an offsetting provision or the policy must be amended by endorsement.
17. Pollution liability insurance and the impact of the contamination or pollution exclusion are treated more fully in Chapter 11.
18. Despite the fact that mobile equipment is not eligible for physical damage coverage under the fleet form, such equipment still can be covered for physical damage losses at an additional cost as prescribed by the rules of the commercial automobile manual. However, if the mobile equipment is of the type commonly used by contractors, broader coverage usually can be obtained by purchasing a contractors' equipment floater which is an inland marine form. Inland marine exposures and their treatment are discussed in CPCU 3, Chapters 9 and 10.

19. McClelland v. Northwestern Fire and Marine Insurance Co., 86 S.E. (2nd.) 729.
20. Freidman v. Insurance Co. of North America, 91 N.W. (2nd.) 328.
21. Unkelsbee v. Homestead Fire Insurance Co., 41 Atl. (2nd.) 168.
22. Rich v. United Mutual Fire Insurance Co., 102 N.E. (2nd.) 431.
23. Harris v. American Casualty Co., 85 Atl. 194.
24. Ringo v. Automobile Insurance Co., 22 Pac. (2nd.) 887.
25. Washington Fire and Marine Insurance Co. v. Ryburn, 311 S.W. (2nd.) 302.
26. Brainard, pp. 290-291.
27. *Accident Facts* (Chicago: National Safety Council, 1977), p. 54.
28. Joseph E. Glass, "Fleet Evaluation and Loss Control," *The National Insurance Buyer*, March 1968. Quoted in RM 54—*Principles of Risk Management Additional Supplemental Readings*, Insurance Institute of America, 1969, p. 10.
29. For example, the omnibus provision of the standard family automobile policy includes as an insured any person or organization legally responsible for the use of the automobile.
30. *Practical Risk Management* (San Francisco: Warren, McVeigh, Griffin & Huntington, August 1976), p. 7, Automobiles No. C-8.

CHAPTER 10

Professional Liability Exposures and Their Treatment

INTRODUCTION

Professionals and others who undertake work which demands special skill are required to possess a standard minimum of special knowledge and ability. They are also required to exercise reasonable care in the performance of their services. A professional who fails to exercise reasonable care in the performance of services or who fails to perform the services for which he or she was employed can be held liable to the client if the client is injured or damaged by such failure.

Following a description of professional liability exposures in general, this chapter will analyze the loss exposures of various classes of "professionals"—medical personnel, architects and engineers, attorneys, insurance agents and brokers, and other professionals. Following the discussion of the specific exposure characteristics of each of these professional classes, the insurance and noninsurance techniques that may be used to treat those exposures are examined.

THE NATURE OF PROFESSIONAL LIABILITY EXPOSURES

A "professional" is one who possesses the special knowledge and skill necessary to render a professional service. Typically, the special knowledge and skill result from a combination of the person's education and experience in a particular branch of science or learning. For tort law purposes, those whom the law has recognized as professionals include physicians, surgeons, dentists, attorneys, engineers, accountants, architects, insurance agents and brokers, and many others.

The Legal Duties of Professionals

Professionals are bound by law to perform the services for which they were hired and to perform these services in accordance with the appropriate standards of conduct. The first duty is primarily a contractual one; the second duty arises from the principles of tort law.

Contractual Obligations of a Professional   When a client hires a professional to perform a particular service, a contractual arrangement is created. A contract is a promise or a set of promises which the law recognizes as a duty. The law also provides a remedy should this duty be breached.

Requisites of Enforceable Contracts.   To have a valid, enforceable contract, there must be (1) an offer, (2) an acceptance of the offer, (3) some consideration, (4) parties having capacity to contract, and (5) a lawful objective. A contract can be either oral or written, unless specifically required by statute to be written.

In many professions, such as law, a self-imposed code of professional ethics traditionally has prohibited the practitioner from soliciting individual clients. Consequently, the person making the offer to form a contract is usually the person seeking the services of the professional. Although written contracts may be entered into—for example, when attorneys agree to represent injured parties on a contingent fee basis— most professional contracts are undoubtedly oral and usually are created when the professional verbally agrees to perform certain services for the client. Acceptance of the contract usually occurs when the professional either affirmatively indicates willingness to perform the services or actually performs the specified act required.

Performance of Contract.   A professional who agrees to perform services for a client is under a duty to perform as promised and at the specified time. Like any other promisor, however, the professional can be relieved of his or her duty to perform if there is a failure of consideration, failure of a condition precedent, rescission of the contract, impossibility of performance, fraud or misrepresentation, mistake, an illegal bargain, or any one of several other matters.

There are three recognized levels of performance: (1) complete or satisfactory performance, (2) substantial performance, and (3) material breach. Complete or satisfactory performance consists of performance which meets accepted standards; this level of performance entitles the professional to the contract price. Substantial performance falls short of complete performance only in minor respects; it entitles the professional to the contract price less any damages the client may have incurred from not getting complete performance. A material breach occurs when the professional's performance is defective in some major respect. In this case, the professional may not be able to recover the contract price and may be liable in money damages to the client for all injuries suffered by the client as a result.

Breach of Contract. When a professional has failed to perform contractual obligations as promised and the other party has suffered an injury or damage as a result, the injured party is entitled to be placed, as nearly as is practical, in the position he or she would have occupied had the contract been performed as promised. In most cases, especially where professionals are involved, money damages will substantially place the injured party in the position the client would have held had the contract been performed.

Damages. Damages recoverable for breach of contract can be either (1) compensatory, (2) consequential, (3) liquidated, or (4) nominal. Compensatory damages are sums of money which will offset the loss sustained. Consequential damages are awarded when the professional, at the time of contracting, was aware of some special or unusual circumstance which might occur as a result of a breach. Liquidated damages are damages stipulated in the contract as the amount to be recovered if there is a breach. Nominal damages are awarded when there is a technical breach but no actual loss or damages suffered.

The injured party owes a duty to make a reasonable effort to avoid or at least minimize damages. Moreover, to recover compensatory damages, the injured party must prove the amount of loss as well as the fact that he or she suffered the loss as the direct result of the breach of contract. When it is presumed that the parties intended to assume only the chances of loss which are normally incident to the performance of the contract, the breaching party is only obligated to pay damages which would normally result from the breach. However, when the professional is aware that a greater loss would be probable, consequential damages may be awarded.

Tort Obligations of a Professional Each member of society is required to follow a course of conduct which does not fall below a recognized standard in the course of daily activities. Professionals are held to a higher standard. In either case, failure to maintain the accepted standard of conduct will expose the person to liability for any damage caused to another person.

A cause of action for a tort injury arises when a person violates a duty imposed by law. The general duty is to avoid causing harm to others. In determining whether an act was wrongful, the test usually applied is whether a prudent person in the exercise of ordinary care would have foreseen that injury or damage would have naturally or probably resulted from that conduct.

As explained in previous chapters, tort liability may arise from intentional or nonintentional breaches of duty. Intentional breaches include willful interference with person or property; nonintentional torts include negligence, strict liability, or absolute liability.

Contract Versus Tort Violations The primary difference between contract and tort actions lies in the nature of the interests protected. Contract actions are created to protect the interest of the parties in having promises performed; accordingly, contract actions arise because of the intent or conduct of the parties. Tort actions protect a party's right to freedom from various kinds of harm, and the underlying duties of conduct are imposed by the law for social reasons. Damages recoverable in a tort action have a much broader measurement than do damages recoverable in a contract action.

The courts often are not clear whether a particular wrong is a breach of contract, a tort, or both. The line of demarcation may be between *nonfeasance* (not doing the thing at all) and *misfeasance* (doing the thing improperly). Nonfeasance is usually a breach of contract and misfeasance is usually a tort, though there are some exceptions to this generalization.[1]

A professional's violation of a duty owed a client can give rise to a contract cause of action, a tort cause of action, or both. If the professional wholly fails to perform services agreed to, a clear breach of contract occurs. If the professional does not perform the services in the manner expected, either a contract or tort cause of action may arise. If professional performance causes personal injury or damage, a tort action is generally created. All things being equal, an injured client probably would prefer to recover against the professional under a tort action because of the potential for a much larger recovery.

Professional Corporations

In recent years, a large number of states have enacted legislation which permits certain specified classes of professionals to do business as professional corporations (sometimes called "PCs" or "PAs," professional associations). In the absence of such a statute, a professional is limited to practicing either as a sole proprietor or in a partnership.

Generally, a stockholder of a corporation is liable for *corporate* obligations only to the extent of the stockholder's investment in the corporation. Under most professional corporation statutes, the shareholder of a professional corporation can lose no more than the shareholder's interest in the corporation—*except* for professional torts committed by the shareholder or under his or her supervision. This is an important exception—some enabling laws for professional corporations explicitly extend liability arising from the acts of one stockholder-employee to other stockholder-employees.

As may be true with respect to employees of other corporations, any employee or officer of a professional corporation is *personally* liable for his or her own actions. Thus, if a professional's personal performance fails to meet the standards for professionals of his or her class, the professional may still be directly liable to the injured persons.[2] For example, the Illinois Professional Service Corporation Act provides, in pertinent part:

> Any officer, shareholder, agent or employee of a corporation organized under this Act shall remain personally and fully liable and accountable for any negligent or wrongful acts or misconduct committed by him, or by any ancillary personnel or person under his direct supervision and control, while rendering professional services on behalf of the corporation to the person for whom such professional services were being rendered. However, a professional corporation shall have no greater liability for the conduct of its agents than a general business corporation. The corporation shall be liable up to the full value of its property for any negligence or wrongful acts or misconduct committed by any of its officers, shareholders, agents or employees while they are engaged on behalf of the corporation in the rendering of professional services.[3]

A number of states require professional corporations to buy insurance meeting certain minimum standards, usually for errors and omissions arising out of the rendering of professional services.[4] Failure to purchase such insurance may subject the shareholders to unlimited personal liability.[5]

Under some state statutes or rules of the statutorily authorized governing organization (e.g., a medical association for doctors or a state supreme court or bar association for attorneys), there may be derivative tort liability or cross-liability among stockholders and their employees. For example, the Professional Service Corporation Act of Maine provides:[6]

> This chapter does not modify the relationship between a person rendering and a person receiving professional service. The liability of shareholders for the debts of and claims against a professional corporation shall be the same as that of shareholders of a business corporation; except that, in the case of liability arising out of the rendering of professional service:
> 1. *Liability not modified.* This chapter does not modify the liability of the person rendering to the person receiving the service; and

2. *Liability extended.* That liability shall extend, jointly and severally, and regardless of fault, to those shareholders participating in a
professional capacity in such rendering.

Especially in states having such provisions, adequate professional
liability insurance coverage should include not only the professional
corporation or association itself, but also each stockholder and
employee.[7]

MEDICAL PERSONNEL

The Exposure

The law is well established that physicians may be liable under
negligence doctrine for injury to their patients.[8] Seldom, if ever, have
physicians been found even indirectly liable for such injuries under
strict or absolute liability theories.[9] In any case, compensable injuries
may be inflicted by the physician's actions directly, or by the
employment of drugs, medical services, or other less direct means.

Similarly, medical professionals other than physicians have been
liable for negligence in their treatment of patients. Among these are
dentists, optometrists and opticians, pharmacists, anesthetists, and
physical therapists. Another allied area of potential malpractice liability
involves nurses and medical attendants, but most of those cases deal
with physician or hospital vicarious liability.

Practitioners such as chiropracters, osteopaths, chiropodists and
podiatrists, and naturopathic physicians are also subject to malpractice
claims. Theoretically, any person who claims to possess the learning,
skill, or ability to treat a particular ailment is required to utilize the skill
and care that is ordinarily used under the same or similar circumstances
by a reasonably well qualified medical professional.

Legal Standards for Medical Professionals The same rules
which govern other negligence actions also apply in any suit against a
medical professional. No higher degree of culpability is required to
establish liability against a doctor than is required in any other tort
action. In each instance the duty is to use reasonable care to avoid injury
to other persons. The term "malpractice," although commonly used to
describe suits against physicians, is actually imprecise and potentially
misleading, since it fails to define either the type of action or the type or
measure of proof required to establish liability. It is a colloquialism
which at best means an actual or alleged breach of the applicable
standard of care.

Usually, in nonprofessional cases, the conduct of the parties may be evaluated in the light of the general experience and background which each juror possesses. For example, there is no special knowledge required to judge that a driver who failed to stop at a stop sign was negligent. Professional liability cases are different. Without special knowledge, jurors would often have difficulty in determining whether the professional defendant used the standard of skill and care required. Therefore, the jury needs to be informed of the standards which pertain to that particular profession. However, integrating this element of proof into court actions against medical professionals has created substantial evidentiary and procedural problems from both a legal and practical standpoint.

Standard of Care. The law generally requires that the plaintiff prove the proper standard of care applicable to the medical treatment which was received (and which he or she claims caused injury). Most courts require the production of expert testimony in order to establish the appropriate standard of care. Other jurisdictions have found that the proper standard of professional care can be established by the use of authoritative journals or treatises, as well as by other secondary or collateral sources. The standard rarely may be established merely by cross-examining the defendant. However, certain medical societies do publish standards to which they expect members to adhere, and these can be used in some states. In any event, the court will require the plaintiff to show that some recognized standard was breached.

Locality Rule. Historically, courts in the United States have adhered to the rule that a doctor's treatment must be measured by the skill and care used by other doctors in the same community. A variation of this rule broadens the standard to encompass the skill and care practiced by doctors in similar communities. However, the "locality rule" and its variations have been criticized as being outmoded, and in some states it has been thoroughly repudiated by recent decisions. One court has held that medical conduct which conforms to the standard of the profession will not necessarily insulate a physician against liability. Indeed, the more modern and slowly developing view is that evidence of custom in the profession is relevant in determining the standard of care, but that custom should never be conclusive.

Specialists and Duty of Referral. Specialists are required to possess and apply that extra degree of skill and care used by specialists practicing in the same field.[10] While some states cling to the locality rule with regard to specialists, the reasons for applying a broader geographical standard are even more compelling in evaluating the acts of a specialist.

There is also a rule stating that if a patient's condition requires consultation or care by a specialist, the attending physician has a duty to so advise the patient or to make the referral. In most instances, the violation of this duty can only be shown through expert testimony or other authoritative evidence. Moreover, the attending physician is generally not liable for the acts of a surgeon whom the physician does not assist in the performance of a surgical procedure. Nor would the attending physician be liable for the acts of a substitute physician, unless the attending physician failed to use reasonable care in the selection of the substitute.

Delegation. There are still diverse views in the courts of the United States regarding the duty of a doctor who delegates a task to a hospital employee, particularly during surgery. For years, many states held that a physician could not be charged with the negligence of a hospital employee, if it was customary to delegate the particular task to hospital personnel, unless the physician directly supervised the performance of the work. Other states have, however, imposed liability on a physician in such a situation. Under these rules, hospital employees are considered to be temporary servants of the operating surgeon, and the surgeon may be found liable for failures which occur under his or her implied direction and supervision. Some courts have gone even further, suggesting that the duty of an operating surgeon may be broader than prior decisions indicate. These courts have held that a physician who retains control or supervision over a hospital employee may be found liable for the negligence of the employee, if the physician fails to exercise that supervision and control with reasonable care. Generally these courts would leave it to the jury to decide whether or not a surgeon was negligent in the supervision of others who negligently performed their duties.

Diligence and Abandonment. Other issues of importance in the field of medical malpractice are those concerning abandonment and diligence in treatment. A doctor is not the sole judge of the necessity or frequency of treatment, but has a duty to treat a patient as long as treatment is required. Further, the physician has a duty to be diligent in the treatment of patients. When a physician refers a patient to a specialist and the referring physician is not required to provide further treatment, the latter cannot be held to have abandoned the patient unless, of course, the referring physician assured the patient or the patient's relatives that he or she would do so.

If the refusal to render medical treatment is beyond the bounds of decency or is otherwise outrageous, some courts have allowed the patient's spouse who observed the events to recover damages under the doctrine of "intentional infliction of mental suffering."

Common Allegations Against Medical Professionals   Among the more common allegations against medical professionals are those which involve charges of improper diagnosis, improper tests, surgical error, lack of informed consent, and use and administration of anesthetics or drugs.

Improper Diagnosis.   It is one of the fundamental duties of a physician to make a properly skillful and careful diagnosis of the ailment of a patient. If a physician fails to bring to a diagnosis the proper degree of skill or care and makes an incorrect diagnosis, the physician may be held liable to the patient for any damage thus caused. However, a mistake in diagnosis is not actionable where the physician uses the proper degree of skill and care. That is to say, liability is not imposed on a physician for making an error in judgment, except where the error results from a failure to comply with a recognized standard of medical care which is exercised by physicians in the same specialty under similar circumstances. (In jurisdictions which still use the locality rule, the applicable standard would be that of the geographical area where the physician practices.) A physician does not guarantee the correctness of his or her diagnosis. But he or she is obligated—in diagnosing a patient's malady—to use ordinary skill and diligence; to apply the means and methods ordinarily and generally used by physicians of ordinary skill and learning to determine the nature of the ailment; and to act upon the honest opinion and conclusion reached.

Improper Tests.   It is also incumbent upon the physician, in the exercise of due and reasonable care and skill, to employ the proper tests and examinations to determine the condition of a patient about to undergo a proposed treatment or operation. Whether or not the failure to make such tests or examinations constitutes want of due and reasonable care and skill depends on whether the standards of skill and care require such a test or examination in a particular case. Failure to make the following tests have led to physicians' liability: biopsy, x-rays, standard diagnostic procedures, allergy tests, and glaucoma tests.

Surgical Error.   A surgeon who performs an operation is under the duty to exercise such reasonable care, skill, and diligence as are usually exercised by surgeons in similar cases. This rule exacts a higher degree of skill and care of the surgeon than it does of the average general practitioner of medicine. The duty of care, skill, and diligence extends throughout the entire operation, and it applies equally to making a diagnosis and prescribing treatment. The fact that the consequences of a surgeon's negligence in performing an operation are aggravated by the physical condition of the patient does not preclude the patient from the recovery of damages for negligence.

One of the most common types of negligence for a surgeon is

leaving a foreign object in the wound. Failure to remove surgical sponges or other foreign substances from the wound before the incision has been closed has been held to be at least prima facie negligence on the part of the operating surgeon. Even though the ultimate burden of persuading the court and jury that the surgeon has been negligent remains with the plaintiff, proof that a foreign substance was left in the wound is prima facie proof that the operating surgeon has been negligent. Thus, the *res ipsa loquitur* doctrine may apply. There are other cases where it is alleged that failure of a surgeon to remove all sponges and foreign substances from a surgical wound constitutes negligence per se. Evidence of negligence in foreign substance cases can be shown by failure of the physician to follow an established procedure with regard to such requirements as a sponge count. Some courts have held, however, that if an operating surgeon exercises due and reasonable skill and care with respect to foreign objects in the wound, the surgeon cannot be held liable for negligence based on the sole fact that a sponge was left in the patient's body.

Lack of Informed Consent. In an operative procedure, the consent of the patient (or someone legally authorized to give such consent) is required, except under emergency conditions or in unanticipated situations. The failure to disclose in advance the danger of any particular procedure or treatment may render the physician or surgeon liable. The surgeon or attending physician must reasonably disclose to the patient or the patient's qualified representative the potential problems which are associated with the treatment, so that the patient or representative can decide whether to accept the treatment or not. Whether a physician should inform the patient of the potential problems of treatment depends a great deal on the severity of the potential harm. Thus, where the severity of the potential harm could be great, the patient should be informed of that possibility, even if it is believed by competent physicians to have a low probability of occurrence; however, where the severity of the potential injury is minimal, the physician need only inform the patient of those dangers which have a high probability of resulting in minimal harm. The modern view is that the burden is not on the physician to disclose every risk conceivable and known to exist by competent physicians, since excessive disclosure might do more harm than good to the patient.

A recent development has been the adoption, in roughly half of the states, of informed consent statutes. These statutes do not radically change the doctrine of informed consent, but the statutes do attempt to give more force and meaning to the signed consent form (discussed later under "defenses").

Use and Administration of Anesthetics or Drugs. The duty and liability of a physician or surgeon in administering an anesthetic or drug to a patient are substantially the same as those which govern the treatment of patients generally; that is, the physician is bound to exercise such reasonable care and skill as is usually exercised by average physicians or surgeons. In some cases, however, the standard of reasonable care and skill has been declared to be that possessed by other persons whose occupation and study give them an equal or better knowledge of the right methods of the use of anesthetics or drugs than is possessed by the general practitioner of medicine. For instance, it has been held that a brochure which accompanied the delivery of an anesthetic or drug and explained how the substance was to be used, was not alone sufficient to establish the standard of care to be used in administering it.

In most of the cases involving the question of negligence or malpractice, the physician has been held liable for an injury to the patient resulting from the mistaken administration of the wrong drug or medicine. Where a choice of drugs is available, the questions become much more complex. Allied areas of liability involving anesthetics and drugs are those involving failure to properly sterilize instruments, drugs, or operative fields; breaking of needles used in administering injections; explosions; the alleged use of harmful drugs instead of the proper ones; the improper employment of spinal injections; and the death or injury of a patient under excessive or improper anesthesia.

Other Allegations. Other allegations to which medical professionals are subject include failure to inform parents of their baby's chances of birth defects, or malpractice causing injuries due to poor eye treatment, poorly fitted eyeglasses, and unsterile techniques of ophthalmologists. Further, a recently developing area involves organ transplants and the question of negligent treatment of the donee or donor.

Post-operative treatment has created questions of malpractice when the surgeon has failed to continue care after the patient leaves the operating room. Another area of liability has been the improper treatment of fractures or dislocations due to the negligent application of a cast, splint, or other treatment.

In some cases, death or injury has resulted from the transfusion of the wrong type of blood. Further, the implantation or insertion of a prosthetic or other corrective device had led to negligence actions when such medical devices were incorrectly installed. Often, insufficient evidence has been presented to make negligence in the use of a prosthetic device a triable issue or, in the face of conflicting evidence, to warrant the jury's finding for the patient.

When a physician or surgeon has been sued for malpractice because a patient was injured by hospital equipment, the courts have applied the general rule that liability will attach only if the doctors fail to use reasonable skill, care, or diligence. Negligence has been found on the basis of the doctrine of *res ipsa loquitur*, however, in that the defendant physician in charge of the equipment causing the injury was in the best position to control the use of the instrument. Other cases have taken the opposite view, the rationale being that to have applied the doctrine would mean that the surgeon would have had the duty of examining all the equipment furnished by the hospital for the operation, and that this would demand more than ordinary care.

Recovery for damages alleged to have resulted from the failure of a sterilization operation has been sought on a number of grounds, the court being required to rule on allegations of negligence in the performance of the operation, breach of a contract or warranty to sterilize a patient successfully, and also fraud, deceit, and misrepresentation in statements made to the patient and the patient's spouse.

Common Defenses Available to Medical Professionals Various defenses may be used in responding to allegations of professional liability—the statute of limitations, good Samaritan statutes, releases, contributory negligence, and informed consent.

Statute of Limitations. The use of the statute of limitations as a defense in a medical malpractice action creates two questions. First, which section or sections of the statute are applicable to this action? Second, what event triggers the running of the statute? A subsidiary question is: What kind of fraud will toll or stop the running of the statute?

Generally, most American jurisdictions apply the personal injury statute of limitations to medical malpractice actions, absent a special medical malpractice statute which creates a limitation for that type of litigation. Some states have a special statute of limitations which extends the period if a foreign substance is negligently permitted to remain in the body and causes harm. Further, when a drug or other product is used in connection with the prescribed treatment of a patient, the provisions of the Uniform Commercial Code concerning the limitation for personal injury actions and predicated on a breach of implied warranty may come into play. Regarding the second question as to what event triggers the running of the statute, some courts have held that the statute of limitations period runs from the end of the medical treatment. However, by far the majority of American jurisdictions has held that the cause of action accrues and the statute begins to run at the time of the wrongful act. Recently, some courts have adopted the "discovery of injury" rule. This last rule states that the cause of action accrues and the statute begins to run when the injured person learns of the injury or should reasonably have learned of it.

When one has fraudulently concealed the cause of action from the person entitled to it, the person entitled to the action may bring the action at any time within a certain period after discovering the right of action.

Generally, the statute cannot begin to run until the treatment is ended. This is especially important if the physician-patient relationship and treatment are continuous.

Good Samaritan Statutes. Most American jurisdictions have adopted some sort of "good Samaritan" statutes. These statutes exempt from civil liability persons licensed to practice treatment of human ailments when they give emergency care without compensation (for instance, at the scene of an accident). The question as to what constitutes an emergency has been the only issue discussed by the cases construing a statute of this sort.

Releases. Exculpatory clauses or releases executed prior to treatment frequently have been held invalid. Early cases had held that a release given by a plaintiff to the original tortfeasor applies as a bar to a malpractice action against a defendant physician in a subsequent action. More recent cases have held that two causes of action rather than one are involved in actions involving negligence of the original tortfeasor and the subsequent negligence of the treating physician.

Contributory Negligence. If the plaintiff's contributory negligence is simultaneous and cooperating with the fault of the physician, and if it enters into the creation of the cause of action, it will usually bar a recovery or, in some states, reduce the recovery. However, where the negligence of the patient is subsequent to the malpractice and the patient's negligence merely aggravates the injury inflicted by the physician, it only affects the amount of damages recoverable by the patient. There have been few medical malpractice cases which involve the defense of assumption of risk. However, one jurisdiction has applied the assumption of risk defense to x-ray treatment burns, whereas others have applied it to cases where patients refuse the physician's advice and are thus contributorily negligent for resulting injuries. Otherwise, the defense of assumption of risk generally has not been recognized in malpractice cases.

Informed Consent. The doctrine of informed consent is a relatively new defense to malpractice actions. If the medical professional discloses the details of a particular procedure, it has been held that the patient, in agreeing to the procedure, waives a technical "battery." Thus, the defense of consent may not be necessarily applicable to malpractice cases, because the patient generally would not have agreed to negligence, but rather to the battery.

In recent years, the law has focused on the quality of the consent given by the patient. Where the consent was given but knowledge of the collateral risks reasonably conceivable and known to competent physicians is withheld, the consent is said to be vitiated because it is not informed. Recently, courts have taken the view that the action can be either in negligence or battery; moreover, expert testimony, although necessary for certain aspects of the case, may not be necessary on the issue of whether or not consent is informed.

Medical Professional Liability Insurance

Medical "malpractice" insurance is a form of protection for various medical-related institutions and medical professionals in the event claims are made against them because of their actual or alleged malpractice, error, or omission in rendering or failing to render professional services of their specialty. Institutions which desire professional liability or "malpractice" insurance primarily for their vicarious liability arising from errors or omissions of professionals include hospitals, sanitariums, nursing homes, blood banks, and clinics. Individual professionals who desire this protection include physicians, surgeons, dentists, nurses, medical technicians, opticians, optometrists, veterinarians, and numerous specialists.

Although the "medical malpractice crisis" to be discussed later has reduced the availability of medical professional liability insurance, both standard and nonstandard forms are still in use on a limited basis through traditional markets. This section of the chapter discusses (1) the nature and scope of standard and/or nonstandard provisions concerning various coverages for professionals and institutions, (2) the medical malpractice crisis—the factors contributing to it and legislative attempts to deal with the problems, and (3) noninsurance techniques for dealing with the exposures of medical professionals.

Nature · and Scope of Medical Professional Liability Insurance Despite the variety of professional services which are performed by medical institutions, by individual professionals, and by members of professional partnership and corporate entities, virtually all medical professional liability exposures are handled by three policies: (1) hospital professional liability, (2) physicians' and surgeons' professional liability, and (3) druggists' liability, the forms to be analyzed here.

Hospital Professional Liability Policies. Hospital professional liability policies geared to the aforementioned institutions, whether government owned, operated for profit, or nonprofit, provide protection in the event of injury to others stemming generally from malpractice, error, or omission of physicians, surgeons, nurses, and the like with respect to the following professional services:

1. medical, surgical, dental, or nursing treatment, including the furnishing of foods and beverages to patients;
2. drugs, medical supplies and/or appliances which are furnished or dispensed by institutions, provided injury occurs after such drug or item has been relinquished to others;
3. post-mortem examinations; and
4. service performed by a member of an accreditation board of an institution. (This coverage is directed at institutions which are sued by physicians, surgeons, and other professional staff who claim that their reputation was wrongfully harmed as the result of directives issued by the accreditation board or similar professional board.)

INJURY. The fact that most policies apply to "injury" rather than to "bodily injury" may suggest that coverage is not necessarily limited to bodily harm but also could include coverage against property damage, or personal injury because of such intentional torts as mental anguish, false imprisonment, and wrongful eviction. Sometimes it does and other times it does not. Much depends upon individual policy interpretation and the claim in question. Those disputes which have been taken to the courts have been interpreted both ways, i.e., some courts have restricted coverage to bodily injury, whereas other courts have taken the broader viewpoint.[11] But whether coverage is limited to bodily injury or is extended to encompass personal injury, medical institutions are generally protected for injury sustained by patients as well as other persons such as visitors, provided the injury results from the rendering or failure to render professional services. For example, if a visitor were injured by the actions of a deranged patient and the hospital or other institution were held liable for not exercising the proper degree of professional supervision required by the circumstances, the institution should be protected by its policy.

INSUREDS. Those who are insureds under hospital professional liability policies may include such persons as trustees, directors, executive officers, or partners, depending upon the type of entity (e.g., government owned, privately owned, or charitable). But regardless of who may be included as insureds, policies generally do not cover the personal acts of a professional nature committed by professional people such as physicians, surgeons, and nurses. Professionals must also obtain their own professional liability policies. Hospitals nonetheless are protected against their vicarious liability which results from malpractice, error, or omission of professional persons who serve the hospitals, even if the professionals are without proper protection in their own name.

DEFENSE, SETTLEMENT, SUPPLEMENTARY PAYMENTS. For the most part, hospital professional liability policies contain the typical supplementary payment provisions concerning such matters as defense coverage and various expenses incurred by insureds, much like those supplementary provisions of the standard general liability policy, with two important exceptions. First, hospital professional liability policies do *not* cover expenses incurred by insureds for first aid given to others at the time of an accident on the premises because hospitals and similar institutions undoubtedly would perform that service without expecting reimbursement for first aid services rendered. Second, the aforementioned professional liability policies usually contain an important provision to the effect that an insurer is precluded from making settlements of claims or suits unless it has the written consent of the insured. This provision prevents an insurer from making an unwarranted settlement which could adversely affect the reputation of the institution.

PERIOD OF COVERAGE. One of the principal differences between standard and nonstandard hospital professional liability policies (and other professional liability policies, for that matter) involves the period of coverage. The standard policy is written on an occurrence basis, whereas many nonstandard policies (those of Lloyd's of London and independently filed forms of insurers) are written on a claims-made basis.

When a policy is written on a *claims-made basis*, the criterion for coverage is that the claim for actual or alleged injury be reported or made during the current policy period, even though the malpractice, error, or omission giving rise to injury, or the injury itself, happened sometime earlier. When a policy is written on an *occurrence basis*, the controlling factor for coverage is that the injury must arise during the policy period regardless of when the claim ultimately is reported. Thus, it is not unusual for an insurer with coverage written on an occurrence basis to be confronted with a claim long after its policy has expired.

In comparing the claims-made and occurrence coverage arrangements, the former presents many advantages to insurers because insurers are made aware of the malpractice claims made against them during the policy period and are better able to estimate what it may cost to settle outstanding claims and to promulgate responsive rates. With coverage on an occurrence basis, there usually is a lapse in time between the injury and the claim, thereby making it difficult for insurers to ascertain their loss experience and to promulgate responsive rates. This is frequently referred to as the "long-tail" problem because a graph of malpractice loss experience tends to show a long "tail" due to the long delay in reporting and settling claims under the occurrence policy. Because of the long-tail problem, an increasing number of professional liability policies written today are on a claims-made basis.

EXCLUSIONS. What few exclusions apply under hospital professional liability policies are meant to preclude coverage of loss exposures which either are best covered under other policies or are not insurable. No coverage applies to an insured's employees who are injured during the course of their employment for their employer nor for workers' compensation, unemployment compensation, disability benefits, or similar statutory coverage for which the insured or its insurer may be liable.

There also is an exclusion of liability of individual owners of hospitals and kindred institutions stemming from their personal acts of a professional nature. Since the hospital professional liability policy is not designed for the protection of individual professionals, this exclusion requires individuals to purchase their own professional liability insurance. Losses stemming from war and the nuclear hazard are also excluded because of their catastrophic potentials, but radioactive contamination to property is insurable and bodily injury liability and/or property damage liability stemming from radioactive isotopes and other by-products usually is covered if the exposure does not otherwise come within the scope of the broad form nuclear energy exclusion.[12] Liability arising out of the ownership, maintenance, use, loading, or unloading of motor vehicles, aircraft, and watercraft is excluded because these exposures can best be covered under other liability policies.

While not specifically excluded, no coverage applies to liability of a nonprofessional nature which occurs in connection with the premises or operations of hospitals. (An exclusion is not necessary for the latter exposure because the insuring agreements of hospital professional liability policies restrict coverage to liability arising from professional services.) Because many insurers no longer provide hospital professional liability insurance, it is often difficult for insureds to combine their general liability, automobile liability, and professional liability insurance with one insurer. However, whenever it is possible to combine coverages, it reduces the problem of "gray areas" between the exposures of those three policies. For example, if a nurse were to fail to adjust the side bars to a hospital bed and a patient were to fall and sustain injuries, the general liability insurer may. argue that the claim arose from the omission of a professional service, whereas the professional liability insurer might argue that the claim arose from the omission of a nonprofessional act. However, if both hospital professional liability and general liability were to be provided by one insurer, the issue would be avoided.

Two limits apply to hospital professional liability policies—a limit for any one claim and an aggregate limit for all claims during the policy period. The aggregate limits operate the way the aggregate limits of various general liability policies do—if one or more claims equal or exceed the aggregate limit during the policy period, the insurance is considered to be exhausted.

Physicians', Surgeons', and Dentists' Professional Liability Policies. Physicians', surgeons', and dentists' professional liability policies are flexible as to the types of professionals who can be covered. With modifications of various provisions by endorsement, coverage also can be provided to nurses, various types of surgeons, such as neurosurgeons, heart surgeons, plastic surgeons, psychologists, psychiatrists, optometrists, various technicians, therapists, and even veterinarians.

These policies, like hospital professional liability forms, do not cover the general liability exposures of a nonprofessional nature, although some insurers write combination liability policies which can include general liability insurance for an additional charge.

INSURING AGREEMENTS. The insuring agreements of physicians', surgeons', and dentists' policies vary. The agreement of the standard ISO policy, which is on an occurrence basis, covers damages because of "injury arising out of the rendering of or failure to render, during the policy period, professional services by the individual insured, or by any person for whose acts or omissions such insured is legally responsible ... performed in the practice of the individual insured's profession described in the declarations. ..."

Reference to the term "individual insured" restricts coverage to individuals. If an individual is a member of a professional partnership or corporate entity, the policy must be modified to reflect that exposure, subject to an additional premium. While this policy will cover the individual insured's vicarious liability arising from the acts or omissions of others, such as a laboratory technician or nurse, the policy will not protect others; they must purchase coverage to protect themselves. Finally, the reference to the aforementioned insuring agreement concerning the "individual insured's profession described in the declarations" is necessary to make coverage compatible with other types of professionals.

When these policies are written on a claims-made basis, the insuring agreement usually refers to any claim or claims made against the insured during the coverage period and arising out of the performance of professional services rendered or which should have been rendered by the insured or by any persons for whose acts or omissions the insured is legally responsible. Some of these policies do not restrict coverage to individual insureds but, instead, define "insured" as the individual, partnership, or corporation designated in the policy declarations.

EXCLUSIONS. Despite the differences among insuring agreements of physicians', surgeons', and dentists' professional liability policies, the few exclusions are quite uniform. Two common exclusions exclude the insured's liability as a proprietor, superintendent, or executive officer of a hospital, sanitarium, clinic, laboratory, or business enterprise, and the nuclear energy hazard. The rationale of the former exclusion is to require persons in that capacity to obtain coverage for their professional liability in connection with institutions under hospital professional liability insurance. Since none of the physicians', surgeons', and dentists' professional liability policies excludes liability stemming from the use of automobiles, professional liability also extends to acts or omissions in rendering or failing to render professional services in vehicles such as ambulances.

OTHER PROVISIONS. Most other provisions of these policies correspond to the provisions of hospital professional liability policies, particularly the requirement that the insurer have the insured's written consent to settle any claims or suits. The dual limits of liability for each claim and annual aggregate also are identical.

Druggists' Liability Policies. Druggists' liability policies provide two coverages: (1) professional liability and (2) products liability. Against these two exposures, the policies cover liability of druggists for bodily injury and/or property damage arising from goods or products, *including* drugs and medicines which are prepared, sold, handled, or distributed after possession has been relinquished to others, whether bodily injury or property damage occurs on or away from the business premises. The products are not restricted to drugs or medicines. Also included are other products of the type sold by drug stores, such as food and beverages. However, not included within the coverage of druggists' liability policies is protection for claims of bodily injury and property damage arising from premises and operations liability exposures. Therefore, druggists should purchase OL&T or CGL coverage to close that coverage gap.

Druggists' liability policies have supplementary payments provisions identical to those of general liability policy provisions and have the same approach to dual limits of professional liability policies—a limit for each claim, and an annual aggregate limit. But there is one important difference—the druggists' policies, unlike other professional liability policies, do *not* require the insured's written consent before claims or suits may be settled by the insurer.

Exclusions. Most of the exclusions which apply to druggists' liability policies are common to general liability policies. These policies do not cover:

1. Bodily injury sustained by any employee of the insured when such injury arises out of and during the course of the employee's work for the insured. Workers' compensation insurance covers this exposure.
2. Bodily injury which directly or indirectly results from any willful violation of any penal statute or ordinance by the insured or by his or her store manager.
3. Liability assumed under any contractor agreement, except warranties concerning goods or products of the insured.
4. Liquor liability at common law or as imposed by ordinance or statute. This exposure may be treated with the purchase of liquor liability insurance.
5. Damage to the insured's own property. This exposure should be covered under some form of property insurance.
6. Liability for damage to property used by, rented to, or occupied by the insured, or property which is in the care, custody, or control of the insured. These exposures also are the subject of property insurance or bailee insurance.

OTHER PROVISIONS. Most other provisions and conditions of the druggists' liability policy correspond to other professional liability policies. With the addition of appropriate forms, this policy can be used to provide somewhat similar protection for opticians and hearing aid service establishments.

The Medical Malpractice Crisis The year 1975 is commonly viewed as the year of the "medical malpractice crisis"—the turn of events that resulted in the withdrawal of insurers from the medical professional liability insurance market, the unavailability of insurance protection to some health care providers or exorbitant insurance costs to others, and more defensive, costly medicine to the public. The "crisis," however, is not something that developed suddenly. The underlying factors leading to the crisis have existed for years in some form or another.

Factors Contributing to the Medical Malpractice Crisis. By and large, the factors which have contributed to the crisis are attributable to an interplay of socio-economic and political conditions. The following are the major factors, not in any particular sequence, which together are blamed for the crisis.

CHANGING RELATIONSHIP BETWEEN MEDICAL PRACTITIONER AND PATIENT. Medical practitioners, unlike those commonly exemplified on television, no longer maintain the warm, personal relationship which was common among hometown physicians who worked seven days a week, made house calls at all hours, and accepted credit or goods in exchange for services rendered. Whether physicians now devote more time to keeping up with advancements in medical technology or to family life and leisure, few medical practitioners now make house calls or work a seven-day week. Many doctors require advance notice for nonemergency office visits, long waiting periods during office visitations, and evidence of insurance or credit as a condition precedent to receiving medical attention. Specialization is also a factor, particularly when people are required to see two or more specialists for what may seem to be exorbitant fees. The result is that people are now more likely to seek monetary redress for the slightest error or omission of these medical professionals than if the relationship were more personal.

THE INFLUENCE OF THE MEDIA. Newspapers, magazines, radio, and television influence people by publicizing first, the advancements of medicine, thereby giving people the impression that modern medicine is a cure-all and, second, verdicts and huge settlements as well as large dollar damages sought by claimants. This publicity makes people more aware of litigation as a recourse against their injuries.

CHANGING ROLE OF TRIAL LAWYERS. With the advent of automobile no-fault insurance, some trial lawyers have turned their attention toward the more lucrative fields of medical malpractice and products liability. These lawyers, some of whom have medical degrees, have become more knowledgeable about the common defenses mentioned earlier and their weaknesses; and, with fees on a contingent basis ranging from one-third to one-half of the damages, they seek judgments or settlements which appear to be more than enough to compensate their clients.

LEGAL DEVELOPMENTS FAVORING PLAINTIFFS. A number of legal developments favor plaintiffs—statute of limitations, informed consent, and the collateral source rule—and these have been in some way responsible for the increase in medical malpractice suits and in high awards.

GROWING PUBLIC AWARENESS OF LEGAL RIGHTS. All of the preceding factors which contribute to the "crisis" have made the public more aware of its legal right to seek remedies however slight their claims may be. The number of claims has been rising consistently and if measures are not taken to check their numbers, the situation can worsen with each passing year.

The size of the awards made is also increasing. While the preceding factors play an important role in the size of awards, it is the public who serves on juries and who, in a large way, is responsible for the size of awards being made.

PROFESSIONAL ERRORS AND OMISSIONS. Many claims and awards legitimately redress injuries caused by professional errors and omissions. Incompetence of medical practitioners plays a significant role in mounting claims. Court digests describe many cases in which people have been maimed needlessly through the errors or omissions of medical professionals.

UNDERWRITING LOSSES. Mounting claims and awards, complicated in part by the "long-tail" of professional liability insurance policies, have brought about insurer losses which are so high as to cause insurers to withdraw from the market.

FACTORS OF THE ECONOMY. The inflationary spiral of the 1970s and simultaneous losses in the stock market have also had a large, unfavorable impact on insurance companies. With spiraling inflation, insurers are required to pay tomorrow's claims with yesterday's premium dollars. And when the stock market goes down, the assets and surplus of insurers also decrease, with the result that insurers' capacity is decreased.

Legislative and Other Attempts to Deal with the Problems. Because of the severe conditions in a number of states and the growing severity of the problem in other states, a number of short-term and long-term solutions were proposed by medical professionals. The former solutions were implemented first until state legislatures could approve some of the long-term solutions.

The short-term solutions which are thought to ease the crisis include (1) putting lawyers' contingency fees on a sliding scale so that the higher the award, the lower the percentage of the award used to determine the fees; (2) eliminating the *ad damnum* (dollar demand of damages) so as to prevent the public from thinking that the amount demanded, as reported by the media, actually is the amount received by a claimant; (3) shortening the statute of limitations regarding the time limit on when claims may be made; (4) eliminating the collateral source rule to avoid duplication of payments; (5) placing a maximum limit on awards, such as $500,000; (6) eliminating awards for punitive damages; (7) imposing mandatory arbitration upon claimants; (8) implementing joint underwriting associations; and (9) providing state funds.

Joint underwriting associations (JUAs), nonprofit arrangements which operate for durations ranging from two to three years, have been implemented in a number of states, including California, Florida, Hawaii, Maryland, and Ohio. Although JUAs operate differently in various states, they generally require all insureds (medical professionals) desiring to participate to pay an additional amount over their premiums, which is used to accumulate a reserve fund for losses in the event the premiums are insufficient to cover the losses. Investment income derived from the reserve fund and the paid premiums are also used for operating the JUAs. Since they assume no chance of loss, insurance companies which are selected to service these associations derive no underwriting profit, but rather receive a service fee for issuing policies and handling claims.

State funds, such as those in Indiana and Louisiana, serve a dual purpose by providing a market for residual applicants who cannot find other forms of protection and for excess liability limits. The state fund in Indiana requires that the residual market be funded by state appropriations and policyholders' assessments, whereas the excess liability is funded by all health care providers. Coverage is provided for limits of $100,000 (and up to an additional $500,000 excess). In addition to the fund, Indiana has reduced its statute of limitations to two years and also regulates lawyers' contingent fees. Finally, all claims and/or awards against medical practitioners are reported to the practitioners' licensing board for disciplinary action if necessary. The state fund of Louisiana differs from that of Indiana in that no assessment is made for residual coverage, only for excess limits; the statute of limitations is three years from the occurrence; the *ad damnum* clause has been eliminated; and arbitration is authorized.

Insurers still willing to write medical malpractice insurance on a limited basis, particularly for large professional groups, have attempted to write coverage on a claims-made basis. However, insurers have met with resistance in many states because some state insurance departments are not totally convinced that the claims-made basis of coverage is advantageous to insureds. Insurers maintain, however, that while claims-made coverage is not a solution to the crisis, it will help enable insurers to tabulate their incurred losses more quickly and promulgate more responsive rates.

All these measures are temporary, meant merely to provide relief until some more permanent solution can be found. A number of long-term solutions have been suggested. These include federal reinsurance, a plan resembling accident and health insurance whereby benefits are provided on a scheduled basis, and a change from the present tort system to a no-fault concept.

Despite what has been and continues to be done in a number of states to alleviate the crisis, some medical groups also have taken the initiative to provide their own protection by establishing reciprocals, mutual insurance companies, and captive companies.

Noninsurance Techniques
for Treating the Medical Malpractice Exposure

Because of the malpractice crisis and the difficulty of obtaining insurance (or the unaffordability of available protection), medical professionals and institutions have had to utilize noninsurance measures either to maintain what little insurance protection they may have been able to obtain or to insulate themselves from personal loss without the aid of insurance. These noninsurance measures include loss control, loss transfer, loss retention, and loss avoidance.

Loss Control Loss control has always been important to medical professionals. Loss control is particularly important as a measure which can reduce the hazards which are the primary source of claims. One insurer's brochure entitled "Ways to Help Avoid a Malpractice Suit," provides some sound loss control guidelines for physicians.

- The physician should not tell the patient or his attorney that he has professional liability insurance. The mere statement can plant the seed of a suit in their minds or induce them to raise the amount for damages should a suit be filed.
- The physician should not make it a habit to diagnose and instruct patients over the phone regarding treatment. The patient might misunderstand the instructions, which in turn could result in a malpractice suit. If the physician has diagnosed or instructed by phone, it should be carefully noted on his records.
- The physician should not press for the collection of fees unless he is positive that the patient has received proper treatment and has no basis for a malpractice suit.
- The physician should not perform any operation until the hospital chart has been checked thoroughly to be sure of the patient's identity and of the operation to be performed.
- The physician should not make any statement which might constitute, or be construed as, an admission of fault on his or her part.
- The physician should maintain a sound attitude, professional manner, and tactful approach toward each patient and the patient's family.
- The physician should carefully delegate and supervise the duties of his or her employees.
- The physician should frequently check the condition of his equipment and make use of every safety precaution available.

- The physician should maintain a complete and accurate history of each patient's case. If the physician knows that a patient has failed to follow instructions, his or her records should show it.
- The physician should refrain from an over-optimistic prognosis and avoid promising too much to the patient.
- The physician should keep inviolate all confidential matters.
- The physician should arrive at an understanding with the patient in advance as to the matter of fees.
- The physician should, when absent from practice, make available or recommend a qualified substitute.
- The physician must know and abide by his legal duties to the patient.
- The physician must be careful to instruct properly, render sufficient care and make himself available to all his patients.[13]

Physical and operations hazards of medical institutions can also be reduced with the assistance of loss prevention experts from insurance companies and other firms which specialize in offering loss control services. And because medical institutions can be held vicariously liable for the errors and omissions of their medical staffs, institutions are being required to improve their employment practices by hiring more competent applicants and monitoring employees once they are hired.

Medical professionals are also practicing "defensive medicine" by requiring extensive tests which sometimes are deemed to be unnecessary and costly to patients before rendering opinions or performing services.

Noninsurance Transfer. The medical professional liability exposure is difficult to transfer to others. Perhaps an early retirement, accompanied by the sale of an ongoing medical practice to another professional, could be deemed a transfer. More likely this would appropriately be considered avoidance.

It might seem possible to transfer the activity-producing exposure to another or to retain the activity but to transfer the financial consequences by use of an exculpatory agreement or release. It is doubtful whether such transfers could be effectively accomplished in the medical profession since the law holds to be unenforceable transfers of liability when (1) the performance of work is inherently dangerous; (2) injury is apt to result not from the way in which the work is performed, but by the very performance of such work; and (3) the law imposes a positive duty to someone, in which case liability for injuries cannot be delegated to others, whether or not the one performing the work has accepted liability under contract.

Avoidance Avoidance is never creating an exposure, or voluntarily or involuntarily doing away with an exposure before it causes any losses. Exemplifying the former are the students in medical school who change their aspirations and enter other professions to avoid the medical malpractice crisis. Avoidance is also used when a general surgeon decides against becoming a cardiac surgeon because of the high number of claims being made against cardiac surgeons.

Avoidance as a technique for handling loss exposures has always existed, but it has seldom been practiced by professionals until the medical malpractice crisis of the 1970s. Until then, insurance was always available at reasonable costs to handle any problems stemming from errors and omissions of medical practitioners.

Retention Medical professionals can retain some portion of every loss through deductibles, or the professional may retain all of his or her losses. This method may seem ridiculous in view of the potential for very severe losses. However, some professionals have threatened to go unprotected either because they cannot obtain insurance or because they cannot afford it. How many professionals have actually followed through with this threat is uncertain.

THE PROFESSIONAL LIABILITY
OF ARCHITECTS AND ENGINEERS

The Exposure

Architects and engineers, who are in the so-called design professions, have exposures to malpractice claims from aggrieved clients and third parties. Both architects and engineers may and frequently do have similar functions—including the design and drafting of plans for structures of a wide variety and, in some cases, supervision of actual construction. Both are exposed to substantial liability in the course of their work. Here, architects and engineers will be treated as one, since the law is similarly applied to both.

State governments have long recognized that the public has an interest in assuring that only qualified, knowledgeable persons practice the design professions. This is why states require architects and engineers to register and to be licensed before entering practice. Practicing beyond the scope of the license—for instance, an engineer drafting architectural plans—is not only a statutory violation but could also be used as persuasive evidence against the design professional in a civil action for damages by a client.

The relationship between an architect and the property owner is typically controlled by a contract of employment which sets forth the specific obligations of the owner and the architect, and establishes the framework within which the two parties must act. The American Institute of Architects publishes a suggested draft contract which is widely used. The breach of any of the conditions found in the employment contract may give rise to a claim for damages by the owner. For instance, an architect who contracts to supply drawings by a certain date and fails to do so may be liable to the owner for any increased costs which result and may also be liable to suppliers and workers who are idled by the delay. Similarly, if an architect is hired to draft plans for a building not to exceed a certain cost of construction, the architect may be liable for overruns beyond the costs contemplated in the plans. Indeed, the possibilities for contractual exposures are as numerous as the clauses in the contract.

When an architect or engineer is hired, an agent-principal relationship is also established. The architect owes a duty of loyalty to the owner and cannot engage in activities counter to the interest of the owner. For instance, it would generally be unethical for the architect to have a financial interest in a contractor or supplier for the project, unless this fact were clearly disclosed to the principal. An architect with such a conflict of interest might therefore be liable to the principal for damages based, at least in part, on the former's profit.

By far the greatest exposure to liability comes from allegations that the design professional was negligent in the preparation of plans or in the design of a particular structure. Although many cases hold that the architect's undertaking, in the absence of a special agreement, does not imply or guarantee a perfect plan, the architect is obligated to prepare plans and drawings which conform to the ordinary skill and expertise of architects. An architect, like other professionals, will be judged by at least the average capacities of other members of the profession. Every claim of negligence involves a fact question. The judge or jury must determine whether the architect's performance was reasonably consistent with the competence and skill of architects in the area.

Some instances clearly show negligence—for example, when a floor or roof collapses because the design did not provide for adequate structural support. Other cases inevitably involve highly subjective determinations.

In cases involving negligence of design, damages can be measured in two different ways. If the defect in the building is relatively minor, damages are usually measured by the cost of repairing the defect. If the defect is major, the damages are generally measured by the difference between the value of the building as it was built and the value it would have had if it had been built according to correct plans and specifications.

The measure of damages also applies to cases where the architect has defrauded the owner, for example, by failing to reveal flaws or by devising shortcuts in construction.

One of the more troublesome areas of exposure arises from the architect's duty to supervise construction. The architect's liability is separate and distinct from the liability of those who are engaged in the actual construction. The architect's obligation is not inherent in the architect-owner relationship, but it is often established by the contract. Originally, courts held that the duty to supervise was limited to insuring that the construction conformed to specifications and materials contemplated by the plans. More recently, some courts have held that the duty to supervise, once accepted, may additionally include overseeing the construction techniques and procedures. This duty carries with it the concomitant responsibility to condemn work which is unfit. In jurisdictions where structural work acts are in effect, this can significantly increase the exposure.

At one time, the architect's responsibility was solely to the owner, the other party to the contract. However, as in other areas of the law, the concept of privity of contract has been eroded, so that now third parties who are injured or suffer property damage as a proximate result of the architect's negligence are potential plaintiffs.

Often architects are required by a three-way contract to be arbitrators of differences between the owner and the contractor. Generally, cases against the architect which arise from performance of the arbitrator function are successfully defended. The architect-arbitrator is said to have some limited immunity in this function as a go-between. Difficulties arise when an architect performs several roles, all of which overlap. Defining these roles and their inherent liabilities through careful drafting of contracts is essential.

The defenses generally available in negligence cases are also available to architects. With the proviso that the statute of limitations may begin to run only upon discovery of a defect by the owner, that defense has often been used. Acquiescence in acceptance of faulty plans may provide a contract defense, as will contributory negligence and assumption of risk in a tort case.

Architects' and Engineers' Professional Liability Insurance

Architects and engineers, like medical professionals, sometimes find it difficult to obtain protection against their errors and omissions because of their potentially large loss exposures and the adverse experience of insurers over the years. But, from time to time, some domestic insurers and Lloyd's of London underwriters will provide coverage on a limited basis, either for large groups or for individuals, depending upon their loss experience, nature of work, and territory of operation.

All architects' and engineers' professional liability policies are nonstandard—the provisions are drafted by the insurers which offer the coverage. Insurers also promulgate their own rates which usually are based on judgment and make their own underwriting rules. The coverage provisions nonetheless do not vary much because, over the two decades since this coverage was first introduced, insurers have learned from experience and/or court interpretations what terminology is to be avoided.

Because it is uncertain what insurers are or will be writing this coverage at any given time, the approach here is to discuss in general the important provisions which usually form a part of this professional liability coverage.

The format of architects' and engineers' professional liability policies is similar to other professional liability forms. They are composed of the declarations page, insuring agreements, definitions, exclusions, conditions, and the requirement that the application be part of the policy.

Insuring Agreement The insurer generally agrees to pay on behalf of the insured all sums which the insured shall become legally obligated to pay as damages because of liability arising out of the negligent act, error, mistake, or omission of the insured in rendering or failing to render professional services as an architect or engineer.

The definitions section of these policies defines the terms "insured" and "damages" as well as other pertinent terms. For the most part, the named insured and employees acting within the scope of their duties are included as insureds. Damages are usually defined to include loss, judgments, and settlements, barring fines and penalties imposed by law.

These policies almost always make provision for defense, settlement, and supplementary payments in much the same way as do general liability policies. Insurers are not, however, permitted to make settlement without the consent of insureds. However, to protect themselves against unreasonable insureds, insurers add the stipulation that if an insured desires to contest a claim, the liability of insurers is not to exceed the amount for which the claim could have been settled if not contested, subject to the limits of liability.

Territorial Scope Policies vary as to their territorial scope. Most apply anywhere in the world, provided claim is brought within the United States, its territories, possessions, or Canada. But insurers have broadened coverage to apply wherever the suit is brought, with the exception of Communist bloc countries. Insureds who perform work in Puerto Rico must make sure the territorial provision is amended to specifically show that location.

Policy Period—Claims Made Virtually all architects' and engineers' professional liability insurance is written on a claims-made basis—the claim must be made during the policy period.

Amount Payable The amount eventually payable as the result of a covered claim depends upon the limit of liability and the deductible provisions.

The limits of these policies universally apply on a per claim/aggregate basis. The insurer's obligation for paying damages, including defense costs, ceases at the level specified in the policy for each claim, and if one or more claims amount to the aggregate specified in the form during any one annual period, the insured no longer has protection. In the latter event, the insured either will have to renegotiate additional coverage from the same insurer or seek coverage elsewhere. Considering market conditions for this coverage, both alternatives present difficulties.

In addition to the limit per claim and aggregate limit, a deductible is deducted from the amount of a claim decided by settlement or judgment. When an insured consents to a settlement and the insurer makes the necessary negotiations and payment, most policies provide the stipulation that the insured must reimburse the insurer for the deductible amount.

Exclusions The number and nature of exclusions vary considerably from one policy to another. Some policies contain a minimum of exclusions common to all types of operations, subject to additional exclusions by endorsement depending upon the nature of the work or professional services to be performed—for example, civil, electrical, structural, mechanical, or design and construction operations. The latter exposure usually involves an architect who does the actual planning and designing of work specifications as well as the managing of construction operations.[14]

Among the common exclusions of architects' and engineers' professional liability policies are:

1. Liability assumed by the insured under *any* contract, except liability which would have applied in the absence of any such contractual assumption. The reason for this exclusion is to require insureds with that exposure to report and to insure it, because it can encompass broad forms of assumption which require contractual liability insurance.

2. Liability arising out of the conduct of any business enterprise, including a partnership or joint venture of which the insured is an officer, partner, or member and is not specifically designated in the policy declarations or in any endorsement attached to the policy. This exclusion prevents the insurer from covering exposures without having the opportunity to underwrite them and to charge a premium commensurate with the exposure. Were it not for this exclusion, insurers might not become aware of other business ventures of their insureds until after a loss occurs. Therefore, it is important for an insured either to declare all of his or her business interests with the insurer of professional liability insurance or to insure all other business interests under a separate policy.

3. Failure to complete drawings, specifications, or schedules, as well as losses stemming from express warranties, guarantees, or estimates of probable construction costs. The exposures and losses are the subject of suretyship and should be treated with performance and maintenance bonds.

4. Loss arising from the advising, requiring, or failing to advise, require, or maintain any type of bond or insurance involving the insured or someone else. This is an exposure developed when architects specify what insurance coverages are to be maintained by others in performing work. The exposure can usually be covered for an additional charge.

5. Dishonest, fraudulent, criminal, or wrongful acts or omissions committed by or on behalf of the insured. This exclusion prevents the insurer from covering criminal acts, which are uninsurable.

6. Liability arising from the ownership, maintenance, or use of any premises owned, occupied by, rented to, or leased by the insured. This exclusion requires the insured to obtain some form of general liability insurance, such as a CGL policy, to cover its losses of a nonprofessional nature.

7. Bodily injury sustained by any employee of the insured which arises out of and during the course of his or her employment; or any obligation for which the insured or its insurer may be held liable under any workers' compensation, disability benefits, and other similar law. The reason for this exclusion is to require the insured to obtain workers' compensation insurance or the appropriate statutory coverage which may be required for the protection of the insured's employees.

8. Liability arising out of the ownership, maintenance, use, or operation of any automobiles, mobile equipment, watercraft, or aircraft. This exclusion is deemed necessary because the

preceding exposures are best covered under other liability forms.

There are other exclusions which may apply, depending upon the type of operation. For example, an architect or engineer who is involved in any work with bridges or tunnels usually will be subject to an exclusionary endorsement concerning those exposures. Or, if an engineer's operations sometimes involve the testing of underground structures or subsurfaces, an endorsement will usually be attached to the policy precluding coverage from such loss exposures because the exposures are commonly deemed to be extra-hazardous in nature and not always insurable. Finally, all policies are subject to the broad form nuclear energy liability exclusion.

Conditions The policy conditions of architects' and engineers' professional liability insurance do not vary much from one policy to another. In fact, the conditions generally are quite similar to provisions of standard and nonstandard general liability policy forms. These conditions specify the duties of the insured in the event of claim or suit; require insurer consent in writing for policy assignment; hold that coverage is excess over other valid and collectible insurance; allow the insured to cancel the policy at any time simply by notifying the company in writing, whereas the company usually must give written notice stating when, not less than ten to thirty days (depending upon insurer) thereafter, coverage may be terminated; and the requirement that the insured assign its rights of subrogation to the insurer in the event that the insurer pays the claim.

Noninsurance Techniques

Considering the loss experience of architects and engineers as a class, and the conditions of the professional liability insurance market, it would appear that all noninsurance techniques, short of avoidance, are a necessary supplement to the design professionals' insurance program. Determining which of the noninsurance techniques may be most appropriate in any given case depends upon the exposures of these professionals.

According to one authority, the claims exposures of these professionals, based upon loss experience, can be grouped into the five following categories:

1. Between 20 and 25 percent of all claims against architects and engineers stem from the "negligent preparation of plans and specifications."

2. Another 20 to 25 percent of all claims made against these professionals arise in connection with "site survey, profiles, soil conditions on the surface and subsurface, grades and elevations." These exposures are said to be particularly troublesome, because it is not always possible to determine who is at fault (i.e., the project owner who supplied the information, the contractor who performs additional survey work, or the architect who relied upon the information which is supplied or who modifies it). It is stated that the architect or engineer seldom can escape liability in any event, because a contractor cannot construct a building or structure without a plan for which the former usually is responsible.

3. Approximately 15 to 20 percent of all claims involving architects and engineers deal with the "selection of materials or equipment." While the architect may not warrant the materials to be used, the architect still is required to designate the type of materials to be used. It therefore is difficult for professionals to limit their liability with respect to materials or equipment and, while the professionals may be able to protect themselves from the owners of projects, the former undoubtedly will be confronted with claims from contractors and subcontractors if the materials turn out to be defective and the equipment fails to perform as specified. It is stated that of all the claims involving this exposure, most are between the professionals and their clients. However, there have been circumstances when a third party institutes a claim against the owner, who in turn impleads the architect or engineer.

4. About 10 percent of all claims are in the nature of third-party claims instituted by contractors against the professionals and prompted by increased construction costs because "(1) the 'quantities' shown on the plans and specifications were wrong and/or the design was defective; (2) the designated construction procedures cost him (contractor) too much money; and (3) the insured (professional) won't approve the work, the estimate and/or the materials or equipment which the contractor has installed."

5. Another 10 percent of the claims made against architects and engineers involve bodily injury sustained by workers or by the public following completion of the work. It is stated, furthermore, that an architect or engineer who supervises the progression of work, or who sets up the procedures under which work is to be performed, undoubtedly will be brought into any suit by a claimant.[15]

The preceding information regarding types of claims common to these professionals could be helpful in deciding upon the degree to which each of the noninsurance techniques could be used in handling loss exposures. Architects and engineers who cannot altogether avoid any exposure can use loss control, noninsurance transfer, retention, and methods of supplementing whatever insurance they may have against their loss exposures.

Loss Control   The following are viewed as loss control measures important to architects and engineers.

Management and Personnel Support.   No loss control program will produce results unless it has the support of management and personnel. It therefore is important for firms to establish some type of written policy on the objectives of their loss control program, including the responsibilities of each individual who has a role in producing quality work. If the firm is large enough to employ a full-time risk manager, it should have a statement of policy which outlines the assignment of responsibility for all risk management functions, including safety, training, security, the purchase of insurance, and the establishing of retention amounts. The need for communication and cooperation by personnel with the risk manager also is essential to the success of the program.

Record Keeping.   Maintaining records is a key element to any loss control program, because records can help to (1) identify the costs of such a program, (2) determine the sources of loss and their underlying causes, (3) determine retention levels, and (4) serve as post-loss measures in aiding the firm in its defense of any claim and/or suit.

Quality Control.   Procedures must be established which will help to prevent or reduce the chance that plans, specifications, and surveys are negligently prepared or performed. Quality control techniques will help to fulfill that objective. In some cases, quality control will be required under various government regulations and laws, such as the Occupational Safety and Health Act of 1970, which requires the compliance of various standards concerning the safety of operations and materials.

Noninsurance Transfers   Architects and engineers, like medical professionals, are limited in the types of noninsurance transfer techniques they may use. Perhaps the most common type of transfer involves the use of hold harmless, exculpatory, or indemnity agreements for the financial consequences emanating from nonprofessional activities in which they are directly involved. There is even a limit to what can be transferred under these agreements. Not too many years ago, architects and engineers required others, particularly contractors, to assume any and all liability stemming from operations, including losses caused by the professionals themselves, and over which the contractors had no control. Many states have since enacted statutes which hold such broad agreements to be unenforceable. The American Institute of Architects has now developed standard contract provisions, including indemnification agreements which are not as stringent as they once were. These contract provisions serve to transfer the potential contingent liability of architects and project owners to those whose negligence results in a claim or suit. For example, an indemnification agreement could require a contractor to indemnify and hold harmless the owner and architect from all claims, losses, and expenses which arise out of the performance of work and which is caused in whole or in part by the negligence of the contractor. The firm which transfers its liability with an agreement such as the aforementioned also will require certificates of insurance showing that the assumption of liability is insured.

Retention All purchasers of professional liability insurance probably should retain some portion of their losses, whether the retention is in the form of a mandatory deductible or is a planned retention of losses up to a limit deemed tolerable to the professional or the firm. Some firms, unfortunately, also retain losses which are inadvertently not covered. Although the latter circumstance should be avoided, some degree of retention always is advisable, particularly for those losses which occur frequently. A firm which actively retains part of its losses is not only more apt to find a market for its professional liability insurance, but will also reduce its insurance costs, because rates are loaded for insurance company expenses and margin for profit, and neither directly benefits the buyer of insurance.

Based upon the preceding discussion of noninsurance techniques and the common loss exposures confronting architects and engineers, firms should not choose from among loss control, retention, or transfer but, instead, should use all of the techniques to the degree suitable to the exposures facing them. Reliance upon one technique is not enough.

ATTORNEYS' PROFESSIONAL LIABILITY

The Exposure

The law regarding the liability of attorneys to others is, like other areas of professional liability, rapidly developing after a long period of relative inactivity. In recent years, attorneys have been increasingly faced with claims from nonclient third parties. For example, shareholders of corporations may be able to sue attorneys for negligent preparation of corporate securities filings and other papers involving the securities laws. However, the bulk of professional liability claims are still brought by former clients.

Liability of Attorneys to Clients   It has long been established that a lawyer can be held liable for negligence in the performance of professional duties on behalf of a client, if the negligence results in damage to the client. However, the attorney can not guarantee the correctness of his or her work. Nor is it possible for an attorney to guarantee results that will be accomplished. If a lawyer unequivocally promises a certain result and it is not accomplished, the client may not be able to collect consequential damages. It may be that an absolute promise to achieve a certain result might constitute negligence in and of itself, depending on the facts and law under which such a promise was made.

In the past attorneys were only held liable for gross negligence. It is now well established that attorneys can also be liable for ordinary negligence, that is, for failing to meet the standard of care ordinarily required of attorneys.

Standard of Care.   An attorney is required to possess that degree of knowledge and skill ordinarily possessed by other attorneys who are similarly situated; an attorney must use reasonable care and diligence; and must, in good faith, exercise his or her best judgment in attending to the matter committed to the attorney's care. If an attorney acts in good faith and in an honest belief that the advice given and actions taken are well-founded and in the best interest of the client, the attorney is not answerable for a mere error of judgment. Nor is an attorney liable for a mistake in a point of law (1) which has not been settled by the court of last resort in the attorney's state, and (2) on which reasonable doubt may be entertained by well-informed lawyers.

Though there appears to be some difference of opinion among the various jurisdictions as to whether the standard to be applied is that of the local bar association in the area where the attorney practices or some more general standard, the courts agree that the standard of care required of attorneys is a question of fact which must be determined by expert testimony.

A question which has not been settled is whether a higher standard of care should be applied to attorneys who specialize. This question will definitely become more significant as the trend continues toward specialization and certification of specialties within the legal profession.

When Suit Must Be Filed.   When the client's cause of action begins, and how soon after the attorney's error the client must sue the attorney before the claim is barred by the statute of limitations, are points on which there have been some recent and noteworthy developments. As might be expected, these developments have been in favor of the client.

It has generally been held that a cause of action for malpractice against an attorney accrues at the time the error is committed, and the statute of limitations commences to run from that time. Because of many inequities which occurred as a result of that rule and, in part, because of the extensions of time created by the courts in cases in which a patient sued a doctor for medical malpractice, the attorney rule came under severe attack. As a result, in a number of states the courts have extended the time within which the client may sue the lawyer for malpractice before the client's claim is barred by a statute of limitations.

Some states have applied the "continuous treatment" doctrine, which was previously limited to medical malpractice cases. According to this doctrine, the statute of limitations does not start to run as long as the attorney continues to represent the client in connection with the matter which is the basis of the client's complaint. Other courts have held that the statute begins to run when the client discovers or should discover the malpractice. Still other courts have used the "date of injury" as the date on which the statute starts to run. Thus, to answer the important question of when the cause of action accrues, one must carefully study the applicable law in the jurisdiction involved.

Regardless of the theories which various courts have thus far embraced, there is a definite trend in the direction of extending the time within which the injured client may sue his or her attorney. And it appears highly likely that when questions of time limitations in attorneys' malpractice cases are presented to courts without precedence on the issue, the tendency will be to favor the client.

Kinds of Liability to Clients. The majority of cases in which attorneys have been held liable for malpractice damages have involved litigation errors. For example, damages have been awarded where an attorney allowed the statute of limitations to run, improperly drafted pleadings, improperly served or failed to serve the defendant, failed to file an appearance, failed to discover readily-available material facts, failed to prosecute an action once begun, prepared erroneous trial findings and court orders, improperly entered judgment, improperly distributed funds received, failed to perfect a valid appeal, abandoned his clients, or disregarded a client's instructions.

Other sources of attorney liability have involved matters other than litigation. They include: failing to observe a title defect or outstanding creditors, giving erroneous advice to a trustee, drafting an unenforceable contract, improperly recording an instrument, improperly drafting or attesting a will, failing to attach a lien on a debtor's property in a timely manner, or improperly managing a client's funds.

The above lists are by no means exhaustive, but they point to the conclusion that virtually no aspect of the practice of law is immune from potential liability.

Liability of Attorneys to Third Parties   It used to be said that an attorney could not be liable to a third party (i.e., someone other than the attorney's client) for damages arising out of professional services rendered to a client, except for fraud and collusion. New York is one of the states that still holds that an attorney cannot be held liable to a third party for damages arising out of negligence in the performance of professional duties.

However, the law is subject to change, and there is a trend toward holding the attorney liable to third parties for simple negligence. To date, the bulk of the cases in this area have involved wills and the rights of persons who would have been heirs under the wills but for the lawyer's negligence. But there are clear indications that the liability of attorneys to third parties will continue to expand, just as we have seen liability to third parties expand in cases involving the negligence of architects, engineers, abstractors, title companies, banks and others.

Liability of Attorneys Under the Securities Laws   One of the most controversial topics of discussion in recent years has been the rapid developments affecting the liability of attorneys and accountants under the securities laws. The most famous case in the area is the National Student Marketing case, decided in 1972.[16] The Securities and Exchange Commission's (SEC) complaint in that case, which involved an allegedly misleading registration statement, named as defendants not only the corporate officers, directors, and independent accountants, but also two of the most prestigious law firms in the securities field. Although the complaint sought an injunction rather than damages, it is a well-known phenomenon that civil suits by stockholders (usually class actions) for large damage claims usually follow or accompany the prosecution of an SEC injunction action. Thus, the impact of the National Student Marketing case was tremendous, particularly since the law firms and others involved were charged with violations of the antifraud provisions of the federal securities acts.

Perhaps the greatest significance of the National Student Marketing case was the SEC's contention that the attorneys had an obligation to the SEC and to the public which transcended the attorneys' obligation to their respective clients. These contentions of the SEC are still causing great concern to securities lawyers and the legal profession in general. In addition to huge potential liability on the part of the lawyers for claims against them by securities holders, it creates a dilemma for lawyers whose traditional position has been that their first and foremost duty is to their client. However, if the SEC's contentions are upheld, lawyers with knowledge of such things as fraudulent or misleading financial statements face potential liability to third-party claimants for (1) failure to refuse to issue their legal opinion letters supporting their client's statements; (2) not demanding that a particular transaction cease, that the securities holders be advised of the questionable statement, and that their approval and consent be obtained again on the basis of the new facts; (3) failing that, to cease representing their clients; and (4) thereupon notifying the SEC of the alleged fraudulent or misleading nature of the financial statements contained in the documents on file with the SEC. In short, instead of being attorneys representing their clients' interests, the lawyers would, in effect, become public-interest lawyers as part of the enforcement arm of the SEC. (The Justice Department has even suggested from time to time that attorneys should reveal conspiratorial activities involving price-fixing schemes of their clients.) On the other hand, if they act as the SEC contends they should act, not only would they stand to lose their clients, but they might also subject themselves to potential lawsuits for violating their duty to their clients and for damages which allegedly resulted from the lawyers' actions.

The matter has not been resolved. However, it has led to much discussion within the legal profession and to a number of suggestions, such as that the lawyers be "expertized" under the SEC laws (i.e., be totally independent of their clients in securities matters, as are public accountants).

Defenses The defense of contributory negligence on the client's part occasionally bars recovery. One court, assessing contributory negligence in a divorce action, held the client-wife's failure to investigate or even to inquire as to whether she was getting her share of community property raised a sufficient issue for jury consideration. A lay person has a duty to inquire whether the attorney is taking action on his or her behalf if the matter relates to something a lay person in the exercise of reasonable prudence should know that the attorney should do. On the other hand, when clients fail to act regarding matters specifically within attorneys' expertise, e.g., clients' failure to file agreement of sale with the registrar of deeds as required by the Bulk Sales Act, such acts do not constitute contributory negligence if the attorney failed to advise the clients to do so.

Attorneys' Professional Liability Insurance

Attorneys have not had the kind of adverse loss experience which presently confronts other professionals, particularly those within the medical field, but the loss potential of attorneys is nevertheless great. The net result is that the market for professional liability insurance of attorneys is rapidly being reduced to a few insurers which will provide the coverage subject to stringent underwriting requirements, high deductibles, and large premiums.

Coverage Features What coverage is currently written is on nonstandard forms and often on a claims-made basis. (The ISO form, though not withdrawn is not currently being sold, particularly since it is on an occurrence basis.) The policy will pay on behalf of the insured attorney all sums which he or she becomes legally obligated to pay as damages because of any negligent act, error, or omission in rendering or failing to render professional services of the type common to attorneys.

The provisions concerning defense costs, supplementary payments, and policy territory are virtually identical to those of the physicians', surgeons', and dentists' professional liability policies. The conditions precedent of coverage on a claims-made basis also are the same (i.e., the policy in force at the time claim is made applies to an otherwise covered loss, including a claim prompted by a negligent act, error, or omission which occurred prior to the policy inception if the attorney had no knowledge of such circumstances giving rise to loss, and no other insurance is available). The policy conditions of attorneys' professional liability policies also follow those conditions of physicians', surgeons', and dentists' professional liability policies, including limits of liability which apply on a per claim basis, subject to mandatory deductibles varying in size with the exposure, and an annual aggregate.

Exclusions Although the exclusions of attorneys' professional liability policies will vary with the exposure, the common types of exclusions found in the basic provisions of these policies are meant to preclude coverage of exposures which either are better covered by other insurance policies or are not considered to be insurable. These exclusions are:

1. Dishonest, fraudulent, or criminal acts or omissions. A fidelity bond will handle the first two offenses but criminal acts are uninsurable.
2. Bodily injury and property damage stemming from nonprofessional acts or omissions. These two exposures are insurable under various general liability forms which are usually used to round out the insurance protection of these professionals.
3. Claims of a professional nature stemming from errors or omissions of an attorney in his or her capacity as a public official or as an employee of any governmental agency. This exposure can be covered under various liability forms designed for public entities, such as public officials' liability insurance.
4. Losses stemming from any other business venture in which the attorney has an interest. This exposure either should be insured under an existing professional liability policy, if the exposure concerns professional errors or omissions, or it should be insured under some more appropriate form, depending upon the exposure.

Noninsurance Techniques

Attorneys are not likely to resort to avoidance as a way to eliminate their losses. And, while noninsurance transfers may be useful for handling various nonprofessional liability exposures, that technique is not particularly suited for handling professional liability exposures, for the reasons given earlier in connection with medical professionals. Thus, about the only noninsurance techniques of any current importance to attorneys are loss control and retention.

Loss Control Loss control for attorneys should be practiced to reduce the types of errors and omissions which commonly result in losses. One author who has published a great deal on this subject has identified nine situations that frequently lead to errors and omissions suits and has suggested loss control measures to reduce the likelihood of such suits. These suggestions are summarized in the following paragraphs.

1. *Statute of limitations.* An effective docket control system, diligently adhered to, can reduce problems due to missed deadlines.
2. *Real estate practice.* Attorneys should keep alert because

procedures and advice in this area tend to become routine and generalized.

3. *Abuse of process/wrongful garnishment or attachment.* These claims result mostly from lawyer carelessness. Office procedures should encompass the requisite procedures and the correctness and service of forms prepared by legal assistants or secretaries should be verified.

4. *Improper handling of tax or estate matters.* This area requires special expertise, and the general practitioner should consider associating specialists when his client's matter goes beyond the elementary stages.

5. *Conflicts of interest.* Attorneys should beware of falling into the conflict trap through dual representations, such as representing both lender and borrower in a transaction.

6. *Generating false client hopes.* Errors and omissions claims based on these grounds generally prove fruitless. However, attorneys can reduce the chance of a claim by giving their clients realistic appraisals of their problems so as not to generate false hopes.

7. *Commingling of funds.* Attorneys should institute workable office management procedures to assure proper protection and prompt disbursement of a client's funds or property.

8. *Unreasonable delay.* Delay per se is neither negligence nor unethical. However, procrastination can lead to an ethical violation. A method of practice should recognize the personal concerns of the client, avoid unreasonable delay, answer client phone calls, and provide the client with copies of correspondence whenever possible.

9. *Fee disputes.* Most fee disputes do not involve ethical violations. However, a disgruntled client may lodge a malpractice claim or a counterclaim for malpractice if the attorney sues for his or her fee. Effective attorney-client communications can reduce such problems. A clear, written contract with clear statements as to the responsibilities of all parties, detailed records of the attorney's time, and consistent procedures are specific measures that can be taken to reduce this problem.[17]

Retention   Although retention is beyond the control of attorneys to the extent that deductibles are mandatory under professional liability insurance, a considerable amount of control over the ultimate retention rests with attorneys. The rationale for selecting high retention amounts for professional liability loss exposures of attorneys is no different than it is for other professionals.

INSURANCE AGENTS' AND BROKERS' PROFESSIONAL LIABILITY

The Exposure

The potential liability of insurance producers has increased in recent years. As agents and brokers become better trained and assume greater advisory responsibilities, they are exposed to greater liability. This increased exposure has, in turn, resulted in additional professional liability insurance claims. Because the policies usually exclude from coverage fraudulent conduct, dishonest or criminal acts, defamation, and direct property damage and bodily injury, the following discussion will focus only on liability loss exposures premised on negligence, omissions, mistakes, and errors arising out of the performance of the duties of insurance agents or brokers.

At the outset, a distinction should be drawn between a broker and an agent. Often this distinction will be made by statutes which generally provide that an insurance agent is to be the agent for the *insurer*, while the insurance broker is generally to be the agent for the *insured*. These relationships are examined in greater detail in CPCU 6.

However, irrespective of the title bestowed upon or adopted by insurance representatives, their status in the eyes of the law will be determined by their acts rather than by what they are called. This distinction becomes especially important in determining the liability of an insurance representative, when suit is brought by the insurer against the representative.

Sources of Loss When a loss is due to an error or omission on the part of an insurance agent or broker, the damaged party may seek a monetary recovery by claiming that the loss resulted from a breach of duty by the representative. It is necessary, therefore, to examine exactly what duties and responsibilities must be fulfilled by agents and brokers. In general, agents and brokers must act in good faith and within the scope of their authority or instructions, and they must exercise such skill as might reasonably be expected from a person in those circumstances. Insurance representatives thus not only have obligations to their client, but also to the insurance company, and they must act in good faith with respect to both.

Concerning liability to the insured, recovery against an agent or broker may be predicated upon (1) breach of contract; or (2) negligence.

Breach of Contract. Courts have long held that an insurance agent or broker may be held accountable to his or her client for failing to procure insurance requested by the client and for failure to ensure that coverage remains in force. For example—when the client who proposes to be insured pays a premium, and the representative agrees to procure insurance and states the period, the amount, and the applicable rate— the representative will usually be held to have entered into a contract to procure insurance for the client. When the applicant suffers a loss and discovers that the representative never procured the promised insurance coverage, the representative will be held to have breached the contract, and he or she will be liable in damages for the injuries sustained by the customer as a result.

Negligence. In addition to breach of contract, negligence may serve as a basis for the liability of an agent or broker to an insured. Insurance representatives owe a duty to their clients. If they undertake to procure insurance for their clients and unjustifiably (or through their own fault or negligence) fail to accomplish this, their customers may maintain an action for any damages that result.

There are many other common sources of claims which are based on the insurance representatives' failure to exercise the skill and diligence required of them as experts in the insurance business. Examples include the representative's (1) neglect to renew coverage when the representative has either promised to renew or when the representative's previous conduct has led the insured to believe that coverage would be renewed; (2) failure to obtain proper or adequate coverage—liability for this often depends on the extent to which the client relies on the representative's expert advice as to premiums, terms, or coverage; (3) failure to notify an insured that the company had canceled coverage or to advise the client of failure to obtain a renewal of the policy; and (4) breach of a duty to place insurance with an authorized and solvent carrier.

In addition to the duties owed to an insured, agents and brokers also have certain duties and responsibilities to insurers. For the most part, the insurance representative who will be held liable for negligent performance of duties will be one who is characterized as an *agent* of the insurer rather than a broker. This is because the law recognizes differences between the duties owed to an insurance company by a broker and those of an agent. While a broker is generally unrelated to the insurance company and deals at "arms length," an agent is deemed a fiduciary of the company. That is, an agent occupies a position of trust with respect to the company and has a correspondingly high obligation to act in good faith and in honesty in all transactions affecting the company. An agent is thus required to make known to the company all material facts of which he or she is aware that in any way affect the insurance transaction and the issuance of coverage.

Therefore, when agents exceed the scope of authority granted to them by the company or when their negligence, errors, or omissions in their dealings with the company causes the insurer damage, they may be subject to liability. There are a number of common situations in which insurance agents have been held liable to insurers for such breach of duty. For example, agents will be held accountable for their clerical neglect when this results in the company assuming coverage for an applicant it did not intend to insure or for whom coverage would have otherwise expired. Also, an agent is accountable if the agent neglects to cancel a policy at the request of the insurer, or if the agent fails to follow the insurance company's rules, regulations, and instructions, and a loss subsequently follows for which the company is liable. In such cases, the agent may ultimately be held responsible for the loss. Again, if the agent breaches the duty to disclose fully all relevant facts, and the company insures an individual or business that it normally would not have insured, the agent may be held responsible for any losses which occur.

Defenses The defenses available to an agent or broker who is faced with potential liability depend upon the theory that the injured party utilizes. In an action charging that the insurance representative breached a contract to procure insurance for the client, the representative can utilize the standard contract defenses and can thus take issue with the contention that he or she was obligated to provide such coverage. For example, the representative could argue that a contract to procure insurance was never entered into because sufficient information to write the insurance was never provided by the prospective client.

Alternatively, the agent or broker can show that the loss in question would not have been covered in any event. Thus, an insurance representative would not be liable for failure to procure insurance which would have been void as contrary to public policy, or which would have been unenforceable if it had been procured in accordance with the directions of the insurance company. In a tort action charging that the representative breached a duty to obtain insurance, the insured must show that the negligence of the representative was the proximate cause of the loss sustained by the insured, and that the loss would have been covered by the policy the representative had been authorized to procure.

In some jurisdictions, a defense based upon the contributory negligence of the insured may be permitted. Thus, if an insured's obvious and glaring misconduct occasions a delay in the renewal of the insurance coverage, during which delay a loss is suffered, the courts may not permit a recovery, because of the insured's contributory negligence. In actions based on contract, the defense of contributory fault may be stated in terms of the doctrine of "avoidable consequences"—for instance, when an insured's failure to read his or her policy to learn whether it furnishes the desired coverage results in consequences (a loss not covered under the policy) that were avoidable by his or her exercise of reasonable care (reading the policy). Similarly, in an action against an insurance agent for recovery of a loss incurred by the insurer on a policy issued in violation of company instructions, an agent might successfully defend on the ground that the insurer, on prior occasions, had disregarded strict conformity with the rules and had accepted similar policies for an additional premium cost.

Agents' and Brokers' Professional Liability Insurance

The preceding discussion concerning the errors and omissions exposures of agents and brokers leads to some rather convincing arguments in favor of the purchase of errors and omissions liability insurance. In at least one state, Kentucky, a statute now requires all licensed agents and brokers to purchase professional liability insurance, in the minimum amounts prescribed, or to post cash or an acceptable surety bond. In the wake of rising claims, many agents and brokers are voluntarily purchasing such coverage, much of it on a mass-marketed basis through their membership in various insurance related associations. Mass-marketed insurance is not necessarily more economical. However, it is often somewhat easier to obtain coverage as a member of a group rather than as an individual.

Coverage Features Being a nonstandard form of coverage, agents' and brokers' errors and omissions liability insurance will vary from insurer to insurer. There are nonetheless many characteristics of these policies common to those of other professional liability policies.

Generally, agents' and brokers' errors and omissions liability policies apply to claims which result from the negligent act, error, or omission of the insured agent or broker, including his or her vicarious liability stemming from negligent acts, errors, or omissions of others for whom the insured is legally liable, such as licensed solicitors and employees. Insureds also receive defense protection and various other supplementary coverages comparable to most general liability policies. However, some insurers reserve the right to settle any claims as may be deemed to be expedient, whereas other insurers will agree not to make any settlements without the consent of their insureds.

Coverage most often applies on a claims-made basis. More important to insureds is the type of protection which is available once the policy is canceled, because claims-made policies only apply to claims made during the policy period. While some insurers offer no protection against errors or omissions which lead to claims after a policy is canceled, other insurers sometimes offer to extend protection for a year or two after policy termination. Still others will provide coverage if the insured notifies the insurer that a certain act, error, or omission during the policy period might culminate sometime after coverage has been terminated.

Agents' and brokers' errors and omissions liability policies, like other professional liability policies, also are written with per claim and aggregate limits often subject to mandatory deductibles.

Exclusions The exclusions of agents' and brokers' errors and omissions liability policies are comparatively few, applying essentially to exposures which are better protected under other forms. The exclusions common to these policies apply to claims stemming from dishonest, fraudulent, criminal or malicious acts, libel, slander, and other intentional torts, bodily injury and property damage liability and, of course, nuclear energy liability.

Noninsurance Techniques for Handling Agents' and Brokers' Errors and Omissions

Aside from avoidance, the single, most important noninsurance technique which can serve to curb the number of errors and omissions of agents and brokers is loss control. The leading causes of claims for property-liability producers are (1) failure to follow up on binders, (2) failure to explain the scope of coverages and their limitations, (3) failure to obtain the type of insurance required by clients, (4) failure to renew coverages, and (5) failure to abide by the agency contract provisions of insurers concerning the types of coverages which can be bound and/or written. Many potential claims can be prevented or reduced with knowledge of the proper procedures to effect coverage according to insurer specifications, knowledge of the various coverages available, written recommendations for coverages, written confirmation to clients of coverages sold and important limitations, and a record-keeping system which will reduce the oversights of binders and renewals.

Noninsurance transfer, though limited in its application, can be an especially useful measure for the large agency or brokerage firm which does not want its loss record or experience rating plan adversely affected by the errors or omissions of its subagents, brokers, or solicitors. Instead of including any of these as insureds under the policy of the agency or brokerage, the insured could require its subagents, brokers, or solicitors to obtain their own errors and omissions protection. This step also should reduce the overall insurance costs of the agency or brokerage itself, since the addition of subagents, brokers, or solicitors could undoubtedly raise the costs of insurance protection under the policies of some insurers.

Retention also has its advantages. For professionals, partial retention is often utilized in the form of mandatory deductibles. But additional amounts of voluntary retention may reduce premiums and enable professionals to obtain higher primary and/or excess limits.

OTHER PROFESSIONAL LIABILITY EXPOSURES

To the extent that someone claims to possess special "professional" qualifications in connection with the performance of a specific service, the law will hold that person to the standards of conduct reasonably expected of a person so qualified. Professionals may be held to even higher standards of conduct in instances involving specialization or warranties they have given.

The Exposure

It is not easy to determine who may be deemed a "professional," in the sense of being legally liable for rendering or failing to render *professional* services. There was a time when it was widely agreed that a professional was one who was engaged in medicine, law, or theology. The concept is no longer that limited. At law, the term now extends to a wide variety of persons who are not members of these time-honored professions.

As noted at the beginning of this chapter, court cases generally hold that a professional is one who "professes" special knowledge and skills which enable him or her to render a professional service. Typically, the special knowledge and skills result from a combination of education and experience in a particular branch of science or learning.

A more empirical means of attempting to determine who is exposed to professional liability is to examine court cases in an effort to determine who has been legally held to be a professional. In addition to those already discussed in previous sections, the following have been found to be professionals: accountants, chemists, editors, electricians, journalists, landscape architects, musicians, shorthand reporters, teachers, and translators. This information is not too helpful when it is noted that in other cases the following have been found not to be professionals: beauty culturists, brokers, insurance agents, labor relations consultants, real estate appraisers, and undertakers. Investigation reveals the fact that there has not been any consistent determination of the status of persons in the fields mentioned above. Within each classification there may be persons who are true "professionals" and others who do not meet the criteria. Thus, while the exposure in any given situation will not depend upon the particular individual's occupation, it may very well depend, from a legal standpoint, upon the qualities of knowledge and skill the individual claims to possess, as well as the services rendered.

Another empirical means of attempting to determine who is exposed to professional liability is to examine the applicable state statutes, i.e., statutes such as that of Illinois requiring practitioners of specified occupations to register with the Department of Registration and Education.[18] These occupations include veterinary medicine and surgery, horseshoeing, architecture, structural engineering, medicine and midwifery, embalming and disposal of corpses, dentistry, nursing, optometry, and barbering. The courts may not deem all these occupations as "professions" for liability purposes. Yet, such statutes may indicate certain relevant social policies within the state which justify professional classification.

Another clue to the professional classification may be the existence of standardized qualifying examinations as a prerequisite to practice, as is usually the case with insurance agents and brokers, real estate sales personnel, registered nurses, and others.

Standards of Care What difference does it make, as far as potential liabilities are concerned, whether one is or is not a "professional"? The difference probably depends on the rigidity of the applicable definition—the more rigid the definition of professional, the more significance the term should have. Of course, those engaged in "skills," "trades," "occupations," or "businesses," may be held to a standard of conduct higher than that of unskilled laypersons; however, the true professional, who professes special knowledge and ability, may be held to even higher standards.

In the event that an assertion of malpractice is made against a professional, the precise standard by which the conduct in question is measured is usually established by the expert testimony of others engaged in the same profession. It is not the witnesses' expert opinions which decide the issue of liability, however, since that is the province of a court or jury. The standard to be established is the reasonable conduct of one satisfactorily qualified in the given profession. Often, the witnesses will testify as to the common customs or usages of the profession. If the defendant's conduct fails to measure up to such customs and usages, liability may be established.

On the other hand, the professional may not necessarily be safe in relying on such customs or usages. A court or jury could conclude that, given the state of the profession, a reasonable person engaged in that endeavor, after assessing the particular custom or usage, would have deemed it an unsatisfactory level of performance and adopted a better, different, or more up-to-date practice. Thus, to avoid liability, the professional must not simply rely on customs and usages. The professional is always under the additional duty to keep abreast of new professional developments.

Liability to Third Parties In addition to the problems involved in determining who is a professional and what standard of care should be applied, it also becomes difficult to determine whether or not a loss exposure exists. This is made more difficult by the fact that the courts are changing in their application of the privity requirement. For example, a recent United States Supreme Court decision considered an allegation by a corporation's shareholder that an independent auditing firm engaged by the corporation to audit various statements failed, on account of its own negligence, to discover a material inaccuracy in those financial statements. The court assumed the allegation of negligence to be true but concluded that the auditing firm could not be held liable to the shareholders.[19] The court concluded that the parties lacked "privity." Because there was no direct contract between the auditing firm and the shareholder, the court refused to hold that the auditing firm had undertaken (or voluntarily obliged itself) to exercise its professional skills in a way which would protect the shareholder's interests. The Supreme Court's decision is significant if only because it tends to depart from a recent trend of state cases disregarding the privity element. The court's decision does not mean that those state decisions are necessarily wrong, however, since its decision was in the context of federal securities laws.

Nevertheless, it is clear the Supreme Court's decision will be influential, and the events which flow from it will be important with respect to potential professional liability. It is likely that privity may become a more important barrier to establishing certain professionals' liability. One factor in determining the importance of privity is whether or not personal injuries were involved. If so, the privity element has quite often been overlooked. On the other hand, the closer a given situation is to a commercial or business loss, the more likely privity is to play a significant role.

Insurance for Other Professionals

Professional liability policies are available for numerous professional individuals and firms, such as risk management consultants, barbers and other hair stylists, bank trust departments, public officials, real estate brokers, stock brokers, employment agencies, employee benefit trustees, notary publics, and social workers, to name just a few. However, most coverage provisions of the above policies follow much the same format and include essentially the same protection as that provided to the professionals mentioned earlier in this chapter. The only differences are that (1) coverage against negligent acts, errors, or omissions applies to a certain type of specified professional services; and (2) some additional exclusions may be necessary due to extra hazardous exposures which, if insurable at all, can only be covered upon payment of an additional premium or by the use of an additional coverage form.

Noninsurance Techniques

The importance of noninsurance techniques varies depending on the characteristics of each given profession. For the most part, however, loss control is usually the most important noninsurance technique for any professional liability exposure. Whether and to what extent it may be necessary or advisable to use noninsurance transfer, retention over the usual mandatory deductibles, or avoidance depends very much on each individual situation.

Chapter Notes

1. William L. Prosser, *Handbook of the Law of Torts*, 4th ed. (St. Paul: West Publishing Co., 1971).
2. Illinois Institute for Continuing Legal Education, Professional Corporations and the Alternatives (hereafter referred to as I.I.C.L.E., Professional Corporations), Sec. 3.10.
3. Ill. Rev. Stats. Ch. 32, Sec. 415-8 (1975).
4. One example of this is the Calif. Business & Professions Code, Sec. 6171.
5. An example is found in I.I.C.L.E., Professional Corporations, Sec. 2.20 and the chart of state statutes in Chapter 14.
6. Maine Rev. Stats. Anno., Title 13, Sec. 708.
7. I.I.C.L.E., Professional Corporations, Sec. 2.20.
8. A breach of professional duty must be shown in any malpractice suit, whether or not an actual contract for patient care existed between the plaintiff and defendant physician. Hoover v. Williamson, 236 Md. 250, 203 A. 2d 861 (1964). Generally, absent a contract between physician and patient, neither professional judgment nor cures can be guaranteed. Huffman v. Lindquist, 37 Cal. 2d 465, 234 P. 2d 34 (1951); Moore v. Guthrie Hospital, 403 F. 2d 366 (4th Cir. 1968).
9. See 54 *A.L.R.* 3d 258 and Cunningham v. MacNeal Memorial Hospital, 47 Ill. 2d 443, 266 N.E. 2d 897 (1970); see also 45 *A.L.R.* 3d 1353. But see Carmichael v. Reitz, 17 Cal. App. 3d 958, 95 Cal. Rptr. 381 (1971) which states the general rule exempting physicians from strict liability because they perform professional services.
10. See for example, Hart v. Steele, 416 S.W. 2d 927 (Mo. 1967) and King v. Flamm, 442 S.W. 2d 679 (Tex. 1969). At least one state imposes no higher degree of care than that which it requires of general practitioners. Grosjean v. Spencer, 258 Iowa 685, 140 N.W. 2d 139 (1966).
11. Phillip E. Hassman, "Coverage and Exclusions Under Hospital Professional Liability or Indemnity Policy," 65 *A.L.R.* 3rd 969.
12. The exposure of radioactive contamination to property can be insured through the use of the limited or broad form radioactive assumption endorsements for use with fire policies or through the use of radioactive contamination forms which are available for use with inland marine forms. These coverage forms are discussed more fully in CPCU 3.
13. Aetna Life & Casualty, February 1973.
14. See Chapter 5 under the heading "Construction Management." Construction management professional liability insurance is available as described in the *F.C.&S. Bulletins*, Management & Sales Section, Surveys Cm 7-9.
15. Norbert A. Drake, "Adjusting and Defending Claims Under Architects' and Engineers' Professional Liability Policies," *Adjusters Reference Guide* (Louisville: Insurance Field Company), Liability—23.
16. SEC v. National Student Marketing, Inc., 402 F. Supp. (D. D.C. 1975).

17. Duke Nordlinger Stern, Ph.D., "Avoiding Legal Malpractice Claims," *Legal Malpractice Review*, February-March 1978 (St. Paul: St. Paul Fire and Marine Insurance Company).
18. Ill. Rev. Stat. Ch. 127, Sec. 58.01-58.11 (1975).
19. Ernst & Ernst v. Hochfelder, 425 U.S. 185 (1976).

CHAPTER 11

Special Liability Exposures and Their Treatment

INTRODUCTION

Since virtually every legal liability exposure has a quality, character, or identity of its own, there is a sense in which every liability exposure is "special." Nonetheless, for want of a better generic title for this chapter, the term "special" is used simply as a convenient label for the grouping of selected liability exposures which merit separate discussion but do not fit neatly into traditional categories. Specifically, the chapter is devoted to a consideration of the liability exposures associated with corporate officers and directors, environmental pollution, employee benefit programs, data processing, and the foreign operations of domestic companies. Within each of these areas, to the extent that space permits, emphasis is placed upon the general nature of the exposures and the corresponding liability insurance coverages, followed by a brief description of noninsurance treatment techniques that may be applied.

DIRECTORS' AND OFFICERS' LIABILITY

A corporation provides a mechanism for the centralized management of labor and capital and shields the personal assets of stockholders from the claims of third parties. The stockholders of the corporation delegate the management of corporate affairs almost entirely to the board of *directors,* which, in turn, elects *officers* to manage the daily operations of the corporation.

Corporate officers and directors are being exposed, at an ever-increasing rate, to lawsuits resulting from alleged violations of their corporate duties and responsibilities. In this age of litigation, officers and directors have become (often undeservedly) the targets of claims by parties who allege that they have suffered as a result of negligent or illegal acts by corporate officials. Instances of corporate wrongdoing often receive a great deal of public attention, as witnessed by the recent publicity surrounding corporate bribery and payoffs to foreign governments and officials. Because of the publicity surrounding real or alleged misdeeds, officers and directors of corporations must be extra mindful of and attentive to the duties and responsibilities they owe, not only to their shareholders, but also to interested third parties and to the general public.

Directors' and Officers' Liability Exposures

In order to fully understand and appreciate the various liabilities to which officers and directors may be exposed, it is essential to recognize and comprehend the nature of their legal duties vis-à-vis the corporation they serve and its constituent shareholders. After an analysis of the legal duties of directors and officers, we will examine the acts which may subject officers and directors to liability, types of legal actions which may be brought, and damages that may result.

Legal Duties of Officers and Directors The duties and responsibilities of officers and directors are prescribed for the most part by various state statutes which, although couched in differing terms, essentially set forth the same governing principles. For example, under Section 717 of the New York Business Corporation Law it is stated that:

> Directors and officers shall discharge the duties of their respective positions in good faith and with that degree of diligence, care and skill which ordinarily prudent men would exercise under similar circumstances in like positions. . . .[1]

It is generally held that officers and directors occupy a fiduciary relationship to the corporation and its stockholders. As part of their fiduciary obligations to the corporation, the officers and directors owe the following duties: (1) *diligence*—the duty to exercise due care in the management of the corporation's business and to avoid being negligent; (2) *loyalty*—the duty to refrain from engaging in personal activity in such a manner as to injure or take advantage of the corporation, or, in other words, the duty to refrain from self-dealing; and (3) *obedience*—the duty not to permit the corporation to engage in illegal acts or acts beyond the power of the corporation.

Duty of Diligence. Consistent with the standard of due care and diligence, officers and directors have a duty to keep themselves informed of corporate developments and to be knowledgeable concerning the corporation's business and activities.[2] In a landmark case decided by the New York Court of Appeals, the court, in defining the duties of a director, stated that he was bound to exercise not only proper care and diligence but also ordinary skill and judgment, and that gross ignorance was no excuse for damage caused by his lack of judgment.[3]

Familiarity by the director with the provisions of the corporate charter and bylaws is indispensable in carrying out the director's duties. As one court has held, the director owes a "stewardship obligation to the corporation and its stockholders" which entails the selection of qualified officers, particularly the chief executive, and supervision of officers' activities.[4]

While most courts, in defining the duty of due care imposed upon a director, equate the standard with the duty to refrain from committing acts of ordinary negligence, some courts apply a less stringent standard and hold a director liable only for "gross" negligence, which is sometimes defined as a willful failure to perform a manifest duty with a reckless disregard of the consequences.[5] On the other hand, some courts hold a director liable for mismanagement only if the director is guilty of actual or constructive fraud.[6]

Duty of Loyalty. Distinct from the duty of diligence is the duty of loyalty or, as the latter is sometimes phrased, the duty to avoid conflicts of interest. Corporate officers and directors "must devote themselves to corporate affairs with a view to promote the common interests and not their own. They cannot, either directly or indirectly, utilize their position to obtain any personal profit or advantage other than that enjoyed also by their fellow shareholders."[7]

The duty of loyalty encompasses the duty to avoid self-dealing with respect to corporate transactions in which directors receive private profits for themselves. Such private profits are recoverable by the corporation, and it is immaterial if the transaction itself was advantageous to the corporation,[8] because the potential conflict of interest creates the possibility of a compromise of a director's duties to the corporation.[9] On this subject, a Pennsylvania court has stated that an officer or director of a corporation must furnish to it his or her undivided loyalty and cannot seize a business opportunity advantageous to the corporation and within the scope of its activities.[10] A fiduciary, however, is not generally precluded from engaging on his or her own behalf in a profitable business opportunity that is outside the scope of his or her corporation's normal business.[11] But even if the opportunity is one outside the scope of the corporation's normal business, the fiduciary may be required to present the opportunity to the corporation if it has some relation to the corporate activity or to a corporate need.[12]

In some states, the duty of loyalty is prescribed by statute. For example, Section 309 of the new California Corporations Code sets forth the requirement that directors perform their duties:

> . . . in good faith, in a manner such director believes to be in the best interests of the corporation and with such care, including reasonable inquiry, as an ordinarily prudent person in a like position would use under similar circumstances.[13]

The statutory standard encompasses both the directors' duty of loyalty to the corporation and the directors' duty of care in managing the corporate affairs. "Good faith," in the context of the director-corporation relationship, has been judicially defined as a "state of mind denoting honesty of the purpose, freedom from intention to defraud, and, generally speaking, . . . being faithful to one's duty or obligation."[14] The cornerstone of the fiduciary duty is the prohibition against any sort of personal gain from one's activities as director unless all who have an interest in the corporation are informed and have consented.[15]

Many states have also legislated standards governing the validity of transactions entered into between a corporation and a director or officer. These statutes generally provide that a contract or transaction between a corporation and a director or officer shall not be void or voidable for that reason alone if the transaction is approved by a vote of disinterested directors with a knowledge of the material facts or if the transaction is approved by the stockholders with knowledge of the material facts. If neither of these tests is met, the contract or transaction is voidable unless the officer or director establishes affirmatively that it is fair to the corporation.[16]

Duty of Obedience. The third duty owed by a director to the corporation is the duty of obedience, which contemplates that *ultra vires* corporate activities are to be avoided. (*Ultra vires* activities are those activities beyond the express or implied powers of the corporation or those illegal or contrary to public policy.[17]) "Directors are supposed to contain their activities within the powers conferred upon them by the articles of incorporation and code of regulations."[18] If the corporation does commit an *ultra vires* act, a corporate officer or director may be held liable.[19] It is essential, therefore, that directors be familiar with the provisions of the corporate charter and bylaws.

Duties of Inside Directors Vis-à-vis Outside Directors. Directors are not all treated alike. Some courts have drawn a distinction between "inside" and "outside" directors when judging whether the director has fulfilled his or her responsibilities towards the corporation and its shareholders. Traditionally, an *inside director* is one who is also part of the corporation's management. As such, the inside director-manager is charged with the daily operation of the corporation and is subject to the supervision of the entire board of directors. *Outside directors*, on the other hand, are not full-time employees of the corporation, and they are not involved in managing its day-to-day operations. Another type of director, known as the *professional or specialist director*, is frequently characterized as an outside director who is expected, usually for additional compensation, to spend more time on the affairs of the corporation than the typical outside director. In view of the expertise possessed by the specialist director, he or she is usually held to a higher standard of care than the ordinary director.

The respective duties of inside and outside directors have generally been described and defined in the context of securities law violations, and the Securities and Exchange Commission (SEC) has been a leading force in defining and enforcing these duties. Although the duties and liabilities of directors under the Federal Securities Acts are treated more extensively later in this chapter,[20] it may be of interest to comment briefly on the attitudes of the SEC on this subject. In the "Report of Investigation in the matter of Stirling Homex Corp. relating to activities of the Board of Directors of Stirling Homex Corp.,"[21] it was stated that outside directors violate their duty to protect shareholders if their presence has no impact whatever on the company's operations or affairs. The commission remarked that an outside director could not blindly rely on the fact that the corporation employs accountants, lawyers, investment bankers, and other professionals. It also noted that directors should familiarize themselves with the company's business and should question management in more than a perfunctory manner, whereas management should make available to outside directors sufficient information concerning corporate affairs to enable them to discharge their responsibilities adequately.

Duties of Officers Vis-à-vis Directors. Although the standards of conduct described above will apply, for the most part, to officers as well as directors, the courts have drawn certain distinctions concerning the duties of a corporate officer vis-à-vis a director. This is based upon the fact that a nonofficer director of a corporation is not required to devote the same amount of attention to the business as an officer of the same corporation, nor would he or she be likely to receive the same compensation.[22] For example, the president—an officer of a corporation—is generally expected to exercise a more personal supervision than an ordinary director.[23] Likewise, since the duties of an officer such as a general manager are more extensive than those of a mere director, the general manager's liability for misdeeds of subordinates, based upon their negligence, is more extensive than the liability of a mere director for like misdeeds.[24]

Stated another way, directors and officers share responsibility for management, but their functions are by no means the same. Officers have a more direct responsibility for the operation of the business than directors who are not officers. The latter are entitled to rely upon the officers' reports of the corporation's affairs in the absence of reasonable grounds to believe that such reports are erroneous. Moreover, nonofficer directors who cannot spend more than a limited amount of their time on the affairs of the corporation normally will not be held to the same degree of accountability as officers.[25] In applying different standards of conduct to a corporate officer and director, one court held an officer liable to the corporation when the officer engaged in a competing enterprise. The court stated that since *officers* are generally engaged upon a full-time, best-efforts basis on behalf of their corporation, their efforts on behalf of a competing enterprise necessarily detracted from the corporation's business, not only because of the usual effects of such competition but also because the time and effort they devoted to the competing enterprise was lost to the corporation. In this respect, the court commented that the position of a mere *director*, i.e., one who is not also an officer, was different. The court indicated that the time and efforts of an outside director would be primarily engaged elsewhere, and that when he became involved in a second competing enterprise, the effect upon the first company was no different from that of a third-party competitor, assuming, of course, that the director acted in good faith and did not use information gained from his relationship to the company to its disadvantage and for the benefit of his competing business.[26]

Summary. In summary, it may be fairly stated that the specific duties a court will impose upon an officer or director will depend upon the particular facts and circumstances involved. The kind of corporation, its size and financial resources, the magnitude of the transaction, the participation or nonparticipation of the officer or director in the transaction, and the extent of injury or damage involved are all factors that are taken into account. As one court has stated, a director (or officer) is called upon to "bestow the care and skill which the situation demands."[27]

Acts Subjecting Corporate Officers and Directors to Liability
The preceding section dealt with the duties imposed upon corporate officers and directors by either statute or common law. In this section, we will examine some of the legal theories upon which corporate officers and directors *have been held liable* to corporations, shareholders, and third parties for breach of their corporate duties.

Negligence. A corporation, being a legal entity created by law, can only act and conduct business through its agents—including its directors, officers, and employees. The liability of officers and directors to the corporation (for damages caused by negligent or unauthorized acts) rests upon the common-law rule, which renders liable every agent who violates his or her authority or neglects his or her duty to the damage of his or her principal.[28] As will be seen from the cases recited below, some courts draw a distinction between ordinary and gross negligence and hold the officer or director liable only for the commission of an act constituting gross negligence. Whether these cases would retain their validity in the present day may be open to some question. In any event, it is often contended that the conduct of all officers and directors should be judged by the application of ordinary negligence principles, and they should be held liable for any violation of the standards of due care and diligence.

STANDARDS OF NEGLIGENT CONDUCT. Before considering cases dealing specifically with negligence of corporate officials, it may be helpful to review some of the guidelines that courts have utilized to determine the standards of negligent conduct. There is no inflexible rule in defining what is or is not negligent conduct, because each case must be decided on its own facts. Generally speaking, however, the degree of care required is the ordinary care that would be exercised by reasonably prudent men under the circumstances.

Ordinary Care. In determining the standard of ordinary care, two general tests have been applied. The first test is the care *of ordinary prudence required in the exercise of one's own affairs.*[29] The second test, which is the one applied in most jurisdictions, is that an officer or director is required to use not the degree of care in the exercise of his or her own affairs, but the ordinary care of a *director or officer of a corporation in a like position* or under similar circumstances. The second test, held to be a more fair and satisfactory rule, is the rule adopted by the Supreme Court of the United States.[30] In the landmark case of Briggs v. Spaulding,[31] the Supreme Court of the United States held that directors of a bank were not insurers of the fidelity of agents whom they had appointed, nor were they responsible for losses resulting from the agent's negligence, unless the loss was a consequence of neglecting their own duty either to supervise the business adequately or to use proper care in the appointment of the agents. The court further stated that directors of a bank, in managing bank affairs, must exercise such degree of care as ordinarily prudent and diligent persons would exercise under the circumstances.

Standard of Negligence. In determining the standard of negligence, the nature and character of the business being conducted by the corporation may be of significance. For example, a higher standard of care may be imposed upon the director of a bank than upon the director of an ordinary corporation. Also, the standard of negligence may be prescribed by statute or limited by charter.

EXAMPLES. The following are specific examples of negligent acts for which the corporate officer or director was held liable. In one case, the president of a corporation who willingly or unintentionally, but by culpable negligence, received forged municipal bonds in exchange for the stock of the corporation was held personally liable for the loss.[32] Bank directors have been held guilty of negligence in paying dividends when the capital of the company was seriously impaired, when the reserves were deficient, and when the surplus and guaranty were adversely affected.[33] In another situation, the court found a director liable for the sale of assets of the corporation for an amount substantially less than the cost to the corporation and without the payment of any cash or assets or the furnishing of any security by the purchaser. The court stated that the directors of the corporation were liable for permitting the corporate funds or property to be lost or wasted by their gross or culpable negligence.

In one case dealing with mismanagement by an employee of a corporation, the court stated that a corporate director who fails to acquire the information necessary to supervise investment policy, or who consistently fails to attend meetings at which such policies are considered, has violated his or her fiduciary duty to the corporation. The court held the director liable, not under any theory of *respondeat superior*, but independently liable by virtue of his own negligent act.[34] Along the same lines, a director cannot escape liability merely by selecting able and apparently trustworthy persons to manage the business, and then pay no attention to corporate affairs.[35] One may also be held liable when he or she recklessly appoints an officer who is untrustworthy or incompetent.[36]

As alluded to previously, directors of a banking corporation have been held to a higher standard of care than directors of an ordinary corporation.[37] On the same subject, reference should be made to the National Bank Act,[38] which provides in part that directors who shall knowingly violate any provisions of the act shall be personally liable for all damages that the bank, its shareholders, or any other person shall have sustained in consequence of such violation.

A director has also been held liable for failure to attend meetings of the board of directors, as well as for failure to keep abreast of corporate developments.[39] In a case involving the negligent mismanagement of funds, the court found directors liable for spending excessive amounts on a plant that was totally unsuited for production, the purchase having resulted in the corporation's insolvency.[40] In the same vein, courts have held directors liable for negligently permitting the officers and employees to misappropriate corporate assets[41] and for failing to carefully supervise major corporate changes such as mergers, sales, or purchases involving substantial assets.[42]

A frequent source of directors' liability is the negligent or illegal payment of dividends.[43] In most states there are statutory limitations on dividend distributions. The statutes, generally speaking, fall into one of two categories: (1) those which provide that dividends may be paid only out of the surplus shown on the balance sheet, i.e., the excess of assets over liabilities, plus stated capital (the balance sheet test); and (2) those which provide that dividends may be paid only out of current or past net profits (the net profits test, sometimes called the earned surplus test).[44] The New York statute makes directors liable for the declaration of dividends in violation of the statute, but provides a defense for the director who has discharged his statutory duty of due care and good faith.[45]

BUSINESS JUDGMENT RULE. In considering the question of whether a corporation officer or director has been negligent in the performance of duties, the courts have sometimes been faced with the application of what is generally known as the "business judgment rule." Some courts have utilized the rule to shield negligent corporate officials from liability. Essentially, the business judgment rule provides that, in the absence of fraud, breach of trust, or the commission of an *ultra vires* act, the conduct of directors is not subject to attack if the challenged acts are discretionary and are performed in good faith with a reasonable belief that they are in the best interests of the corporation.[46]

Some courts have reconciled the conflict between the business judgment rule and the standard of due care required by stating that the business judgment rule is applicable only where directors have acted with reasonable prudence.[47] It is not applicable when the loss results from the failure to exercise proper care and diligence.[48] In any event, the business judgment rule continues to be cited by the courts as a reason for not interfering with the judgment of a board of directors.[49]

Breach of the Duty of Loyalty. Of the various duties that corporate officers and directors owe to their corporations and shareholders, the duty of loyalty best exemplifies the fiduciary nature of the obligations imposed upon corporate officials. Jealously guarding the corporate right to loyalty from management officials, the courts ordered such officials to turn over any private or secret profits they may have recovered in corporate transactions, regardless of whether the corporation was injured or whether the transaction was, in fact, favorable to the corporation.[50] The following cases provide examples of violations of the duty of loyalty owed by corporate officers and directors.

A director purchased property for himself, knowing that the corporation wanted it, and then resold it to the corporation. The director was required by the court to transfer the property to the corporation at cost.[51] In another case, a vice-president and general manager of a corporation, knowing of the corporation's desire to buy a quantity of asphalt, contracted to buy the asphalt himself in order to make a personal profit from the resale to the corporation. The court found the official liable to the corporation, stating that it was the official's duty to obtain the asphalt for his corporation on the most advantageous terms possible. He was not allowed to make a secret profit out of the transaction.[52]

A corollary to the principle prohibiting self-dealing among corporate officers and directors is the principle prohibiting them from seizing for themselves a corporate opportunity within the scope of the corporation's own activities and of potential advantage to it.[53] However, it has been held that a director violates no legal or moral duty to the corporation merely by engaging in a competitive enterprise if the profits made therein are not deemed to have been made at the expense of the corporation.[54] Though a director is generally permitted to compete, any conduct beyond mere normal competition may not be permissible. For example, it has been held that an officer or director who, to the detriment of his or her corporation, actively engages in a rival or competing business is liable to the corporation for the injury it sustains,[55] and, solicitation of the corporation's customers for a rival business goes beyond the scope of permissible conduct.[56]

It may be expected that *directors* who are not also officers will engage in business activities outside the scope of the corporation's business, but an *officer* normally is required to devote full time and energy to the affairs of the corporation. Accordingly, any outside activity that may detract from an officer's obligations to the corporation may constitute a breach of duty, especially when the outside activity is of a competitive nature. In one case, the president of a company organized a second company which, while not in direct competition with the first company, did require him to spend considerable time in managing the business of the second company. The court, in an action brought by the president for reinstatement to his position as president of the first company, held that the defendant corporation was not required to "endure the unfaithful officer and employee while he diverted to a rival the business he might have obtained for the corporation had he employed his best efforts in its behalf."[57] However, if the new business or transaction engaged in by the officer or director is clearly noncompetitive and the officer does not otherwise breach any duty owed to the corporation, there is no liability.[58] Nevertheless, once a conflict of interest is present, liability may be found, even though the officer or director, in good faith, exercised due care and honest business judgment, since the duty of undivided loyalty is held to be paramount.[59]

Contractual Liability. A corporate officer or director may also be exposed to liability arising from the officer's having entered into a contractual relationship on behalf of his or her corporation. In the law of agency, the general rule is that if a corporate officer or director makes an authorized contract *in the name of the corporation* so as to bind the corporation, the contract is with the corporation only. The other party to the contract cannot hold the officer personally liable. But, when the agent enters into a contract in his or her own name for an *undisclosed principal*, the other party to the contract may hold the agent personally liable. Moreover, if the agent acts in excess of authority so that the principal is not bound, the agent will be liable, provided the other party did not know of the agent's lack of authority—even if the agent acted with due care.[60]

An agent may not escape personal liability merely by notifying the third person that he or she is acting in a representative capacity. The identity of his or her principal must be disclosed.[61] In a leading case holding an agent personally liable, the court commented that the fact that the contract was negotiated by an agent under a trade name was not of itself a sufficient disclosure of agency. Furthermore, the court indicated that the fact that the plaintiff had dealt with the corporation on previous occasions did not preclude a finding that, in the transaction at issue, he contracted with the agent in his individual capacity.[62]

Ultra Vires Acts. Even though an officer or director may have exercised due care and diligence, he or she may be held liable if he or she engaged in activities outside the scope of the express or implied powers of the corporation.[63] *Ultra vires* acts for which corporate officials have been held liable include the use of corporate funds to speculate in the commodities market and the making of payments to the widow of a deceased officer, without any valid consideration.[64]

Violation of Antitrust Laws. Corporate officers and directors may also be held liable for violating both state and federal antitrust laws. In the case of United States v. Wise,[65] the Supreme Court of the United States ruled that a corporate officer may be criminally prosecuted under Section 1 of the Sherman Antitrust Act[66] if, while acting on behalf of the company, he or she knowingly participates in effecting an illegal contract, combination or conspiracy, regardless of whether he or she authorizes, orders, or helps perpetrate the crime or whether acting in a representative capacity.[67]

Under Section 14 of the Clayton Act,[68] when a corporation violates any of the penal provisions of the antitrust law, "such violation shall be deemed to be also that of the individual directors, officers or agents of such corporation who shall have authorized, ordered, or done any of the acts constituting such violation in whole or in part."[69] Of course, an officer can also be held liable for violation of a state antitrust act[70] and can be held liable in damages to the corporation itself.[71]

Criminal Liability. Corporate officers may be criminally liable for their own acts, whether or not such acts are performed in their official capacity as corporate officers.[72] Moreover, it is no defense in a criminal prosecution that the officer was ordered by the corporate management to perform the criminal act.[73]

As a general rule, an officer will be held criminally liable only when the crime charged involved his or her knowledge of guilt or criminal intent or the officer actually and personally participated in the acts which constituted the offense, or the acts were committed at his or her direction or with his or her permission.[74] But in a case involving the violation of the federal Food, Drug and Cosmetic Act, the Supreme Court of the United States found the president of a drug company liable for violations of the act, even though he did not personally participate in the unlawful conduct.[75] This case is cited to convey the general principle that the directing heads of a corporation may be held liable for such unlawful acts of subordinates as are committed in the normal course of business, regardless of whether or not the directing heads personally supervised the particular acts involved or were personally present at the time and place of the commission of those acts. In a 1974 ruling by the United States Supreme Court, the court held the president of a supermarket chain criminally liable for the violation of a federal regulatory statute and stated that liability under the statute did not turn on conscious fraud or awareness of wrongdoing, but rather that the statute permitted the conviction of a responsible corporate official who had the power to prevent or correct violations. It is not necessary that the corporate official personally participate in the situation to be held liable, the court remarked, if it can be proven beyond a reasonable doubt that he or she "had a responsible relation to the situation."[76]

The laws of every state have statutes which prohibit certain conduct by corporate officials. Although reference must be made to each particular statute for the nature of the specific offenses prohibited, it may be helpful to list briefly a few representative state statutes and the kinds of conduct they declare unlawful. For example, an Ohio statute prohibits the issuing of false statements, prospectuses or reports by an officer or director of a corporation,[77] as well as unlawful loans, dividends or distribution of assets.[78] A New York statute declares it to be a misdemeanor for a director to concur knowingly in any vote or act of the directors by which it is intended to pay a dividend, except in the manner provided by law; or to divide, withdraw, or pay to any stockholder any of the capital stock, except in a manner provided by law; or to discount or receive a note or other evidence of debt to pay for an installment of the capital stock; or to use corporate funds to purchase its stock, except in the manner provided by law.[79]

Fraud. Officers and directors owe the corporation and its stockholders the duty of honesty and good faith and will be held liable for the commission of fraudulent acts even though they may be acting for the benefit of the corporation.[80] Funds of a corporation can be used only for corporate purposes. If funds are misapplied by directors, they will be held personally liable to the corporation for any loss caused thereby.[81]

Situations in which corporate officers or directors have been held liable for fraud include (1) the issuance of a large amount of stock to the officers for a grossly inadequate consideration,[82] (2) a sale of corporate property without authority,[83] and (3) the payment of attorneys' fees from corporate funds for services rendered to directors in an individual capacity.[84]

Violation of Securities Laws. Directors' and officers' liability has seen particularly rapid development in the field of securities law violations, i.e., violations of state "blue sky" laws and violations of the Securities Act of 1933[85] and the Securities Exchange Act of 1934.[86] Though it would be impossible to present a full and comprehensive treatment of this subject in the limited space available, its overwhelming significance requires at least a brief recognition of the particular sections of the securities acts that impose liability upon officers and directors, and some reference to several significant court decisions in this respect.

STATE LAWS. Despite the inroads of federal statutory and common law on this subject, the states still retain jurisdiction and control over securities transactions that fall outside the scope of federal review. Various state statutes prohibit certain conduct in the issuance, purchase, and sale of securities. When Kansas passed the first such act in 1911, a state congressman commented that the laws should prevent unscrupulous stock sellers from "promising the blue sky" to unsuspecting citizens.[87] The so-called "blue sky" statutes often specifically provide that a sale of securities is voidable at the purchaser's election if there is a statutory violation, and those personally participating or aiding in the sale are liable to the purchaser for the amount paid.[88] Since the provisions of "blue sky" statutes vary substantially from state to state, the law governing a given transaction must be consulted to determine the extent of the officer's or director's responsibility in a particular situation.

SECURITIES ACT OF 1933. The Securities Act of 1933 deals primarily with the distribution of new issues and securities. The purpose of the act is to provide the prospective investor with full and accurate data with which to judge the respective chances of financial loss and gain of the proposed investment. It accomplishes this purpose by requiring the filing with the Securities and Exchange Commission of a registration statement which contains information concerning the corporation's business and affairs. The registration statement is made available to the public, thus allowing prospective investors the opportunity to judge for themselves the desirability of the investment.

The basic liability section of the 1933 Act, Section 11,[89] provides that if a registration statement, at the time it became effective, "contained an untrue statement of a material fact or omitted to state a material fact required to be stated therein or necessary to make the statements therein not misleading, any person acquiring such security" may sue, among others, every person who signed the registration statement, every person who is a director of the corporation when the registration statement was filed, and every person who has consented to be named in a registration statement as a person who is to become a director.

A plaintiff who shows a misstatement or omission in the registration statement, and can show that it is material, will have established a case. There are, however, three defenses available to any defendant other than the issuer, and the most important is the so-called *due diligence defense.*

The due diligence defense involves different standards of diligence, depending upon whether or not the defendant in question is an expert and whether the error or omission occurred in an expertized—for example, a financial statement—or a nonexpertized part of the registration statement. To prove due diligence with respect to the nonexpertized part of the registration statement, the defendant must show that he or she made a "reasonable investigation" and that he or she had "reasonable ground to believe and did believe" that there were no material misstatements or omissions in the registration statement. It is this requirement of a *reasonable investigation* that is commonly referred to as the duty of due diligence.

With respect to the expertized part of the registration statement, the *expert* on whose authority it is made must show that he or she made a "reasonable investigation" and that he or she had a "reasonable ground to believe and did believe" that there were no material misstatements or misrepresentations in this part of the registration statement. Any defendant *other than an expert* on whose authority it was made must show only that he or she "had no reasonable ground to believe, and did not believe" that there were material misrepresentations or omissions in the registration statement.

A leading case describing the duties and obligations of directors under Section 11 of the Securities Act of 1933 is Escott v. Bar Chris Construction Corporation.[90] This case is important because of its analysis and application of the Section 11 defenses and its description of the standard of care required of a person attempting to take advantage of those defenses.[91] The case involved a class action brought by purchasers of convertible debentures. The plaintiffs asserted that the registration statement included material false statements and omitted other material facts as well.

The Bar Chris court divided the director-officer defendants into three categories for the purposes of analysis. The first category was the corporate insiders, including the company president, who, the court decided, because of intimate knowledge of the corporation's business, must have known that the registration statement contained material misstatements. The second category consisted of those defendants who were actively involved in the process of preparing the registration statement although they did not have factual knowledge of the misstatements. The third category was the outside directors who had no actual knowledge of the facts and played no part in drafting the registration statement. In its decision, the court held the defendants in all three categories liable, but the court distinguished among the degrees of diligence that were required of each.

Since the defendants in the first category had actual knowledge of the misstatements, the court held that they had no possible defense. Because of their key role in drafting the registration statement, the court imposed upon the defendants in the second category a higher duty of diligence than it did upon the defendants in the third category, and it indicated that if the second category defendants had been reasonably diligent, they would have discovered many of the errors. With respect to the outside directors, less was expected of them than of the other defendants; nevertheless, the court held that they were required to exercise some degree of diligence. (In fact, they had done virtually nothing.)

Following the decision of Bar Chris, the court, in Feit v. Leasco Data Processing Equipment Corp.,[92] again had the opportunity to interpret the due diligence defense under Section 11, and also drew a distinction between duties owed by outside and inside directors. The case involved a class action suit seeking damages in connection with a registered exchange offer, and the defendants included the issuing corporation and three individual director defendants, two of whom were also chief executive officers. The court interpreted Bar Chris as requiring "independent verification of the registration statement by reference to original written records" and concluded that the liability of the inside directors approached that of the issuer as guarantor of the accuracy of the prospectus. The court found that the directors both lacked reasonable ground to believe in the accuracy of the registration statement and failed in their duty to make a reasonable investigation into the facts.

Although Section 11, just discussed, is the most important part of the 1933 Act, directors and officers can also be held liable under Section 12(1) of the act, which provides that any person who offers or sells a security in violation of Section 5 of the act (which requires sales of securities to be registered unless an exemption is available) shall be liable to the person purchasing such securities from him or her.[93] Section 12(2) of the act provides that any person who offers or sells a security in interstate commerce (whether or not the security is exempt from registration) by means of a prospectus or oral communication containing a material untruth or omission shall be liable to the person purchasing such securities.[94]

Liability under the Securities Act of 1933 can also be found under Section 17(a), which basically makes it unlawful to sell securities by means of a fraudulent device or material misrepresentation or omission.[95]

SECURITIES EXCHANGE ACT OF 1934. By far the most prolific source of litigation involving officers' and directors' liability under the federal securities laws can be found under Section 10(b) of the Securities Exchange Act of 1934[96] and Rule 10b-5 promulgated thereunder.[97] Essentially, Section 10(b) makes it unlawful "to use or employ, in connection with the purchase or sale of any security . . . any manipulative or deceptive device or contrivance in contravention" of the Commission's rules. Rule 10b-5 makes it unlawful

> for any person, directly or indirectly, by the use of any means or instrumentality of interstate commerce, or of the mails or of any facility of any national securities exchange, (a) To employ any device, scheme, or artifice to defraud; (b) To make any untrue statement of a material fact or to omit to state a material fact necessary in order to make the statements made, in the light of the circumstances under which they were made, not misleading; or (c) To engage in any act, practice, or course of business which operates or would operate as a fraud or deceit upon any person, in connection with the purchase or sale of any security.

In the famous case of Securities and Exchange Commission v. Texas Gulf Sulphur Co.,[98] the United States Court of Appeals for the Second Circuit found various defendant officers and directors liable for purchasing shares of Texas Gulf Sulphur stock without disclosing material inside information—a rich copper strike in Canada. Under a settlement formula, the defendants were required to pay into court the profits received from their purchases of stock.

In another case involving a 10b-5 violation, the court held that a director, in his capacity as a director (a nonparticipant in the transaction), owes no duty to insure that all material adverse information is conveyed to prospective purchasers of the stock of the corporation on whose board he sits.[99] In Ernst & Ernst v. Hochfelder,[100] the Supreme Court held that *scienter* (knowledge of fraud) is required in a Rule 10b-5 action. However, the Supreme Court reserved its decision on whether a reckless misrepresentation made without any basis upon which to judge truth or falsity would violate the rule.

Although Section 10(b) of the act imposes only criminal liability, it was soon recognized as the basis for a civil action.[101] It is generally held that Rule 10b-5 does not apply to all the kinds of deception that are commonly found in "fraudulent mismanagement of corporate affairs,"[102] but the fact that a securities transaction is part of a larger scheme of corporate mismanagement will not bar a federal action under Rule 10b-5.[103]

Other situations in which the courts have found directors and officers to have violated the Securities Exchange Act of 1934 include the making of unduly low payments to stockholders in connection with a merger,[104] the purchase of shares from insiders at too high a price,[105] the issuance of shares to insiders at too low a price,[106] and the sale of control under circumstances detrimental to future prospects of the corporation.[107]

In contrast to the aforementioned actions, it has been stated that claims of corporate mismanagement or the breach of fiduciary duty are not of themselves violations of Section 10(b) and Rule 10b-5, in cases where the sale of securities is only incidental to a major mismanagement issue cognizable primarily under state law.[108] The general rule appears to be that "where the duty allegedly breached is only the general duty existing among corporate officers, directors, and shareholders, no cause of action is stated under Rule 10b-5 unless there is an allegation of fact amounting to a deception."[109] As the Sixth Circuit has said, to do otherwise would "open the door to federal jurisdiction in claims for damages against corporate directors and officers arising out of breach of their fiduciary duties."[110]

Section 16(b) of the Securities Exchange Act of 1934 has also been used to hold corporate officers and directors liable in purchasing or selling securities of their corporations. This section essentially provides that a director or officer or beneficial owner of more than 10 percent of any class of any equity security of an issuer is liable to the corporation for the profit realized within a six-month period from a purchase and sale—or a sale and purchase—of any equity security of the corporation. This standard is applicable whether or not insider information was actually available, obtained, or utilized.[111]

Yet another source of considerable litigation has been Section 14(a) of the 1934 Act,[112] which makes it unlawful for any person to solicit proxies in violation of SEC rules and regulations. Under Rule 14a-9[113] promulgated thereunder, officers and directors have been held liable for issuing false or misleading statements in proxy solicitation materials.[114] And there are several other provisions of the federal securities laws that impose liability upon corporate officers and directors for certain violations stated thereunder.[115]

Types of Legal Actions There are two broad types of legal actions that may be brought against corporate officers and directors: (1) nonderivative or third-party actions and (2) derivative actions of shareholders. Each will be considered in turn.

Nonderivative or Third-Party Actions. Third parties include, for example, a creditor, a competitor, a government agency, or a stockholder, as distinguished from the corporate entity. If such a third party is damaged as a result of an officer's or director's breach of duty, the remedy is by way of a third-party action. The general rule holds that a corporate officer or director, like any other person, is personally liable for all torts he or she commits, notwithstanding that he or she may have acted in a representative capacity as an agent for his or her principal. It is immaterial that the corporation may also be held liable.[116] However, an officer or director cannot be personally liable for the torts attributable to the corporation merely by reason of his or her office; it must be shown that he or she personally participated in the tort.[117]

With respect to officers' and directors' negligence liability to third parties, some courts draw a distinction between acts of misfeasance and acts of nonfeasance, in which case the officer or director is held liable only for acts of misfeasance.[118] Misfeasance is generally defined as the performance of an act in an improper manner, and nonfeasance as failure to perform an act one has the duty to perform. However, it would appear to be the better rule that, regardless of whether the act is classified as misfeasance or nonfeasance, the officer or director should be held liable if his or her breach of a duty owed to the plaintiff proximately caused the damages alleged.[119]

CREDITORS. As mentioned, creditors of a corporation may assert a third-party action for damages sustained. In one such instance, officer-directors were held personally liable to a payee for causing issuance of a corporate check when they knew or should have known that there were insufficient funds in the bank to cover the check.[120] However, some cases hold that directors and officers will not be liable to creditors for mere negligent mismanagement; there must be fraudulent or intentional conduct resulting in injury to the creditor to sustain an action.[121]

On the other hand, there are cases which support the proposition that if the injury is to the corporation, the creditor is not the proper party to bring suit. In one such case, the court determined that directors, as agents of the corporation's stockholders, are accountable only to their principal, whereas the creditors of the corporation are strangers to the obligation owed by the directors to the corporation.[122] Thus, in order to sustain a cause of action by the creditor for mismanagement or for wasted assets, commission of actual fraud must be proven, not just negligent mismanagement.[123] Directors have also been held liable to creditors of a corporation when the directors willfully or negligently misapplied the assets of the corporation by the payment of dividends, and there were no surplus profits out of which they could lawfully be paid.[124]

Under the statutes in some states, directors who engage in certain prohibited acts may be held jointly and severally liable to the corporation for the benefit of its creditors to the extent of any injury suffered by such persons.[125]

STOCKHOLDERS. A stockholder may sue a corporate officer if a wrong has been done to him or her individually, as distinguished from a wrong done to the corporation. For example, a stockholder who purchases stock in reliance on false representations of a director or officer may sue such officer or director in an action in tort.[126] On the other hand, if the injury is primarily inflicted upon the corporation, the appropriate remedy would be a stockholders' derivative suit (to be discussed below).

OTHER THIRD PARTIES. Other third parties also may sue officers and directors for a violation of their duties. In Spivek v. United States,[127] certain officers were held liable to the U.S. Government for failing to pay federal withholding and social security taxes, and, as indicated previously, the government may bring suit against corporate officials for violation of the federal antitrust laws[128] or other federal statutes.[129]

Competitors may also sue officers and directors for violation of antitrust laws,[130] as well as for violation of the securities laws.[131]

Stockholders' Derivative Actions. The liabilities of a corporate officer or director may arise from suits brought by shareholders *on behalf of the corporation*, as well as from suits by third parties. Shareholders' derivative suits are brought by stockholders, on behalf of the corporation, to enforce corporate rights against insiders who have allegedly breached their duty to the corporation. Since the suit enforces *corporate* rights, all benefits derived therefrom accrue to the corporation and not to the stockholder directly.[132] Derivative suits may be brought for a variety of reasons, including conflicts of interest on the part of an officer or director;[133] personal appropriation of a corporate opportunity;[134]

negligence in permitting antitrust violations to occur;[135] misuse of corporate funds;[136] and, performance of *ultra vires* acts.[137]

In the leading case of Diamond v. Oreamuno, the New York Court of Appeals held two officers liable to the corporation in a derivative action for failing to disclose inside information in connection with the sale of their stock. The court held that the inside information to which the insiders had access was a corporate asset and that "a corporate fiduciary who is entrusted with the potentially valuable information may not appropriate that asset for his own use, even though in so doing he causes no injury to the corporation."[138]

Frequently, a question arises as to whether the wrongful act committed results in injury to the corporate entity (the stockholders collectively) or to the stockholders in an individual capacity. To distinguish between the two, there is authority that a stockholder who sustains no loss in addition to the loss sustained by the corporation cannot sue at law. The test is whether the injury to the complaining shareholder is the same as to every other shareholder; if it is, then the proper remedy is a derivative action. Since the injury resulting from mismanagement or wrongful use of corporate property by corporate officers is primarily to the corporation itself, a suit for damages should be by the corporation, rather than by the stockholders individually.[139]

The stockholders' derivative action is also to be distinguished from a stockholders' class action which is brought by one or more shareholders in their behalf and in behalf of all others similarly situated to redress a wrong done to the shareholders individually, as opposed to a wrong done to the corporation per se.

Stockholders' derivative suits have been maintained to recover short-swing insider profits under Section 16(b) of the Securities Exchange Act of 1934.[140] They also have been maintained to recover damages for violation of the antifraud provisions of Section 10(b) of the Securities Exchange Act and Rule 10b-5 promulgated thereunder.[141]

As a procedural matter, stockholders cannot sue on their own behalf in equity unless they can demonstrate that they have unsuccessfully made every reasonable effort to have the corporation sue or that any such effort would have been futile.[142] Reference should be made to the various state statutes and Rule 23.1 of the Federal Rules of Civil Procedure to determine whether a stockholder has standing to sue.

Damages

When there is a violation of the duties owed by the corporate officer or director, the types and amount of damages to which the injured party is entitled are dependent upon the nature of the action brought and whether the violation is of statutory origin or based in common law. To illustrate, in an action against directors of a corporation to recover damages for fraud and deceit in the sale of stock, the plaintiff is entitled to recover an amount equal to the difference between the actual value of the stock at the time of purchase and the value the stock would have had if the false representations had been true, less any dividends the plaintiff has received.[143] In private civil actions brought pursuant to the Securities and Exchange Act and the rules and regulations promulgated thereunder, recovery is limited to actual damages sustained and the recovery of punitive damages is precluded.[144]

Remote and speculative damages generally may not be recovered, but corporate officers may be held liable for profits lost by management.[145] In some circumstances, punitive damages may be allowed by the court for the fraudulent breach of a fiduciary duty.[146]

In the area of federal law, the courts may invoke a wide variety of legal devices to redress wrongs committed by corporate officials. These may include injunctions,[147] rescission,[148] accounting and restitution,[149] an award of compensatory[150] but probably not punitive damages,[151] attorney fees[152] and, in some instances, litigation expenses.[153]

Regarding criminal penalties, the penal law of each state prescribes fines and prison terms for violation of the statutory act, whether it may be applicable only to corporate officials or to all persons, including corporate officials.[154] The Federal Securities Act of 1933 imposes criminal penalties, not to exceed a $5,000 fine and five years in jail, for the willful violation of any of the provisions of the act or the rules and regulations promulgated by the Securities and Exchange Commission under authority thereof.[155] Under Section 1 of the Sherman Antitrust Act, a director who knowingly makes any contract or engages in any combination or conspiracy in restraint of interstate commerce may be punished by a $50,000 fine, imprisonment up to one year, or both.[156] Likewise, under the Clayton Act, an officer or director may be subjected to a $5,000 fine or a one year imprisonment for violation of its terms.[157]

Indemnification of Corporate Officers and Directors

When a director or officer becomes a defendant in a suit of the types which have been discussed, there has been considerable debate over the director's or officer's right to be indemnified by the corporation for costs incurred in the suit. This debate obviously has a bearing on the subject of directors' and officers' liability insurance. Of particular importance is the question whether individual directors or officers or the corporate entity will ultimately bear the burden of any loss, and what type of insurance may be used to treat the exposure. In a given situation this question is answered by the effect of any applicable statutes and by any indemnification agreements the corporation might have made with directors and officers. However, the numerous situations, statutes, and indemnification agreements make this a difficult subject to describe in general terms.

Legal Background At common law, a corporate officer or director who had been unsuccessful in the defense of a derivative suit had no right to indemnification from the corporation. It was reasoned that a wrongdoing insider cannot justifiably be reimbursed by the very party that his or her misconduct had harmed. Although this rationale would seem inappropriate when the insider was successful in defense of a derivative suit, early cases denied indemnification in such situations, because the expenditure of corporate funds would not produce a benefit to the corporation and thus would be *ultra vires*.[158]

In the landmark case of New York Dock Company v. McCollum,[159] the corporation brought a declaratory judgment action to determine whether it had an obligation to indemnify the insider. The court held that there was no obligation to indemnify. It implied that there was no power to do so in the absence of any benefit conferred on the corporation by a successful defense. In contrast, the Supreme Court of New Jersey determined that there was a common-law obligation to indemnify the insider for a *successful* defense of a derivative suit, even in the absence of any direct benefit to the corporation.[160]

As a result of the confusion surrounding the right to corporate indemnification—especially in the context of a stockholders' derivative suit—the legislative bodies of various states have enacted statutes granting the right to indemnification in certain situations. Some of the statutes permit indemnification; others require it; and still others make court approval or a court order a necessary prerequisite. Some of the indemnification statutes are "exclusive" in that they authorize indemnification only to the extent provided by the statute. Other statutes declare that statutory indemnification will not be considered exclusive of any of the rights to which the officer or director may be entitled under any bylaw, agreement, vote of shareholders or disinterested directors, or otherwise.[161]

Indemnification Agreements In most states, as a prerequisite to indemnification, the corporation must have adopted some form of contractual provision that sets guidelines for reimbursement, since the statutes are merely permissive. This provision, whether incorporated in the bylaws, a corporate resolution, or other written agreement, such as an employment contract, can obligate the corporation to indemnify the corporate official as long as the standard of conduct that must be followed is in harmony with the statute.[162]

The basic difference among corporate indemnification agreements is the standard of conduct that must be maintained by the insider in order to obtain indemnification. Some agreements deny indemnification to the insider who has been adjudged liable for negligence or misconduct, while others deny indemnification only when the official's action constituted gross negligence or willful misconduct.[163]

Courts have been quite restrictive in interpreting the legality of corporate resolutions or bylaws. For example, one court ignored the nonexclusive clause in the statute and disallowed indemnification even though the board of directors had passed a resolution providing it. The court stated that an exception provided in the statute mandated that there could be no indemnification if the insider had been adjudged to be liable.[164] In another situation, a derivative suit, an insider was held liable for negligence, and a charter provision of the corporation permitted indemnification therefor; but the court disallowed indemnification by interpreting the nonexclusive clause of the statute quite restrictively and holding that it permitted bylaw but not charter provision indemnification.[165]

With respect to the Securities Act of 1933, the SEC has taken the position that it is against public policy to indemnify a director against personal liability for damage caused by misrepresentations or omissions in registration statements.[166] However, insurance coverage is treated differently from corporate indemnification. The SEC has declared that insurance against liabilities arising out of the 1933 Act is not contrary to the public's interest, whether the cost of the insurance is born by the registrant, the insured, or some other person.[167]

In the case of Globus v. Law Research Service, Inc.,[168] the court stated that it would be against the public policy embodied in the federal securities legislation for an underwriter (investment banker) to enforce an indemnification agreement if he were found guilty of actions graver than ordinary negligence. There is no sound reason the same logic should not apply to the activities of a director as well.

In certain situations an officer or director has the right to obtain indemnification from the corporation pursuant to the principles of agency law and independent of any corporate or statutory obligation to indemnify. For instance, an agent, whether an officer or director, is entitled to reimbursement for legal liability arising out of his or her principal's acts, but not for liability arising out of his or her own wrongful conduct.[169] An agent is also entitled to be indemnified against loss and liability for acts he commits at the principal's direction when such acts are not manifestly known by the agent to be wrong.[170]

DIRECTORS' AND OFFICERS' LIABILITY INSURANCE

Many corporations have adopted resolutions to indemnify officers and directors for legal expenses they incur in defending suits based on their alleged wrongful acts as directors or officers. As mentioned, most states permit such indemnification provisions. Furthermore, a number of states have enacted legislation permitting corporations to have the power to purchase and maintain liability insurance covering corporate officers, directors, and employees.[171]

The Internal Revenue Service has also made a ruling under which premiums paid by a corporation for directors' and officers' liability insurance are deductible by the corporation as an ordinary and necessary business expense. The insurance protection afforded by payment of the premiums allows directors and officers to make business decisions without fear of unfavorable consequences.[172]

The stakes are not small. Some evidence of the growing magnitude of the overall exposure is provided by the Wyatt Company surveys which are conducted annually. For example, the 1976 survey involved 1,730 United States and Canadian corporations and institutions ranging in size from under $25 million to over $1 billion in assets. According to this report, it was estimated that the average directors' and officers' liability claim cost was $750,000 ($550,000 for awards to claimants and $200,000 for defense costs).[173] In the 1975 survey involving 1,720 corporations and institutions, the average claim cost was $582,000 per claim ($468,000 for awards to claimants and $114,000 for defense costs).[174] Average figures can be misleading, of course, in the absence of appropriate measures of dispersion or variability. The quoted figures are presented here only to confirm that the exposures are more than theoretical. This information, combined with other available data and the knowledge that some claims may be closed without payment, suggests that some claims are resulting in multimillion dollar settlements.

One actual case concerned eight shareholder suits against nineteen former and current directors and officers of Gulf Oil Corporation who either were directly involved in or who failed in their duty to prevent others from making illegal political campaign contributions between 1960 and 1973. The out-of-court settlement was $4 million, half of which was paid by the insurer and the other half with the corporation's stock options.[175] Another actual case, considered to be one of the largest on record, concerned five class action suits by stockholders against Mattel, Inc., alleging that the corporation committed security law violations by falsifying its financial records in order to inflate the value of its stock.

The result was that three insurers agreed to pay $13.8 million out of a $30 million out-of-court settlement.[176] As this text went to the printer, several lawsuits had been filed against directors and officers of the defunct W. T. Grant Company. The largest of these suits seeks damages in excess of $800 million.[177]

The theoretical chance of being confronted with such claims has long existed. Yet, even in the early 1970s, skeptics questioned whether directors' and officers' liability insurance was really worth purchasing at all. Insurers contended that many lawsuits were pending, but published data on losses and loss reserves were virtually nonexistent. Thus, to many corporate officials, the price of the insurance seemed far too high in relation to known, paid losses. To other officials, it was a moot point. The insurance simply was not available to them at any price.

The situation is somewhat different today. The need for directors' and officers' liability insurance is more widely recognized, and coverage is more readily available in the worldwide marketplace. In the earlier years, only certain types of large publicly held corporations (those with $25 million or more in assets) were eligible for this insurance, whereas today it is also available to most banks, savings and loan associations, condominium corporations, closely held corporations, and nonprofit organizations. However, some firms still find it difficult to procure insurance at a premium level which management regards to be commensurate with the loss exposure.

The basic purpose of the insurance is to protect corporate or institutional officials in the event of claims made against them because of wrongful or allegedly wrongful acts or omissions made while acting in their individual or collective capacities as directors and officers. There is no standard form of directors' and officers' liability insurance—that is, each insurer has its own policy provisions. Therefore, it is important for the prospective insurance buyer to compare the differences among available policies. Some of the differences are significant, despite the fact that most policies are similar in format and contain somewhat similar exclusions.

Coverages Afforded Under Available Contracts

What many people call "directors' and officers' liability insurance," or "D&O," actually consists of two separate coverages. The two coverages, which may be described under one insuring agreement, under separate insuring agreements, or even in separate polices, are (1) directors' and officers' liability coverage and (2) company reimbursement or company indemnification coverage. The former covers the personal liability of directors and officers who are not indemnified by the corporation; the latter covers the corporation's loss from indemnification of directors and officers.

Directors' and Officers' Liability Coverage This first basic coverage protects *executives* against their liability *when they are not otherwise protected by their corporations under bylaw or charter provisions calling for indemnification.* The coverage is in essence a form of professional liability insurance.

Under the typical form of directors' and officers' liability coverage, the insurer agrees to pay on behalf of the insured (directors and officers), loss (as defined) that emanates from any claim or claims made against the insured, jointly or severally, during the policy period, because of any wrongful act (as defined and not otherwise excluded) in their respective capacities as directors or officers. Thus, of importance in determining the extent of coverage are the meanings of the terms "insureds," "loss," and "wrongful acts."

Although the persons actually insured do not necessarily differ from policy to policy, the methods used to describe or define them vary. Some insurers require that directors be specifically named in the policies, along with the holders of other named positions. Other insurers cover all director and officer positions listed in the policy declarations, an approach similar to that taken with blanket position fidelity bonds. Still others list only excluded positions; this means that all positions not excluded are considered to be covered. Most policies also automatically insure each director and officer who "was, now is, or hereafter may be" a director or officer of an existing position. However, persons who fill newly created positions of existing firms, or positions of subsidiaries formed or acquired during the policy period are usually not automatically covered unless insurers are advised of the exposure in writing within a certain period.

Since liability of directors and officers is personal in nature, these policies also cover heirs, estates, and legal representatives of deceased executives who have been directors and officers, and the legal representative of directors or officers who are insolvent, bankrupt, or adjudged to be incompetent.

The term "loss" is generally defined to mean any amounts which the insureds are legally obligated to pay as a result of claims made against them for wrongful acts. Included in such amounts are court judgments or other settlements and costs, charges, and expenses incurred in the defense and appeal proceedings. However, the term loss usually does not include (1) the payment of fines or penalties imposed by law, or (2) other matters deemed to be uninsurable according to the law under which the policy is interpreted. Presumably, the fines or penalties mentioned in (1) above refer to violations of antitrust or other federal laws, whereas the other matters referred to in (2) above are presumably meant to encompass principally punitive damages. Note that punitive damages may be covered if coverage is not otherwise prohibited by law. Some insurers feel that punitive damages should not be insured under any circumstance and add exclusions to their D&O policies specifically precluding coverage for such damages.

Finally, to be payable by the insurer, the loss must not only be one an insured is legally obligated to pay. It must also stem from a "wrongful act." The term wrongful act is commonly defined to encompass any breach of duty, neglect, error, misstatement, misleading statement, omission or other act that is done, wrongfully attempted, or so alleged by any claimant. Since the term itself also includes "any" claim made against the insureds solely by reason of their being directors or officers of the company, it would appear to cover virtually any civil or criminal act that culminates in a loss. But, as mentioned later, there are many exclusions that narrow the coverage to its intended scope. The net effect is somewhat akin to the "all-risks" coverage concept—there is coverage for loss by any wrongful act except those acts that are specifically excluded.

Company Reimbursement or Company Indemnification Coverage The second of the two basic coverages covers any loss the corporation sustains by having to reimburse an officer or director for any judgment and defense costs (to the extent that the corporation is permitted or required to do so under common or statutory law and under the applicable provisions of the corporation's bylaws or charter). So, if a corporation does not agree to indemnify directors and officers under such circumstances, the corporation does not need the indemnification coverage.

There is nothing mandatory about either directors' and officers' or company reimbursement coverage. Thus, if a corporation does not adopt a policy of indemnification and it is not required to do so by law, the corporation itself is not exposed to the losses covered by reimbursement coverage or directors' and officers' liability coverage. Even if a corporation desires or is required to adopt a policy of indemnification, it still does not have to purchase insurance. However, executives may demand that the corporation purchase at least directors' and officers' liability coverage even if the executives have to pay for part of the insurance costs themselves.

Directors' and officers' liability coverage may be particularly desirable when there is a potential for loss due to derivative actions, since indemnification of directors and officers is usually not permitted by law following a successful derivative action, because it is the corporation that has benefited from such suit in the first place. And, while reimbursement of legal expenses is sometimes permitted when the defendants are proved to be innocent of the allegations, directors' and officers' liability coverage provides for the expensive defense costs an executive may not be able to afford until he or she finds out if the costs can be reimbursed by the corporation's indemnification coverage.

In effect, the two insuring agreements complement one another for corporations with indemnification agreements. For directors' and officers' claims that are legally within the scope of the indemnification agreement and not excluded by the policy, the corporation is protected by its reimbursement coverage for indemnification it must make. In some situations, directors' and officers' liability coverage would protect directors and officers against losses for which corporate indemnification is prohibited by law or for which the corporation will not respond, as, for example, when the corporation is insolvent. Of course, coverage is subject to policy limits, deductibles, and exclusions. Although directors' and officers' liability coverage is in some ways broader than reimbursement coverage, the policy does not, and probably should not, protect directors and officers against certain losses, such as those caused by self-dealing or conflict of interest.

Common Exclusions and Their Rationale Directors and officers who are included as insureds, by name or by position, are covered for any "loss" which is attributable to any "wrongful act," as these terms are defined in the policy subject to various exclusions. Although directors' and officers' liability policies are nonstandard, most contain exclusions that are similar in scope and intent. Below is a summary of the exclusions that commonly apply to the directors' and officers' liability insuring agreement. This is followed by a summary of exclusions that commonly apply to the company reimbursement insuring agreement.

D&O Liability Coverage Exclusions. Not included as a wrongful act covered by the policy is *libel* or *slander*. Both of these offenses are specifically excluded. However, coverage for them is not only available by endorsement to general liability policies, it is also provided automatically in special forms of liability insurance, as well as in most umbrella liability policies.

The term "loss" does not include *any personal profit or advantage to which directors or officers are not legally entitled.* The intent of this exclusion is to preclude coverage in situations where claims are brought against executives for their unlawful use of inside information to obtain a personal profit. If the allegations are proven, the director or officer must relinquish such profit to the corporation. In no event is the insurance to be used to defend an executive who is claimed to have gained a personal profit, nor is it to be used to pay another for any loss of personal profit to which an executive is not entitled.

The term "loss" does not include *remuneration, such as salaries and bonuses illegally paid to executives without the approval of stockholders.* The applicability of this exclusion hinges on whether such action by executives is illegal, and it may ultimately be a question for the courts to decide. In any case, it must be determined whether the approval of stockholders was actually necessary. If it is determined that approval should have been obtained, the executives are required to return that portion received by them, along with any defense costs which might have been expended by the insurer. On the other hand, if it is determined that approval of stockholders was not necessary, the executives would at least have their defense costs paid by the insurer.

Profits made by executives from the purchase or sale of securities of the company within the meaning of Section 16(b) of the Securities Exchange Act of 1934 or similar provisions of any statutory law are not covered losses within the meaning of the policy. (Some policies also mention here the provisions of any pertinent common law.) The purpose of Section 16 (b) of the aforementioned federal law is to prevent the unfair use of information which may be available to executives. It is also intended to prevent any short-swing profits that may be realized from the purchase and sale, or the sale and purchase, of an equity of the corporation for whom the executives work, within any period of less than six months. Any short-swing profits realized by company executives must be returned to the company, and neither insurance nor defense costs would be provided to the executives involved.

Covered loss does not include *loss brought about or contributed to by deliberate acts of dishonesty by executives.* Claims of this nature are rightfully the subject of fidelity insurance. Nevertheless, most such exclusions contain exceptions which in effect provide insureds with defense protection under directors' and officers' liability policies. This protection applies to claims that allege dishonesty on the part of executives. In other words, those against whom claims are made are innocent until proven otherwise. However, this protection can be negated if it is ultimately established that the acts of the insureds were deliberately committed for dishonest purposes.

The policy does not include *loss covered by and paid under other valid policies.* The intent of this exclusion is to make other valid and collectible insurance primary and to make coverage under directors' and officers' liability insurance excess. If payment is not made under other policies, the directors' and officers' liability policy becomes primary.

Coverage is not provided for *losses based on or attributable to any failure or omission on the part of the insureds to effect and maintain insurance.* This is commonly referred to as the insurance exclusion. Its purpose is to avoid covering suits that hold executives accountable for having procured insufficient corporate property-liability insurance or insufficient limits. (Not all policies contain this exclusion. Others contain the exclusion, but insurers sometimes will delete it following the submission of particulars, with or without an additional premium charge.)

Not covered within the terms of the policy is *any loss for which the insureds are entitled to indemnity under any policy previously in force.* When a policy is canceled by an insurer, the insured usually is given the opportunity to purchase, within a certain period, an extension of coverage ranging from three to twelve months. The insurer that provides the coverage extension is liable for any covered claim that is discovered during the extended period, provided the circumstances giving rise to such claim actually occurred prior to policy termination. This exclusion, therefore, avoids holding the current insurer answerable in cases where a claim is rightfully covered under a prior policy.

Directors' and officers' liability coverage does not apply to *any claim dealing with loss covered under company reimbursement coverage.* The effect of this provision was mentioned earlier. Its purpose is to avoid double coverage.

The policy does not cover *claims based on or attributable to bodily injury, sickness, disease or death. It also does not cover damage to or destruction of any tangible property, including any loss of use.* Since bodily injury liability and property damage liability losses caused by negligence of officers and directors are covered under the provisions of general liability, umbrella liability, and umbrella excess liability policies, these claims need not be covered by directors' and officers' liability insurance. The purpose of this exclusion, therefore, is to prevent an overlapping of coverage.

Loss is not covered for *bodily injury or property damage stemming from contamination or pollution unless loss is sudden and accidental.* This exclusion is commonly found in all liability policies. Note the exception to loss which is sudden and accidental. This exception is also common, but it is only on an excess basis insofar as directors' and officers' liability insurance is concerned (if there are other valid policies under which payment is made).

Most directors' and officers' liability policies contain a provision that states, in a variety of ways but with the same purpose, that the negligent act, error, omission, or breach of duty of any one insured shall not be imputed to any other insured for purposes of determining the applicability of the foregoing exclusions. The end result of this provision is that coverage still applies to other insureds who are found not to be involved in an excluded wrongful act or loss, in spite of their being implicated in a suit.

Some policies also exclude direct or indirect losses incurred by directors and officers in their capacities as fiduciaries of pension and other employee benefit plans, though there is the opportunity to buy back the coverage for an additional premium charge. While the fiduciary exposure has existed for many years, and while directors' and officers' liability policies were broad enough to cover it, there had not been much concern about the exposure or the coverage until the passage of the Employee Retirement Income Security Act of 1974 (ERISA). The act broadened the potential liabilities of fiduciaries to such an extent that insurers of directors' and officers' liability insurance became unwilling to provide coverage under existing policy language and for existing premiums. Insurers therefore inserted an exclusion that makes it quite clear that corporate officials are not covered in their capacities as fiduciaries of pension and other employee benefit plans. The exclusion forces those who have need for such insurance to obtain it either by the purchase of an endorsement to the directors' and officers' liability policy or by the purchase of separate errors and omissions insurance for trustees and fiduciaries of employee benefit plans. (The latter subject is discussed in a subsequent section of this chapter.)

Company Reimbursement Coverage Exclusions. The company reimbursement coverage insuring agreement of most policies usually has but two exclusions, and they relate to other insurance that may be applicable. The first of these bars *any liability for payment when the insureds are entitled to indemnity under any policy which was previously in force.* The second exclusion *precludes recovery, except on an excess basis, when coverage applies under another valid policy which was in force at the time the loss occurred.* However, if no other valid policy applies to the loss in question, coverage is considered primary under the company reimbursement insurance.

Additional exclusions are considered unnecessary, because the company reimbursement coverage is already confined to reimbursing the corporation for only such losses as are legally reimbursable. An act such as a breach of duty, which results in an excluded loss under directors' and officers' liability coverage, would also not be covered under the company reimbursement insuring agreement, if the loss is not legally reimbursable.

Mandatory Retentions and Other Important Policy Provisions
The insurer, under practically all directors' and officers' insurance policies is liable for 95 percent of any covered loss that exceeds the amount retained (deductible) by the insured, subject to the applicable limit of liability stated in the declarations. Furthermore, almost all policies warrant that the insured's 5 percent participation (the deductible) *must* be assumed—i.e., it cannot be insured—and an

insured's breach of that warranty can void coverage under the policy. The apparent reason for this requirement is to reduce moral hazard and to provide insureds wth an incentive to prevent losses. Thus, an insured must pay 100 percent of every loss that is less than the deductible amount, and on every loss that is greater than the deductible, the insured must pay (1) the deductible amount, plus (2) 5 percent of any amount in excess of the deductible but within the policy limits, and (3) 100 percent of any amount that exceeds the policy limit. The deductible and 5 percent participation provisions also require the insured to share in the payment of defense costs, but only when defense costs are not provided in addition to the limits of liability. However, unlike most other liability policies, the typical directors' and officers' policy does *not* provide for the payment of defense costs as an addition to the limit—defense costs are paid to the extent that they, combined with loss payments, do not exceed the limit of liability.

The mandatory retention or deductible may take one of several forms, depending upon what is purchased. The first involves a *single deductible* in the minimum amount of $5,000 and commonly as large as $20,000. Whatever that amount may be, it is first deducted before the insurer becomes liable for the remaining 95 percent, subject to the limit of liability. Moreover, losses arising out of the same act or interrelated acts of one or more of the executives are considered to be a single loss. This means that only one retention amount is deducted from the aggregate amount of covered loss.

A second form of retention involves *split deductibles*. One deductible of $5,000 or more applies to each director or officer, and another deductible of $20,000 or more serves as an aggregate deductible in any one occurrence. For example, suppose five officers are involved in a single covered loss in a situation where split deductibles of $5,000 and $20,000 apply. The aggregate deductible of $20,000 would serve as the maximum deductible (not $25,000 or $5,000 for each of the five officers) assuming, of course, that the interrelated acts of the officers are considered to be a single loss.

Under some policies it is a requirement that the aggregate deductible, when it applies, be prorated among the officers involved, in proportion to their respective losses. If $20,000 is the retention and the judgments against each of the five officers are the same, each would be responsible for one-fifth, or $4,000. But if the judgment against each varies in amount, it would be necessary to determine the ratio each judgment bears to the total judgment and then multiply each ratio by the aggregate retention amount in order to determine the dollar retention that must be borne by each of the officers.

Corporate reimbursement coverage is also subject to a deductible. The minimum deductible available is usually $20,000.

Other provisions of both coverages include thirty days' notice of cancellation by the insurer; three to twelve months' extension of coverage in the event of cancellation by the insurer for claims discovered during the period of extension but which occurred prior to policy termination; and the right of subrogation by the insurer. Finally, the policy usually warrants that statements made in the application or proposal, as well as those in the declarations, constitute part of the policy.

Availability and Cost   Although the eligibility requirements for directors' and officers' liability insurance have been broadened over the years to include smaller corporations and even nonprofit institutions, insurers are still extremely selective. In fact, even when coverage is readily available, some prospective buyers believe the premium to be excessive, and if claim frequency and severity continues to increase, premium rates are bound to increase even more.

No standard rates apply, of course. Rates are determined largely by the judgment of underwriters. In determining the rates and deciding whether to insure an applicant, underwriters assess the exposure by taking into account such factors as: the size of the corporation or institution; the policy limits desired; the number of directors and officers to be covered; the deductibles desired; and the type of corporation or institution and its acquisition activity, diversity, loss experience, and overall profitability. Also considered are the number of subsidiaries that may be involved and the degree of their control by the parent company, the nature of stock distributions, and special features of coverage.

Noninsurance Techniques for Handling Directors' and Officers' Liability Exposures

Though legal liability for breach of their fiduciary duties falls initially upon directors and/or officers as individuals, there is ample reason for their corporations to be concerned with the legal, financial, and managerial aspects of the exposure. The corporation is a party to derivative actions; it may be a codefendant in third-party actions; it may incur substantial litigation expenses in either type of action; it may agree to reimburse directors and officers for defense expenses and/or liability judgments, where permitted; and it faces the practical problem of convincing qualified individuals to serve as corporate officers and directors, particularly outside directors, in an age when they have become increasingly vulnerable to litigation. Hence, the corporation, as an entity, has an obvious financial interest in the legal liability exposure of its individual officers and directors.

Whether or not the corporation purchases directors' and officers' liability coverage and company reimbursement coverage, due consideration should be given to the noninsurance techniques available to deal with the underlying exposures. In the context of directors' and officers' liability exposures, the techniques of avoidance and noninsurance transfer are not practical options for the corporation per se. Retention and loss control, on the other hand, are of indispensable importance.

Retention When directors' and officers' liability coverage and company reimbursement coverage are purchased, both the corporation and its individual officers and directors must partially retain the insured losses, in effect, because of the mandatory deductibles and percentage participation provisions that were discussed in the previous section. The typical policy warrants that the mandatory retentions cannot be insured; they must be "assumed" by the individual (or the corporation, under company reimbursement insurance). Losses excluded from coverage are totally retained by the parties held legally liable for them.

Total retention also occurs when the insurance is not available or is not available at a price that management is willing to pay. Total retention can be dangerous to the corporation, especially when it has entered into legally enforceable agreements to reimburse officers and directors, but it is particularly dangerous to the individuals whose personal assets are at stake. One certainly could not blame an individual for avoiding the exposure by refusing to serve as a corporate director unless the corporation provides appropriate insurance to cover his or her individual exposure.

Loss Control Even when insurance is purchased, the importance of loss control cannot be overemphasized. Once losses occur, they must be at least partially retained by the parties involved. Poor loss experience will adversely affect the cost and availability of insurance.

Theoretically, there is no better way to treat the liability exposures of officers and directors than to prevent the acts and omissions that give rise to the corresponding legal actions. While this goal is more easily expressed than achieved, corporate officials could go a long way toward insulating themselves from liability if only they would honor the duties and obligations imposed upon them by common and statutory law and stay knowledgeable and aware of corporate developments, both inside and outside the corporation. Very simply, if corporate officials are faithful to their duties and do what the law tells them to do, they will be in a favorable position to avoid liability.

Negligence. As a specific example, the law imposes upon the officers and directors a standard of due care and diligence in the performance of their duties. In order to protect themselves against allegations of negligence or failure to exercise reasonable care, the directors should attend as many board meetings as possible. At these meetings it is important that significant matters of corporate policy and material corporate developments be discussed in depth. They should take active roles in discussing matters that come before the board and should register dissent if they disagree with corporate policies. Although directors are entitled to rely upon reports prepared by officers or accountants, they should not merely accept such reports at face value but should make an honest attempt to evaluate them. The directors should insist upon receiving periodic reports from management, get to know the officers, and make a sincere effort to evaluate their performance. In the case of mergers or acquisitions, the directors should analyze each transaction to insure that the corporation is receiving fair consideration.

Of course, it is essential that the officers or directors be knowledgeable about the rules and regulations governing the corporation's conduct and spelled out in its articles of incorporation and bylaws. They should fully understand all laws, whether statutory or common, that may regulate their own conduct. To assure that this knowledge is conveyed, the advice and assistance of competent legal counsel are imperative.

Conflicts of Interest. Since many claims against officers and directors involve allegations of conflict of interest or self-dealing, it is necessary for the corporate official, in averting liability of this kind, to recognize the existence of potentially actionable conduct. Any contract entered into by the officer or director with his or her corporation should be scrutinized with the utmost care, since many state statutes declare transactions of this kind to be void or voidable unless certain conditions are met. Moreover, the charters of many corporations, as well as the bylaws, may contain prohibitions of one kind or another. Other areas of potential concern include those where the officer or director sells or leases property of the corporation or buys property from the corporation; the officer or director appropriates a corporate opportunity or competes with the corporation; or the officer or director owns stock in a supplier or customer of the corporation. In all the aforementioned situations, it may be helpful for the corporate official to seek the assistance of an outside legal consultant before entering into the transaction. Furthermore, it is essential that there be full disclosure to the board of directors or to the stockholders when engaging in a transaction that may be advantageous to the corporate insider.[178]

Antitrust Problems. To increase awareness on the part of corporate officers and otherwise protect against liability that may arise from an antitrust proceeding, many companies have instituted internal antitrust compliance programs. It is imperative that knowledge of antitrust liabilities be conveyed to every management person involved in pricing, marketing, and other areas of antitrust sensitivity, and periodic legal conferences between company lawyers and management personnel can be useful in disseminating information about antitrust problems.[179]

Criminal Liability. To protect against criminal liability, corporate officers or directors should be ever mindful of the oft-quoted admonition that "ignorance is no excuse." They should be cognizant not only of the penal statutes that may be applicable to their conduct but also to the recent court decisions that have imposed liability upon officers and directors, even though they may not have participated in the unlawful conduct.[180]

Ultra Vires *Acts.* Obviously, to avoid the commission of an *ultra vires* act, the corporate officers and directors must be aware of the express and implied powers granted to the corporations by their charters or bylaws; and, when in doubt as to the propriety of certain activities, they should consult with company counsel.

Securities Laws Violations. No discussion of the prevention of officers' and directors' liability would be complete without mentioning preventive measures necessary to avoid liability under the federal securities laws. In fact, many of the guidelines set forth below are useful, not only in avoiding liabilities arising out of securities transactions but also in avoiding common-law liability.

With respect to protecting against liability under the federal securities laws, the director should read registration statements very carefully and make sure that there are no misstatements or omissions of a material or misleading nature. The Bar Chris case, cited earlier, teaches that it is not sufficient merely to glance at a registration statement and blindly rely upon others concerning its accuracy. Indeed, it is good practice to hold a directors' "due diligence meeting," during which time the entire registration statement can be reviewed carefully and discussed by the directors. As a general rule, it may be stated that the degree of diligence required increases with the directors' proximity to the registration statement; i.e., those directors and officers who are charged with preparing a registration statement will probably have a more difficult time establishing a due diligence defense than those directors not so intimately involved.[181]

To prevent liability under Section 10 of the 1934 Act and Rule 10b-5, the director (or officer, if he is possessed of material inside information) should refrain from trading in the company's securities until such information has been disseminated to the public. In order to assist directors and officers in determining when it is safe to buy company stock, the New York Stock Exchange has issued a set of guidelines[182] which advises the corporate insider to buy or sell stock only after the annual report has been sent to stockholders, or after the release of current or quarterly results. The guidelines also suggest a periodic investment program in which the insider makes regular purchases in a program outside the control of the insider.

Moreover, to prevent incurring liability under Section 10, the insider should disclose material information necessary to enable the public investor to make a reasonable and informed decision concerning whether to buy the company stock. Examples of material information that should be disclosed are: an important invention or new products; a new contract significantly affecting earnings; a change in the dividend or a significant increase or decrease in earnings; a merger or acquisition; a proposed tender offer; and a stock split.[183]

Prevention of Section 16(b) liability is largely a matter of being aware that acts other than ordinary purchases or sales for cash may constitute purchases or sales for purposes of the statute; for example, contracts, mergers, and exchanges of securities.[184]

Some general guidelines for preventing liability under provisions of the securities laws, proposed jointly by the New York Stock Exchange and the Securities and Exchange Commission, recommend that there be established a board-level audit committee composed entirely of outside directors and able to provide an objective appraisal of corporate management and corporate affairs.[185] It has also been recommended that the corporation have a morally strong and highly capable general counsel and that, in a corporation which has a high degree of public ownership, a majority of its board of directors, preferably two-thirds, be outside directors.[186]

It has also been suggested that directors should be adequately compensated at a rate that realistically encourages them to spend the time necessary to become informed concerning the corporation's affairs; that the board of directors frequently review long-term corporate policy and goals with respect to capitalization, diversification, expansion, marketing, disclosure practices, and other major areas of concern; and that a director should be prepared to resign when he believes management is not providing timely and meaningful information. A corporation should also make available professional consultants, attorneys, and independent accountants to render professional advice, and the corporate attorney should play a major role in insuring against directorial liability, both by providing the legal framework within which preventative programs may be adopted and carried out and by monitoring disclosure programs to insure continued compliance with legal requirements.[187]

It should be apparent to all concerned that the day of the "dummy director" is over. At the least, any individual who accepts a position as a director of a corporation should be aware that he or she will be held strictly accountable for failing to carry out managerial responsibilities. Unless the director is able to expend the necessary time and effort required to serve on the board of directors, he or she should decline to accept the position, or, if presently sitting on the board, it may be more prudent for him or her to resign.

As publicity surrounding corporate wrongdoing becomes more widespread, there will be increasing demands upon officers and directors to be faithful to their fiduciary obligations. It is imperative, therefore, that the corporate officer or director devote the necessary time and effort to corporate affairs, if only to carry out the duties and responsibilities imposed by law.

Noninsurance Transfer and Avoidance Because a corporation must have officers and directors, it cannot literally avoid or transfer its directors' and officers' liability exposures except through insurance. A corporation could avoid a portion of the exposure by refusing to enter into an agreement to reimburse its officers and directors for defense expenses or judgments, or it could transfer a portion of the exposure to the officers and directors by terminating an existing reimbursement agreement. Neither is likely, since the officers and directors themselves have the power to approve or disapprove such agreements (assuming the agreements are legally permitted in the jurisdiction(s) involved). Moreoever, the statutes of some states require indemnification under specified circumstances, and the corporation might also be required to indemnify under principles of agency law.

An individual could avoid the exposure entirely by refusing to accept a position as a corporate officer or director, especially if the corporation does not have directors' and officers' liability insurance or a written reimbursement agreement. In the case of a prospective outside director, who would typically serve for a very nominal compensation, avoidance might well be the best alternative. A prospective officer would want to weigh the liability exposure against the salary and other benefits of the position.

If an officer or director resigns from an existing position, the resignation could be viewed either as avoidance or as a noninsurance transfer of the directors' and officers' liability exposure, since the exposure would be transferred to the incoming director or officer. However, the transfer would only be partial, since the former executive would still be accountable for acts or omissions he or she committed prior to resignation. Such acts might be covered under the former employer's directors' and officers' liability insurance, if any.

ENVIRONMENTAL POLLUTION LIABILITY

The Exposure

Common-Law Grounds for the Imposition of Tort Liability
Prior to the twentieth century, most law in the environmental field
arose from (1) legal decisions aimed at narrowly defined nuisance
problems and designed to serve narrow and specific purposes, and (2)
legislation enacted to regulate governmental police power over health
and disease control. The legal devices that evolved were concerned
largely with methods of resolving private disputes, and the courts
utilized a balancing test that weighed the seriousness of the injury
against the economic benefits flowing from the activity that produced
it.[188]

Today the common-law causes of actions, including nuisance,
trespass, negligence, and others, are of only limited utility to the
individual plaintiff seeking relief against the alleged polluter. Not only
are more effective statutory remedies increasingly available, but also the
common-law remedies are applicable only in situations where it is
possible to isolate the alleged polluter (from others who may be
polluting) and assess the damages caused by the alleged polluter.[189]
Nonetheless, before examining some of the major federal and state
statutes applicable to polluters, we should first review the common-law
grounds for the imposition of tort liability.

Negligence. Pollution that arises from careless or reckless conduct
will give rise to a cause of action for negligence, in which case the
plaintiff may seek either damages or an injunction. The plaintiff who has
sustained damages *and* fears future injury should seek both remedies.[190]

Unless negligence per se can be shown, i.e., a violation of a statute
or regulation, the plaintiff must prove that the defendant failed to
exercise reasonable care. For example, if discharging pollutants into a
stream creates a hazard for downstream users and the hazard could be
averted by a warning, proof of a failure to give a warning may indicate
actionable negligence;[191] but when damage is caused by conditions that
could not have been foreseen by ordinary care, there is no liability for
injury occurring prior to notice of the injurious effect of those
conditions.[192]

Negligence can create liability for the pollution of a well or spring,
the pollution of a water supply by industrial waste products, and noise
created by the operation of aircraft in violation of statutory
standards.[193] The degree of care demanded of a person in a particular

situation depends upon the likelihood that his or her conduct will injure others, taken with the seriousness of the injury, if it happens, and balanced against the interest he or she must sacrifice to avoid the risk.[194]

In a negligence action, the plaintiff may be able to recover punitive damages as well as actual damages. In Reynolds Metals Co. v. Lampert,[195] flower growers sued an operator of an aluminum production plant for actual and punitive damages that resulted from the settling of fluoride particles on the plaintiff's property. The court held that the question of punitive damages was for the jury to decide, in view of the fact that the jury could have found the defendant acted with disregard of property rights of the plaintiff, operated recklessly so as to imply a disregard of social obligations or with other improper motives in failing to control the discharge of fluorides from their plant.[196]

Strict Liability. The rule of absolute or strict liability has been applied where harmful gases or fumes escape from one person's property to that of another, and where waste material is permitted to escape from one person's land into the underground water supply of an adjoining owner.[197]

The leading case on strict liability is Rylands v. Fletcher,[198] in which it was held that when land is used in a special or extraordinary manner and the use, in turn, creates increased danger to others and causes harm, the owner is liable for all damages that are the natural consequences of the use of his or her land in that manner.[199] This rule has been applied to the discharge of water onto another's land, the fumigation of a building with cyanide gas, the dusting of crops with dangerous chemicals, and the emission of smoke, dust, and noxious gases by factories.[200]

In Rylands v. Fletcher the court predicated the absolute liability on the proposition that since the use of land for the artificial storage of water was not a natural use, the landowner was bound to keep the waters on his own land. Though proof of negligence is not necessary in strict liability cases, it is necessary to establish the relationship of the defendant to the dangerous and defective condition, and to show that there was a causal connection between the plaintiff's damages and the defective or dangerous condition.

The theory of strict liability is frequently applied to one engaged in abnormally hazardous activities. A person so engaged is liable to another whose person or property is injured by such activities, even though the utmost care is exercised to prevent harm. The Restatement of the Law of Torts states:

> . . . in determining whether an activity is "abnormally hazardous," the following factors are to be considered: (a) existence of a high degree of risk of some harm to the person, land or chattels of others; (b) likelihood that the harm that results from it will be great; (c) inability

to eliminate the risks by the exercise of reasonable care; (d) extent to which the activity is not a matter of common usage; (e) inappropriateness of the activity to the place where it is carried on; and (f) extent to which its value to the community is outweighed by its dangerous attributes.[201]

INTENTIONAL INTERFERENCE. Intentional interference with real property is analogous to the concept of battery in that unpermitted contact with real property is also a tort.[202] A battery is an intentional, unprivileged, unconsented touching that is offensive. There need only be knowledge on the part of the actor that contact or apprehension will occur. Thus the touching can be caused by the intentional spewing forth of pollutants or the vibrations of air pressure caused by a loud noise.[203]

In an action based on intentional interference with property, the plaintiff will usually seek exemplary or punitive damages. Recovery of exemplary or punitive damages in a pollution action is based upon the same rules that govern the recovery of such damages in other actions.[204] The principal requirements are (1) proof of an independent cause of action, since there is no cause of action for punitive damages only; (2) proof of actual (or compensatory) damages; and (3) evidence that the defendant's wrongful act was characterized by either willfulness, wantonness, maliciousness, gross negligence or recklessness, oppression, outrageous conduct, insult, indignity or fraud.[205]

PRIVATE "NUISANCE" AND "TRESPASS" THEORIES. Every person has the right to have the air diffused over his or her premises in its natural state and free from artificial impurities. An unreasonable interference with this right constitutes a nuisance.[206] Whether atmospheric contamination is a nuisance is generally a question of fact to be determined from the circumstances of the particular case.[207] The injury from air pollution must be substantial; the question is whether the proven acts or conduct either materially interfere with the comfort of human beings or are materially detrimental to the reasonable use or value of property.[208]

Trespass is the invasion of a protected interest in the exclusive possession of property.[209] The doing of an act that will, with substantial certainty, result in the entry of foreign matter into another's land suffices for an intentional trespass to land upon which liability may be based. Liability frequently has been imposed for the settling on another's land of airborne gases, particulates, and fluorides, and for the pollution of a landowner's water supply by industrial wastes.[210]

Distinctions have been made between nuisance and trespass. Whereas a nuisance consists of a use of one's own property so as to cause injury to the property or interest of another, usually as a result of the commission of an act beyond the limits of the property affected, a trespass is a direct infringement of another's right of property. Also, in a trespass action no damage need be shown in order for a plaintiff to prevail, while in a nuisance action actual damages must be proved.[211]

Unless there is a physical invasion of the plaintiff's property, the cause of action is generally for nuisance rather than for trespass. For example, an encroachment on the space above another's land but not upon the land itself is a nuisance and not a trespass.[212] However, a distinction has also been made between trespass as a theory of recovery and trespass as a form of action. It has thus been held that trespass may be a proper *form of action* to assert a claim for damage or injury resulting from the escape of gases or fumes from another's premises. A trespass by fluoride fumes and particles may constitute a nuisance, and recovery may be obtained on that theory; or it may be treated as an action in trespass, if only to take advantage of a longer statute of limitations.[213] In general, statutes of limitations are considerably longer for trespass actions than for nuisance actions.

Under the Restatement, one intentionally entering land in another's possession or causing some person or thing to enter thereon is liable as a trespasser, even in the absence of harm, while one entering recklessly, negligently, or as a result of ultra-hazardous activity is liable only if harm results. Nuisance liability obtains if there is a substantial and unreasonable invasion which is intentional, negligent, reckless, or ultra-hazardous.[214]

It is difficult to distinguish between actions of nuisance and those based on negligence, particularly where the acts or omissions will give rise to both torts. Nuisance and negligence actions are both grounded in a breach of some duty, but lack of due care is ordinarily relevant only in a negligence action.[215]

Although there is legal authority to the effect that liability for a nontrespassory invasion (by fumes and gases) of another's interest and property exists only if it is shown that the actor acted intentionally or negligently, the prevailing view is that liability may be imposed without a showing of negligence. Moreover, the fact that a business causing the nuisance is carried on in a careful and prudent manner does not constitute a defense.[216]

In McElwain v. Georgia Pacific,[217] a nuisance action, it was held that punitive damages would be awarded, if the jury "found that the defendant had not done everything reasonably possible to eliminate or minimize damage to adjoining property." The court used none of the harsh words like "willful," "wanton," and "reckless disregard," which are commonly heard in connection with punitive damages. The decision thus implies that a manufacturer who pollutes the atmosphere must utilize the most adequate technology. Failure to do so will not simply bear on the determination of whether a wrong, such as negligence or trespass, has been committed, or whether an action for damages due to nuisance will lie; rather, given the special knowledge and expertise of the defendant, such failure will result in punitive damages above and beyond the ordinary form of relief.[218]

Liability Under Federal and State Statutes In addition to common-law liability, liability for contamination or pollution has been imposed by many statutes, as described in the following paragraphs.[219]

River and Harbor Act.[220] This act prohibits the obstruction of various waters of the United States by the building of structures, unless the work has been recommended by the Chief of Engineers and authorized by the Secretary of the Army. It also prohibits the discharge or deposit of any refuse matter of any kind or description (other than that flowing from streets and sewers and passing therefrom in a liquid state) into any navigable water or any tributary of navigable water of the United States.

Every person or corporation that violates the provisions of the act is guilty of a misdemeanor. On conviction, the violator is liable to punishment by (1) a fine of not less than $500 nor more than $2,500, (2) imprisonment for not less than thirty days nor more than one year, or (3) both fine and imprisonment at the discretion of the court. One-half of any fine is to be paid to any person or persons giving information that leads to conviction.

The requirements of this act could have restricted any and all discharges from factories into waterways during most of its seventy-odd years of existence, but it was formerly interpreted to apply only when a discharge would impede navigation. In recent years, however, environmental considerations have prompted the government to use the authority of the statute to force corporations to cease water-polluting activities.[221]

The Oil Pollution Act.[222] The Oil Pollution Act was enacted on August 30, 1961, and amended in 1973. It prohibits the discharge of oil or oily mixtures from a tanker or ship, unless such discharge is for the purpose of securing the safety of a ship, preventing damage to a ship or cargo, or saving a life at sea. Section 1005 provides both criminal and civil penalties for violations, as follows:

> . . . (a) any person who willfully discharges oil or oily mixture from a ship in violation of this chapter or the regulations thereunder shall be fined not more than $10,000 for each violation or imprisoned for not more than one year, or both; (b) . . . in addition to any other penalty prescribed by law any person who willfully or negligently discharges oil or oily mixture from a ship in violation of this chapter or any regulation thereunder shall be liable to a civil penalty of not more than $10,000 and any person who otherwise violates this chapter or any regulation thereunder shall be liable to a civil penalty of not more than $5,000 for each violation.

The Pollution Control Act.[223] The Federal Water Pollution Control Act stipulates that any pollution (of interstate or navigable waters in or adjacent to any state or states) which endangers the health or welfare of any person shall be subject to abatement as provided within the statute. It encourages local action in the abatement of water pollution, seeks to identify sources of such pollution, and encourages local solutions to pollution problems. Any person who violates either the act, any permit, condition, or limitation implementing any section thereof, or any order issued by the administrator, shall be subject to a civil penalty not to exceed $10,000 per day of such violation.

In U.S. v. Detrex Chemical Industries, Inc.,[224] the court held that under the aforementioned section, the maximum civil penalty for violation of a permit is $10,000 per day, regardless of the number of violations occurring on that date. It also held that an Environmental Protection Agency Order that required the holder of a permit to comply with terms of the permit before a specified date did not preclude the assessment of civil penalties for violations occurring before that date. In U.S. v. Phelps-Dodge Corp.,[225] the court stated that while the administrator must act upon any violations, he has alternative methods of acting (that is, either by civil or criminal proceedings), and he is not required to proceed first to effect a correction by civil means before instituting criminal proceedings.

The Federal Water Pollution Act Amendments of 1972 provide that any person who willfully and negligently violates its provisions is guilty of a crime and punishable by a fine of up to $50,000 per day of violation (or up to two years' imprisonment for second offenses). The statute specifically states that "for the purposes of the" . . . (criminal prosecution subsection) . . . "persons shall mean, where appropriate, any responsible corporate officers." Section 309(c)2 makes it a crime, punishable by not more than a $10,000 fine, imprisonment for not more than six years, or both, for "any person who knowingly falsifies information required under the Act" or who "knowingly renders inaccurate" any monitoring equipment which is required to be maintained. It is also important to note that the "anti-discrimination clause" of the 1972 amendments protects employees against discharge or discrimination that results from their initiating or participating in proceedings under the act.[226]

The Clean Air Act.[227] Under the Clean Air Act, the administrator, upon receiving information of a violation, is given authority to proceed to abate the violation. If the violation is of a federally set emission limitation, such as a hazardous emission standard or a standard of performance, the administrator has the authority to proceed directly and immediately. At his or her discretion, he or she may issue an administrative abatement order, seek criminal prosecution (in the case of a knowing violation), or obtain injunctive relief directly in a federal district court.

The sanctions that accompany the act provide that for first violations the court may impose maximum fines of up to $25,000 per day or imprisonment for not more than one year. These sanctions escalate to up to $50,000 per day or imprisonment for not more than two years in the case of subsequent violations. However, since the sanctions are expressed in terms of maximum penalties, the court has wide latitude in applying them.[228]

In order to preserve enforcement proceedings undertaken pursuant to earlier law and to assure a procedure for abatement of international air pollution, the 1970 amendments continue the authority of the abatement conference in the international abatement procedures. The act provides that no order or judgment under an abatement procedure shall relieve any person of any obligation to comply with any requirement of any implementation plan or other standard required under the 1970 amendments.[229]

National Environmental Policy Act.[230]   The National Environmental Policy Act requires that federal agencies file an "Environmental Impact Statement" on all projects that will have a significant impact on the environment. Generally speaking, the guidelines require the preparation of an impact statement at an early stage in the decision-making process. The draft should be prepared and available prior to any public hearings, to insure that other federal, state, and local agencies with relevant expertise, as well as the public, can comment on the draft statement prior to the making of even a tentative decision or recommendation. The chief function of the National Environmental Policy Act is administrative in nature. It does not define civil or criminal penalties.

Water Quality Improvement Act of 1970.[231]   This act initially provided that the President should determine those discharges which were deemed harmful for the purposes of the act. Upon the occurrence of a harmful discharge, the person in charge of the vessel or facility that made the discharge had to notify the appropriate agency. If the discharge was not then appropriately cleaned up by the discharger, the federal government could remove the oil or arrange for its removal. The discharger would then reimburse the government for any removal costs it incurred, up to a specified dollar limit, unless the discharger could show, as a defense, that the discharge was solely due to an act of God, an act of war, negligence of the government, an act or omission of a third party, or a combination of these causes. Vessels of over 300 gross tons had to maintain evidence of financial responsibility, through insurance or other means, to cover a cleanup liability of up to the lesser of $100 per gross ton or $14 million. Onshore and offshore facilities were liable to a limit of $8 million per occurrence. The statutory liability limits did not apply where the government was able to prove "willful negligence or willful misconduct in the privity and knowledge of the owner." A third party who caused the discharge was held to the same limits. When an owner or operator acted to clean up the discharge, the removal costs from the government could be recovered if one of the aforementioned defenses to a liability suit could be proven to exist. Authority was also given to establish procedures to be used in containing, dispersing, or removing oil.[232]

The 1972 amendments to the Federal Water Pollution Control Act added a major change to the provision of the Water Quality Improvement Act of 1970. Hazardous substances were folded into the structure of the oil section on a par with oil.

Under the old act, the civil penalty was imposed only if the discharge was a "knowing one." Since controversy arose over the Coast Guard's implementation of the knowledge requirements, Congress deleted them from the section when making the 1972 amendments. Congress also reduced the maximum possible penalty to $5,000 (from $10,000). Discharges of almost any quantity of oil or hazardous substance are subject to a penalty of up to $5,000.[233]

Other Federal and State Statutes. Section 10 of the Noise Control Act prohibits the sale or importation of products in violation of Noise Emission or Product Labeling Regulations under the act, and the section also prohibits the removal (except for repair) of noise control features built into a product in compliance with EPA (Environmental Protection Agency) regulations. The use of a product after such tampering has occurred is also prohibited. Labels affixed in compliance with the EPA regulations may not be removed before the product reaches the consumer.

Knowing violations by a manufacturer or importer are criminal offenses punishable under Section 11 by a fine of up to $25,000 per day of violation, or by a maximum prison term of one year, or both. The maximum penalties are doubled for second offenders. Each day of a continuing violation is punishable as a separate offense. The government may either sue in Federal District Court to restrain a violator or may issue an order specifying such relief as is determined to be necessary to protect the public health and welfare.[234]

New York Environmental Conservation Law makes it unlawful to discharge directly or indirectly into the waters of the state, substances that would create a condition in violation of standards adopted by the Environmental Conservation Department. Willful violations are punishable by a fine of not less than $500 or more than $2,500, or by a year's imprisonment or both. Each day of violation constitutes a separate offense.[235]

New York's version of the Federal Refuse Act of 1899 is found in Section 33C of the Navigation Law, but it applies only to discharges from watercraft, marinas, or moorings. Strict liability is imposed upon persons, meaning corporations or individuals, who place, throw, deposit, discharge, or cause to be placed, thrown, deposited, or discharged, any liquid or solid material detrimental to either the public health and safety or the recreational use of the water. A violation is a misdemeanor that subjects the actor to a fine of not more than $100, or to imprisonment of not more than sixty days, or both. A similar fine is placed on littering without regard to its effect on public health.[236]

Chapter 715 of the Laws of 1971 added criminal penalties to New York's air pollution legislation. For willful violations of the air pollution statutes by a person, which is defined as either an individual or a corporation, the applicable penalties are the same penalties that apply to water pollution offenses.[237]

Summary of Potential Liability and Penalties for Pollution
We have seen that, in addition to the common-law liability for wrongful acts by polluters, the trend of modern legislation has been to impose criminal, as well as civil, sanctions against polluters. Examples of the trend include jail sentences and rather heavy fines provided for in the Clean Air Amendments of 1970. The reader will recall that such penalties are imposed upon any person who knowingly falsifies information required by the act or who knowingly renders a required monitoring device inaccurate. As also is true of the Water Amendments, the use of heavy jail sentences, along with the requirement that corporate officials be given notice of violations, makes it apparent that prosecution of corporate executives was very much the intent of Congress when this section was passed.[238]

Courts have also begun to use criminal contempt powers in pollution cases. Corporations and corporate officials have been found guilty of criminal contempt for willful violations of injunctions restraining various forms of pollution. Including legislation designed to encourage and reward informants who identify sources of pollution and the laws which seek to impose the monetary burden of cleaning up the effects of environmental pollution on the polluters themselves, the developments heretofore described make it clear that the trend of modern society is to discourage pollution by the imposition of strict penalties.

Class Actions: Status and Implications The class action can be an effective means by which a large number of plaintiffs (those with relatively small claims and who may be economically unable to litigate individually) can join together as a group. There are four requirements to a class action: (1) that the class is so numerous that joinder of all members is impractical; (2) that there are questions of law or fact common to the class; (3) that the claims or defenses of the representative parties are typical of the claims or defenses of the class; and (4) that the representative party will fairly and adequately protect the interests of the class.[239]

Class actions have been used effectively by environmentalists, especially where polluters of water or air adversely affected large numbers of persons in a given area. In 1973, however, the Supreme Court dealt a major blow to the use of class actions.

In Zahn v. International Paper Company a majority of the Supreme Court agreed that each plaintiff, and therefore each member of the class, must allege a claim exceeding $10,000 in order to maintain a class action under Federal Rule 23(b)(3).[240] Justice White, speaking for the majority, stated that each plaintiff "must satisfy the jurisdictional amount and any plaintiff who does not must be dismissed from the case—one plaintiff may not ride in on another's coat tails." On remand, since the District Court was unable to determine how many of the 240 proposed class members actually met the $10,000 requirement, the court denied class action status to all.[241]

Furthermore, in Eisen v. Carlisle and Jacquelin, et al.,[242] a majority of the court held that individual notice must be provided to all class members who are identifiable through reasonable efforts. There were over two million class members involved in that action. Yet, the court held not only that individual notice was mandatory but also that the named plaintiff must bear the initial cost of notice to each member of the class.[243]

These decisions have, at least for the time being, restricted the use of class actions at the federal level. Nevertheless, the environmental movement continues to grow. Legislatures, government agencies, private businesses, and individuals are becoming increasingly aware of the consequences of pollution and the need to comply with the standards set down by society for its control.

Pollution Liability Insurance

After an overview of the history and impact of the contamination or pollution exclusion of most liability policies, this section will analyze the commercial insurability of pollution liability losses and the availability of insurance against both intentional and unintentional pollution exposures. Since pools have been formed to provide insurance against some pollution exposures, the Water Quality Insurance Syndicate and the Tanker Owners Voluntary Agreement on Liability for Oil Pollution (TOVALOP) will be briefly examined before the discussion proceeds to the topic of noninsurance techniques.

Contamination or Pollution Exclusion Prior to 1966 most liability policies were written on an "accident" basis which, in effect, provided coverage only for events that were sudden and accidental. There were exceptions, of course. Manuscript policies and even some standard policies provided coverage under the broader "occurrence" basis. However, as demand for and use of occurrence coverage heightened, standard liability policies were revised in 1966 to provide coverage on an occurrence basis.

By definition, occurrence includes both sudden and prolonged exposure to conditions that ultimately result in bodily injury or property damage that is neither expected nor intended from the standpoint of the insured. Many were satisfied that the wording was sufficiently clear to rule out cases involving intentionally caused injury or damage. But there were times when insureds successfully argued that, while their *acts* may have been intentional, they did not expect or intend the resultant *damages*. Furthermore, as the national concern over environmental pollution heightened, ultimately bringing about a number of new laws, insurers soon realized that the occurrence provision could very possibly subject them to claims for virtually every pollution or contamination incident. At the very least, insurers would sustain heavy expenditures in providing defense coverage. It therefore was decided that a change in policy provisions was needed.

In June 1970, two exclusions were issued for use with most standard liability policies. Not all insurance companies implemented the particular exclusions that were promulgated by the Insurance Rating Board (now the ISO). Some elected to file their own versions (most of which closely corresponded to the IRB language).

One of the IRB exclusions deals with all pollution or contamination exposures other than oil, and the other concerns only oil pollution exposures. The former excludes bodily injury or property damage arising out of any contamination or pollution into or upon land, the atmosphere, or any body of water—except when the discharge, dispersal, release, or escape is sudden and accidental. The latter excludes bodily injury or property damage arising out of the discharge, dispersal, release, or escape of oil or other petroleum substance or derivative into or upon land, the atmosphere or any body of water—whether or not it is sudden and accidental. The net effect of the latter provision is to preclude all coverage for damages claimed by oil pollution, however caused.

When these exclusions were first introduced, one insurance company executive explained the rationale for them this way:

> We will no longer insure the company which knowingly dumps its wastes. In our opinion, such repeated actions, especially in violation of specific laws, are not insurable exposures. Moreover, we are inclined to think that any attempt to provide such insurance might well be contrary to public policy.[244]

Since liability for contamination or pollution is an exposure faced by many firms, it is important to analyze factors that affect the commercial insurability of pollution liability losses. In this context, it is necessary both to consider traditional tests of insurability and also related social issues.

Commercial Insurability of Pollution Liability Losses Business leaders who are truly concerned about the environment and its inhabitants have already taken some admirable voluntary actions to prevent further environmental pollution. For those who have not yet taken the necessary preventive steps, perhaps the potential common-law consequences will combine with the newer statutory penalties to provide the motivation to do so.

Complementing pollution law is the almost complete absence of liability insurance for nonaccidental contamination and pollution claims. The absence of liability insurance may serve to the detriment of those who are harmed by polluters, but it may also be viewed as a much-needed motivation for the observance of existing pollution laws.

Some insurers now offer environmental pollution liability insurance to firms that implement antipollution control devices. In addition, some insurers participate in pools or syndicates to handle specific types of pollution or contamination liability claims, such as those resulting from nuclear radiation and oil spillage. Nonetheless, acts of intentional pollution cannot be insured at any price, and other aspects of pollution liability continue to pose insurability problems for private insurers.

When pollution liability is considered in the light of the usual tests for determining the insurability of losses, the various problems become rather evident. The usual tests (loosely referred to as "requisites" but more accurately described as ideal characteristics of insurability) are that (1) the losses should be definite in time, place, and amount; (2) the losses should be accidental, i.e., unforeseen, fortuitous, and unexpected to the applicant or insured; (3) the losses should not have an unmanageable catastrophe potential; (4) there should be a large number of homogeneous exposure units so that, through the law of large numbers, losses may be satisfactorily predicted; (5) the losses should be measurable in terms of money; and (6) the insurance must be economically feasible. An analysis of these tests as applied to pollution liability follows:

1. *Losses must be definite in time, place, and amount.* Many pollution losses cannot be definitely pinpointed as to time and place, nor to any one source. They are attributable to prolonged misuses or exposures by many sources. If insurance were provided, legal problems could result. For example, it would be almost impossible to determine whether, and to what extent, illnesses or property damages are solely attributable to an insured. Another difficulty would be to prove that the actual cause of some diseases—emphysema for example—is the air pollution. Such diseases can be caused by other factors, such as smoking, or working in a hazardous industry. Multiple causes of loss could pose problems, even when a pollution incident is sudden and accidental. In addition to these legal problems, there would be severe actuarial problems in trying to predict losses that are not definite in time, place, and amount.

2. *Losses must be accidental in nature.* Without question, some of the pollution that culminates in damages is willful or done with flagrant disregard to its possible effects. Also, some *acts* are intentional, but the *results* are unforeseen. A typical example is the dumping of mercury into streams and rivers, an occurrence that went on for a number of years. It was thought that mercury would sink and do no harm. However, it was subsequently discovered that mercury so disposed of would produce another harmful substance.

   Of course, not all pollution is intentional. Accidents can happen. Large, harmful amounts of pollutants or contaminants can be emitted or dumped through mechanical failure or human error. Furthermore, products can be manufactured without any reasonable expectation that they can add to ecological problems. For example, not too many years ago it was discovered that phosphates in household detergents produced harmful effects on streams, rivers, and lakes. The results were probably unexpected and unforeseen, but in waters that have been polluted by many substances and many polluters, it would be nearly impossible to single out the damages caused by a particular manufacturer.

3. *Losses should not have an unmanageable catastrophe potential.* Catastrophes are said to be losses of great magnitude sustained by many people at the same time (or within a comparatively short period of time). Pollutants and contaminants are obviously capable of producing catastrophic results. Dangerous concentrations of industrial pollutants commonly produce stagnant air masses detrimental to the health of people in large segments of

the country. Chemical wastes dumped into rivers can also affect the drinking water of thousands of people who consume it, and the available legal actions could result in aggregate liability losses amounting to untold millions of dollars.

It is possible to insure losses that have a catastrophe potential, of course, but, to do so successfully, insurers must be able to "manage the catastrophe potential"—that is, insurers must be able to achieve satisfactory operating results, over time, by the use of underwriting, rating, contract design, reinsurance, and other techniques. The catastrophe potential of windstorm is "manageable" in this sense, whereas the catastrophe potential of war is not. Whether the catastrophe potential of pollution liability can be managed now or in the future is not yet clear, but the severe consequences of an error in making this judgment justify some caution on the part of insurers.

4. *There should be a large number of homogeneous exposure units.* In order that losses may be predicted accurately enough, there should be a large number of homogeneous exposure units—i.e., similar type businesses or organizations in order to permit satisfactory predictions of the losses that will be incurred by firms who are actually insured. There should also be a substantial volume of credible loss experience and an acceptable means of forecasting significant increases in future losses. It would seem that there are ample numbers of similar firms interested in purchasing pollution liability insurance if the price is reasonable. Nonetheless, it is still no easy task to predict the frequency and severity of insurable pollution liability losses for those who would constitute the insured group.

5. *Losses should be measurable in terms of money.* Measuring the dollar costs or equivalents of property damage, bodily injury, sickness, death, loss of earning power, and loss of consortium and other such intangibles is sometimes difficult, though it is not impossible in the context of most types of legal liability. However, in some pollution cases, as mentioned earlier, it may well be impossible to determine the proper portion of a total dollar loss that was caused by a particular insured. There may be many causes involved, as well as many different polluters. Moreover, additional problems will surely arise if insurers are required to pay damage for such things as the aesthetic and/or enjoyment value of recreational areas or lakes. Intangible or so-called "general" damages are not new to liability insurers, of course, but such damages have already served as a contributing cause of skyrocketing premium increases for other types of

liability insurance, and they could conceivably have the same effect on premiums for pollution liability coverage.

6. *Insurance must be economically feasible.* If the statutory goals of curbing water, air, noise, and thermal pollution are met in the future, and if antipollution control devices and other effective techniques are implemented on a widespread basis, perhaps pollution liability insurance will become more readily available at economically feasible premiums. At present, however, these are not the realities; pollution is still rampant; pollution costs are enormously high; and appropriate insurance is difficult to obtain, especially for premiums prospective buyers would pay.

The Environmental Protection Agency estimates that the toll on human health from air pollution alone amounts to $6.1 billion annually; damage to materials amounts to $4.7 billion each year; and damages to residential property is estimated to cost $5.2 billion yearly.[245] Combined with the costs of other types of pollution, these figures strongly suggest that it may not be possible to have economically feasible pollution insurance premiums, at least not if the insurance is to respond to all pollution damages in the foreseeable future.

Lest the situation seem utterly hopeless, it is desirable to note that the insurability problems just discussed can be overcome—at least in part—if *most* of the insurability criteria can be met by a combination of contract design, rating, underwriting, reinsurance, and other insurance techniques (as opposed to noninsurance techniques). There is also the possibility that development of compulsory private insurance, social insurance, or some other governmental action may alter the insurability of the pollution exposure. However, no insurance or quasi-insurance approach by itself is capable of reducing the total social costs of pollution, and any such approach could even create a moral hazard to forestall further attempts to deal effectively with the problem of pollution prevention.

It does not seem likely that the conceptual problems associated with the insurance of intentional pollution will ever be solved. Unless and until society makes much greater progress in pollution abatement, even the liability aspects of unintentional pollution will surely continue to pose insurability problems that will adversely affect the availability and price of commercial insurance. And, despite the problems, some forms of commercial insurance are available, as discussed in the next subsections.

Intentional Pollution and Commercial Insurance. No insurer is presently willing to offer protection to firms that *intentionally* pollute the environment. In addition to the previously discussed problems, also applicable to the insuring of accidental pollution, intentional pollution presents some inherent insurability obstacles. First, an insurance contract that purports to cover intentional pollution may not be a contract "for a legal purpose" in the legal sense, because there is merit in the argument that encouragement of intentional pollution by "financing" it would be contrary to public policy. Apart from the legalities, moreover, intentional pollution quite obviously is not fortuitous. To that extent, the losses would be so inevitable that the premiums would have to be prohibitively high (essentially a trading of dollars plus the insurer's overhead and profit. Or, perhaps even worse, the losses of intentional polluters would have to be shared in a highly inequitable manner by insureds who do not intentionally pollute. In the unlikely event that such an inequity would be approved by rate regulatory authorities, it probably would not work anyway as a practical matter, unless the inequity and the purchase of the insurance is mandated by law.

Unintentional Pollution and Commercial Insurance. Even *un*intentional pollution has not been free from insurability problems, as we have seen. In fact, between 1970 and 1974 there was no commercial insurance available for the liability associated with unintentional pollution other than for damages resulting from sudden and accidental discharge, dispersal, release, or escape of pollutants or contaminants.

Then, in 1975, underwriters at Lloyd's of London took what many acclaimed as an affirmative approach to the problem by offering liability insurance to firms that had taken specified precautions against environmental pollution and had been certified to be in compliance with all environmental laws. In other words, the insurance was (and is) provided to firms that make an earnest attempt to reduce, control, and eliminate their pollution and contamination.

Pollution insurance programs are not standardized, so their coverages, exclusions, and conditions, as well as their rating methods, naturally vary to some degree. Even so, they have similar criteria for eligibility. Under one such program, referred to as environmental protector liability insurance, the following are the minimum criteria for coverage:

1. The insured must comply with all federal, state, or local laws, regulations, or ordinances concerning pollution or contamination of air, water, or the environment.
2. A pollution control engineer must certify that the insured is in compliance with all environmental laws and is eligible for insurance. (The engineer is selected by the insurer, but it is the insured's responsibility to pay for the professional services.)

3. The insured must be audited by an environmental control engineer in order to certify that all facilities are operated at design efficiency.
4. A detailed application is required and information is sought that will indicate, in part, the potential environmental effects of the applicant's operations on water, air, and noise pollution, and on solid wastes and other nuisances.

A noteworthy point about this program is that coverage applies for liability imposed by law or assumed under contract, but the cause of any such claim must *neither* be sudden nor accidental. This may appear to be an unusual stipulation until one considers the fact that sudden and accidental losses are already covered as exceptions to the contamination or pollution exclusion under standard general liability policy provisions. If it is determined that general liability coverage does not apply, the environmental protector policy then responds, subject to its own exclusions.

Whether the desired limits of liability are available at reasonable cost obviously needs to be considered. In situations where underlying limits are insufficient, firms may be able to purchase additional layering. In any event, as more firms attempt to abide by environmental laws, perhaps more insurance programs will be devised to offer higher limits and more competitive rates.

Water Quality Insurance Syndicate The so-called Water Quality Insurance Syndicate is a pollution liability pool made up of U.S. and alien insurers of ocean marine exposures. Its primary purpose is to provide coverage to owners, operators, and charterers of vessels, in the event they become liable to the United States for oil pollution cleanup costs and the spillage of other hazardous substances. The insurance thus parallels the needs that are made explicit by the previously discussed Water Quality Improvement Act of 1970 and the Federal Water Pollution Control Act Amendments of 1972.

The first of these two acts prohibits the discharge of oil in harmful quantities into or upon the navigable waters of the United States and adjoining shorelines. The limit of liability corresponds to the lesser of two amounts: (1) $100 per gross ton of the vessel, or (2) the statutory limit set by the laws. The second act bans the spillage of elements and compounds that present an imminent and substantial danger to public health and welfare.

Although not required by any federal antipollution law, property damage liability insurance is also made available by the syndicate to complement the basic "clean-up" insurance. Coverage to vessel owners for polluting incidents is written on a worldwide basis. The maximum limit of coverage is $5 million, while the minimum amount can be no less than the value of the insured hull of the vessel.

Offering property damage liability insurance on a voluntary basis may prevent states from having to enact legislation to protect their resources—legislation that could create obligations for which insurance may not be readily available.[246]

At least one state, Florida, has enacted a stringent anti-oil-pollution law which was upheld by the United States Supreme Court in 1973. This law can make shippers and dock owners liable for damages, to the state and to owners of private property, regardless of fault. In essence, the law imposes strict and unlimited financial liability without exceptions, even for acts of God, or war. At the time of the ruling, the maritime industry feared that posting insurance or a surety bond for purposes of financial responsibility would be extremely difficult. [247]

TOVALOP. Another similar pool is known as Tanker Owners Voluntary Agreement on Liability for Oil Pollution (TOVALOP). This group of tanker owners provides financial responsibility requirements for cleanup costs by oil spillage.

Noninsurance Techniques.

By and large, the utilization of loss prevention and loss reduction techniques is the ultimate key to dealing effectively with ecological exposures. Perhaps nearly all firms should employ the services of environmental specialists or engineers who can identify problems, provide assistance on the most economically feasible methods to solve or handle them, and assure compliance with the applicable laws. Large firms will have engineering specialists on their staffs, while smaller firms will have to look to outside specialty firms.

Engineers and specialists are able to identify and suggest alternatives in curbing high, harmful noise levels in such places as canneries, bottling works, and computer facilities. Noise levels in places of employment are the subject of regulation by the Occupational Safety and Health Administration. Supplying employees with ear plugs and other protective headwear is sometimes permitted (or required) if the protective equipment does not interfere with other exposures. Carpeting floors and walls is also a suggested method for controlling noise. Engineering staffs often assist in designing noise emission standards for certain products, such as construction equipment, motors, and electronic equipment subject to regulation by the EPA under the Noise Control Act of 1972.

Solid waste disposal can also be a problem, because open dumping or open burning is usually no longer permitted. However, it is sometimes possible for firms to hire the services of solid waste consulting companies to determine the best methods and locations for disposal of wastes. Those that discharge wastes and liquids into sewage systems need to be concerned with the biological oxygen demand of water. In reducing pollution, such devices as holding tanks and filtering systems are often effective. It is also suggested that firms work closely with federal, state, and local government, as well as with water companies and chemical laboratories. In some areas of commercial enterprise, pollution control is satisfied merely by changing to different heating fuels for processing.[248]

While engineers and environmental specialists provide beneficial services in identifying and suggesting solutions for pollution problems, their services are also necessary in preventing the occurrence of incidents once various devices are being utilized. For example, a mining company was held to be in violation of a pollution law, despite its implementation of substantial and costly control equipment, and a meat processing plant was held to be in violation of a pollution control statute by accidentally emitting odors into the atmosphere, even though the emissions were caused by an equipment breakdown that was repaired as soon as it was discovered.[249]

In spite of the obvious advantages of loss prevention and engineering in pollution control, whether insurance applies or not, some companies have not been able to withstand the costs of controls. For many, this has meant going out of business. The total costs of pollution controls are likewise formidable. In a joint study by the EPA, the Council on Environmental Quality, and the Department of Commerce, it was determined that the costs (over the period 1971 to 1980) of controlling air and water pollution, improving solid waste management, abating noise, reclaiming strip mined lands, and increasing radiation safety would total $287.1 billion. Of that total, air pollution costs were estimated at $106.5 billion or an average of $10.65 billion annually.[250]

BENEFIT PROGRAMS LIABILITY

Employee benefit programs have become an integral part of our society's economic security. Indeed, their growth in size, composition, and numbers has been remarkable. In addition to social security, workers' compensation, and unemployment compensation programs, voluntary private plans now commonly provide life, basic and major medical expense, and disability income insurance, as well as pension, profit sharing, and other retirement benefits. Numerous factors account for the growth of privately sponsored plans, including inadequacies of social insurance benefits, competition in the labor market, tax advantages for the employer and the employees, and the demands of organized labor.

At the end of 1976, it is estimated that fifty million people in the United States were participating in major private and public pension and retirement programs, other than social security. In 1975 private pension and retirement plans paid some $13.3 billion in benefits. Of this amount, private pension plans, other than those with life insurance companies, paid out $10.8 billion in benefits. Government retirement plans for civilian employees, on the other hand, paid a total of $17.6 billion in benefits. Social security benefits paid to retired workers, (including those on disability) during the same year, amounted to $45.0 billion, along with almost $19.7 billion paid in benefits under old age, survivors, disability and health insurance (OASDHI). Moreover, the accumulation of assets under privately sponsored employee benefit programs has become an important source of capital for the financial markets of the United States.[251]

The Exposure

No one will deny that employee benefit plans can (and usually do) play an important role in meeting people's financial needs and otherwise enhancing the social and economic stability of this nation. Unfortunately, however, the history of employee benefit plans contains a significant number of instances in which various factors have served to deny beneficiaries of their anticipated security.

One such factor is that many employees have not been given sufficient information or counsel about their eligibility for benefits and the kinds and amounts of benefits they should expect, or the advice or counsel given them by employers, union leaders, personal advisers, or administrators has been erroneous or misleading. Many pension plans, for example, have eligibility or vesting requirements that involve a certain minimum number of years of continuous employment. Information as to whether temporary layoffs or temporary absences can nullify previously earned continuous service credits is important and should be effectively communicated to employees.

Because of a technicality involving an employee benefits program of a union some years ago, many members are without adequate retirement benefits today. Those involved were under the impression that when they were transferred from one union shop to another, their previous service credits would also be transferred. Instead of being cumulative, all prior service credits automatically were invalidated upon transfer. This meant that, at retirement age, these persons had insufficient tenure to be eligible for benefits under the plan. Many of these sad occurrences might have been avoided if employees had been properly advised at the proper time. Of course, it would be unfair to blame employers for all such misfortunes. Some are beyond their control. Moreover, tax, insurance, and other laws account for much of the complexity of employee benefit plans. A prudent employee will make personal efforts to know and understand the benefits available.

Another problem is that assets of these programs, involving thousands and even millions of dollars, too often have led to such serious abuses as careless management of funds, imprudent investments, and embezzlements. Since proper safeguards had not been enacted, at least not until recently, these and other abuses ultimately deprived prospective beneficiaries of their benefits at the time of need.

Implications of Gediman v. Anheuser Busch[252] The inherent complexities of many employee benefit programs and the errors and omissions that may occur in administering them can adversely affect many people, but those who ultimately may have to pay heavily are the employers. In what is considered to be a very significant court decision, an employer was held liable to the estate of an employee for providing incorrect information. The employee in this case had a vested pension plan interest with a present value of $78,356 in 1956. Because of his health, he decided to take early retirement and file an election in writing to take his benefits in cash or in the form of an annuity. His employer advised him that if he were to defer his election until 1958, his vested interest would increase to $84,582. Relying upon that representation, he elected to defer the payment of his benefits. However, when he died in 1957, his former employer refused to pay that sum and offered, instead, $32,000 as the death benefit.

The executor refused this offer and commenced action against the employer, claiming that the employer violated its duty by not correctly and fully informing the decedent of the potential reduction in benefits in the event of death prior to the activation date of the pension. The lower court ruled in favor of the executor. On appeal by the employer in 1962, the lower court's decision was affirmed, and the employer was ordered to pay $78,356, plus interest from 1956.

This case, no doubt, had an influence upon the renewed interest in employee benefit programs liability insurance. A variety of such policies had been on the market for a number of years, but the demand for them had been relatively insignificant because the imposition of liability always had been subject to the "prudent man" rule of common law, and various interpretations of that rule had made it rather difficult and costly to prove negligence of administrators. Also, some of the statutes and regulations governing the operating efficiencies of benefit plans had not been adequately enforced.

Implications of the Employee Retirement Income Security Act of 1974 (ERISA)   Injurious effects and abuses of employee benefit plans persisted into the 1970s. Finally, the demands of reform advocates having been heard, Congress passed the Employee Retirement Income Security Act of 1974 (ERISA), which is commonly and loosely referred to as the Pension Reform Act of 1974. This act, which became effective on January 1, 1975, is considered to be one of the most significant and far-reaching developments in the entire history of employee benefit plans.

The act, which also has been termed a "bill of rights for employees," is too comprehensive and complex to describe here in any detail. But some of its provisions are germane to the subsequent discussion of corresponding liability insurance. First of all, the law encompasses virtually all firms that are involved in interstate commerce (though some plans, such as those of governmental bodies are exempt from its provisions). It therefore affects a large number of businesses. Another aspect of the law is that it regulates a variety of employee benefit plans, not just pension and retirement plans. The act also has far-reaching effects on plan fiduciaries, i.e., administrators, trustees, executors, and other fiduciaries because it supersedes all other statutes and regulations previously dealing with such persons and imposes, instead, an all-encompassing and uniform standard of federal control upon them. A fiduciary who breaches the requirements of this act now is *personally* liable for any losses which result from that breach. In addition, the act voids any exculpatory provisions designed to relieve fiduciaries from their liability.

The stringent provisions dealing with the liability of fiduciaries set off a wave of concern and panic because no insurance was then available with which to treat in full this new loss exposure. The act requires all fiduciaries to be bonded against fraud and dishonesty losses, but the purpose of the bonds is to protect *plans* against losses to their assets and funds, not the fiduciaries. While the demand for employee benefit programs liability insurance increased, this did not fully cover the exposure.

Employee Benefit Programs Liability Insurance

Employee benefit programs liability insurance came into existence in the early 1960s, largely as a result of the landmark case of Gediman v. Anheuser Busch. Generally, the intent of this insurance is to protect firms, their partners, officers, directors, and stockholders, as well as employees who are authorized to act in the administration of any plan, in the event of any claims made against them by prospective, present, or future employees and their beneficiaries and legal representatives. The damages insurers agree to pay must stem from negligent acts, errors, or omissions in the administration of various plans.

However, not all plans are covered by this insurance, nor are all acts that ultimately lead to claims. The plans usually covered are group life and health insurance, profit sharing and pension plans, employee stock subscription plans, workers' compensation and unemployment insurance, social security, and disability benefits coverages. Some policies also include travel, savings, and vacation plans. The kinds of acts of administration that are covered usually include (1) giving counsel to employees; (2) interpreting employee benefit programs; (3) handling records in connection with those benefits; and (4) handling enrollment, termination, or cancellation of employees under the various benefits. Even then, coverage may not apply. Policies usually stipulate that, to be included as an insured, an employee must be authorized to act in the administration of the plan.

These policies contain few exclusions. Dishonest, fraudulent, criminal, or malicious acts are not covered, although the first two can be treated with the purchase of fidelity bonds. As a matter of fact, ERISA requires the purchase of fidelity bonds covering dishonesty and fraud. Also excluded are claims based upon libel, slander, discrimination, or humiliation, and bodily injury or property damage losses. The latter two are covered under general liability policies, and the other ones—with the possible exceptions of discrimination and humiliation—are covered under personal injury liability insurance.

No coverage applies if an insurer of the plan fails to meet the requirements of its contract or when an employee benefit program fails. Also beyond the scope of these policies are claims resulting from the insured's failure to comply with the laws dealing with workers' compensation, unemployment insurance, social security, or disability benefits. Claims involving unsatisfactory stock performances are also excluded. In this latter category are losses to employees because stocks do not perform as represented, losses resulting from advice given to employees concerning participation in stock subscription plans, and claims based upon the investment and noninvestment of funds.

Most conditions of these policies correspond to those of other liability policies. However, the policies in question usually carry a mandatory deductible—typically $1,000—which applies on a per-claim basis. If any insurer decides to settle a claim by paying the full amount of the policy, the insured is obligated to reimburse the insurer for the deductible amount.

Fiduciary Liability Insurance

The development of ERISA stimulated another type of insurance, commonly referred to as fiduciary liability insurance or pension trustees errors and omissions insurance. Since these are nonstandard policies, they carry a variety of names and there is substantial variety in their provisions. Yet all of them are directed toward protecting administrators, trustees, and the like in the event they become liable for damages as the result of their negligence, errors, omissions, or breach of duties in handling any of the affairs dealing with employee benefits. While all such policies share a common purpose, the method of achieving that purpose lacks uniformity. Policies are so broad and diverse that it is difficult to summarize their provisions.

At least one insurer agrees to provide coverage stemming from any breach of fiduciary duty of its insureds, or from any such breach by any other person for whom the insured is legally responsible, and arising out of an activity of any plan named in the policy. Quite obviously, the meaning of the phrase, "breach of fiduciary duty," is important in determining the scope of coverage. This particular policy defines that phrase to mean "the violation of any of the responsibilities, obligations or duties imposed upon fiduciaries by the Employee Retirement Income Security Act of 1974 or amendments thereto with respect to any plan named in Item (1) of the declarations."

Other insurers provide coverage stemming from any wrongful act. Though the definition of that term varies, it is defined by one insurer to mean "any actual or alleged breach of duty, neglect, error, misstatement, misleading statement, omission or other act done or wrongfully attempted ... or so alleged. ..."

Most policies contain numerous exclusions. Among the claims, losses, or events specifically excluded are fines or penalties imposed by law, as well as other matters deemed uninsurable under laws. Also not covered are claims made against insureds for libel, slander, bodily injury, property damage, fraudulent acts or dishonesty, and failure of the insured to effect or maintain bonds or insurance.

If coverage is not excluded, the insurer's liability for any claim depends upon two amounts. The first of these is the policy limit—which is the maximum payable during the policy year or in the discovery period. (The discovery period is essentially the same concept that applies to directors' and officers' liability insurance when coverage is canceled and the insured desires to buy an extension to cover claims that may arise because of any wrongful act or breach of duty committed before such date of cancellation.) Some policies include defense costs as part of the limit of liability, while others pay for such costs in addition to the limit of liability. The other amount deals with mandatory deductibles ranging from $1,000 to over $100,000.

When an employer decides to purchase insurance for its fiduciaries, it must make sure the policy does not contain the recourse provision. Otherwise, the very purpose for which an employer purchases that fiduciary liability policy is defeated. The act requires that when fiduciary liability insurance is purchased by an *employee plan* for the benefit of its administrators, trustees, etc., the policy must include a so-called recourse provision which gives an insurer the right to subrogate against fiduciaries who breach their duties. However, when the *employer* or *sponsor* of such plan purchases the fiduciary liability insurance, the recourse provision is neither mandatory nor desirable from the employer's standpoint.

Noninsurance Techniques

The chance of liability arising out of improper administration of employee benefit programs can be avoided if benefit programs are not provided. In fact, ERISA has been directly responsible for the termination of many pension plans. The reason for this lies, not in the loss exposures involved, but in the complex reporting and disclosure requirements of the act, which create significant administrative expenses, particularly when dealing wth only a small group of employees.[253] Regardless of the motivation for avoidance, it is a successful risk management technique. Not all those who are subject to ERISA law are purchasing insurance, although they are, of course, purchasing the mandatory fidelity bond. Some firms, particularly small partnerships and closely held corporations, forgo the purchase of fiduciary insurance, for at least three reasons. First, they feel the insurance costs too much in relation to their exposure to loss. (Many of these same firms do not purchase directors' and officers' liability insurance for the same reason.) Second, some firms transfer all of their responsibilities of administering employee benefits, or at least a large share of them, to outside professionals. However, while firms may be able to reduce their liability through such transfers, they cannot wholly avoid their responsibilities under law, and, hence, their liability. Third, some firms have but a few employees, thereby making it relatively easy for them to exercise various internal controls, thus avoiding pitfalls that often lead to claims.

Some of the larger firms and labor unions may also elect to utilize retention as their principal tool in handling ERISA liability loss exposures, and partial retention is usually forced upon purchasers of insurance (by policy exclusions and mandatory deductibles). However, regardless of whether a firm is large or small or whether it buys insurance, loss prevention and other complementary techniques should be utilized. To a large extent, the provisions of ERISA specify what is required for compliance therewith, but mere observance of the statutory requirements will not totally eliminate the possibility of costly claims.

For example, the opinion of one executive, Harry C. Anderson, president of Corporate Policyholders Counsel, Inc., is that profit-sharing plans rather than pension plans will be the primary target of lawsuits in the area of fiduciary liability because of claims alleging poor investment performances. Yet, to a large extent, claims of this nature can be reduced by using outside investment counsel. In fact, the more often outside expertise is sought and used, the less are the chances successful suits will be made against inside fiduciaries.[254] Thus, using outside expertise could be viewed as a form of noninsurance transfer or loss prevention.

Internal controls can reduce the chances of loss by fraud and dishonesty, and such controls are desirable for all firms, whether or not they are subject to ERISA. Also desirable is a formal organizational plan designating the authority and the responsibility of each person involved in any way with employee benefits. A system of checks and balances to ensure that each person fulfills the roles properly is likewise needed. There should be an unobstructed system of communication among those persons who handle employee benefits, company executives, and any outside professional assistance. Furthermore, the administrators should be competent and able to explain benefit provisions in language most people can understand. There should also be a system of proper claims handling and control. Finally, firms should produce written material in accurate but easy-to-read language explaining the various benefits provided, as well as their eligibility and termination provisions.

Regardless of the care and the skill exercised in managing employee benefits, claims of negligence, errors and omissions will continue to occur; but, by exercising precautions and keeping good records, many costly claims can be prevented.

DATA PROCESSORS' ERRORS AND OMISSIONS LIABILITY

Computer technology is one of the most significant and far-reaching achievements of our time. Its growth, sophistication, contribution, and use now affect all segments of society. In fact, nearly all businesses, institutions, and levels of government are dependent upon electronic data processing equipment today, not only in handling the menial tasks usually associated with paperwork, but also in handling complicated technological processes.

EDP systems became commercially available in 1952,[255] and their demand and growth continue to be phenomenal. But they are costly investments. Such costs include not only their purchase or rental prices, but also the expenses required to train competent operators, maintain the equipment properly, and establish controls to prevent any conditions that can damage or impair their usefulness. For these reasons, many firms that require the services of EDP systems cannot afford to purchase or lease them. Instead, many hire out their work to specialty service organizations whose function is to perform data processing work for others.

The Exposure

Service organizations, including some commercial banks that offer their computer facilities and expertise to *others*, must exercise a high degree of skill and care, because they are vulnerable to costly damages in the event their performance does not meet the level of expectation they may warrant or represent. (Those who process their own data may also make errors, but this business peril cannot be transferred.) The possibilities for liability are innumerable. Errors in accounting records may preclude the user of such services from collecting many of its receivables. A mistake in the color coding program of a concrete mix may result in expenses for a concrete supplier who must pay for the costs of removing and replacing the concrete section of a structure of a different shade from that specified. Negligence in programming the input on inventory controls may cause a firm to make unnecessary expenditures or to refrain from making certain necessary expenditures.

The consequences of these and other errors or omissions are easy to imagine. They may result in damages of such magnitude as to destroy or seriously impair the assets of an EDP service organization. Various loss prevention procedures can and should be implemented by such organizations, of course. But many service organizations also purchase a special type of errors and omissions insurance.

Insurance Coverages Available

The available data processors' errors and omissions liability policies are nonstandard forms. However, some generalizations can be made. Most such policies contain the agreement that payment will be made on behalf of insureds when they are determined to be legally obligated to pay others for damages arising from their negligent acts, errors, or omissions in the performance of data processing services for others. Those usually protected as insureds include officers, directors, and stockholders of corporations (and sometimes nonofficer employees). When the firm is a partnership, coverage extends individually to its partners. In addition to liability coverage per se, insurers commonly provide the usual supplementary benefits for the costs and expenses incurred in investigating, defending, and settling any claims.

These policies are almost always subject to mandatory deductibles. The deductibles are directed primarily toward firms that offer to rerun erroneous work as a means of satisfying clients and preventing claims. While the extra expenses of reruns probably are insurable, deductibles serve to place on insureds the assumptions of such expenses as costs of doing business.[256]

Exclusions vary among the available policies. Commonly excluded are any dishonest, fraudulent, criminal or malicious act or omission of insureds; liability of others assumed by the insured under any contract or agreement; loss or damage to property in the care, custody, or control of insureds, or of property which is in transit; bodily injury or property damage, as well as any liability stemming from loss caused intentionally by or at the direction of the insured; liability for punitive or exemplary damages; and liability of the insured arising out of the giving of advice on methods, practices, procedures, or opinions on financial statements, as well as for any liability for the preparation of any income tax returns. Many of the excluded claims are insurable under other policies or bonds. Others are simply uninsurable.

Noninsurance Techniques

Regardless of the liability insurance that may be available for those processing the data of others, certain kinds of loss exposures are either uninsurable or insurable only for prohibitive premiums. Therefore, it is important for service organizations to establish and maintain effective controls if they wish to keep their clientele and remain solvent. (Of course, it is also important for firms processing their own data to practice sound loss control measures.)

Since many errors and omissions are the result of incompetence, data processors should continuously train their operators, programmers, and supervisors on the complexities of EDP systems. Continuing education helps to develop skills that can prevent costly errors.

As noted earlier, data processing service organizations frequently offer to make adjustments in the event of faulty work, even to the extent of redoing all faulty work. Since many such expenses are retained, data processors may desire to set up a formal system of funded retention to take care of their loss costs, particularly if the frequency and severity of such incidents are high.

Finally, some service firms probably should refuse certain kinds of work, particularly work that has produced a history of claims in the past. Unless clients are agreeable to assuming by contract some of the potential problems that can arise, the noninsurance transfer technique would not seem to be available to data processors.

INTERNATIONAL EXPOSURES AND THEIR TREATMENT

The basic principles of risk management and insurance are universal; but the unique cultural, social, legal, regulatory, economic, and political environment in each country requires some modifications of risk management techniques. The sources of liability facing the foreign affiliate of an international company (subsidiary, licensee, joint venture, etc.) are basically the same as those facing its domestic (home country) counterpart—premises and operations, products and completed operations, professional, contractual, automobile, pollution, and others. In addition, the legal system in each foreign country may present unique liability situations. For example, some countries determine liability according to a code rather than through common law. The Napoleonic Code determines liability by statute in certain situations, such as damage caused to a landlord's property by a tenant. In these situations the common-law defenses are ineffective, and strict (or absolute) liability often applies.

Similarly, recent events, such as pollution incidents, have resulted in harsh legislation imposing punitive damages and even the threat of imprisonment of executives. Intense nationalism and the resulting distrust of "foreign" business interests have contributed to the adverse legal environment in many countries.

Insurance

Insurance management in the foreign affiliates of an American-based corporation is usually more complex than in the United States because of each country's regulations regarding *admitted* and *nonadmitted* insurance. Admitted insurance consists of insurance contracts that are in conformance with the laws and regulations of the country in which the subject of insurance is located. It is usually written in the language of that country, and its insuring clauses and conditions reflect the business customs and practices peculiar to that country. Losses are usually payable in local currency and may present serious problems if there are currency controls in effect, such as inconvertibility to U.S. dollars. The advantages of admitted insurance are: tax benefits (premiums are deductible as a business expense), compliance with government insurance regulations, claims settlement handled by a local insurer aware of cultural sensitivities, and good will generated by supporting the local insurance industry.

Nonadmitted insurance refers to insurance policies issued on forms or through companies not approved by the regulatory authorities of the country in which the subject of insurance is located. Prohibitions against nonadmitted insurance exist in about two-thirds of the countries of the world. Penalties for noncompliance vary greatly in terms of severity and enforceability but may include heavy fines, attachment of assets, and even jail sentences for top management. Advantages of nonadmitted insurance (especially comprehensive U.S. policies) are that it is usually broader in coverage, less costly, easier to understand, and enforceable in U.S. courts.

To capitalize on the advantages of each kind of insurance, most international companies use a combination approach. One study showed that the most popular method of insuring foreign operations is to purchase admitted insurance from a local insurer for basic (or compulsory) coverage and superimpose nonadmitted coverage to provide the breadth of coverage needed.[257]

Noninsurance Techniques

Retention Retention is not as widely practiced abroad as it is in the United States for several reasons.[258] First, in autonomous foreign affiliates, the decision concerning commercial insurance users' retention is often made by the affiliate manager, who may be unfamiliar with retention programs. In addition, due to tradition and to pressures from insurance brokers, the affiliate manager may be insurance-oriented.

Second, few local insurance companies have the flexibility, the experience, or the desire to design insurance rating programs with adequate credit for substantial deductibles. This negative attitude towards large deductibles has found its way into local insurance laws and customs in many countries.

The third factor discouraging retention abroad is that only a few countries have a work injury program that functions separately from the social security system. Workers' compensation is the most common loss exposure retained by U.S. companies, but there is no comparable exposure to retain in foreign operations.

Loss Control Loss control programs in most foreign countries are not as widespread as in the United States. The variance in the quality of loss control activities is great and is influenced by such factors as:

- the attitudes of local nationals toward safety rules (smoking, wearing of hard hats and safety shoes), and
- the responsiveness of less than wholly owned affiliates to costly loss control devices suggested by American management.

The availability and quality of loss control services vary from a standard that equals that of the United States (in Great Britain and a few other industrialized countries) to a complete absence of such services in some developing countries.

Avoidance Avoidance can be practiced for individual foreign exposures in much the same manner as for domestic exposures. More significant is the initial decision of whether a firm should expand its operations into foreign countries. Even when other business indicators are favorable, foreign exposures are often avoided simply because of the complexity and increased uncertainty of operating within a strange environment.

Noninsurance Transfer Noninsurance transfers can be used in treating foreign loss exposures, but the variety of legal environments involved are beyond the scope of this text.

In general, despite a desire by American firms to treat their foreign loss exposures in the same manner as their domestic exposures, conditions usually demand a different mix of risk management techniques, depending on the availability of insurance coverages, the incentives for retention and control, and the regulatory forces in effect.

Chapter Notes

1. McKinney's, *Consolidated Laws of New York, Business Corporation Law*, Sec. 717 (1963); see also Model Business Corporation Act, Sec. 35 American Bar Association (1974).
2. Barnes v. Andrews, 298 F. Supp. 614 (S.D.N.Y. 1924); Cohen v. Cocoline Products, 309 N.Y. 119, 127 N.E. 2d 906 (1955).
3. Hun v. Carey, 82 N.Y. 65, 74 (1880).
4. Cohen v. Cocoline Products, supra, note 2.
5. Jones v. Foster, 70 F. 2d 200 (4th Cir. 1934); see also, Parrish v. Maryland and Virginia Milk Producers Assn., Inc., 250 Md. 24, 242 A. 2d 512 (1968).
6. Levitan v. Stout, 97 F. Supp. 105 (W.D. Ky. 1951).
7. Seaboard Industries, Inc. v. Monaco, 442 Pa. 256, 276 A. 2d 305, 309 (1971), quoting from Lutherland, Inc. v. Dahlen, 357 Pa. 143, 151, 53 A. 2d 143, 147 (1947).
8. Stanton v. Schneck, 140 Misc. 621, 251, N.Y.S. 221 (Sup. Ct. 1931).
9. Western States Life Insurance Co. v. Lockwood, 166 Cal. 185, 193, 135 P. 496, 499-500 (1913); see also Fleishhacker v. Blum, 21 F. Supp. 527 (N.D. Cal. 1937), aff'd in part, rev'd in part, 109 F. 2d 543 (9th Cir.) cert. den. 311 U.S. 665 (1940).
10. Lutherland, Inc. v. Dahlen, supra, note 7, 357 Pa. at p. 151, 53 A. 2d at p. 147.
11. Lancaster Looseleaf Tobacco Co. v. Robinson, 199 Ky. 313, 250 S.W. 997 (1923).
12. Johnston v. Green, 35 Del. Ch. 479, 121 A. 2d 919 (Sup. Ct. 1956).
13. California Corporations Code Section 309 (1976).
14. Efron v. Kalmanovitz, 249 Cal. App. 2d 187, 192, 57 Cal. Rptr. 248, 251 (1967).
15. Sheppard v. Wilcox, 210 Cal. App. 2d 53, 26 Cal. Rptr. 412 (1962); see also Wiita, 7 Pacific L. J. 613 "California's New General Corporation Law, Directors' Liability to Corporations" (1976).
16. McKinney's, *Business Corporation Law*, supra, note 1, Section 713, Del. General Corporation Law, Section 144 (1976).
17. Henry Campbell Black, *Black's Law Dictionary*, 4th ed. (St. Paul: West Publishing Co., 1957).
18. William E. Knepper, *Liabilities of Corporate Officers and Directors* (Indianapolis, IN: The Allen Smith Co., 1973), p. 6; see also Diedrick v. Helm, 217 Minn. 483, 14 N.W. 2d 913 (1944).
19. See section dealing with "Liabilities of Corporate Officers and Directors," infra.
20. Ibid.
21. C.C.H. Fed. Sec. L. Rep. Section 80, 219 (1975).
22. Duncan v. Williamson, 18 Tenn. App. 153, 74 S.W. 2d 215 (1933).
23. Davenport v. Prentiss, 126 App. Div. 451, 110 N.Y.S. 1056 (1908).
24. San Pedro Lumber Company v. Reynolds, 121 Cal. 74, 53 P. 410 (1898).

25. Morton Feuer and Joseph E. Johnston. *Personal Liabilities of Corporate Officers and Directors*, 2nd ed. (Englewood Cliffs, NJ: Prentice-Hall, 1974).
26. Fells v. Katz, 256 N.Y. 67, 175 N.E. 516 (1931).
27. New York Central Railroad Company v. Lockwood, 17 Wall 357, 382, 383, 21 L. Ed. 627 (1873).
28. Bown v. Ramsdell, 227 App. Div. 224, 237 N.Y.S. 573 (1929).
29. Hanna v. Lyon, 179 N.Y.107, 71 N.E. 778 (1904).
30. Briggs v. Spaulding, 141 U.S. 132, 35 L. Ed. 662, 11 S. Ct. 924 (1890).
31. Ibid.
32. Fidelity & Deposit Company of Maryland v. Wiseman, 103 Tex. 286, 124 S.W. 621 (1910).
33. Prudential Trust Co. v. McCarter, 271 Mass. 132, 171 N.E. 42 (1930).
34. Stern v. Lucy Webb Hayes, 381 F. Supp. 1003 (Dist. of Columbia 1974).
35. Fletcher v. Eagle, 74 Ark. 585, 86 S.W. 810 (1905).
36. Graham v. Allis-Chalmers Manufacturing Co., 41 Del. Ch. 78, 188 A. 2d 125, aff'g 40 Del. Ch. 335, 182 A. 2d 328 (1962).
37. Coddington v. Canaday, 157 Ind. 243, 61 N.E. 567 (1901).
38. 12 U.S.C. Section 503.
39. Platt Corp. v. Platt, 42 Misc. 2d 640, 249 N.Y.S. 2d 1 (1964).
40. Selheimer v. Manganese Corporation of America, 423 Penn. 563, 224 A. 2d 634 (Penn. 1966).
41. Syracuse Television, Inc. v. Channel 9, Syracuse Inc., 51 Misc. 2d 188, 273 N.Y.S. 2d 16 (Sup. Ct. 1966).
42. De Pinto v. Landoe, 411 F. 2d 297 (9th Cir. 1969).
43. See, e.g., Southern California Homebuilders v. Young, 45 Cal. App. 679, 188 P. 2d 586 (1920); Gordon v. Elliman, 306 N.Y. 456, 119 N.E. 2d 331 (1954); Robertson's, Inc. v. Renden, 189 N.W. 2d 639, (N.D. 1971).
44. See e.g., McKinney's, supra, note 1, Business Corp. Law Sec. 510, 719; Del. General Corp. Law Sec. 170.
45. McKinney's, supra, note 1, Bus. Corp. Law Sec. 719 (a)(1), Sec. 719(e).
46. Burt v. Ervine Co., 237 Cal. App. 2d 828, 47 Cal. Rptr. 392 (1965).
47. Chance v. Guaranty Trust Co., 32 N.Y.S. 2d 412 (Sup. Ct. 1941).
48. Wangrow v. Wangrow, 211 App. Div. 552, 207 N.Y. Supp. 132 (1924).
49. Sinclair Oil Corp. v. Levien, 280 A. 2d 717 (Del. 1971); Miller v. American Tel. & Tel. Co., 344 F. Supp. (E.D. Penn. 1972).
50. Stanton v. Schneck, supra, note 8; Fleishhacker v. Blum supra, note 9.
51. New York Trust Co. v. American Realty Co., 244 N.Y. 209, 155 N.E. 102 (1926).
52. Asphalt Constr. Co. v. Bouker, 150 App. Div. 691, 135 N.Y.S. 714 (1912) aff'd 210 N.Y. 643, 105 N.E. 1080 (1914).
53. See, e.g., Guth v. Loft, Inc., 23 Del. Ch. 255, 5 A. 2d 503 (1939).
54. New York Auto Co. v. Franklin, 49 Misc. 8, 97 N.Y.S. 781 (Sup. Ct. 1905) aff'd 135 App. Div. 908, 118 N.Y.S. 1127 (1909) aff'd 202 N.Y. 557, 95 N.E. 1134 (1911).
55. Foley v. D'Agostino, 21 A.D. 2d 60, 248 N.Y.S. 2d 121 (1964).
56. Universal Electric Corp. v. Golden Shield Corp., 316 F. 2d 568 (1st Cir. 1963).
57. Fells v. Katz, supra, note 26, 256 N.Y. at p. 70, 175 N.E. at p. 517.
58. Broderick v. Blanton, 59 N.Y.S. 2d 136 (Sup. Ct. 1945)

59. Chelrop, Inc. v. Parrott, 293 N.Y. 442, 57 N.E. 2d 825 (1944).
60. Mueller v. Nugent, 187 Ky. 61, 218 S.W. 730 (1920).
61. Anderson v. Smith, 398 S.W. 2d 635 (Tex Cir. App. 1966).
62. Saco Dairy Co. v. Norton, 140 Me. 204, 35 A. 2d 857 (1944).
63. Holmes v. Willard, 125 N.Y. 75, 25 N.E. 1083 (1890).
64. Adams v. Smith, 275 Ala. 142, 153 So. 2d 221 (1963).
65. United States v. Wise, 370 U.S. 405, 8 L. Ed. 2d 590, 82 S. Ct. 1354 (1962).
66. Sherman Anti-Trust Act, 15 U.S.C. Sec. 1.
67. See also United States v. American Radiator & Standard Sanitary Corp., 433 F. 2d 174 (3rd Cir. 1970).
68. Clayton Anti-Trust Act, 15 U.S.C. Sec. 24.
69. See also Cott Beverage Corp. v. Canada Dry Ginger Ale, Inc., 146 F. Supp. 300 (S.D.N.Y. 1956) app. dismissed 243 F. 2d 795 (2d Cir. 1957).
70. Kugler v. Koscot Interplanetary, Inc., 120 N.J. Sup. 216, 293 A. 2d 682 (1972).
71. Wilshire Oil Co. v. Riffe, 409 F. 2d 1277 (10th Cir. 1969).
72. United States v. Andreadis, 366 F. 2d 423 (2d Cir. 1966); United States v. Knox Coal Company, 347 F. 2d 33 (3rd Cir. 1965).
73. People v. Trapp, 20 N.Y. 2d 613, 286 N.Y.S. 2d 11, 233 N.E. 2d 110 (1967).
74. State v. Thomas, 123 Wash. 299, 212 P. 253 (1923).
75. United States v. Dotterweich, 320 U.S. 277, 88 L. Ed. 48, 64 S. Ct. 134 (1943).
76. United States v. Park, 421 U.S. 658, 44 L. Ed. 2d 489, 95 Sup. Ct. 1903 (1975) rev'g 499 F. 2d 839 (4th Cir. 1974).
77. Ohio Rev. Code Ann. Sec. 1701. 93.
78. Ibid. Sec. 1701.95.
79. McKinney's, Consolidated Laws of New York, Penal Law Sec. 190.35.
80. Hines v. Wilson, 164 Ga. 888, 139 S.E. 802 (1927).
81. Dome Realty Co. v. Rottenberg, 285 Mass. 324, 189 N.E. 70 (1934).
82. Beaudette v. Graham, 267 Mass. 7, 165 N.E. 671 (1929).
83. King Realty, Inc. v. Grantwood Cemeteries, Inc., 4 Ariz. App. 76, 417 P. 2d 710 (1966).
84. Griesse v. Lang, 37 Ohio App. 553, 175 N.E. 222 (1931).
85. Securities Act of 1933, 15 U.S.C. Sec. 77a. et seq.
86. Securities Exchange Act of 1934, 15 U.S.C. Sec. 78a. et seq.
87. See generally Louis Loss & Edward M. Cowett, *Blue Sky Law* (Boston: Little, Brown and Co., 1958).
88. See cases cited in Louis Loss, *Securities Regulations* Sec. 1638, n. 38 (Boston: Little, Brown and Co., 1961); C.C.H. Blue Sky Law Rep. Sec. 3615.
89. 15 U.S.C. Sec. 77 k.
90. Escott v. Bar Chris Constr. Corp., 283 F. Supp. 643 (S.D.N.Y. 1968).
91. Ernest L. Folk, III, "Civil Liabilities Under the Federal Securities Acts: The Bar Chris Case," 55 *Virginia L. Rev.* 1 (1969).
92. Feit v. Leasco Data Processing Equip. Corp., 332 F. Supp. 544 (E.D.N.Y. 1971).
93. 15 U.S.C. Sec. 77 l(1).
94. Ibid. Sec. 77 l(2); see also Hillyork v. American International Franchises, Inc., 448 F. 2d 680 (5th Cir. 1971).
95. 15 U.S.C. Sec. 77 q.

96. 15 U.S.C. Sec. 77 j(b).
97. 17 C.F.R. Sec. 240.10b-5.
98. Securities & Exchange Comm. v. Texas Gulf Sulphur Co., 258 F. Supp. 262 (S.D.N.Y. 1966); Securities and Exchange Comm. v. Texas Gulf Sulphur Co., 401 F. 2d 833 (2d Cir. 1968).
99. Lanza v. Drexel & Co., 479 F. 2d 1277 (2d Cir. 1973).
100. Ernst & Ernst v. Hochfelder, 425 U.S. 185, 47 L. Ed. 668, 96 Sup. Ct. 1375 (1976).
101. Kardon v. National Gypsum Co., 69 F. Supp. 512 (E.D. Pa. 1946).
102. Birnbaum v. Newport Steel Corp., 193 F. 2d 461 (2d Cir. 1952) cert. den. 343 U.S. 956, 96 L. Ed. 1356, 72 Sup. Ct. 1051 (1952).
103. New York Park Mining Co. v. Cranmer, 225 F. Supp. 261 (S.D.N.Y. 1963).
104. Vine v. Beneficial Finance Co., 374 F. 2d 627 (2d Cir. 1963) cert. den. 389 U.S. 970, 19 L. Ed. 460, 88 Sup. Ct. 463 (1967).
105. Dasho v. Susquehanna Corp., 380 F. 2d 262 (7th Cir. 1967) cert. den. Bard v. Dasho, 389 U.S. 977, 19 L. Ed. 2d 470, 88 Sup. Ct. 480 (1967).
106. Pappas v. Moss, 393 F. 2d 865 (3rd Cir. 1968).
107. Perlman v. Feldmann, 219 F.2d 163 (2d Cir. 1955) cert. den. 349 U.S. 952 (1955).
108. Jannes v. Microwave Communications, Inc., 325 F. Supp. 898 (N.D. Ill. 1971); Lester v. Preco Industries, Inc., 282 F. Supp. 459 (S.D.N.Y. 1965).
109. O'Neill v. Maytag, 339 F. 2d 764, 767 (2d Cir. 1964) aff'g 230 F. Supp. 236 (S.D.N.Y. 1964).
110. Simmons v. Wolfson, 428 F. 2d 455, 456 (6th Cir. 1970).
111. S.E.C. v. Chenery Corp., 318 U.S. 80 (1943).
112. 15 U.S.C. Sec. 78 n (a).
113. 17 C.F.R. Sec. 240.14a-9.
114. See e.g. Gerstle v. Gamble-Skogmo, 298 F. Supp. 66 (E.D.N.Y. 1969); Norte & Co. v. Huffines, 288 F. Supp. 855 (S.D.N.Y. 1968) cert. den. 397 U.S. 989, 90 Sup. Ct. 1121 (1970).
115. See e.g. 15 U.S.C. Sec. 78-1 (Williams Act, Section 12); 15 U.S.C. Sec. 80a (Investment Company Act of 1940).
116. Faulk v. Milton, 25 App. Div. 2d 314, 268 N.Y.S. 2d 844 (1966); Wampler v. Palmerton, 250 Ore. 65, 439 P. 2d 601 (1968).
117. Ellingson v. World Amusement Service Association, Inc., 175 Minn. 563, 222 N.W. 335 (1928); Patrons State Bank & Trust Co. v. Shapiro, 15 Kan. 856, 528 P. 2d 1198 (1974).
118. Michaels v. Lispenard Holding Corp., 11 App. Div. 2d 12, 201 N.Y.S. 2d 611 (1960).
119. Hoeverman v. Feldman, 220 Wis. 557, 264 N.W. 580 (1936).
120. Klockner v. Keser, 488 P. 2d 1135 (Colo. App. 1971).
121. Equitable Life & Casualty, Inc. v. Inland Printing Co., 44 P. 2d 162 (Utah 1971).
122. Hart v. Evanston, 14 N. Dak. 570, 105 N.W. 942 (1905).
123. Ibid.
124. Walker v. Man, 142 Misc. 277, 253 N.Y.S. 458 (1931).
125. See e.g. McKinney's, supra, note 1, *Business Corporation Law* Sec. 719(a).
126. Gordon v. Elliman, 306 N.Y. 456, 119 N.E. 2d 331 (1954) .

127. Spivek v. United States, 370 F. 2d 612 (2d Cir. 1967).
128. United States v. Wise, supra, note 65.
129. United States v. Park, supra, note 76.
130. Bergjans Farm Dairy Co. v. Sanitary Milk Producers, 241 F. Supp. 476 aff'd, 368 F. 2d 679 (1966).
131. Securities & Exchange Commission v. Texas Gulf, supra, note 98.
132. Bert S. Prunty, Jr., "The Shareholder's Derivative Suit: Notes on its Derivation," 32 *N.Y.U.L. Rev. 980 (1957).*
133. Fleishacker v. Blum, supra, note 9.
134. Fayes, Inc. v. Kline, 136 F. Supp. 971 (S.D.N.Y. 1955).
135. Graham v. Allis-Chalmers Manufacturing Co., supra, note 36.
136. Bennett v. Propp, 187 A. 2d 405 (Del. Ch. 1962).
137. Rogers v. Hill, 289 U.S. 582 (1933).
138. Diamond v. Oreamuno, 24 N.Y. Ed. 494, 301 N.Y.S. Ed. 78, 248 N.E. Ed. 910 (1969).
139. Stephan v. Merchants Collateral Corp., 256 N.Y. 418, N.E. 824; Weingand v. Atlantic Savings & Loan Association, 1 Cal. 3rd 806, 83 Cal Reptr. 650 464 P. 2d 106 (1970).
140. Roth v. Fund of Funds, Ltd., 405 F. 2d 421 (2d Cir. 1968).
141. Schoenbaum v. Firstbrook, 405 F. 2d 215 (2d Cir. 1968).
142. Sias v. Johnson, 86 F. 2d 766 (6th Cir. 1936).
143. Morrow v. Frank, 289 Mo. 549, 233 S.W. 224 (1921).
144. Kohler v. Kohler, 208 F. Supp. 808 aff'd 319, F. 2d 634 (2d Cir. 1963).
145. Goodwin v. Milwaukee Lithographing Co., 171 Wis. 351, 177 N.W. 618 (1920).
146. Jacobson v. Yaschik, 249 S.C. 577, 155 S.E. 2d 601 (1967).
147. Mutual Shares Corp. v. Genesco, Inc., 384 F. 2d 540 (2d Cir. 1967).
148. Myzel v. Fields, 386 F. 2d 718 (8th Cir. Minn. 1967).
149. Securities and Exchange Commission v. Texas Gulf, supra, note 98.
150. Kohler, supra, note 144.
151. Globus v. Law Research Service, Inc., 418 F. 2d 1276 (2d Cir. 1969) cert. den. 397 U.S. 913, 90 Sup. Ct. 913 (1970); Cf. deHaas v. Empire Petroleum Co., 302 F. Supp. 647 (D. Colo. 1969).
152. Mills v. Electric Auto-Lite Co., 396 U.S. 375, 24 L. Ed. 2d 593, 90 Sup. Ct. 616 (1970).
153. Ibid.
154. See e.g. McKinney's, *Consolidated Laws of New York,* Penal Law Sec. 190.35, 55.10 and 80.05.
155. 15 U.S.C. 77x.
156. 15 U.S.C. Sec. 1.
157. 15 U.S.C. Sec. 24.
158. See generally, "Indemnification of the Corporate Insider: Directors and Officers Liability Insurance," 54 *Minn. L. Rev.* 667 (1970).
159. New York Dock Company v. McCollum, 173 Misc. 106, 16 N.Y.S. 2d 844 (Sup. Ct. 1939).
160. Solimine v. Hollander, 129 N.J. Eq. 264, 19 A. 2d 344 (1941).
161. See generally William F. Knepper, "Indemnification and Liability Insurance—An Update, Officers and Directors: 30 *Bus. Law* 951 (1975);

McKinney's, N.Y. B.C.L. Sec. 721-726, Del. Code Ann. Tit. 8, Sec. 145(F) (Cum. Supp. 1968) Ohio Rev. Code Ann. Sec. 1701.13(E)(6) (Page Supp. 1973).

162. Note 158, supra; and George T. Washington and J. W. Bishop, *Indemnifying the Corporate Executive: Business, Regal and Tax Aspects of Reimbursement for Personal Liability* (New York: The Ronald Press Co., 1963).

163. Ibid., Washington & Bishop, p. 293.

164. Teren v. Howard, 322 F. 2d 949 (9th Cir. 1963).

165. S.E.C. v. Continental Growth Fund, C.C.H. Fed. Sec. L. Reptr. Sec. 94, 719 (S.D.N.Y. 1964).

166. 17 C.F.R. Sec. 230.460, Note A (1974).

167. See S.E.C. Securities Act, Release No. 4936 (Dec. 9, 1968).

168. Globus v. Law Research, Inc., supra, note 151.

169. Monnet v. Merz, 127 N.Y. 151 (1891).

170. Powell v. Newburgh, 19 Johns 284.

171. *PF&M Analysis* (Indianapolis: The Rough Notes Co., March 1977), Specialty Coverages, 384.1, p. 5.

172. Ibid.

173. Warren G. Brockmeier, "Status of D & O Liability Coverage," *Risk Management* Vol. 24, No. 1, January 1977, p. 20. No survey was conducted in 1977, and 1978 survey results are not available as this book goes to print.

174. The Wyatt Company, "Directors and Officers Liability and Fiduciary Liability Survey," *Summary Report*, 1975, p. 1.

175. "Insurer would pay half of Gulf directors' settlement," *Business Insurance*, Oct. 4, 1976, p. 1.

176. Joanne Gamlin, "Record D&O settlement in Mattel case," *Business Insurance*, Nov. 17, 1975, p. 1.

177. Ellis Simon, "Huge Grant Suit Clouds D&O Market, Experts Say," *Business Insurance*, 1 May 1978, p. 1.

178. Joseph F. Johnston, Jr., "Practical Considerations in Developing an Officers and Directors Protection Program," *Protecting the Corporate Officer and Director from Liability* (New York: Practicing Law Institute, 1976); see also Herbert S. Wander, "Protecting Directors Against Securities Liability," Preventing Directors' Liability Under the Securities Laws 1976 (P.L.I. 1976).

179. Johnston, supra, note 178.

180. United States v. Park, supra, note 76.

181. Escott v. Bar Chris Constr. Corp., supra, note 90.

182. New York Stock Exchange Manual, Page A-24 reprinted in C.C.H. Fed. Sec. L. Rptr. Sec. 26, 100.

183. Feuer, supra, note 25, Chap. 15.

184. Ibid.

185. Brooks Wilder, "Mobilizing the Use of the Board's Talents," Preventing Directors' Liability Under the Securities Laws (P.L.I. 1976).

186. Samuel P. Brown, "Criteria for Judging Preventative Programs—The View of One Outside Director," *Preventing Directors' Liability Under the Securities Laws* (P.L.I. 1976).

187. Wander, supra, note 178.

188. Frank P. Grad, *Environmental Law*, Sec. 1.01-1.02 (New York: Matthew Bender, 1973).
189. C.C.H., *Topical Law Reports*, Vol. 2, *Pollution Control Guide*, Sec. 6203 (Commerce Clearing House, 1976).
190. 61 *Am. Jur.* 20, "Pollution Control," Sec. 141 (Rochester, NY: The Lawyers Co-operative Publishing Co., and San Francisco, CA: Bancroft-Whitney Co., 1973).
191. American Cyanamid Co. v. Sparto, 267 F. 2d 425 (1959).
192. Chapman v. American Creosoting Co., 220 Mo. App. 419, 286 S.W. 837 (1926).
193. 61 *Am. Jur.* 2d, "Pollution Control," Sec. 141 (Rochester, NY: The Lawyers Co-operative Publishing Co., and San Francisco, CA: Bancroft-Whitney Co., 1973).
194. Conway v. O'Brien, 111 F. 2d 611 (2d Cir. 1940).
195. 324 App. 2d 465 (1963).
196. Julian Conrad Juergensmeyer, "Control of Air Pollution Through the Assertion of Private Rights," *Duke L. J.*, 1967.
197. 6 *Am. Jur.* 2d, "Pollution Control," 142 (Rochester, NY: The Lawyers Co-operative Publishing Co., and San Francisco, CA: Bancroft-Whitney Co., 1973).
198. 3 H. L. 330 (1865).
199. Robert J. Meyers, "The Viability of Common Law Actions for Pollution Caused Injuries and Proof of Facts," *New York Law Forum*, Vol. 18, 1972-1973, p. 948.
200. Ibid.
201. Restatement, Second, Torts, Sec. 520 (Philadelphia, PA: The American Law Institute, 1966).
202. Charles A. Gregory & Harry Kalven, Jr., *Cases and Materials on Torts*, 2d ed. (Little, Brown & Co., 1969), p. 23.
203. Robert J. Meyers, p. 949.
204. 61 *Am. Jur.* 2d, "Pollution Control," 168 (Rochester, NY: The Lawyers Co-operative Publishing Co., and San Francisco, CA: Bancroft-Whitney Co., 1973).
205. 22 *Am. Jur.* 2d, "Damages," 241 et seq. (Rochester, NY: The Lawyers Co-operative Publishing Co., and San Francisco, CA: Bancroft-Whitney Co., 1973).
206. DeLongpre v. Carroll, 331 Mich. 474, 50 N.W. 2d 132 (1951); Cochran v. Consumer Wirebound Box Co., 246 Miss. 398, 149 So. 2d 844 (1963); State ex. Rel. Board of Health v. Sommers Rendering Co., 66 N.J. Super. 334, 169 A. 2d 165 (1961).
207. Patterson v. Peabody Coal Co., 3 Ill. App. 2d 311, 122 N.E. 2d 48 (1954).
208. 61 *Am. Jur.* 2d, "Pollution Control," Sec. 43 (Rochester, NY: The Lawyers Co-operative Publishing Co., and San Francisco, CA: Bancroft-Whitney Co., 1973).
209. C.C.H., *Topical Law Reports*, Vol. 2, *Pollution Control Guide*, 6203 (Commerce Clearing House, 1976).
210. 61 *Am. Jur.* 2d, "Trespass," 143 (Rochester, NY: The Lawyers Co-operative Publishing Co., and San Francisco, CA: Bancroft-Whitney Co., 1973).

211. 61 *Am. Jur.* 2d, "Trespass," 149 (Rochester, NY: The Lawyers Co-operative Publishing Co., and San Francisco, CA: Bancroft-Whitney Co., 1973).
212. Victor J. Yannacone & Bernard S. Cohen, *Environmental Rights & Remedies*, Vol. 1, Sec. 4:6 (The Lawyers Co-operative Publishing Co., Bancroft-Whitney Co., 1972).
213. Juergensmeyer, supra, note 196.
214. "A Trend Toward Coalescence of Trespass and Nuisance: Remedy for Invasion of Particulates," *Washington University Law Quarterly*, Vol. 1, 1961, p. 64.
215. C.C.H., *Topical Law Reports*, Vol. 2, *Pollution Control Guide*, 6203 (Commerce Clearing House, 1976).
216. 61 *Am. Jur.* 2d, "Pollution Control," 48 (Rochester, NY: The Lawyers Co-operative Publishing Co., and San Francisco, CA: Bancroft-Whitney Co., 1973).
217. 245 Ore. 247, 427, P. 2d 957 (1967).
218. John C. Esposito, "Air and Water Law Pollution: What to Do While Waiting for Washington," *Harvard Civil Rights—Civil Liberties Review*, Vol. 5, 1970, p. 37.
219. 33 USC Sec. 407.
220. Act of March 3, 1899, C. 425, Sec. 16, 32 Stat. 1151.
221. Ralph C. Nash, Jr., and Susan Linden, "Federal Procurement and the Environment," *Federal Environmental Law*, Environmental Law Institute (St. Paul, MN: West Publishing Co., 1974), p. 488.
222. Public Law 93-119, 87 Stat. 424.
223. Public Law 87-88, 75 Stat. 204.
224. 393 F. Supp. 735 (D.C. Ohio 1975).
225. 311 F. Supp. 1181 (D.C. Ariz. 1975).
226. "Criminal Responsibility of Corporate Officials for Pollution of the Environment," *Albany Law Review*, Vol. 37, 1972-1973, p. 84.
227. 42 USC, Sec. 1857 et seq.
228. Thomas Jorling, "The Federal Law of Air Pollution Control," *Federal Environmental Law*, Environmental Law Institute (St. Paul, MN: West Publishing Co., 1974), p. 1108.
229. Ibid., p. 1072.
230. Public Law 91-190, 83 Stat., 852, 42 United States Code, Sec. 4321 et seq.
231. Public Law 91-224, 84 Stat. 91.
232. Charles F. Lettow, "The Control of Marine Pollution," *Federal Environmental Law*, Environmental Law Institute (St. Paul, MN: West Publishing Co., 1974), pp. 606-607.
233. Ibid., p. 612.
234. William Lake, "Noise: Emerging Federal Control," *Federal Environmental Law*, Environmental Law Institute (St. Paul, MN: West Publishing Co., 1974), p. 1228.
235. "Criminal Responsibility of Corporate Officials for Pollution of the Environment," p. 88, supra, note 226.
236. Ibid., pp. 88-89.
237. Ibid., pp. 84-85.
238. Ibid., pp. 84-85.

239. C. J. Stanley Mosk, "Finding a Direction for Our Environment," Barrister, Vol. 3, No. 2 1977, p. 16.
240. 414 U.S. 291 (1973).
241. Mosk, supra, note 239.
242. 417 U.S. 156 (1974).
243. Mosk, supra, note 239.
244. Thomas J. Slattery, "INA Excluding Pollution Cover in All Policies," *The National Underwriter Co.*, Property and Casualty Edition, April 17, 1970, p. 1.
245. Marvin Zeldin, *The Campaign for Cleaner Air* (New York: Public Affairs Pamphlet, 1973), p. 15.
246. *F.C.&S. Bulletins* (Cincinnati: The National Underwriter Co., 1974), Companies & Coverages, Large Lines, M-3.
247. Reubin O'D. Askew v. The American Waterways Operators, Inc., 411 U.S. 325 (1973).
248. Norman Hoffman, "How to Face Your Company's Many Ecology Exposures," *Business Insurance*, February 14, 1972, p. 25.
249. 46 *A.L.R.* 3rd 758.
250. Zeldin, *The Campaign for Cleaner Air*, p. 15.
251. *Life Insurance Fact Book '77* (Washington, D.C.: American Council of Life Insurance), p. 35.
252. Gediman v. Anheuser Busch, 193 Fed. Supp. 72 (1961).
253. Jerry Geisel, "ERISA Wrecks Some, But Not All, Pensions," *Business Insurance*, March 20, 1978, p. 1.
254. Joanne Gamlin, "Profit Sharing Plans Stand to Suffer Significant Lawsuits Under ERISA," *Business Insurance*, November 3, 1975, p. 4.
255. Robert H. Catherwood, *E.D.P. Risks, The Management of Insurable Risks Incident to the Use of Electronic Data Processing Equipment* (Toronto: Canadian Underwriter Magazine, 1963), p. 5.
256. Norman A. Baglini, *Risk Management in International Corporations* (New York: Risk Studies Foundation, 1976), pp. 111-142.
257. Ibid., pp. 95-97.
258. Ibid.

CHAPTER 12

Aviation Exposures; Liability Exposures of Charitable, Governmental, and Educational Entities

INTRODUCTION

This chapter continues the discussion of special liability exposures and their treatment. It analyzes two types of liability exposures which have unique characteristics. For a variety of reasons, aviation exposures are in a class by themselves. The analysis of aviation exposures and their treatment here will include not only the liability exposures, but also a discussion of the property loss exposures of aircraft hulls. The operations of charitable, governmental, and educational entities are, by and large, similar to those of other commercial enterprises. However, their liability exposures are often different from those of other entities because of doctrines affording immunity for certain types of acts. In addition, a variety of court decisions and statutes have made some special distinctions regarding the liability of such enterprises. Because of these factors affecting the exposures, there are special considerations involved in the risk management of charitable, governmental, and educational entities.

AVIATION EXPOSURES AND THEIR TREATMENT

Aviation Liability Exposures

In 1822 the New York Supreme Court held a balloonist liable, in an action in trespass, for the damage to crops caused when the balloon descended into a private garden.[1] The court also required him to pay for the damages of curiosity seekers and those who were intent on rescuing him. The court compared ascending in a balloon to throwing a lighted firecracker into a crowd or letting loose a dangerous animal. The judge agreed that ascending in a balloon was not an unlawful act, but he did say: ". . . it is certain that the astronaut has no control over its motion horizontally; he is at the sport of the winds, and is to descend where and how he can; his reaching the earth is a matter of hazard." If the phrase "reaching the earth is a matter of hazard" accurately described the advances in the aeronautical sciences, especially during the past quarter of century or so, air transportation could not have attained the position it now holds in the commercial life of the world.[2] Yet, surprisingly enough, as recently as 1955, the intrepid balloonist decision was cited as authority for holding an airline liable, without proof of fault, for damages caused when its aircraft made an off-airport crash landing.[3]

Exposures of Aircraft Owners and Operators

Common-Law Principles. Although the chances of loss in connection with aircraft are exceedingly large, the current trend of the law holds that, ". . . properly handled by a competent pilot exercising reasonable care, an airplane is not an inherently dangerous instrument, so that in the absence of statute, the ordinary (common-law) rules of negligence control."[4] As a general rule, the tort liability of aircraft owners and operators is determined in accordance with the applicable law of the state where the accident occurred. However, it is important to note that this traditional rule has been repudiated in a number of states and replaced by the following principle: the local law of the state which has the most significant relationship with the occurrence and with the parties determines their rights and liabilities in tort.[5] And, while most states apply common-law negligence principles to aviation accidents, a few states have absolute liability statutes and, by treaty and private agreement, absolute liability is imposed upon the commercial airlines for accidents in international flights.

Statutory Modifications and Private Agreements Affecting International Travel. Common law has been modified by a number of statutes, some of which apply to international travel and others to domestic travel.

THE FEDERAL DEATH ON THE HIGH SEAS ACT.[6] This act gives the federal admiralty courts jurisdiction over the cause of action for death caused by a wrongful act which arises out of an aircraft crashing into the high seas beyond one marine league from shore.

WARSAW CONVENTION.[7] A treaty commonly called the Warsaw Convention, among other things, applies to passenger injury and death when the accident occurs in "international" air transportation, as determined from the place of departure and the place of destination appearing in the passenger ticket, when performed by an "air transportation enterprise." The treaty establishes limitations on the amounts recoverable as follows: for a passenger's death or bodily injury, 125,000 francs; for loss of or damage to checked baggage and goods (air freight shipped under an airway bill), 250 francs per kilogram; and for loss of or damage to personal effects of which the passenger takes charge, 5,000 francs.

MONTREAL AGREEMENT OF 1966. This private agreement was the response of the airlines to the United States' Notice of Denunciation of the Warsaw Convention, a denunciation which was based upon the low level of maximum recovery for bodily injury and death. The Montreal Agreement provides that the airlines shall file tariffs with the Civil Aeronautics Board. These tariffs (1) raise the Warsaw Convention limit of liability to $75,000 for a passenger's bodily injury or death, and (2) waive the defenses otherwise allowed by Article 20 (1) of the convention. Had these defenses not been waived, an air carrier would not be liable if it could prove that all necessary measures were taken to avoid the damage or that it was impossible to take such measures.[8] Upon acceptance by the airlines of the Montreal Agreement principles, the United States withdrew its notice of denunciation. The agreement imposes absolute liability on the air carrier, but the amount of liability is not limited absolutely, because an "escape" is provided the passenger by article 25. This article removes the ceiling on the amount recoverable, upon proof that the damage was caused by willful misconduct of the air carrier or its agent.

GUATEMALA PROTOCOL. When the United States withdrew its notice of denunciation, it was with the understanding that the private agreement was an interim arrangement pending the negotiation of a new international convention to replace the Warsaw Convention. Working through the International Civil Aviation Organization (ICAO), negotiations to develop an international convention concluded in the adoption of the Guatemala Protocol in 1971. The major revisions to the Warsaw Convention may be summarized as follows:

1. absolute liability of the air carrier;
2. a $100,000 per passenger limit;
3. automatic and periodic upward revision of the limitation to accommodate changing economic conditions;
4. a settlement inducement provision permitting the limit to be increased by the amount of the legal costs, if the air carrier does not settle within six (6) months of the claimant's demand; and,
5. provision for supplemental protection which will permit countries to devise systems for supplemental compensation in addition to the liability limit of $100,000.

At this writing, the Guatemala Protocol had not been submitted to the United States Senate for the advice and consent required for ratification. One problem has been the development and funding of a supplemental compensation plan which would pay United States passengers up to $200,000 above the Guatemala Protocol limit for provable damages.

Statutes Affecting Domestic Travel. There is no Warsaw Convention type of compensation system for victims of accidents in the *domestic* transportation of passengers by air in the United States. A jury instruction states the general rule: A common carrier is not a guarantor of its passengers' safety. But it has a duty to its passengers to use the highest degree of care consistent with the mode of conveyance used and the practical operation of its business as a common carrier by air. Some jurisdictions make a distinction between the duty to protect a passenger from the perils of operating an airline when boarding, alighting, and being transported versus the perils of operating a waiting room or ticket-selling operation, which normally present no hazards unique to a common carrier. In the latter circumstances, only ordinary care may be required; in the former circumstances, a somewhat higher degree of care may be required. It has been said that the degree of care should be commensurate with the danger to which the passenger is subjected, and the degree of care required to be exercised increases as the danger increases.

AVIATION GUEST STATUTES. Many states have currently adopted aviation guest statutes, which closely follow the form of automobile guest statutes.[9] When the guest-passenger status is established, an injured guest's recovery under such statutes is usually dependent upon proof of intoxication or willful misconduct of the pilot. The principal issue of fact in a guest case may be whether the injured person was in fact a guest passenger riding in the aircraft without giving compensation. It is not necessary to show actual payment of funds to establish that the flight was motivated by business considerations and, therefore, outside the application of an aviation guest statute. In deciding that there was substantial evidence to establish that the corporate defendant expected to benefit from a flight which ended in the crash of the aircraft and death of the passenger, the court said:

> We believe that the jury could have found from the evidence that Mr. Halbert was a prospective customer of the corporation, and that Mr. Berlinger, as the president and executive officer of the corporation, was motivated by business considerations in suggesting and making the flight. The fact that the parties also planned to do some hunting would not necessarily mean that the trip was a social venture; it is common knowledge that businessmen often entertain customers and prospective customers for business reasons. This line of testimony

concerns not only the corporation's liability on grounds of *respondeat superior*, but also the status of the Halberts, whether that of passengers or guests.[10]

Statutes limiting or excluding liability for bodily injury are not popular these days. Two states, Idaho and Michigan, have to date held their aviation guest statutes unconstitutional.[11] California has repealed its guest statute.

Strict Liability or Absolute Liability Statutes. Statutes in a few states still impose absolute liability on aircraft owners and operators for injury to persons or property *on the ground* and caused by forced landing of aircraft or the falling of objects therefrom.[12] The absolute liability statutes make technical owners as well as actual owners liable, but a federal law exempts lessors or mortagees from liability, unless they are in actual control of the aircraft.[13] The rule of absolute liability had its beginning in Section 5 of the Uniform Aeronautics Act of 1922, but in 1943, since the act was deemed obsolete, it was withdrawn from the active list of Uniform Acts by the National Conference of Commissioners on Uniform State Law.

Financial Responsibility—The Uniform Aircraft Financial Responsibility Act. This act or some form thereof is law in several states. The act requires the furnishing of acceptable security for the specified limits deemed sufficient to satisfy any judgment which may be recovered as damages resulting from the accident.

Vicarious Liability Statutes. At least two states currently have so-called *vicarious liability statutes* which provide that the owner of aircraft shall be liable for damages in any case in which the user of the aircraft would be liable for the injury or damage if the use of the aircraft is with the express or implied permission of the owner.[14] The California Public Utilities Code, Sec. 21404 and 21404.1 also provides that an owner is vicariously liable for the negligent operation of an aircraft by a permissive user, though it limits the dollar amount of liability to $15,000 for the death of one person, $30,000 for one accident, and $5,000 for property damage.

Summary. Subject to the important exceptions already noted, then, the common-law rules of negligence are the basic legal principles to be applied in analyzing the liability exposures of aircraft owners and operators. The burden is on the person who has been damaged to prove fault as a proximate cause of the accident—i.e., to prove that there was a failure to exercise the requisite degree of legal care owed to the damaged plaintiff—before the owner or operator becomes legally obligated to pay damages.[15]

Other "Aviation" Exposures Our concern has been with liability exposures of aircraft owners and operators in their capacity as owners and operators. However, broadly defined, "aviation" liability exposures include a number of other exposures which are not unique to aviation. The term "aviation exposures" would encompass the liability of airport owners and operators and also that of liability for products used in aircraft operations or in the aircraft themselves.

Airport Owners and Operators. Airport exposures may include operations as diverse as managing the best restaurant in town or operating a fleet of unlicensed surface vehicles and premises similar to those of a central city department store, including those exposures associated with escalators and elevators.

Important liability exposures more peculiar to airport operations stem from the following four activities: (1) maintenance of runways, taxiways, and ramps, keeping them free of obstructions and lighted as required, and providing pilots with appropriate notice of dangers; (2) hangarkeeping—the exposure to loss when aircraft of others are left in the care, custody, or control of the hangarkeeper for repair, storage, or safekeeping; (3) aircraft refueling and defueling; and (4) fire fighting and rescue activities after an aircraft accident occurs.

The rules of law governing the liability of owners and operators of airports are not unique. The owners and operators are liable for all damages caused by their failure to exercise reasonable care. Their duty to exercise reasonable care is owed to lessees, aircraft owners and operators, passengers, spectators, visitors, and members of the public who may be on or about the property and using the premises in accordance with an invitation, express or implied, to be there.

The courts have been nearly unanimous in holding that the operation of an airport is a proprietary, as distinguished from a governmental, function. Therefore, as a general rule, states, counties, and municipalities cannot successfully assert governmental immunity (discussed later in this chapter) as a defense to suits which allege their negligence in the operation or maintenance of an airport.

Aviation Products. There have been a number of damage suits from aviation products alleged to have been defective. The exposure to liability of airframe manufacturers and component parts suppliers may have its origin in many causes, but the principal sources may be summarized as failure to exercise necessary care in one or more of the following particulars: design; selection of material; construction; testing; and, instructions for proper use, including emergency procedures and appropriate warnings. Breach of warranty and traditional tort theories of recovery in products cases are being replaced, in an increasing number of jurisdictions, by a rule of strict liability. This represents an attempt to insure that the costs of injuries are borne by the manufacturers of defective products rather than by the injured persons who are powerless to protect themselves. As discussed in an earlier chapter on products liability, the broad effect of the strict liability rule is to permit the plaintiff to establish the manufacturer's liability, apart from any proof that the manufacturer was negligent.

Aircraft Liability Insurance

The aircraft hull and liability policy is usually written on a combined form—the consolidation of two standard policies—to provide the coverages and limits of liability which are indicated by specific premium charges in the declarations. In the case of major clients, airlines or the large users of corporate aircraft—sometimes referred to as *industrial aid risks,* it is not unusual for the underwriter, the broker and the corporate insurance manager to negotiate the terms of coverage and reduce them to a manuscript policy which is fashioned to meet the needs of the particular insured. Either in manuscript form or by endorsements, the coverage provided under the standard policies may be enlarged or restricted as required.

There are many terms and conditions in the aircraft liability insurance contract (or the liability portion of a combined form) which closely resemble those found in automobile insurance forms. The aircraft policy is designed to protect the named insured and described permissive users against legal liability for bodily injury and property damage caused by an occurrence and arising out of the ownership, maintenance, or use of the insured aircraft. The major divisions of the aircraft hull and liability policy are as follows: (1) declarations, (2) insuring agreements, (3) exclusions, and (4) conditions. The first three will be discussed in the following sections. In general, policy conditions are similar to those already studied in connection with other liability insurance forms.

Declarations The declarations page identifies, among other things, the named insured, the insured aircraft, the approved pilots, the approved purposes of use, and the geographical scope of coverage. Some items here continue to be more controversial than others.

Named Insured and Insured Aircraft. The insured aircraft are described in the declarations by: "Make and Model," Federal Aviation Administration (FAA) identification number (sometimes referred to as the "N" number), "Passenger Capacity" (excluding crew), and "Insured Value." Identification and representations as to licenses and ownership are also required for fairly obvious reasons.

Approved Pilots. The following is an example of how an "approved pilot clause" might appear in the declarations:

It is a condition hereof that, while the aircraft is "in flight," it may be operated only by the following pilots: John Doe and Richard Roe, properly certified commercial pilots with multi-engine ratings, or a pilot holding a valid and effective commercial certificate who has had a minimum of 2,000 hours as a pilot in command of an aircraft, including at least 500 hours in multi-engine aircraft; each of such pilots to hold proper ratings as required by the FAA for the flight involved.

The rather strict pilot requirements in the declarations were inserted in this case because of the nature of the named insured's business—a commercial operator carrying passengers for hire—and because of the use of high performance aircraft which require pilots with appropriate experience for a safe operation. Such limitations on the nature of the use of the aircraft, the type of aircraft to be flown and the qualifications of the pilot limit exposures to those for which the underwriter intends to provide coverage. The conditions with respect to approved pilots may be reinforced by a second provision, an exclusion which provides that the policy does not apply while the aircraft is operated "in flight" by other than the pilot or pilots specified in the declarations.

Purposes of Use. Purposes of use are not only stated in the declarations, they are also the subject of an exclusionary clause which provides that the policy does not apply while the aircraft is used for any purpose other than that stated in the declarations. For example, if an aircraft crashed and was destroyed while on an unauthorized charter flight, coverage has been successfully denied by the insurer based upon the policy exclusion which provided in substance that the policy did not apply while the aircraft was being operated for any purpose other than Industrial Aid or Pleasure and Business.[16] (The term Industrial Aid relates to corporate use when employees and guests of the company are transported in the interest of the company's business and no direct charge or profit is involved.)

The usual use of classifications for rating purposes may be summarized as (1) "Airline"—carriers operating under appropriate economic authority issued by the Civil Aeronautics Board, subject to Part 121 of the Federal Aviation Regulations, and either scheduled or supplemental air carriers engaged in the carriage of persons or property for compensation or hire;[17] (2) "Pleasure and Business"—individual owners and operators of aircraft who make up the bulk of the general aviation fleet; (3) "Commercial"—including transportation of passengers for hire, air taxis, student instruction, rental to others, charter work and similar uses to make a profit in the business of air transportation; and (4) "Special Uses"—a classification judgment-rated to fit the peculiar characteristics of such operations as aerial crop spraying (sometimes written on a policy form drafted specially for the purpose), aerial fire fighting, pipeline patrol, law enforcement, and banner towing.

Insuring Agreements The insuring agreement, in substance, states that in consideration of the payment of the premium and in reliance upon the declarations, and subject to the limits of liability and all the other provisions of the policy, the insurer will pay, on behalf of the insured, all sums which the insured shall become legally obligated to pay as damages because of bodily injury, property damage, or medical expenses, subject to stated limits of liability in one or more of the following categories:

A. bodily injury sustained by any person except a passenger;
B. injury to property;
C. bodily injury sustained by any passenger;
D. single limit bodily injury and property damage;
E. single limit bodily injury (excluding passengers) and property damage; and
F. expenses for medical services.

"Occurrence" is defined in the policy in the customary manner:

An accident, or a continuous or repeated exposure to conditions, which results in injury during the policy period, provided the injury is neither expected nor intended from the standpoint of the Insured. All damages arising out of such exposure to substantially the same general conditions shall be deemed to arise out of one occurrence.

The policy definition of "injury" is:

As respects any person, injury means bodily injury, sickness or disease, including mental anguish or death resulting therefrom; and, as respects any property, means injury to or destruction of property including the loss of use thereof.

Coverage F, expenses for medical services, is written on an "each person" basis, and the limit of liability stated in the declarations is the insurer's limit of liability for all expenses incurred by or on behalf of each person who sustains injury in any one accident. As with automobile insurance, payment under the medical services coverage is not conditioned on the liability of the insured.

A form of coverage available, usually requested in connection with industrial aid use, provides for passenger voluntary settlements, sometimes referred to as admitted liability coverage. The salient features of this coverage include an offer to pay the principal sum stated in the policy for scheduled death or dismemberment benefits (and sometimes weekly indemnity) in exchange for a full release of liability, the offer to be accepted within a stated time limit in lieu of prosecuting a claim based upon negligence. Crew members and employee passengers may benefit from this coverage. The success of the voluntary settlement insurance, as a means to achieve amicable adjustments of third-party passenger legal liability claims, regardless of liability, depends upon whether the principal sum realistically expresses the settlement value of the claim, considering the merits of the liability case and the provable damages.

The passenger coverage, or lack thereof, has been the source of litigated disputes, even though the policy definition of the term "passenger" seems fairly straightforward: "Any person in, on or boarding the aircraft for the purpose of riding or flying therein, or alighting therefrom following a flight or attempted flight therein." One controversy stems from the fact that many deaths and serious bodily injuries in aviation accidents are caused by the impact of a turning propeller. The issue is whether the person struck was a passenger at the time of the accident and therefore excluded from coverage under A— bodily injury sustained by any person except a passenger. Was the act of "alighting" completed? Had the "in, on or boarding" phase commenced?

The property damage liability insuring agreement may be limited by a sometimes overlooked exclusionary clause with respect to injury to or destruction of property carried by, in or on any aircraft for which insurance is afforded by the policy. This excludes coverage for passenger baggage or personal effects, and may be construed to exclude coverage for clothing while being worn. A passenger, for example, tears a coat on a sharp-edged ash tray. A broad form policy will cover damages, not exceeding a stated limit, for injury to the personal effects and baggage of guest passengers, including wearing apparel. Airlines insure against passenger baggage and personal effects losses, but it is common for them to retain the exposure to liability for the checked baggage of each fare paying passenger, usually $500, as established by published tariff.[18]

Under the provisions of the insurance policy, the insurer agrees to conform the policy to state financial responsibility laws with respect to liability for the ownership, maintenance, and use of aircraft. This extends only to the minimum coverage actually required by the law and certified to the responsible regulatory authority. Moreover, when policy defenses are unenforceable because of the application of financial responsibility laws, the insured assumes the obligation to reimburse the insurer for the sums required to be paid pursuant to this policy agreement.

Defense, Settlement, and Supplementary Payments. The defense, settlement, and supplementary payments provision of the policy imposes a number of important obligations, one of which is the insurer's duty to defend. In major crash cases, this becomes a formidable and expensive duty which requires involved investigations and preparation for the typically complex litigation. The investigators will frequently cooperate with those of the National Transportation Safety Board which has aircraft accident investigative responsibilities.[19]

The defense, settlement, and supplementary payments provision also provides: ". . . the company shall have the right to make such . . . settlement of any claim or suit as it deems expedient. . . ." When claim settlements are being negotiated and an insured angrily denounces his or her defenders as lacking resolution, as sometimes happens, the insured's views should be carefully considered. However, the company must be the final arbiter. The insured does have a financial stake in the litigation when the prayer for damages and the loss potential is in an amount exceeding the limits of primary coverage and the excess is uninsured. The insurer's right to settle within the policy limits, depending upon all the facts of the case, may now become a duty to settle. The rationale of transforming a right into a duty stems from the policy language which gives the insurer exclusive control of the settlement process. Space is not available here to develop all of the problems relating to liability of an insurer in excess of its limits of coverage for "bad faith" refusal to settle within the policy limits. It is a basic rule, however, that the insurer's representatives must conduct themselves at all times in a reasonable manner, behaving as though the policy afforded unlimited coverage.[20]

The so-called *first aid* insuring provision, under which the insurer agrees to pay expenses incurred by the insured for immediate medical attention imperative at the time of the occurrence, has produced controversies in the past, mainly due to the construction of the words "immediate" and "imperative" in deciding the need for surgical and medical relief to others. This agreement, and also other supplementary payments obligations with respect to bonds and expenses, are nearly uniform in various liability insurance forms. Thus, through the years they have been interpreted by the courts a number of times, particularly as used in the automobile liability insurance policy. The automobile policy interpretations are often applied to the aircraft policy.

Omnibus Clause.   The policy definition of "insured"—the so-called omnibus clause—may restrict the application of coverage to a limited few, or it may refer in broad terms to permissive users (those using the aircraft with permission of the named insured). However, the courts have pointed out that the paragraph defining "insured" must be read and given effect in conjunction with other policy terms and conditions. Thus, merely by giving his or her permission to an unqualified pilot, as defined in the declarations, the named insured does not give that person insured status. Any person or organization legally responsible for the permissive use of the aircraft is also an insured, under the omnibus clause, except when engaged in the manufacture or sale of aircraft and their components or when engaged in repair, rental, or commercial aircraft operations. Finally, coverage does not apply in the case of one employee making claim against another employee of the same employer for injury sustained in the course of such employment.

Liability and medical coverages are extended to apply to newly acquired aircraft, use of other aircraft and temporary use of substitute aircraft. (Hull coverages are also provided under the newly acquired aircraft policy extension.) An identical clause is frequently contained in automobile liability policies.

A crucial question in interpreting the newly acquired aircraft extension is whether ownership of the aircraft had been acquired at the time of the loss (there is also a notice to insurer requirement following acquisition). A lease agreement with an option to buy is not an acquisition within the insuring intent of this provision.

For the coverage of temporary use of substitute aircraft to become effective as an extension of the policy, the specified aircraft must have been withdrawn from normal service for reasons of breakdown, repair, servicing, loss, or destruction, and a nonowned aircraft must be used temporarily as a substitute. In an aviation decision one court said, in part, using an auto case as precedent: ". . . speaking concerning a substitution provision in a policy of automobile insurance, that such a provision should be construed liberally in favor of the insured, if any construction is necessary, and that the terms of such a provision should be given their every day man-in-the-street meaning."[21] Where an insured could not start his airplane and used a flying club airplane from the flight line to make his cross-country trip, the crash on the return segment was held to be covered as a substitute aircraft.

The application of the use of other aircraft provision is restricted to coverage for the owner-named insured, his or her spouse residing in the same household, or an executive officer of a corporate-named insured while acting within the scope of duties as such. Where there is a frequent or regular use of hired aircraft or the purposes item of the declarations permits "commercial" use of the aircraft, the insurance does not apply. Coverage needs might require the purchase of a nonownership liability policy. In the case of a corporate named insured, the underwriter may provide a nonownership liability extension of coverage in the description in the declarations of the aircraft covered. Such an extension might read:

> This policy shall automatically attach and apply in respect to any aircraft owned, maintained or used by the Named Insured or any aircraft operated on behalf of or in the interest of the Named Insured for which the Named Insured is legally liable.

Exclusions The standard exclusions, other than those already discussed or to be discussed later under aircraft physical damage coverages, are summarized in the following paragraphs.

Coverage does not apply to any aircraft not registered under a "Standard" category Airworthiness Certificate issued by the Federal Aviation Administration. By policy definition, "Airworthiness Certificate" refers to the certificate named in the Federal Aviation Act of 1958 as amended and the Civil Air Regulations (CARs) and Federal Aviation Regulations (FARs), but in substance it means a certificate issued by the FAA or a designee which certifies that the aircraft met, at the time of inspection, current airworthiness standards.[22] An experimental aircraft, for example, would not meet the "Standard" category requirement.

Coverage does not apply to liability assumed by contract or agreement, except liability assumed by the named insured under an airport contract. By policy definition "Airport Contract" means a written agreement required as condition to the use of an airport or airport facility. For example, a state or municipal airport authority may require a hold harmless of some sort as a condition to the use of hangar, tie-down, or transient parking facilities.

Coverage does not apply to intentional injury to persons or property by or at the direction of the insured, except for injury resulting from an assault and battery committed to prevent dangerous interference with the operation of the aircraft.

Coverage does not apply to injury to property owned by, rented to, in charge of, or transported by the insured. This exclusion may be modified to provide a limited amount of coverage for the personal effects and baggage of any one guest passenger in any one occurrence, and for damages not exceeding a total stated amount per policy period for injury to hangars and contents not owned by the insured (for example, damage to a rented hangar).

Coverage does not apply to any obligation for which insured or the insurer may be held liable under any workers' compensation, unemployment compensation, or disability benefits law.

As mentioned earlier, the coverage provided under the standard policy may be extended or restricted by the underwriter in a given situation. For example, contractual liability coverage may be provided by endorsement. And, too, there are separate policies to cover such exposures as flight instructor's professional liability, loss of license, and nonownership liability, the latter of which becomes applicable in excess of other valid and collectible insurance.

Aircraft Physical Damage Exposures

Aircraft physical damage exposures are incurred when airplanes are at rest—either sheltered in hangars (which sometimes collapse or burn) or are tied down in the open (which makes them vulnerable to windstorms, hail, and moving vehicles). Aircraft are exposed while taxiing or being towed—movements which subject them to the collision exposures of surface vehicles in motion. Aircraft are, of course, exposed while in the air where they face an environment sometimes made hostile by severe weather and a lack of forgiveness for human mistakes. Aircraft physical damage exposures run the gamut of potential losses, including a bent wing tip caused by an airport employee moving the airplane from a gas pump, total loss of an aircraft blown from its tie-down moorings in a windstorm, and the major crash of two commercial jet aircraft. In direct physical damage to the hull alone, a loss may be of multimillion dollar proportions.

Aircraft Physical Damage Insurance

The purpose of aircraft physical damage insurance, hereinafter referred to as hull coverage, is to protect the owner or a secured creditor (whose interest will be described in the declarations) against loss involving physical damage to the insured aircraft. There is a policy exclusion which provides that the hull coverages do not apply to loss or damage due to conversion, embezzlement, or secretion (the act of hiding something) by any person in lawful possession of the aircraft under a lease or rental agreement, conditional sale, mortgage, or other encumbrance. Upon its payment to the lienholder or mortgagee, the insurer will become subrogated to the rights of the lienholder or mortgagee to the extent of the payment.

The interest of the lienholder or mortgagee may be further protected by a breach of warranty endorsement which will provide that, to the extent of the lien or mortgage, the holder's rights under the policy will not be prejudiced by any act or neglect of the insured except an act of conversion, embezzlement, or secretion by the insured in possession of the aircraft.

Declarations An examination of the hull coverages begins with the declarations, where information pertinent to hull coverages will be found, as described in the following paragraphs.

Ownership. Specified here are the named insured's interest in the aircraft and, if it is encumbered, the type of encumbrance and the name of the mortgagee or lienholder. The importance of this declaration is signaled by a policy exclusion which provides that the hull coverages do not apply while the aircraft is subject to any bailment lease, conditional sale, mortgage, or other encumbrance not specifically declared and described in the policy or if the interest of the named insured is or becomes other than owner or as stated in the declarations.

Loss Payee(s). The loss payable clause contains the identity of those to whom losses will be payable, the named insured, and the secured creditor, if any, which holds a mortgage or a lien on the aircraft.

Hull Coverages A number of insurance options may be open to the named insured, but for present purposes they may be reduced to three—"all-risks" of physical loss or damage to the aircraft *while not in motion;* "all-risks" of physical loss or damage to the aircraft *while not in flight;* and "all-risks" of physical loss or damage to the aircraft. Not in motion and in motion deductibles, if any, are included in this section, and spaces are provided within which to enter the amount of insurance.

The policy contains a definition of *lost in flight* which provides that "the aircraft shall be presumed lost in flight if it disappears after take-off and is not located nor its whereabouts reported within sixty days." The terms *in flight* and *in motion* are defined in the policy. "In flight" means the time commencing when the aircraft (other than a rotocraft) moves forward in attempting to take off and continuing thereafter until it has completed its landing run. A rotocraft shall be deemed to be "in flight" when the rotors are in motion as a result of engine power, the momentum generated therefrom, or autorotation. "In motion" means all times when the aircraft is "in flight" and, *in addition,* whenever the aircraft is moving under its own power or the momentum generated therefrom. Upon the successful completion of an off-airport emergency landing precipitated in flight when the pilot noticed the odor of smoke in the cockpit, and while the aircraft was motionless at its emergency landing place, it burst into flames and was completely destroyed by fire. It was held covered, within the not in motion coverage provided.[23]

Hull coverages may also be expressed as a combination "all-risks" while not in flight and limited risks while in flight. The combined coverage is for "all-risks" of physical loss of or damage to the aircraft while not in flight and only such physical loss of or damage to the aircraft while in flight which is directly caused by theft, robbery, vandalism, lightning, fire or explosion, excluding fire or explosion caused by or resulting from crash or collision of the aircraft with the ground, water, or any object. "All-risks" coverage means all risks of physical loss of, or damage to the aircraft are insured against, except as thereafter specifically excluded by other policy provisions.

Valuation. When accidents occur, the insurer's obligation for hull damage is the provable damage which is *the least of* (1) the amount of the agreed value less any deductible; (2) the repair costs, which include costs for material and parts of like kind and quality, wages paid for labor at predetermined rates, and transportation costs; or (3) the replacement cost of another aircraft of like kind and quality.

The amount of insurance entered under the hull coverages, therefore, is usually the agreed upon value. The insurance may be written with no deductible. In general, lower premium rates apply to higher deductibles, and conversely higher rates are charged when lower deductibles apply. The use of deductibles is important in the overall concept of insuring airline fleets. Subject to the application of any deductible, the insurer will pay up to the agreed upon value specified in the policy.

Insured value, too, is the basis upon which the annual premium is developed. Subject to a fixed maximum, automatic insurance for increased value may be provided to cover the cost of modifications or additional equipment, but the increased value must be reported to the insurer usually within thirty days.

In the event of loss or damage to the aircraft, the amount of insurance is reduced by the amount of the loss or damage. When repairs are commenced, the automatic reinstatement clause becomes effective. It increases the amount of insurance by the value of the completed repairs until the amount of insurance is fully reinstated or the policy has expired. Where there has been a replacement aircraft acquired, insurance on the replaced aircraft terminates, and the amount of insurance on the newly acquired aircraft is equal to the lesser of its actual cost, or the limit of the highest amount of insurance upon any described aircraft.

Loss Adjustment. The named insured must file a proof of loss within a specified time after the occurrence of the loss or damage, and the amount of loss for which the insurer may be liable is payable within a stated time thereafter. The insurer is permitted to make reasonable investigations and examine the named insured and others under oath to verify the claimed loss or damage. Proof of loss clauses are strictly enforced, but courts may find a waiver of policy requirements, including the requirement to file a sworn proof of loss based upon the insurer's conduct over the entire course of the investigation, negotiation, and litigation.

The hull loss adjuster will have the responsibility to survey the loss and in the case of a partial loss may offer solutions, sometimes innovative and imaginative, to recover the aircraft and repair and restore it to its previous condition. Disputes sometimes arise when the named insured claims a total loss of the aircraft and the insurer says that there was a partial loss and, thus, its liability extends only to the cost of repairs. The following definition of "total loss" has been submitted to a jury:

> . . . the term "total loss" means such destruction of the airplane that, after the crash, if any, there remains no substantial remnant thereof which a reasonably prudent owner, uninsured, desiring to restore the airplane to its original condition, would utilize as a basis for such restoration.[24]

APPRAISAL. In the event of failure to agree on the amount of the loss, the appraisal provision of the policy provides that the insured and the insurer may each appoint an appraiser, the appraisers to select an umpire, and if they cannot agree on an umpire, then either the named insured or the insurer can petition "a court of record," in the state in which the property is located, to appoint such umpire. The appraisal procedure is final and binding.

SUBROGATION. Upon payment of the claim, the insurer becomes subrogated to the insured's rights of recovery against any person or organization. The insured agrees to cooperate and do nothing to impair or prejudice such rights of recovery. Release of rights against third parties relieves the insurer from any liability under the policy. A loss payee is an additional insured for purposes of hull coverage. The insurer cannot maintain an action against one of its insureds, even though the loss payee may be a person or an organization against whom liability for the loss or damage may be established.

PROTECTION FROM FURTHER LOSS. Following an accident to an aircraft to which the hull coverage applies, the named insured has the duty to protect the aircraft from further loss or damage, and further loss caused by failure to protect is not covered. On payment of a total loss, the insurer, at its option, is entitled to all remaining salvage value. However, there can be no abandonment of the aircraft to the insurer without its consent.

Other Exclusions. Important exclusions not already considered involve:

1. loss or damage to tires, unless the direct result of other covered physical damage, except the policy will apply to loss or damage from theft, vandalism, or malicious mischief;
2. loss or damage due and confined to wear and tear or deterioration or to freezing or mechanical or electrical breakdown or failure, unless the direct result of other covered physical damage (for example, the failure and destruction of engines traceable to the negligent work of a mechanic or due to design defect have been held to come within this exclusionary clause); and

3. loss or damage from the risks of capture or seizure or war risk, the latter covered in certain circumstances by government war risk insurance.[25]

Aviation Insurance Markets

There are many markets today for insuring aviation exposures. Some of these insurance markets are managed by professional aviation underwriters, "groups," or "pools," whose portfolios are solely in aviation insurance and whose own fortunes necessarily rise and fall with the successes and failures of aviation enterprises. Their policies may be issued in the names of company members of the "group," all of whom agree to be jointly and severally bound to the terms and conditions of the contract. Other insurance companies manage aviation underwriting as a department of their casualty or fire operations, writing the insurance on their own contracts. Depending upon the amount of insurance required, the character of the exposures, and the capacity of the primary insurer, a certain share of the exposure will be ceded by the original insurer to reinsurers under either treaty or facultative plans. There is nothing peculiar to aviation insurance in the distribution and disposal of surplus risks through reinsurance.

Noninsurance Techniques

Retention Devices may also be employed to retain specific casualty exposures and coordinate partial retention with hull insurance coverages in the insurance buyer's overall plan, in order to obtain the required quality and quantity of protection for the premium dollar. After appropriate analysis, a larger corporation may find it economically advantageous to retain the bulk of its exposures, looking to the commercial market for claims handling and defense needs, and the protection afforded by excess liability insurance in the event of a catastrophe loss. Cash flow considerations and cost of an adequate layer of primary insurance have stimulated the development of retention plans.

Loss Control To be successful, an aviation risk management program requires an active accident prevention and flight safety program. The hazards of aviation may be minimized through recurrent pilot training at regularly established intervals and maintenance of a corporate fleet to Federal Aviation Administration standards or better. It is also wise to delegate the flight dispatching decision solely to the chief pilot. (This is the decision whether the proposed flights can be conducted safely, weather and equipment considered.) Supervision at the corporate level is required to establish the objectives and standards of the flight department and make sure that those objectives and standards are met.

Handling Catastrophe Exposures

Any decision regarding the mix of risk management techniques should consider the catastrophe loss potential. Although the catastrophe exposure has always been present in airline insurance underwriting, jumbo jets—with their high hull values and unprecedented passenger capacities—have created challenges to conventional methods of handling the exposures. The aviation insurance markets of the world seem to have met the challenges of the jumbo jets, just as they did the challenges of the jet age. Insurance and aviation have come a long way together since the days when the Aero Club of America—a club which was recognized by the Federation Aeronautique Internationale in the early days of aviation as the governing authority for aviation in the United States—issued its first license to Glen H. Curtis on June 8, 1911.

LIABILITY EXPOSURES OF CHARITABLE, EDUCATIONAL, AND GOVERNMENTAL ENTITIES

Liability Exposures of Charitable Organizations

In the majority of jurisdictions in the United States, charitable organizations have the same exposure to tort liability as individuals and noncharitable enterprises. As with noncharitable entities, negligence liability is imposed upon a charity only if it is established that the charity owed a duty of care to the victim, that this duty was breached by the charity, and that the negligent act of the charity was the cause of the victim's injury.

In a number of jurisdictions, however, charitable entities enjoy either total or qualified immunity from tort liability.[26] The doctrine of charitable immunity derived from a nineteenth century English case which held that trust funds in the hands of a charity could not be utilized for the payment of tort claims, because such payment would divert the funds to purposes other than those intended by the donor.[27] The doctrine also derived from the public policy notion that the effectiveness of charities would be unduly impaired if such organizations were exposed to tort liability.

A growing number of jurisdictions have repudiated the doctrine of charitable immunity, recognizing the paramount importance of a victim's right of recovery against an organization which negligently inflicts injury. The trend of recent decisions is clearly toward abandoning charitable immunity.

The Doctrine of Charitable Immunity

Underlying Legal Theories. The doctrine of charitable immunity has been propounded in a variety of theories, the earliest of which was the *trust fund theory,* enunciated in Victorian England. Immunity under this theory is predicated upon an idea that the assets of a charity constitute a trust fund which may not be diverted for noncharitable uses. Diversion of trust funds for payment of tort liability claims would ostensibly cripple the charitable organization and also thwart the intent of the donor. Most jurisdictions adhering to this theory hold that, while trust property is exempt from satisfaction of a judgment, nontrust property owned by the charity may be used to satisfy a tort claim.

The trust fund theory has been criticized on the ground that a trust fund is normally liable for torts committed in administering the trust. Moreover, the funds would not be exempt from execution in the hands of the donor, and thus should not be shielded merely because they are placed in trust.

Immunity is also accorded to charities under the theory that the rule of *respondeat superior* does not apply to charities, because they derive no pecuniary gain from the actions of their employees. Under this theory, therefore, charities are not vicariously liable for tortious acts of their employees and agents. The theory has been criticized on the ground that the vicarious liability of an employer derives from the employment relationship, and it is not limited, under principles of agency law, to profitable enterprises.

Charitable immunity is based in some jurisdictions on the theory that individuals who accept the benefits of a charity waive liability or assume the risk of negligence by the charity. This theory derives in part from the notion that a "Good Samaritan" should not be held liable to beneficiaries for charitable, albeit negligent actions. Under the *waiver theory,* a charity remains liable for negligent acts which injure nonbeneficiaries, such as employees, invitees, and strangers, because such individuals do not waive their right to sue the charity. The waiver theory has been criticized as a blatant fiction. Individuals who seek the services of a charitable organization expect competent service. They certainly do not consent to negligent treatment.

Public policy theories are also invoked in jurisdictions which accord immunity to charities. Policy-minded courts in early decisions reasoned that charities would be stifled if they were exposed to tort liability, because donors would be reluctant to contribute to charitable enterprises if contributions could be used to cover tort claims. There is no evidence, however, that contributions have diminished in those jurisdictions which have abrogated charitable immunity. Furthermore, the financial consequences of tort liability are readily transferred through the purchase of adequate insurance, and the expense of liability insurance is recognized as a routine "cost of doing business" for charitable, as well as profit-oriented, enterprises.

Degree of Immunity Accorded Charitable Institutions. Charitable enterprises are presently accorded total immunity from tort liability in only three jurisdictions in the United States.[28] Total immunity was judicially created in these jurisdictions. It is based upon public policy considerations, as well as the judicial notion that the legislature, and not the courts, should abrogate the doctrine.

Charitable organizations currently enjoy qualified immunity from tort liability in nine jurisdictions.[29] Qualified immunity is generally based on the trust fund or the implied waiver theory, and several jurisdictions confer qualified immunity upon charities under the theory that charities are not vicariously liable for the negligent acts of their employees. Statutes control the question of charitable immunity in North Carolina and Nevada, where the common-law defense of charitable immunity has been statutorily abolished.[30]

A few jurisdictions hold that physicians are independent contractors, and therefore hospitals are not liable for a physician's negligence, as long as reasonable care was exercised in hiring the physician. In contrast, Nebraska has abolished charitable immunity as to hospitals, but not as to other charitable institutions.

An increasing number of jurisdictions have abrogated the doctrine of charitable immunity, placing charities on an equal footing with noncharitable entities. The gradual erosion of the doctrine of charitable immunity is of particular importance for insurance underwriting purposes, because the insurance losses of a charitable organization are directly dependent upon the tort immunity accorded the charity. Decisions abrogating the doctrine of charitable immunity have usually been prospectively applied, thereby allowing charities and insurers to adjust the price and terms of coverage of insurance policies to account for increased liability exposure. However, one decision abrogated the doctrine of charitable immunity retrospectively, to the extent of the maximum amount of insurance coverage of two defendant hospitals.[31]

Effect of the Status of Persons Injured. In several jurisdictions, particularly those adhering to the waiver theory of charitable immunity, the tort liability of a charitable organization is dependent upon the status of the victim. It has been held that the beneficiaries of a charity or recipients of the charity's services waive their right to sue a charity in tort. This immunity, however, does not generally extend to torts committed against a stranger, defined as one who is unrelated to the purpose of the charity and who receives no benefits from it. Similarly, the doctrine of charitable immunity does not generally apply to torts committed against a servant or employee of the institution. It has also been held, in several jurisdictions, that immunity does not extend to those who pay for services of a charitable organization.

Additional Factors Limiting the Doctrine. In jurisdictions where charitable immunity rests upon the trust fund theory, it is generally held that immunity does not prevent suit and liability, but only exempts trust assets from levy and execution. Thus, where nontrust assets are available, a plaintiff may appropriate such assets for the satisfaction of a tort judgment.

In those jurisdictions where a charity is immune from vicarious liability for negligent acts of its employees and agents, such immunity does not generally extend to acts of corporate or administrative negligence. Corporate negligence refers to negligence on the part of officers or managing directors of the charity, as distinguished from the negligence of ordinary employees. Such acts of corporate negligence include negligence in hiring personnel and supplying instrumentalities. For instance, a charitable hospital may be held liable for failing to ascertain whether its staff physicians are qualified for the positions for which they were hired, for failing to maintain equipment, or for failing to adequately supervise its nursing staff.

It has also been held that the doctrine of charitable immunity does not extend to negligent acts committed in the course of noncharitable, commercial activities. A charity does not lose its charitable status merely because it charges fees or because it receives funds from other operations. However, activities which are primarily commercial in nature are not immune from liability, notwithstanding the fact that the revenues derived from such activities are used for charitable purposes. Similarly, charitable immunity does not extend to intentional torts, or to the maintenance of a nuisance.

Exposure of Employees, Officers, and Trustees. The immunity from tort liability accorded charitable organizations does not insulate the employees, officers, and agents of charities from personal liability for tortious acts. The liability of such individuals is governed by normal principles of tort law. In contrast, a trustee of a charitable trust who is sued individually for a tortious act of the charity is personally liable only if the trustee was personally at fault while administering the trust.

Impact of Insurance Coverage. Insurance has no unique impact upon the liability exposure of a charitable organization in jurisdictions where charities are not afforded immunity. Similarly, in the majority of jurisdictions which confer immunity upon charities, the immunity is not lost or otherwise affected by the fact that the charity carries liability insurance. However, where the charitable immunity is limited to the exemption of trust property from levy and execution on a tort judgment, liability insurance may be appropriated for the satisfaction of a tort judgment because insurance is regarded as nontrust property.

Several jurisdictions have statutes called "direct action statutes," which allow an injured party to proceed directly against an insurance company or to join the insurer as a party defendant. An insurer, however, may not be held liable for injuries for which the insured charity may not be liable.

Other Exposures to Liability Charities are also exposed to liability losses under workers' compensation statutes, products liability law, OSHA, and ERISA.

Workers' Compensation Statutes. Jurisdictions vary considerably with respect to the applicability of workers' compensation statutes to charitable institutions. In some jurisdictions, charities are excluded from the workers' compensation act on the ground that charities are not conducted for profit within the meaning of the state statute. In contrast, courts in other jurisdictions have held that employment with a charitable institution constitutes "other employment" within the meaning of the compensation act. Statutes in some jurisdictions explicitly provide that workers' compensation coverage extends to employees of charitable organizations. However, it has been held in several jurisdictions that where charitable organizations are accorded immunity from tort liability, such organizations are also exempt from the workers' compensation act.

Where an employee of a charitable institution is covered under a workers' compensation statute, statutory compensation for a job-related injury is the employee's sole remedy, and a separate recovery under common law is barred.[32] In some jurisdictions, an employee of a charitable institution who is not covered under the workers' compensation statute may be denied recourse against the employer altogether if the jurisdiction also affords the employer charitable immunity from tort liability. However, in other jurisdictions where such an employee is not covered by the workers' compensation statute and there is no charitable immunity from tort liability, an employee may resort to a common-law remedy.

In a common-law action predicated upon negligence, the employee of a charitable institution must prove that the employer breached a duty of care owed the employee. In some of those jurisdictions permitting a common-law suit, however, the employer may invoke the defenses of contributory negligence, assumption of risk and the fellow servant rule. The assumption of risk defense means that an employee assumes the chance of loss due to hazards normally incident to the employment. Under the fellow servant rule, an employee is deemed to have assumed the chance of loss due to negligence on the part of other employees, and the employer, therefore, is not liable for injuries resulting from such negligence.

Liability for Products. Charities which engage in the manufacture, distribution, or retail sale of products may be held strictly liable in tort for injury caused by defective products. Under the doctrine of strict liability, an injured party seeking to hold a manufacturer or vendor liable need only establish (1) the defendant's relationship to the product in question, and (2) a causal connection between the defective condition and the plaintiff's injury. However, strict liability does not apply to enterprises which engage only in the occasional sale of merchandise. Thus, a charitable organization which sells merchandise once a year to raise operating funds might not be exposed to strict liability, whereas a charity which operates retail stores would probably be exposed to strict liability for injuries caused by defective products.

In those jurisdictions which accord immunity from tort liability to charities, the charity may be shielded from products liability. However, where the manufacture or sale of a defective product was part of a noncharitable, commercial enterprise, the immunity would probably not apply. Thus, if a charitable organization operates a manufacturing enterprise to finance charitable activities, it would not be shielded from strict liability for injuries caused by defective products, because manufacturing is a commercial activity.

In some jurisdictions, the manufacture or sale of goods may be regulated by statute. Failure to comply with these statutory requirements could render a charity liable in tort, if the failure to comply with statutory requirements proximately caused the injury to a person within the protective scope of the statute. In several jurisdictions which accord immunity to charities, such immunity does not apply to liability which is predicated upon the breach of a duty imposed by statute.

A charity that regularly engages in the sale of merchandise may also be held liable for breach of warranty of merchantability, if such goods fail to meet the standards of merchantability set forth in the Uniform Commercial Code. On the other hand, a charity that engages only in the occasional sale of goods may not fall within the merchant category and may not be subject to liability for breach of warranty of merchantability.

The liability of a charity for the sale of defective products may also be predicated upon negligence theories, which are governed by general principles of tort law.

Charities are subject to liability for breach of contract to the same extent as individuals and noncharitable enterprises. Such liability is governed by principles of contract law and by state commercial statutes.

OSHA. The Occupational Safety and Health Act of 1970 (OSHA) empowers the Secretary of Labor to establish occupational and health safety standards that bind all employers engaged in business affecting interstate commerce. Charitable organizations which retain employees and engage in business affecting interstate commerce are covered by OSHA to the same extent as other employers. The act provides for civil penalties of up to $1,000 for a serious violation of the act and up to $10,000 for willful or repeated violations. Failure to correct a violation may result in assessment of a civil penalty of up to $1,000 for each day the violation continues. An employee's right to recover for occupational injury under common law or workers' compensation statutes is not affected by OSHA. The act does not provide new civil remedies against an employer for injuries suffered by an employee because of a violation of the act.

ERISA. The Employee Retirement Income Security Act of 1974 (ERISA) sets forth extremely technical provisions governing tax treatment, funding, and reporting requirements for private employee benefit plans. Employee pension plans of charitable organizations are required to comply with the reporting and funding requirements of ERISA, with the exception of church pension plans, which are exempt unless they specifically elect coverage. Church plans which do not elect coverage are governed by pre-ERISA pension plan law.

Any person who is a fiduciary with respect to a pension plan is subject under the act to personal liability for breach of fiduciary duty. An employer is authorized to purchase insurance for its fiduciaries and for itself to cover liability for losses occurring by reason of an act or omission by the fiduciary.

Charitable Versus Noncharitable Entities The liability exposures of charitable institutions, in the majority of jurisdictions, are the same as those of noncharitable entities. Charities, however, enjoy partial or total immunity from tort liability in a number of jurisdictions. Such immunity does not generally extend to commercial activities or to intentional torts, and it is subject to numerous other limitations. Employees of a charitable institution remain liable for tortious acts, even in jurisdictions which adhere to the doctrine of charitable immunity. Insurance coverage does not uniquely affect the exposure of charities to tort liability, except in those jurisdictions which only permit appropriation of nontrust fund property for settlement of tort claims.

Charities may be accorded immunity from liability in workers' compensation and products liability cases, in jurisdictions adhering to the charitable immunity doctrine. The exposure of charities to liability for breach of contract, however, is the same as that of noncharitable entities. The provisions of OSHA and ERISA apply to charitable organizations, with the exception that church pension plans are not required to comply with ERISA.

A growing number of jurisdictions are abandoning the doctrine of charitable immunity. Although decisions abrogating the doctrine have generally been applied prospectively, there is a chance that the abrogation would be retrospective, to the extent of a charity's insurance coverage.

Liability Exposures of Governmental Entities

Until relatively recently, no such thing as a "liability exposure" of governmental units existed. From the earliest times, a sovereign government had been immune from suits brought in its courts or other courts on behalf of persons injured by the negligent acts or omissions of its officers or agents.

The Doctrine of Sovereign Immunity   Historically, the *doctrine of sovereign immunity* rested upon the concept of the divine right of kings. When this ground for exempting the United States from liability ended, American courts explained their continued recognition of the doctrine by the public policy argument that it is better for an individual to go without a remedy than to inconvenience the public by diverting public funds to liquidate private damages. On this reasoning, the doctrine long prevailed over the countervailing and equally well-established principle that every wrong should have an appropriate remedy in law.

Today, a growing number of courts and legislatures recognize that the traditional reasons for exalting the public good over the injured individual cannot withstand analysis. But few courts are willing to abrogate so ancient a doctrine by judicial fiat. Consequently, except in those instances in which the United States has "consented" to be sued by statute, it continues to be immune from suit upon claims against it or debts owed by it. The same immunity from civil liability extends, in varying degrees, to lesser units of government, such as states, counties, municipalities and other governmental agencies.

Differences in the immunity doctrine as applied to the federal government, on the one hand, and units of local government, on the other, make it useful to divide discussion of governmental liability into two sections. The first will deal exclusively with the suits against the federal government and the second with variations in the immunity doctrine as it is applied to local governmental entities.

Federal Liability Exposure   The rule of immunity which protects the federal government from civil suits without its consent applies to all types of actions—from condemnation proceedings and personal injury to contract and injunctive actions against the federal government. A claimant cannot circumvent the doctrine of immunity by bringing an action directly against a federal officer, agency, or department, when the relief sought could operate indirectly to control the action of the government or subject it to liability. If the suit is based upon actions taken by the officer or agency in conformity with the statutory authority conferred upon them, and if those actions would be imputed to the United States as principal under the rules of agency, the suit will be considered one against the United States itself and, thus, it will be subject to the immunity doctrine.

On the other hand, federal officers may be sued in person for acts committed without statutory authority, for acts in excess of their authority, or for acts which are otherwise illegal. The unauthorized acts of the officer or employee are not deemed to be the acts of the United States and the defendant federal officer therefore cannot invoke the immunity of his employer in his own defense. For the same reason, even absent a statute waiving immunity, civil suits may be brought to compel individual officers or employees of the United States to carry out duties which are imposed upon them by law and which involve no exercise of discretion or judgment, or to enjoin them from enforcing an unconstitutional law.

Because the government is not held responsible for the unauthorized acts of its officers and employees, it cannot be taxed with the costs of a court action against it or with interest on the amounts recovered against it. Further, when the government brings a counterclaim against a private plaintiff in a civil action against the United States, the plaintiff will not be permitted to defend against the counterclaim on the grounds that the government failed to assert its claim within a reasonable time or the time allowed by statute for claims of that kind. The government, on the other hand, is fully empowered to assert the plaintiff's delay as a defense to the plaintiff's claim.

Sovereign immunity can thus protect the United States from liability exposure in a variety of ways. In the last fifty years, however, the scope of the doctrine has been increasingly restricted by congressional enactments consenting to suits of many kinds against the

United States. Congress has absolute discretion to give consent to suit or withhold it on whatever terms and conditions are deemed appropriate. Unless the claimant complies precisely with all of the terms of the statute authorizing suits of the type he seeks to prosecute, no court will have the power to hear the suit.

Federal Tort Claims Act. Perhaps the most important legislation waiving immunity is known as the Federal Tort Claims Act (FTCA). The FTCA provides that the United States shall be liable for injuries resulting from the negligence or other tortious conduct of any of its officers, agents, or servants committed in the performance of their duties, to the same extent and in the same manner as a private individual under like circumstances. While this act would appear to open the door to myriad claims against the government, certain procedural requirements and express exclusions on liability for certain common injuries significantly narrow the tort liability exposure of the United States under the act.

The single most effective exclusion exempts the United States from liability for injuries resulting from (1) acts or omissions of government employees, exercising due care, in the execution of a statute or regulation (whether valid or not); or (2) the performance or nonperformance of a "discretionary function" on the part of a federal agency or employee. Under the first branch of this exclusion, the claimant must be in a position to show that his or her injury did not occur while the federal employee was engaged in carrying out the express requirements of a statute. Similarly, a claim will fail under the second branch if the claimant's alleged injury occurred in a situation which required the employee to exercise personal judgment about action to be taken under the law.

Although the distinction between "discretionary" and "nondiscretionary" tasks has not been maintained with much clarity or logic, the courts agree that the following activities which frequently give rise to private injuries are strictly "discretionary": establishing programs, granting, refusing, or revoking licenses, and issuing regulations. A large number of private suits against the United States are thus barred by this double-barreled exclusion.

Other FTCA exclusions preclude recovery against the United States for claims arising out of the loss or negligent miscarriage of mail, and for claims arising out of the intentional torts of federal employees. The latter exclusion bars claims based upon assault and/or battery by a federal employee, false arrest or imprisonment, malicious prosecution, abuse of process, libel, slander, misrepresentation, deceit, and interference with contract rights. Yet another exclusion exempts the United

States from liability for claims based upon the assessment or collection of any item by tax, customs, or other law enforcement officers.

Judicial redress of private grievances against the government under the FTCA is also limited by the procedural requirement that the claimant present the claim within a certain time to the appropriate federal agency for administrative determination prior to going into the federal district courts. Until the claim has been finally denied by the proper agency, the courts lack jurisdiction to entertain the suit. This is commonly called the "exhaustion of administrative remedies."

Furthermore, even on a valid claim, recovery is limited, because the United States can only be held liable for actual or compensatory damages. Punitive damages which may be assessed in private personal injury actions for particularly egregious behavior on the part of a defendant are expressly prohibited under the act. Despite its exclusions and pitfalls, however, the FTCA subjects the United States to potential liability for an enormous range of personal and property damage incurred by private citizens because of the negligent acts or omissions of its officers and employees.

Federal Employees' Compensation Act. The Federal Employees' Compensation Act (FECA) entitles federal employees to payment of compensation for disability or death resulting from a personal injury sustained while in the performance of their duties. Like most state workers' compensation laws, the FECA holds the United States liable to its employees for such compensation even when the injury did not result from any fault on the government's part. No recovery may be had under the FECA, however, for disability or death caused by the willful misconduct or intoxication of the injured employee. As with the Federal Tort Claims Act, a claimant under the FECA must comply with a series of procedural requirements in order to recover the amounts due. Thus, claims must be made within the time allowed and in the manner prescribed under the act.

Other Federal Acts. The same right to recover disability compensation from the United States is extended to dockworkers and longshoremen by the Longshoremen's and Harborworkers' Compensation Act and to military support personnel by the Military Claims Act. Like the FECA, the Longshoremen's and Harborworkers' Compensation Act excludes payment of benefits for disability caused by the intoxication of the claimant or by the claimant's willful intention to kill or injure the claimant or someone else. The Military Claims Act goes further and denies a claimant recovery when his mere negligence fully or partly caused the damage or injury for which recovery is sought.

Recovery against the United States is also possible in many nonpersonal injury cases. The Tucker Act, for instance, subjects the

United States to liability for civil claims arising out of express or implied contracts or other nonpersonal injury situations. Thus, a private litigant may now collect damages against the government for the government's breach of a contract or for its failure to pay its debts, provided that his or her claim meets all the requirements of the Tucker Act. In some instances, a plaintiff's action against the United States may include both breach of contract claims and tort claims based upon the same act or omission. The plaintiff in such situations has the option to sue either under the Tucker Act or the Federal Tort Claims Act, although the courts have sometimes refused to entertain a suit under the particular act invoked when it appears that the suit would more appropriately be brought under the other.

Liability Exposure of Lesser Branches of Government There are many types of governmental entities. In addition to the federal government, there are a great number of lesser entities, such as states, counties, school districts, and municipalities. The early common law applied the rule of absolute immunity, without differentiation, to all governmental entities. In the absence of statutory provisions to the contrary, even today no recovery may be had against local governments for injuries caused by the negligent acts or omissions of their officers or employees. The protection afforded by the doctrine of sovereign immunity, however, varies somewhat with the extent of the governmental authority wielded by the individual entity. For example, states are more fully protected from liability than are municipalities or counties. Further, the gradual erosion of the doctrine has been accelerated in many states by the adoption of laws similar to the Federal Tort Claims Act, as well as by other legislation affording private claimants judicial or administrative relief for injuries caused by local governmental act.

State Governments, School Boards, and Counties. Like the federal government, a state government may waive sovereign immunity on whatever terms and conditions it sees fit. Some states confine waivers of governmental immunity to particular classes of cases or for injuries resulting from activity undertaken by particular state departments or agencies. In other states, statutes waive immunity from liability as to any and all private claims arising from the negligence of state officers, agents, and employees. When a state passes legislation of the latter type, the waiver of immunity has been interpreted by the courts to apply to all branches of state government, including counties, municipalities, townships, and villages.

Examples of more specific waivers of immunity include the common so-called Safe-Place Statutes, which specifically impose liability upon municipalities or other branches of government for injuries caused by negligence in the maintenance or operation of certain areas under their control. Thus, private individuals may be entitled to recover for injuries resulting from dangerous conditions in areas such as streets, highways, public buildings, grounds, works, or property, the maintenance of which has been made the responsibility of the particular governmental entity under the Safe-Place Statute. Another type of common statute provides for indemnification of state employees who are held personally liable for negligent acts and omissions committed in the course of their employment by the state. Still other state statutes make school boards, in particular, liable for personal injury to pupils resulting from negligent failure to supervise their conduct or from negligence in transporting them to and from school and extracurricular activities.

In addition to this erosion of the sovereign immunity doctrine by legislative action, the courts in a few states have themselves abolished the doctrine. In this small minority of jurisdictions, the courts reason that the doctrine is unnecessary to preserve any public interest and, indeed, is subversive to that interest, in view of the hardship the rule may impose upon private parties injured by the state. A few other jurisdictions determine a state's liability by applying a distinction used in municipal law for determining the liability of municipal corporations for personal injuries. In these states, private persons may sue the state when their injuries result from acts committed in the exercise of the government's purely "private" or "proprietary," as opposed to its "public" or "governmental," functions.

Finally, a small but growing number of state courts hold that a state waives its immunity to the extent that it obtains insurance coverage for the activity which allegedly caused the plaintiff's injury. Though these minority views are consistent with the modern trend toward abrogation of the rule of governmental immunity, it should be recognized that most state courts decline to hear private civil suits brought against state governments, in the absence of a state statute waiving immunity to the type of suit brought.

Even in those jurisdictions still recognizing absolute governmental immunity, a state may be held liable for its breach of a contract entered into with a private party. This exception to the general rule of immunity rests upon the rationale that the state implicitly waives its immunity by entering into the contract.

In addition, the doctrine of governmental immunity does not apply where the injury complained of is the taking or damaging of private property for public use without compensation or in cases involving damage to property without an actual taking. This exception stems from federal and state constitutional prohibitions against the taking of private property without just compensation.

For the purposes of determining liability for civil damages, school boards and counties are considered arms of the state which come within the same protection from liability as the particular state of which they form a part. As indicated earlier, statutes in many states have rendered such lesser units of government specifically liable in tort for certain injuries sustained by private parties. Though the entity itself may be immune, individual officials of these lesser units may, like state officials, be personally liable for acts committed in excess of their authority or pursuant to an unconstitutional statute. In many states, however, certain classes of employees are relieved by statute of liability for their negligent acts or omissions in carrying out their duties. School teachers and principals, for instance, are frequently exempted from liability for their negligence while acting within the scope of their employment.

Municipal Corporations. Most of the rules which determine the immunity or nonimmunity of a state or state agency to civil suit apply also in the case of municipal corporations. However, municipalities in most states are more vulnerable to private civil suits, by reason of a long recognized exception to governmental immunity for claims arising out of municipal acts committed in a private or proprietary capacity (rather than in a governmental or public capacity). A few states still recognize the common-law rule of absolute immunity, even for municipal corporations. The courts employing the exception are slowly expanding municipal liability for the wrongful acts of municipal employees and agents, even in the absence of statutes expressly waiving immunity to suit. Faced with the hardship worked upon particular individuals by denial of any remedy, the courts have made irrational and arbitrary characterizations of a particular municipal function as *proprietary* or *governmental* in order to assure the injured plaintiffs some relief.

PROPRIETARY VERSUS GOVERNMENTAL FUNCTIONS. This tendency to tailor characterizations of the governmental activity involved to the exigencies of the plaintiff's situation results in tremendous variation, from jurisdiction to jurisdiction, in the classification of governmental versus proprietary functions. In general, the courts use certain tests to determine whether an act falls within either category. One test frequently applied is whether the act performed is for the common good of all, or whether it is for the special benefit or profit of the corporate entity. Those acts deemed beneficial to all are classified as public and are, therefore, immune. Some courts, applying a second test, rely instead upon the status of the person performing the act. Usually, in performing governmental tasks, a municipality acts through its public officers, while proprietary tasks are performed by mere agents or servants employed by the corporation. Both these tests are sufficiently subjective to permit the courts to bend the rules of immunity to benefit plaintiffs in appealing cases. A third test categorizes a function as proprietary when the municipality derives pecuniary benefits and profits from it. A distinction between activities which produce pecuniary benefits and activities which do not is no more conducive to objective decision-making than the first two tests. A municipality often derives pecuniary benefits from activities recognized as purely governmental. For example, a fee is often exacted from applicants for licenses of various types, a commonly recognized public function.

The real test seems to be the court's perception of the main purpose for which the municipality undertakes the activity that causes the harm, as well as the character of that activity. If it is a purely commercial activity, which might under other circumstances be carried out by a private corporation, the fact that a municipal corporation derives no pecuniary benefits from it would not immunize the municipality from liability. On the other hand, if the municipality makes a small profit from activities such as licensing, which are purely incidental to a governmental function, the fact that income is derived from the activity would not render the municipality liable in tort.

Although any generalization concerning the characterization of particular acts as governmental or proprietary is difficult, the courts of most jurisdictions have consistently classified certain acts and functions as one or the other. Thus, because they are classified as governmental activities in almost all jurisdictions, a municipal corporation is immunized from liability for injuries caused by the grant, revocation, or denial of licenses or franchises; the appointment or discharge of officials or employees; insect or rodent control programs; conducting celebrations for public amusement; the assessment and collection of taxes; malicious prosecution or wrongful legal proceedings against individuals; false arrest; judicial decisions and other discretionary functions; suspension of or failure to enact ordinances or enactment of invalid ordinances; operation of on-street parking meters; free transportation of school children; and failure to erect traffic signals and control devices (although some courts make the government liable for failure to maintain such signals and devices properly, once installed).

It has been previously mentioned that most courts regard operation of an airport as a proprietary activity. Other activities which most courts deem proprietary, and which may thus expose the municipality to tort liability, include maintenance of streets and sidewalks in a reasonably safe manner; operating public utilities such as waterworks, electrical plants, etc.; construction of public improvements in buildings (which must be done with reasonable care after the discretionary function of planning the improvement has ended); operation of metered or unmetered off-street parking facilities; and planning or operating a nuisance of any kind, including public dumps, sewer systems, and the collection and disposal of garbage.

The courts have been less consistent in classifying other activities commonly undertaken by municipalities as either governmental or proprietary. Thus, the liability exposure of municipal corporations for activities such as operating a zoo, public building, or public swimming pool varies from state to state. Similarly, a city's liability for injuries arising from the operation of motor vehicles by its employees or agents depends upon the court's characterization of the functions being performed at the time the accident occurred. Often, a municipality is immune from suit by the injured civilian, when the vehicle causing the accident was operated by the fire department, the police department, the board of health, the street or highway department, or other agency of the municipality in the course of performing the official functions conferred upon it by the corporate charter or by ordinance. On the other hand, liability is often imposed upon municipalities for accidents involving municipal employees engaged in street maintenance and repair, or in the operation of the municipal water departments, electric plants, and municipal airports.

Almost uniformly, the cases exempt a municipal corporation from suits based upon the enforcement or nonenforcement of a municipal ordinance or a state statute. It is usually said that the city's ordinances are adopted and enforced for the benefit of the general public, and they do not impose on the city a duty to the individual harmed by their nonenforcement. An exception to this rule is made in cases in which the police department or some other municipal agency undertakes to protect the individual claimant from harm, and then fails to provide the promised protection or is negligent in so doing. Such is sometimes the case when police protection is given to an important witness in a criminal case.

In most states, a municipality is also immune from torts based on damage to personal property resulting from acts, committed by its employees or officers, which are totally outside the powers conferred on the city by its charter. Thus, a municipality is not answerable in damages for injuries inflicted by police officers using excessive force in effecting an arrest. The court reasons that the municipality cannot confer on its agents any authority which it does not have to commit the complained act. This rule, like the governmental versus proprietary function rule, sets a very flexible standard. In cases where application of the principle would cause unusual hardship, the courts tend to construe the powers of the municipality broadly in order to include the power to perform the act allegedly causing the injury.[33]

In any event, even if the agent's acts are fully authorized under the municipal charter or by ordinance, the city's liability for any injuries may depend upon the status of the person committing the act. If the person is totally independent of the municipal corporation, as to tenure of office and manner of discharging duties, the corporation would not be held responsible for any negligence or wrongful act committed in carrying out those duties. For this reason, a city is rarely answerable for the acts or omissions of its judges. Similarly, the city would not be liable for the acts of a person elected or appointed by the corporation in obedience to a state statute to perform a public service that is not particularly local or corporate in nature.

Even in the absence of statutes waiving their immunity to suit, municipalities are exposed to liability from a wide range of activities. This exposure has been steadily increasing as the courts have narrowed the range of activities characterized as public and therefore immune from suit. Some states and municipalities have even enacted legislation imposing liability on local governments for negligently inflicted damages occurring during the execution of purely public functions. Cities in many states are, for instance, subject to the requirements of workers' compensation acts and similar legislation intended to compensate employees injured in the course of their employment.

Even when the municipality itself cannot be sued, municipal employees, like state and federal employees, must answer for the consequences of their own negligent or unauthorized acts and omissions in carrying out their duties. Statutes in some states, and municipal ordinances in individual cities, may require the city to indemnify municipal employees for any amounts they may be called upon to pay for such injuries.

Thus, insurance coverage is becoming increasingly necessary to protect not only governmental units but also employees and officers individually. Liability insurance coverages are also becoming increasingly necessary for other units of government, such as states and counties, as courts and state legislatures restrict the areas within which these entities may act with immunity. In order to determine the insurance needs of any particular governmental unit or entity, reference must be made to the particular statutory and decisional law of the jurisdiction determining the vulnerability of the particular unit to liability.

Liability Exposures of Educational Entities

The liability exposures of educational entities are affected by both charitable immunity and governmental immunity. Private schools often are a type of charitable institution; public schools, conversely, are an arm of the government.

Private Schools Private schools, colleges, and universities which are generally not-for-profit organizations have traditionally been considered subject to the same immunity from suit for tortious injury as charities. Although this immunity has been abrogated in varying degrees and from state to state, both judicially and by statute, an understanding of the effects of charitable immunity remains a starting point for understanding the liability exposure of a private school.

The charitable immunity of private schools has not been absolute. It has been tempered by a number of traditional limitations which softened the seemingly harsh doctrine of immunity in the face of an actual injury. Not all of these limitations have been used in all jurisdictions.

One traditional limitation on the charitable immunity of private schools has been that if the school runs a profit-making facility and the injury occurs in connection with that facility, there is no immunity. Because a profit-making facility would not involve trust property, any tort recovery would be from nontrust property which is not protected for a charitable or educational use. A private charitable school, although otherwise immune from tort liability, can thus be liable for injuries suffered by persons in connection with noncharitable activities conducted by the school, where such activities are primarily commercial in nature, even though carried on for the purpose of obtaining revenue to be used to carry on the charitable purposes of the school.

As an example of the distinctions made by the courts on this subject, the courts have held that the operation of an office building, with the income from such building going to support the school, was a noncharitable activity, while the operation of a dormitory, for which a fee was required of the student residents, was encompassed within, and incidental to, the general charitable activities of the school. Another noncharitable activity was a medical care plan for school employees, which plan was provided for a fee and managed by the school for a profit.

In some jurisdictions, there has been a limitation that a school may be liable for "administrative" negligence but not for the negligence of its employees. This derives from the theory that while the *respondeat superior* doctrine does not apply to charities, there is no immunity from the negligence of the charity itself. Thus, if a loss arises from administrative negligence, such as the hiring of incompetent faculty, or the failure to issue proper rules and regulations, the injured party may recover, while if it arises from the negligence of employees, the party may not. In many cases this is really just a semantic distinction, because the negligence of a teacher may often be expressed as the negligence of the school in hiring or in failing to fire that teacher.

A third traditional exception, existing in some states, exempted from immunity certain types of property torts, such as trespass or nuisance, the theory being that the ownership of property is noncharitable and *respondeat superior* does not apply.

A further limitation has been imposed on charitable immunity according to the status of the injured party. Thus, in some cases, liability has been either imposed or denied because the injured party is a student, a stranger, or an employee. Frequently, a student may not recover, for example, because the student is considered to be a beneficiary of the charitable trust.

As a general rule, charitable immunity is not lost or affected by the fact that a private school carries liability insurance. However, if a state law requires a private school to carry liability insurance, it may be liable to the extent of such coverage, although otherwise immune from liability.

If there is no immuunity in a particular situation, the injured party does not automatically recover. The injured party must, like any other victim of a tort, still prove that a duty existed, that that duty was breached, and that the breach was the proximate cause of injury.

There are two areas in which school tort cases most commonly fall: those cases in which the injury resulted from the negligence of teachers or other students; and cases in which the injury resulted from a condition existing on the school premises.

Suits based on employee or teacher negligence are founded on a failure to fulfill the duty to supervise, a duty which varies with the circumstances. An institution must provide supervision when it has reason to think supervision is required. But it is not required to provide constant supervision over students at all times. For example, no supervision is generally required of high school students when they are engaged in a nonhazardous activity after normal class hours.

The duty to supervise requires that a school provide supervision if it could reasonably anticipate that supervision is required because of the nature of the activity. Where students, as part of their courses, use potentially dangerous equipment under the supervision of instructors, the school is required to give the students reasonable instructions as to the methods to be used, give warnings as to risks of injury which might otherwise follow, and afford reasonable supervision of the activity being performed. The warnings are particularly important if, because of inexperience, the students might otherwise be unaware of the risks involved. Where an activity is potentially hazardous, the school has the duty of providing that degree of supervision which the situation demands. The fact that a student is required to take a class, particularly if the class involves some danger, may require a greater degree of care for the safety of the students than would be the case if the class were made up of volunteers.

Where an injury is caused by the act of a fellow student during the absence of the teacher, the duty to supervise is measured by whether the circumstances were such that the teacher, if present, could have reasonably foreseen the subsequent incident and would have had sufficient time to take preventive action prior to such incident.

In many cases, the duty of care of a school is considered discharged by the formulation of appropriate rules and regulations and a reasonable effort to enforce them. Under this reasoning, deliberate infraction of the school rules by a pupil or student has barred recovery. Where a third person is injured through the negligence of a student, the school may be liable, if the negligent student is under the immediate control of an employee of the school and the proximate cause of the injury may be said to be that of the school's employee.

With respect to liability of a school for negligence of its employees, the school is liable for injury suffered by third persons under general rules applicable to employers, provided that the employee was acting within the scope of employment at the time of the accident.

An injured pupil may be barred from recovery for a particular injury on the grounds of contributory negligence or assumption of risk. Thus, notwithstanding the possible negligence on the part of a school, if students are injured while voluntarily engaging in an extremely hazardous activity with other students, particularly where such activity is against the rules of the school, a submission of the issue of contributory negligence to the jury is proper, at least where the injured pupil is of high school age.

The other major source of liability for private schools, when not barred by the doctrine of charitable immunity, is for those injuries suffered by students as a result of the allegedly defective or dangerous condition of the school premises. As a property owner, a school has the same duties of any property owner with regard to invitees, licensees or trespassers who enter or remain upon the premises. Whereas a guest on the school premises is considered a mere licensee, a student is considered an invitee, as a general rule. If an employee of a private school is injured, the case is governed by the general rule that an employer has a positive, nondelegable duty to furnish employees with a reasonably safe place to work.

Public Schools Under the doctrine of governmental immunity, public schools, colleges, universities, and school districts, as well as the local governments which operate public schools, have traditionally been immune from suit for tort liability. Although the modern trend is away from this doctrine, governmental immunity is a starting point for consideration of the liability of public schools.

The reasons for governmental immunity of public schools are similar to the reasons given for charitable immunity. The theory is that the school benefits the public and that the public funds it uses are held in trust, in effect, for the purpose of educating its students; hence, such funds should not be used for the payment of tort judgments. There is also an argument that the funds belonging to a school district cannot legally be used for the payment of tort judgments, since the school district has no power which is not given to it by statute.

The major reason for abolishing school district immunity is the same as that for abolishing charitable immunity. It is now felt that it is more appropriate to spread the cost of injury among many, rather than to have the burden fall on the one injured.

For public schools, as well as private schools, there have been traditional exceptions to the immunity rule. In some states, the school district may be liable for property torts such as trespass or nuisance. For example, a school district may be liable if there is damage to neighboring property during the excavation of school property.

A public school may be liable if the injury arose out of a proprietary or business function, rather than a governmental function. Examples of functions found to be governmental include public athletic events; construction, repair, or maintenance of premises; and operation of school cafeterias. Proprietary functions have included leasing the school stadium to another school district and charging admission to an athletic event.

Another potential exception to the traditional immunity doctrine is the distinction between nondiscretionary and discretionary functions. Even where the doctrine of governmental immunity has been abrogated, some jurisdictions still hold school districts immune from liability for the discretionary acts of their employees. A similar distinction has been made between optional and mandatory activities, in which case liability is held for optional activities.

A number of cases have held or recognized that school districts may be liable for injuries resulting from the creation of a nuisance, even though done in the performance of a governmental function. It also has been said that governmental immunity does not extend to willful, intentional, or malicious misconduct. Immunity may not generally be waived by a school district. Recovery may be had, however, through a special bill in the state legislature designed to compensate a particular victim not otherwise entitled to a remedy.

Unlike private schools, the purchase of liability insurance by a public school or school district may be considered a waiver of governmental immunity.

There is a growing trend in many states, both by statute and by court decision, to modify or eliminate the immunity of public school districts. There is a wide variety of solutions to the problem. Some statutes and some state court decisions abolish immunity completely, either by the total abolition of governmental immunity or with special reference to school districts. Some statutes have created administrative boards for hearing claims against school districts. Others have simply authorized school districts, in their discretion, to purchase liability insurance, in which case immunity is waived. Some states provide indemnity protection for the negligent employee. Many of these statutes also limit the amount the claimant can recover.

Even where immunity is abrogated, this does not relieve the injured party of the burden of proving negligence and proximate cause. A public school and a private school have the same duties of supervision, to make and follow regulations, and to warn against not rectifying hazardous conditions. Further, the public school child may be found guilty of contributory negligence of assumption of risk, which would act as a defense against a personal injury claim.

School administrators may be found personally liable if they are found to be individually negligent or acting beyond the scope of their employment but, as a general rule, governmental immunity extends to the individual members of a school board and other school administrators.

TREATMENT OF LIABILITY EXPOSURES OF CHARITABLE, EDUCATIONAL, AND GOVERNMENTAL ENTITIES

It is evident that, with the abrogation of charitable and sovereign immunity in a growing number of jurisdictions, and with numerous other factors which can limit immunity, charitable, educational, and governmental entities can be just as vulnerable to liability loss as commercial enterprises. And, while the erosion of immunities is a growing problem unique to these entities, there are other conditions common to most other businesses which also have an adverse effect— such as society's growing awareness of its legal rights, the resulting frequency of lawsuits, and the size of court awards. Compounding the aforementioned problems are insurer underwriting losses, the withdrawal of some insurers from the marketplace, and the reluctance of some insurers to provide basic forms of protection unless both businesses and charitable, governmental, and educational entities accept higher levels of retention (deductibles) in addition to paying high premiums.

The conditions described above are by no means new or universal in scope. Some charitable, governmental, and educational entities have been experiencing hardships in obtaining insurance protection for years. A growing number of governmental entities, in particular, are at the crisis stage today. Others have yet to encounter significant problems.

The status of problems at any given time depends upon the nature of the entity and its exposures, as well as the extent of immunity which may apply.

Despite deteriorating conditions, many of these entities, perhaps the majority, still rely upon conventional insurance as their primary risk management technique. However, most are finding the traditional approach of buying moderately-priced, first dollar liability coverages on a competitive-bid basis to be a thing of the past. In the usual course of events, these entities are usually finding various forms of insurance protection to be more limited in scope, costlier, and subject to higher retention amounts. As a result of these changing conditions, some entities are being forced to seek alternative risk management techniques to control their costs, while still maintaining some basic forms of protection against liability in areas of need. The trend is toward an increasing awareness of the risk management process and the handling of liability loss exposures primarily with the noninsurance techniques of loss prevention and control, funded and unfunded retention, transfer by contract, avoidance when there are no other alternatives, and the use of insurance at the higher or catastrophic levels of potential loss.

Some of the larger charitable, governmental, and educational entities are able to justify and afford full-time risk managers who can establish, administer and monitor programs which may help to achieve protection against catastrophic losses, along with savings in the overall costs of administering such programs. Smaller entities may have to rely on outsiders with expertise, such as insurance agents, insurance brokers, or risk management consultants. Such outsiders can provide advice and/or administer various segments of risk management programs.

It is also becoming increasingly common, for those cities and counties whose immunities have been abrogated, to retain risk management consulting firms who conduct audits and make recommendations as to how the pure loss exposures can best be handled. These risk management consulting firms can identify and evaluate the pure loss exposures; recommend ways to handle the exposures with a mix of noninsurance techniques and insurance; help to set up unfunded retention levels or funded retention mechanisms; assist in the choice of insurance markets, agents or brokers; obtain excess layers of liability insurance; and help to hire risk managers or to recommend present staff members who can handle the risk management program in a systematic and efficient manner.

At the other extreme, there are some entities which consider insurance to be basically unaffordable, high deductibles to be unrealistic, and the employment of risk management experts to be impractical. Entities in this category may thus rely upon whatever insurance protection they feel they can afford and whatever loss control assistance an insurance company staff can provide. If permitted by law, they may be able to participate with other entities in pools.

Pooling, a form of funded retention shared by many participants or members of the association, is becoming increasingly popular among medium to small governmental entities.[34] The reason for its popularity is that these entities are able (1) to refrain from purchasing insurance for high frequency severity losses which can easily be retained by the group, as a whole; (2) to reduce the unnecessary costs or so-called insurance premium loadings, such as underwriting expenses and producers' commissions; (3) to share their losses and related loss costs, including the expenses of administering the pools; and (4) to utilize their influence, as a group, to bargain for lower costs on the excess insurance which is usually required to protect against any large losses which might occur over their retention amounts.

The preceding overview of the problems of charitable, governmental, and educational entities which are losing their shield of immunity illustrates the measures which sometimes have to be taken when insurance cannot be depended upon as the primary source of protection.

The remainder of this chapter is devoted to a discussion of treating the various liability exposures of charitable, governmental, and educational entities—the insurance forms which are available to cover those exposures and the noninsurance techniques which may be used in lieu of, or in addition to, insurance. But, because of space limitations, much of the emphasis is placed on governmental entities, rather than on charitable and educational entities.

Liability Exposures

Governmental entities, like business enterprises, come in various sizes, ranging from very small operations with two or three employees to very large operations with hundreds of employees. The liability exposures of these entities therefore can range from a few uncomplicated ones to others which are so diverse and numerous that any attempt to identify all loss exposures may seem to be a hopeless, if not an endless, task.

To gain a better perspective on the types of liability exposures which can confront entities, the following is a list of the more common ones, divided into five groups by type of exposures:

Premises and Operations (General). Parks, amusement and recreational, swimming pools, beaches, lakes, stadiums, convention and exhibition halls, golf courses, streets and sidewalks, cemeteries, correctional facilities, dams, reservoirs, firefighting facilities, flood control, utilities, libraries, museums, parking lots and garages, sewage disposal, animal control, housing projects, pipelines, bridges and tunnels.

Premises and Operations (Professional). Asylums, clinics, convalescent homes, hospitals, other medical facilities, including paramedics, police and sheriffs departments, schools, public officials, architects and engineers.

Vehicles—Operations. Owned, nonowned and hired automobiles, trash collection, transit systems, watercraft, wharves, piers, marinas, ferries, aircraft, airports, and helipods.

Owners Protective—Contractual. Work performed on behalf of the entities by independent contractors, including pipelines and other forms of transmission operated by outside interests.

Personnel. Employees of entities, including persons who are hired under the Comprehensive Employees Training Act, as specified and subsidized by the Federal government, to perform various jobs at lower income levels.

As mentioned more fully later, insurance for many of the aforementioned exposures is difficult to obtain. Even when insurance is available, entities are finding various coverages to be unaffordable. Nonetheless, a variety of insurance forms are designed precisely for the exposures of governmental entities.

Insurance Coverages

Various standard and nonstandard insurance coverages are used to cover the exposures of governmental entities, with nonstandard coverage being common today. In most cases, the basic coverage forms have to be amended to fit the liability exposures, not only to broaden some of the coverage features, but also to limit them. Based upon the preceding categories of liability exposures confronting governmental entities, the following are the major coverages which can be used to cover them.

Premises and Operations (General) Coverages which may be required for general premises and operations liability exposures include:

1. Comprehensive general liability insurance which covers all known exposures, as well as those which arise during the policy period, that may cause bodily injury, personal injury, and property damage. Coverage applies not only to the physical hazards of premises, but also to the acts or omissions of entity employees. Generally, the exposures arising out of the existence of streets and sidewalks can be excluded by endorsement, if desired, with a resulting premium reduction, which can be substantial for larger entities. It is particularly important to have personal injury liability coverage to protect entities against

claims frequently caused by civil authorities in law enforcement. However, coverage for injury or damage caused by the attempted control of mob action or violence is generally excluded and difficult, if not impossible, to purchase.

2. Owners, landlords, and tenants liability insurance is a restricted version of coverage which may be used to cover certain known and specified exposures without also automatically covering other like exposures which presently exist or may arise. For example, when a municipality has several reservoirs but desires coverage only on the more hazardous ones, the OL&T policy can be used for this purpose.

3. Buffer layer liability insurance is a form of contract which provides a layer of liability limits on top of primary limits in order for entities to qualify for excess liability insurance. Buffer layer liability insurance is becoming more and more prevalent, with the restricted primary markets and increasing demands of excess liability insurers for higher limits of underlying coverages.

4. Commercial umbrella liability coverage is intended to provide entities with excess protection over coverages of underlying insurance, and additional coverages for exposures not covered by underlying insurance, subject to high retentions. Because of the loss experience of governmental entities, commercial umbrella liability policies are being written to provide protection for very few exposures which are not also covered by underlying general liability policies. Thus, they would often be written to exclude dams and reservoirs, errors and omissions of public officials, aircraft and airports and malpractice exposures of hospitals, clinics and staff, including paramedics.

5. Excess liability policies are used to provide additional limits of liability over primary or excess liability policies without providing any broader coverage.

Premises and Operations (Professional) Generally, the premises hazards of professional liability exposures, such as clinics, hospitals, and schools, are covered by the general liability forms mentioned above. However, operation exposures of a professional nature need to be covered by various professional liability forms, depending upon the exposure. The following are the types of nonstandard forms which may be required:

1. Hospital professional liability insurance is used for asylums, mental health clinics, medical laboratories, and other medical facilities to protect governmental entities for their vicarious liability involving claims resulting from the negligent acts,

errors, or omissions of personnel who render or fail to render professional services. Most such policies also cover injury claims resulting from food, beverages and other products which are necessarily dispensed by these facilities. Not usually within the scope of coverage, however, is the liability of individual professionals.

2. Physicians', surgeons', and dentists' liability, druggists' liability, medical laboratory technicians' and paramedics' liability forms, among others, are commonly required to protect individual professionals against losses arising from their personal acts which may give rise to claims.

3. Public officials liability forms are designed for elected or appointed officials of public entities who wish to be protected against their actual or alleged errors, misstatements, acts, omissions, neglect, or breach of duty in the discharge of their duties. Coverage usually is patterned after directors' and officers' liability and reimbursement coverages, with coverages available to handle claims made against the officials or the public entities, as well as reimbursement to the entities for having to pay officials for any judgments and defense costs to the extent the entities are required or permitted to do so under common or statutory law.

4. Board of education and school district liability forms, patterned after directors' and officers' liability and reimbursement coverages, can cover members of the board of education, trustees, directors, student teachers, administrators, athletic directors, counselors, superintendents, principals, as well as the board of regents, trustees or governors of colleges or universities for their wrongful acts or omissions which give rise to claims.

5. Police professional liability forms provide protection against liability primarily in the nature of such intentional torts as false arrest, wrongful eviction, and wrongful entry. Ordinarily, the personal injury liability coverage of basic general liability insurance would be sufficient to cover the exposure of police. But, because of the exposure, basic liability policies are commonly endorsed to exclude such exposures, although umbrella liability policies will cover any losses over the applicable retained limit.

Vehicles Depending upon the size of these entities, a variety of vehicles and, hence, exposures to liability, could prevail. The more common coverages which are available include the following:

1. Comprehensive automobile liability forms are designed to provide entities with protection in the event of bodily injury or

property damage sustained by the public resulting from the operation, maintenance or use of owned, nonowned, and hired automobiles, trucks, and buses, including vicarious liability of employees who may use their personal automobiles on business. If the automobile liability exposure is not entirely satisfactory to insurers, the latter may impose more restricted forms of insurance, in order to make coverage less comprehensive in scope, particularly with respect to newly acquired and nonowned automobiles.

2. Marine policies are available to provide liability coverage for losses to property on watercraft, or for collision with other vessels and with wharves, piers, and other structures adjoining bodies of water. Depending upon the watercraft exposure, umbrella excess liability policies may not necessarily provide excess protection. In this event, so-called bumbershoot liability (a form of excess marine liability coverage) may have to be purchased.

3. Aircraft liability policies can provide entities with liability protection stemming from the maintenance, operation, and use of owned, nonowned, and hired aircraft and helicopters, as well as the premises liability exposures of airports and heliports. Umbrella or excess liability policies usually do not cover owned aircraft exposures, but such excess coverage may not be necessary, because limits into the millions generally are obtainable from the primary insurers of aircraft liability.

Owners Protective—Contractual Many of the entities which do not have the personnel to perform street and road repair work, maintenance of grounds, and new construction on improvements and betterments of their entity's property often will have to contract out work. Some of the larger entities also may hire independent contractors to perform certain difficult projects. When entities engage outside experts to perform certain services usually under contract, they are vulnerable to loss of a contingent or vicarious nature. To protect themselves with insurance, entities need owners protective liability and contractual liability coverages, both of which are automatically included in most comprehensive liability policies. However, contractual liability coverage may be restricted to designated contracts, whereas the broader, blanket coverage may be desired. When such broader coverage for oral and written contracts cannot be obtained, entities may have to rely upon their umbrella excess liability policies for the coverage subject to the applicable deductible amount.

Personnel The liability coverages which may be required or desired to compensate personnel for their injuries, sicknesses, or deaths are provided under workers' compensation and employers' liability insurance, which were discussed thoroughly in Chapter 7.

Other Coverages The preceding liability coverages are not by any means meant to be an exhaustive list of liability coverages available to charitable, governmental, and educational entities, but merely those which are designed for the more common liability exposures of entities. However, the fact that certain coverages may fit the exposures does not necessarily mean that insurance is a must. Most forms of liability protection are increasingly being viewed as unavailable or unaffordable because of the loss experience of these entities, in general, as well as their lack of interest and/or expertise in implementing measures of loss control. The result is that entities sometimes have to go without insurance for their malpractice and/or errors and omissions liability exposures, and may have no other choice but to retain as much as $500,000 to $1 million of their general liability, automobile liability and workers' compensation losses. While the two foregoing forms of retention may cause financial hardship, they also may be able to motivate entities to take a more active interest in loss control and other noninsurance techniques. In addition, the retention of high loss amounts may open the market for excess limits which may be required against the catastrophic loss exposures. The implementation of noninsurance techniques is therefore becoming increasingly important to entities.

Noninsurance Techniques

In the pages that follow, each of the noninsurance techniques for treating the liability exposures of governmental entities (except on a federal level) is discussed in generalities, because the practicality and application of each technique can vary considerably.[35] Furthermore, to simplify matters, the assumption is made that all entities have no legal restrictions that affect their use of the noninsurance techniques on potential losses which are no longer shielded by immunity.[36]

Loss control, retention, noninsurance transfer, and avoidance are the noninsurance techniques available to entities for treating their liability loss exposure. These techniques are used for the same reasons as when they are applied to business enterprises, i.e., to reduce losses and insurance costs.

There is considerable opportunity for entities to protect themselves against loss and to improve their chances of reaching the insurance market for higher levels of protection at more economically feasible costs by using various noninsurance techniques. However, it is getting so that noninsurance techniques are not a matter of choice—they are essential, particularly when entities no longer have the shield of immunity which they once enjoyed.

Loss Control The noninsurance technique of loss control is commonly viewed as indispensable because, when properly structured, it can reduce the frequency and/or severity of losses and, hence, the financial hardship which otherwise could result. However, an effective loss control program is not easy to manage, especially among the larger charitable, educational, and governmental entities which have widespread operations and premises exposures which can take in miles of sidewalks, streets, and roads. Of those liability claims made against governmental entities, many involve the allegations of hazardous road conditions and malfunctioning traffic signals.[37]

The fact that an entity has a risk manager and/or safety director does not mean that it will have an effective program of loss control, even though either or both of those persons may be expected to perform certain inspections. What also may be required is the cooperation and assistance of all employees, coordinated by the risk manager or safety director. For example, a large charitable or educational entity may have a loss control program whereby each department head has the responsibility for noting and reporting all physical hazards (work-related or not) to the risk manager or coordinator and assisting in the implementation of any corrective action which may be deemed necessary. And, to make the overall program more successful, each of the department heads is also given periodic feedback on losses, such as claim analysis reports which list claim frequencies by department, along with a brief description of claims, to enable each department head to study the frequency patterns and to measure their department's performance. Without this feedback, department heads might not have any way of knowing how effective their loss control efforts are.

A governmental entity, such as a large municipality, may have a similar arrangement of loss control with responsibility placed upon its (1) safety director to handle workers' compensation exposures, (2) public works director to inspect operations performed by municipality employees and independent contractors, (3) director of parks to inspect all recreational facilities and to help plan new developments, (4) street and parkway maintenance director to inspect road conditions and to periodically test traffic signals, (5) utilities director to handle the inspections on power-producing facilities to prevent brownouts or inadvertent power cutouts to commercial and industrial customers, and to inspect dams and/or reservoirs, and (6) automobile maintenance director to inspect vehicle safety, to purchase new vehicles and to repair or subcontract repair of motor vehicles. Each of the foregoing persons also may be expected to note and report work-related exposures involving premises, operations, motor vehicles, watercraft, aircraft, and to administer accident prevention programs for employees as directed by the risk manager.[38] All municipality employees, on the other hand, may be expected to report exposures relating to premises and operations to their respective department heads.

While it is unlikely that all liability loss exposures will be identified, in spite of everyone's commitment to be more safety-conscious, comprehensive loss records, which are considered to be one of the necessary elements of any risk management program, can prove to be invaluable sources of information in pinpointing troublesome or potentially troublesome exposures. For example, a high frequency of motor vehicle accidents may indicate the necessity for implementing a program of driver safety, or an unusually high rate of minor workers' compensation claims among the police force may indicate the need for improving working conditions and morale.

Loss control programs are difficult to organize and even more perplexing to manage on an efficient scale. It also may take a number of years before these programs will produce results. Yet, sound loss control programs can aid entities whose insurance markets are disappearing, and it can complement the technique of retention which also is becoming increasingly popular among such entities.

Retention Businesses and governmental entities alike can use the technique of retention to their advantage for losses which are frequent and, hence, predictable, and for infrequent, potentially large losses which can be wholly or partially absorbed with their own financial resources. There are both tangible and intangible benefits of retention. One of the more cogent benefits is that entities can realize savings, when they forgo the use of insurance on small, predictable losses. Another benefit is that entities are more likely to be aware of the need for loss control when losses are retained rather than insured.

While the retention of small, frequent losses should present no undue hardship, the same cannot be said of the potentially large but infrequent losses—it may only take one catastrophic loss to bankrupt a business or entity which has not taken steps to protect itself. However, full insurance may be uneconomical or unavailable. What often is suggested as an alternative is that entities should decide how much of the loss they can afford to retain without causing financial hardship, and then buy excess liability insurance for the remainder. By taking this approach, entities can apply the savings from retaining losses at lower levels toward the purchase of insurance at more catastrophic levels—which may be more readily available.

The only obstacle is in deciding upon the amount of retention for these infrequent losses. Over the years, a number of guidelines have been offered to aid entities and businesses in establishing their retention levels, but none of them is precise. These guidelines suggest, in general, that the retention level be based upon the percentage at which revenues, earnings per share, or budgeted expenses can fluctuate without causing financial dislocations. The rationale of these guidelines is that there usually is some cushion or alternative source of funds which can be used to handle unforeseeable contingencies. For example, if an entity has a budget of $50 million and it could withstand a fluctuation (a decrease in revenues or an increase in expenses) of no more than 1 percent, that entity could likely retain an aggregate of $500,000, i.e., one or more losses for the fiscal period, over the planned retention of the more frequent and predictable losses of that entity. One major problem with these guidelines is in determining the percentage of permissible fluctuation.

The preceding approaches to retention and the reasons for considering them in treating various liability loss exposures apply primarily to entities which have good loss experience and are not experiencing any difficulties in obtaining insurance for their needs. Unfortunately, a growing number of charitable, governmental, and educational entities are finding that the choice of retention levels is not theirs. This is especially true of those entities in claim-prone areas of the country, such as California and New York, which have (1) exposures that are difficult, if not costly, to insure at any level—such as medical malpractice, public transportation, dams and reservoirs, (2) a general history of poor loss experience, and (3) no formal program of loss control.

It is said that public entities in the foregoing category have brought these problems upon themselves. Here, for example, is what three brokers of California firms which handle insurance on public entities had to say about the reasons for these problems and some of the ways they may be overcome:

> Public entities have looked at insurance as a way of picking up the bills. They haven't cooperated with insurers on safety recommendations or on controlling losses. But that's changing, because many public entities are assuming growing retention levels and paying the bills first themselves. So they are now more safety conscious, more concerned with losses and are even hiring risk managers.[39]

> Within five years you'll all have self-insured retentions of $500,000. No one wants to write the first layer for public entities in California. Sometimes there are seven or more participants in the first $500,000 excess layer of a $500,000 retention.[40]

> To make public entity risks more attractive to the excess and surplus market, risk managers should be involved with loss control. Good loss control can mean more savings in self-insurance for public agencies.

Get specific with your safety and loss control measures. This will present your risk a lot better to primary underwriters.[41]

It might be argued that California is a little out of the ordinary when it comes to public entities and their problems. Perhaps the argument is valid. But what is happening in that state can also occur elsewhere in the country, in time, if losses begin to mount and entities do not take the initiative to control and retain some of them.

Although the alternatives for handling various forms of retention are too diverse and numerous to discuss here in any great detail, the following are a few of the possible approaches which could be considered. First, if general liability loss experience records over a period of at least five years show a high frequency of incurred losses ranging up to a maximum of $25,000 per loss, an entity could decide, if it has the choice, to use an unfunded retention of, say, $50,000 per loss and a $200,000 annual aggregate and seek liability insurance for excess limits. Thus, by taking a higher retention than what its actual experience reflects, the entity may find more insurers willing to provide a market for excess insurance, and the insurance is likely to be more reasonable at the higher level than if excess limits were to be sought for losses at a level of $25,000 or $30,000 per loss. The adjustment of claims within the retention amount could be handled by a claims administrator of the entity or by an independent firm which specializes in claims handling. Any litigation, in turn, could be handled by the entity's legal staff and assisted by outside law firms. However, if an entity cannot obtain excess protection unless it retains at least the first $500,000 in losses, the entity is likely to have no other choice but to follow that route.

Second, if automobile liability losses are insured for primary limits of $300,000 per occurrence, at what an entity considers to be an economically feasible cost, but excess limits are not available at lower than $500,000 primary, the entity may have to obtain buffer layers from one or more insurers (for an amount of $200,000) in order to qualify for the excess protection. If the entity's motor vehicles are parked in areas of high concentration of values but there is no concentration of exposures when the vehicles are in use, the entity may decide to retain all physical damage losses and to exercise some form of loss control on the so-called "terminal hazard," or to use two or more separate parking facilities.

The workers' compensation exposure, on the other hand, may have to be insured in an assigned risk pool if commercial insurance is not available through normal channels and an entity is not large enough to handle the exposure any other way.

It may be to the advantage of some large governmental entities to handle losses with a funded retention of up to $1 million (or another large figure that may be deemed appropriate, depending on past loss records) and to obtain specific excess or aggregate excess coverage of $5 or $10 million for catastrophic losses. The workers' compensation exposure, in turn, could be controlled by the activities of a risk manager or loss prevention engineer, and the funded retention could be administered by the finance director, aided by inside and/or outside expertise to handle the actual adjustment of losses.

Both loss control and retention may be virtually essential to a growing number of entities, not only to reduce losses and overall costs, but also to qualify for insurance protection where it may be needed the most—at the higher levels where entities are least able to handle losses. Although some entities may view loss control and retention as involuntary measures, the technique of noninsurance transfer is still considered to be a purely voluntary measure that entities must use whenever possible.

Noninsurance Transfer Noninsurance transfer, when properly handled, can be a beneficial tool for charitable, governmental, and educational entities. It is a way to transfer losses in whole or in part which might otherwise have to be retained or treated by the entities themselves at considerably more expense. However, noninsurance transfer can have its pitfalls, especially when the entities have no control over the contract-making process and no system for the review of contracts imposed upon entities by others. The result could be costly in at least two ways: (1) contracts required by entities may be deemed to be ineffective because they are unreasonable in scope or ambiguously worded; and (2) contracts accepted by entities may require the assumption of liability beyond what entities might have anticipated.

While the type of system to prevent problems and to meet the objectives of noninsurance transfer will vary by entity, there are certain basic requirements which are essential.

First, a qualified attorney should be involved in drawing up contract provisions, as well as in reviewing the provisions of contracts accepted by entities.

Second, an attorney should be assisted by the risk manager or insurance administrator when it comes to drawing up specifications for the various insurance coverages, limits and other appropriate provisions which are to be required of others by contract. This is an especially crucial step, and one which must be handled by a person who is knowledgeable of the type of exposures which are likely to arise, so that the insurance requirements are in the best interests of the entity. Many legal experts are not skilled in insurance matters.

Third, the risk manager or insurance administrator must obtain insurance certificates as prerequisites to awarding contracts, and the certificates must be maintained, preferably on a diary system, so as to ensure that coverage is maintained on a continuous basis, especially for long-term projects.

Fourth, all contracts received by personnel of entities should be referred to the attorney and risk manager (or insurance administrator) for review before they are signed and accepted.

When the foregoing requirements are met, entities are likely to have fewer problems in meeting their objectives of noninsurance transfer. But, as one can surmise, communication and cooperation of all personnel are also essential ingredients for a successful risk management program, and cooperation can be difficult to achieve—especially among large entities which have numerous personnel and widespread operations.

If there are exposures of entities which are likely to produce catastrophic results and they cannot be satisfactorily handled with insurance or any one of the aforementioned noninsurance techniques, the only other recourse is avoidance.

Avoidance Whether avoidance will be looked upon by educational, charitable, and governmental entities as a way to treat their liability loss exposures remains to be seen. Despite the fact that the abrogation of immunities (in whole or in part) has put some entities on an equal footing with commercial enterprises insofar as potential for liability loss is concerned, charitable, governmental, and educational entities, more than businesses, are likely to use unfunded retention before going to the last resort of avoidance. Many of the more troublesome exposures of these entities—hospitals and universities, dams and reservoirs of cities, and various proprietary operations of charitable organizations—are attributable to activities which are an essential part of the entities' very reason for existence. It is not unusual to read about the less conventional approaches being taken by all entities in handling their difficult liability exposures. Hospitals often attempt to form or join captives, educational entities seek pooling arrangements, and governmental entities are taking higher and higher forms of retention.

In his treatise on governmental risk management, Pfennigstorf makes some interesting observations about governmental entities which serve to answer the question why such entities are more likely to keep and treat exposures by measures other than avoidance. He states:

> Government entities differ in several important respects from private business enterprises even though their risk situations may be similar. First, a government entity could not be wiped out by a large uninsured loss in the same way as a private business, by being forced into liquidation and out of existence. The survival of government units is

subject to political rather than economic forces—as organizations and carriers of public powers and duties they must continue to exist and to function even if their liabilities exceed their assets and even if they are unable to pay their creditors. The alternative would be anarchy. It is true that governments do not always pay their debts. Instances of default or even repudiation of public debts have occurred rather frequently. Municipalities go through formal bankruptcy proceedings under chapter IX of the Bankruptcy Act; states and national governments usually do not even need that formality to get rid of their debts. In either case, the essential functions of government have to go on, though perhaps at a rudimentary scale. The principal losers are the bondholders and suppliers; in more serious cases the population in general also suffers through a reduction of public employment and a reduction of the quantity and quality of public services. Therefore, and because of the politically and economically unsettling side effects of financial crises, it is the duty of responsible governments to avoid them. Governments are expected to operate within the limits of their budgets and to make adequate provision for contingencies to avoid the need for large tax increases. Nevertheless, the double guaranties of perpetual existence and taxing power give them more latitude in dealing with risks than any private business enjoys.

Second, governments, unlike private businesses, are not governed by the principle of profit maximization, and while economy is one objective of responsible government, it is not the only objective or even the most important one. It is often subordinated to other objectives inherent in the democratic structure of government, especially decentralization, municipal self-government (home rule), and democratic procedures for decision making. A third characteristic of governmental management is that the political climate in which governments operate encourages attempts to improperly influence decisions. There are elaborate rules and procedures to ensure integrity, often at the expense of economy and efficiency. Fourth, risk management decisions of governments tend to be influenced by deep-seated political convictions concerning the paramount role of free enterprise. Additional differences with respect to risk exposure, available resources, flexibility of the tax base, legal and budgetary restrictions, decision-making procedures, and general administrative and fiscal policies exist among the different types and levels of government units; state governments and their departments and agencies and businesslike ventures; counties, townships, and municipal corporations, school districts, park districts, hospitals, universities, and similar semiautonomous institutions.

It is not surprising, therefore, that governments have responded in different ways to the challenge of risk management. Some have been more aware of the problems and options than others and have devoted more effort and imagination to developing sound programs. . . .[42]

While the preceding comments provide some interesting insights on why some entities—particularly governmental entities—are not likely to resort to avoidance as a way of handling even serious exposures, there could be circumstances when smaller charitable, educational, and governmental entities might resort to avoidance, especially when the loss potentials are too large to handle by any other means. Avoidance therefore is available if all other measures will not do.

Chapter Notes

1. Guile v. Swan, 19 John Rep. 381 (1822). No record is available to show whether the funds to satisfy the ninety-dollar judgment against the trespassing balloonist were provided by a casualty insurance company. A market for balloonist liability insurance probably was nonexistent, unless some unwary underwriter learned to his sorrow that his policy was held to include performing feats in a balloon. We do know that aviation insurance followed closely after the earliest flights of the flying pioneers.
2. As of December 31, 1975, there were 168,475 active general aviation aircraft and 2,495 aircraft in the fleets of commercial air carriers.
3. Margosian v. U.S. Airlines, 127 F. Supp., 464 (1955).
4. Wood v. United Airlines, Inc., 223 NYS 2d 692 (1962); Aff'd without opinion N.Y. Sup. App. Div. 2nd Dep.
5. Restatement (second) Conflicts of Law as Amended 1968, Sec. 379.
6. 46 U.S.C. 761 et seq.
7. 49 Stat., Pt 2 at page 3,000. For an interesting case in which the plaintiffs recovered for injuries sustained in a terrorist attack in the airport waiting room, see Evangelinos v. Trans World Airlines, U.S. Court of Appeals, 3rd Cir., 1977.
8. See Lowenfeld, "The United States and the Warsaw Convention," 80 *Harv. L. Rev.* 497 (1967). Under the provisions of the Hague Protocol, the Warsaw Convention limit was double to the then U.S. equivalent of $16,000, but its proposed ratification by the U.S. was never acted upon. The Hague Protocol came into force among the thirty ratifying states on August 1, 1963.
9. *Rough Notes Policy, Form and Manual Analyses (P.F.&M.)* 330.6 contains a listing of statutes affecting liability to guests.
10. Halbert, et al. v. Berlinger, et al. 273 P 2d 274 (Cal. Dist. Ct. of App. 1954).
11. Messmer, etc. v. Ker, 524 P 2d 536 (1974); Longnecker v. Noordyk Mooney, Inc. et al., 232 N.W. 2d 654 (1975).
12. *P.F.&M.* 330.5 contains a current listing of state statutes affecting aircraft liability.
13. 72 Stat. 774, 49 U.S.C. Sec. 1404 (Supp. IV, 1963).
14. This is currently true in Michigan and New York.
15. The legal doctrine in tort known as *res ipsa loquitur*, which creates a rebuttable inference of negligence, has been applied in many jurisdictions to aircraft crash cases, but others have rejected it. The factual basis necessary as a premise for the application of the doctrine, generally, is not uniform in all jurisdictions, but briefly and basically the plaintiff's injury must have been proximately caused by an agency or instrumentality under the exclusive control of the defendant, and the accident causing the injury must have been of the kind which ordinarily does not occur in the absence of negligence by the persons having control of the instrumentality.

16. Ringsby Truck Lines, Inc. v. Insurance Company of North America, 496 P 2d 1069 (1972).

17. General aviation aircraft operate under Part 91, General Operating and Flight Rules; Part 135, applies to air taxi operators and commercial operators of small aircraft.

18. By the terms of Sec. 403(a) of the Federal Aviation Act of 1958 as amended, all carriers are required to file with the Civil Aeronautics Board tariffs showing, among other things, the rules and regulations in connection with air transportation.

19. An Independent Safety Board was created by the Transportation Safety Act of 1974 and charged with responsibilities which include investigation of aircraft accidents to determine their cause or probable cause or causes.

20. In Crisci v. Security Insurance Company, 66 Cal. 2d 425, the idea of a rule of strict liability was proposed as the standard for insurer's liability for failure to settle an action within the policy limits. This harsh proposal would provide the insured with excess limits of coverage free of premium charge. For a discussion of this developing law, see Very, Donald L., "The Pennsylvania Unfair Insurance Practices Act: The Sleeping Giant," CPCU Annals, Vol. 28, No. 2, June 1975, p. 109.

21. Whittington, Exrx. v. Ranger Insurance Company, S.C. Sup. (1973).

22. The Federal Aviation Act of 1958 as amended has as its purpose ". . . to continue the Civil Aeronautics Board as an agency of the United States, to create a Federal Aviation Agency, to provide for the regulation and promotion of civil aviation in such a manner as to best foster its development and safety, and to provide for the safe and efficient use of the air space by both civil and military aircraft. . . ."

23. Dillard v. Continental Insurance Company, La. Ct. of App. (1971).

24. Ranger Insurance Company v. Kidd, et al., 478 S.W. 2d 803 (1972).

25. The Federal Aviation Act of 1958 as amended, 49 U.S.C. Sec. 1331 et seq. provides for government war risk insurance in certain circumstances. The program is now administered by the Federal Aviation Administration.

26. Arkansas, Colorado, Connecticut, Georgia, Maine, Maryland, Nebraska (with the exception of charitable hospitals), New Mexico, Ohio (with the exception of charitable hospitals), South Carolina, Tennessee and Virginia.

27. Feoffees of Heriot's Hosp. v. Ross, 12 C&F 507, 8 Eng. Rep. 1508 (1846).

28. Maine, New Mexico and South Carolina.

29. Arkansas, Colorado, Connecticut, Georgia, Maryland, Nebraska (with the exception of charitable hospitals), Ohio (with the exception of charitable hospitals), Tennessee and Virginia.

30. Nev. Rev. Stat., Sec. 41.480 (1977); N.C. Gen. Stat., Sec. 1-539.9 (1975).

31. Myers v. Drozda, 180 Neb. 183, 141 N.W. 2d 852 (1966). The court justified the retrospective impact of the decision on the reasoning that: "The impact of liability upon an insurer should be relatively light because of its ability to spread the loss."

32. William F. Prosser, Law of Torts, 4th ed. (St. Paul, MN: West Publishing Co., 1971), Sec. 80 (Employer's Liability) at p. 531.

33. A small minority of states impose liability on the municipality for all acts, however unauthorized, committed by its agents and employees.

34. Although some governmental entities are pondering the use of pools for their liability exposures, especially in California where insurance is nearly unaffordable, most of the current thought being given to pooling in a number of states is on the workers' compensation exposures. Educational entities, on the other hand, are reportedly having some difficulty in isolated areas of the country and are considering pooling and captives as possible recourses.

35. The federal government is said to operate without insurance on its exposures, unless it is required to insure by law or when it is in the best interest to insure its exposures. For further discussion of this point, see Werner Pfennigstorf, "Government Risk Management in Public Policy and Legislation: Problems and Options," *American Bar Foundation*, 1977, p. 265.

36. There is still a great deal of variance among state and local governments as to the scope of their permission under law to handle exposures with insurance, as well as with noninsurance techniques. For further discussion on the variety of approaches, see pp. 270-274 ibid.

37. See George J. Couch, *Couch on Insurance*, 2nd ed. (Rochester, NY: The Lawyers Co-Operative Publishing Co., 1971), Secs. 44.456; 48:511.1-512. Also Sherwood v. Stein, 259 So. (2nd.) 876 (1972).

38. Numerous other qualified persons can assist with various other loss exposures, such as police personnel on security measures and fire personnel on fire safety.

39. Patrick T. Moore of Worldwide Facilities, Inc., Los Angeles, as quoted from Kathryn McIntyre Roberts, "Retentions Key to Excess for Municipalities," *Business Insurance*, 19 September 1977, p. 19.

40. James A. Bradley of I-West Insurance Managers, as quoted from Margaret LeRoux, "Calif. Cities Face $1 Million Retention," *Business Insurance*, 31 October 1977, p. 38.

41. Robert J. McGrath of Fred S. James, San Francisco, as quoted in ibid.

42. Pfennigstorf, "Governmental Risk Management in Public Policy and Legislation: Problems and Options," pp. 257-258.

CHAPTER 13

Surety Exposures and Their Treatment

INTRODUCTION

The fact that contracts of suretyship are nearly as old as civilization itself should be sufficient proof of their need and importance. Judging from the number of transactions involving people who require assurances of others in fulfilling their part of any contractual agreement, contracts of suretyship are virtually indispensable to modern commerce.

A contract of suretyship is a contract whereby one party engages to be answerable for debt, default, or miscarriage of another.[1] The relationship created by a contract of suretyship involves three parties. The *principal* or debtor is obligated to perform in some way for the benefit of the *obligee* or creditor, and the *obligor* or surety guarantees to the obligee that the principal will fulfill the underlying obligations.

An example of a personal surety contract may clarify these relationships. Assume that a son is caught stealing and is sent to a reformatory. Upon his release, the son cannot get a job because of his record. A satisfactory employment record is necessary, however, if the son is to be rehabilitated, become self-supporting, and develop personal pride. The father goes to a friend and asks that the boy be given a job that will demonstrate the boy's honesty. The friend refuses, fearing that he, too, may suffer a loss. The father then agrees in writing to repay the friend for any loss suffered because of the dishonesty of the boy, if he is hired. On this basis, the friend hires the boy. The agreement is a personal surety contract of the type known as a fidelity bond. The obligation guaranteed the son's honesty. The parties to the contract are

347

the father (obligor or surety), the son (principal), and the friend (obligee) who employs the boy. The exposure being treated is the uncertainty of loss arising from the son's possible dishonesty.[2]

The earliest form of suretyship dates back to biblical times and was personal in nature. Then, the surety was an individual who, because of some wealth, stature, or friendship, was asked to support another person's promise to perform in the future if the principal were unable to do so. The *personal surety* often provided this form of support gratuitously, although others required or were given some form of consideration.

Suretyship has undergone a great deal of development since the days of personal suretyship. Insurance company surety bond premiums in 1976 were approximately $585 million, and the figure continues to grow.[3] The principal function of corporate suretyship today is to provide a service to those who require verification of their ability to satisfactorily perform for others. To enhance the promise of the individual or firm with an obligation to perform, a corporate surety lends its name and reputation, and gives its own promise or guarantee on an instrument called a bond. This promise states that if performance is unsatisfactory and the person or firm is unable to make restitution, the surety is answerable and will fulfill the necessary obligation. In return, the corporate surety charges a fee which solidifies the contractual agreement.

Because of the services of corporate suretyship, a variety of undertakings are possible involving from a few dollars to millions of dollars. The undertakings thus made possible provide employment to many thousands of people, investments in the economy, growth and progress in society, and peace of mind to those who require and depend on performance guarantees.

Following a detailed discussion of the principles involved in surety bonding, this chapter will examine a variety of types of surety bonds, contract bonds, federal surety bonds, license and permit bonds, public official bonds, judicial bonds, and miscellaneous surety bonds. Concluding sections of this chapter will examine the surety bond guarantee program for small contractors, and municipal bond insurance—a form of suretyship against default on municipal bond issues of governmental entities. In many ways the surety exposure differs from other exposures discussed in this course. When suretyship is involved, it is important to examine closely the relationships among the *three* parties involved. As will be seen, a study of surety exposures and their treatment requires closer attention to the underwriting process than has been given in previous chapters of this course.

Development of Corporate Suretyship

The fact that a personal surety was sought in a given transaction signified that the undertaking was a gamble, or at least that the obligee viewed the principal's promise with some uncertainty. As might have been expected, many of the ancient transactions proved disastrous to sureties as well as to obligees. In fact, King Solomon warned in Proverbs 11:15, "He that is surety for a stranger shall smart for it, and he that hateth suretyship is sure." In any event, what often happened was that those who agreed to support the promises of others either lost considerable assets in doing so, or found themselves in the embarrassing position of being unable to fulfill their promises. The ultimate burden of any loss, then, was assumed by the obligees.

Gratuitous personal sureties (as opposed to those who were compensated for their services) were released of their obligations by courts in some jurisdictions, or were at least given the benefit of the doubt in any arguments. The reasoning was that gratuitous personal sureties were not the recipients of any consideration or benefit, as were the principals. Furthermore, gratuitous personal sureties—unlike the other two parties to the contract—had little if anything to gain, but surely a lot to lose. Again, the ultimate loss fell on the obligee.

There were also times when sureties fulfilled their promises, but were then unable to recoup their losses from the principals. Here the ultimate burden of loss was assumed by the sureties. In any case, the persons who should have been exposed to loss—the principals—were anything but loss bearers.

In spite of all these various weaknesses of personal suretyship, its need grew in importance with the growth of civilization. However, it gradually became apparent that, if the concept of suretyship was to fulfill its purposes, it could best serve those who need the assurance of a third party through the use of compensated, corporate suretyship.

The Corporate (Compensated) Surety   A *compensated* surety is one whose function, *as a business*, is to guarantee that it will become answerable to any obligee in the event of nonperformance or noncompliance of its principal under the terms of the contract. In return for that guarantee, a surety charges a fee which solidifies its promise in this contractual arrangement.

A compensated surety has advantages over gratuitous suretyship. A compensated surety is not so readily released from its obligations; in fact, contracts that are given by those who are compensated for them are interpreted strongly against them in the eyes of the law. After all, honoring the contract is precisely what obligees expect or should expect.

Furthermore, those who are in need of some financial guarantee are more apt to locate assistance through a compensated surety than through a gratuitous surety. The availability of a compensated surety thus avoids the sometimes distasteful endeavor of having to search for an acquaintance who is willing to lend some support in time of need. Even compensated suretyship may be too enormous for an individual to handle, which helps explain why the development of compensated suretyship took a long time. Not many individuals had the necessary capital.

One of the earlier forms of *corporate* suretyship to come into being was the Guarantee Society of London. Established to avoid the defects inherent in the system of personal suretyship, its prospectus stated what it intended to accomplish:

> The Guarantee Society undertakes, on the payment of a small premium per cent per ann., to make good in case of default by fraud or dishonesty, any losses which may be sustained to an amount specifically named and agreed upon in their policy, and by such means obviate the necessity for private sureties as well as the obligations arising therefrom, which often prove as prejudicial to the best interest of employers as to the party seeking guarantee.

In 1842, by Act of the British Parliament, the scope of the Society's undertakings were broadened, as was the field of fidelity bonding, because public officials were officially empowered to accept bonds on the honesty of public employees.[4]

It was not until the late 1800s that the first forms of corporate suretyship appeared in the United States. Fidelity coverage was offered first, followed by judicial bonds, and then by contract bonds. Today, a multitude of companies offer a variety of bonds which are mandatory or voluntary but, nevertheless, vital to persons, businesses, and institutions. Some of these companies are international in scope, while others limit their operations within the United States, or even to regions. Some even specialize in certain bonds. Regardless of size, scope of operations, and specialization, each must be licensed in jurisdictions of operation, and they are subject to stringent regulation by the government.

Suretyship as a Tool for Handling Loss Exposures Under instruments referred to as bonds, a corporate or compensated surety lends its name and reputation, and gives its promise to become answerable to obligees, in the event its principals are unable to perform. This provides the kind of assurance that obligees require. It also serves those principals who otherwise would be unable to obtain contracts with others without some reliable source of support. Through these services of a corporate surety, obligees can transfer their exposures to loss to principals knowing that, if the contract is breached and principals cannot make restitution, the burden of any loss then lies with the corporate surety.

However, a corporate surety does not provide these guarantees unless, in fact, principals appear qualified to fulfill their contractual obligations, even after default. When default occurs and the surety meets its commitments as promised, it then has a direct right of recourse against its principals under subrogation. It exercises this right in order to recoup its losses. It is for these reasons—a surety (1) prequalifies its principals, and (2) exercises its rights of subrogation—that sureties do not *expect* losses on *surety* bonds.

Fidelity Versus Surety Bonds Versus Insurance

Fidelity bonds have been discussed in detail in CPCU 3, Chapter 12. Fidelity bonds guarantee the principal's honesty. Surety bonds, in contrast, guarantee that the principal will accomplish certain tasks.

Fidelity bonding more closely resembles insurance than does surety bonding. Fidelity bond losses, like insurance losses, are expected and considered in the rate. In theory, at least, surety bond losses are not expected.

SURETY BONDS

Characteristics of Surety Bonds

There are many different types of surety bonds. There are those that guarantee the faithful performance of public officials or fiduciaries. Some guarantee the performance of work contracts of a statutory or nonstatutory nature. Others guarantee the payment of taxes upon demand of the government, or duties upon the arrival of imports. Yet, surety bonds have some basic similarities which, taken together, set them wholly apart as a class. One of these, as previously noted, is that a surety bond is tripartite in nature—there cannot be a surety arrangement without three parties to the contract. The following paragraphs describe some of the other characteristics of surety bonds—the principal is liable to the surety, the surety theoretically expects no losses, the indeterminate length and noncancelability of many bonds, the influence of regulations and statutes, the bond penalty, the bond premium, and the fact that the bond must be in writing. In varying degrees, these characteristics distinguish surety bonds from insurance, and these distinctions will be summarized following the analysis of surety bond characteristics.

Principal Is Liable to the Surety   In the event the principal should fail in the performance of its obligation to the obligee, the surety becomes answerable. This means that the surety must then fulfill that obligation and/or pay damages. However, the surety's performance does not extinguish the principal's duty to reimburse the surety. On the contrary, the principal still is obligated to indemnify the surety. This right is granted to sureties at common law and need not necessarily be specifically expressed in the bond or in the application. However, bond applications often contain indemnity agreements between principals and sureties. One such indemnity agreement found on a bond application to be signed by the principal reads as follows:

> The Indemnitor(s) will at all times indemnify, and keep indemnified, the Surety, and hold and save it harmless from and against any and all damages, loss, costs, charges and expenses of whatsoever kind or nature, including counsel and attorney's fees, whether incurred under retainer or salary or otherwise which it shall or may, at any time, sustain or incur by reason or in consequence of its suretyship.

Surety Theoretically Expects No Losses   When a bond is issued, the surety is attesting to the principal's integrity, capability, trustworthiness, financial responsibility, or whatever qualities may be required for the undertaking. Therefore, a surety will not provide a bond until it is sure that the principal has the qualifications that are necessary. By prequalifying the principal, the surety does not expect to become involved in any default and thus does not expect to sustain any losses. Bond underwriting requires careful analysis of the principal's character, capacity, and capital—the "three C's." Before a surety bond will be issued, the surety considers the three C's to determine, to its own satisfaction, that the principal is of such character, capacity, and capital that the obligation will be fulfilled. (These points will be discussed in greater detail as they apply to individual types of bonds.)

Sureties frequently require the principal to post collateral of a value equal to all or part of the bond penalty. Usually, the use of collateral results in a premium credit, since it reduces the surety's loss exposure. When the principal deposits collateral with the surety, the surety is assured of funds with which to pay the penalty for any default, even though the principal's financial condition deteriorates during the bond period. The situation with a surety bond involving collateral is similar to that of a bank charging interest on a collateral loan. The bank charges interest for the use of its money despite the fact that the loan is secured by collateral.

Joint control may also be used to reduce a surety's loss exposure, particularly when fiduciary bonds are involved. Joint control means that any disbursements of the assets involved must be with the approval of the surety. For example, this makes it more difficult for a fiduciary administering a trust to divert some of the assets of the trust to the fiduciary's own benefit, or to use the assets unwisely. Because of careful surety underwriting, it is said that the fee a surety charges for its services theoretically contemplates no losses. Nevertheless, losses do occur for many reasons, including poor judgment in underwriting and unforeseen developments in the economy. Losses are also reduced by the rights of the surety in default, and by the possibilities of subrogation and salvage.

Rights of the Surety Upon Default. Should the principal be unable to perform fully, for some reason, the surety must do whatever is necessary to fulfill the undertaking. (Remember, the principal is still liable to the surety.) However, in the event of default the surety acquires no more of an obligation than the principal's original obligation, subject to the bond limit (also called the penalty). If, for some reason, damages exceed the bond limit, the surety's obligation usually ceases; but the liability to the obligee of the principal for any default or damage may be unlimited.

Significance of Subrogation and Salvage. Once having fulfilled the principal's obligation in default, the surety is subrogated to the rights and remedies of the obligee to the extent of any payment it has made. In fact, subrogation was first used in cases involving suretyship.[5] Through subrogation, the surety attempts to recover anything of value, since whatever is recovered is used to offset its losses.

Indeterminate Length and Noncancelability of Bonds Surety bonds usually terminate when the principal's obligations have been fulfilled, so a bond could involve performance over several years. For this reason, surety bonds are considered to be indeterminate in length. This is especially true when the bond is noncancelable. This is not to say that *all* surety bonds are noncancelable or terminate only when performance has been completed. A public official bond, for example, cannot normally be canceled before expiration of an official's term in office, but there are exceptions in such circumstances as premature removal from office, or death. License and permit bonds can usually be canceled, and are usually renewable each year. But a statutory construction contract bond cannot be canceled either by the obligee or by the surety. The reasons for these variations will become more apparent as specific bond types are analyzed later in this chapter.

In view of the fact that many surety bonds are noncancelable and continue until completion of the principal's underlying obligation, it is difficult for a surety to determine its loss experience in the short run.

Influence of Regulations and Statutes on Bonds Surety bonds can be statutory or nonstatutory in form. A *statutory bond* is one that is prescribed by law—a municipal ordinance, or federal or state regulation or statute. Also, the law specifies the conditions of a statutory bond, so the obligations of all three parties are controlled not by the bond provisions, but by the law involved. A *nonstatutory bond*, on the other hand, is one that is controlled by the contract as drawn by the obligee.

Bond Limit (Penalty) The bond penalty is the amount for which the bond is written. It is similar to the limits of a liability policy. If, for some reason, damages exceed the penalty, the surety's obligation usually ceases at the penalty amount, although some bonds pay for court costs and interest on judgments above the bond penalty, as do most liability insurance policies. Although the bond penalty limits the obligation of the *surety*, the obligation of the *principal* for any default or damage may be unlimited.

Bond Premium When a surety gives a bond, it charges its principal a premium or service fee. This fee represents the price of the surety's guarantee that it will answer to the obligee if the principal should fail for some reason. While the *principal* pays the premium, it is the *obligee* who benefits from the bond. Contrary to the belief of some, the service fee is not the legal consideration of the bond. Instead, the principal's consideration is the undertaking secured by the bond, and the surety's consideration is its guarantee to answer to the obligee in the event of nonperformance. Thus, a surety is obligated to fulfill the terms of a delivered surety bond even though the premium has not been paid.

Must Be in Writing A surety bond must be in writing to be binding and enforceable. As a contract of guaranty—i.e., a promise to be responsible for the debt or default of another—it is subject to the Statutes of Frauds and other common-law and statutory requirements.

Surety Bonds Versus Insurance Contracts

With the advent of multiple-line insurance companies, corporate sureties have all but lost their separate identities, so bonds and insurance are not distinct based on the identities of insurers or sureties. Many academic discussions have attempted to contrast suretyship with insurance. There no doubt are some differences, and significant ones at that. But the differences between the two types of contracts have diminished somewhat over the years.

One distinguishing characteristic of suretyship often cited, for example, is that many bonds are noncancelable. While most insurance policies may be canceled, statutes now preclude the cancellation of many property-liability policies without good cause. Some property-liability insurance policies are continuous until canceled, and a few, such as title insurance, provide protection as long as the insured continues to own the property, based on payment of a single premium. So noncancellation is neither a feature of all surety bonds nor is it unique to surety bonds.

Another academic point of difference involves the fact that statutes are virtually read into surety bonds. However, the same can be said of many insurance contracts. For example, financial responsibility laws are often read into automobile policies for the protection of the public, and workers' compensation insurance provides the benefits described by law.

Perhaps the greatest differences between surety bonds and insurance are the following: with a surety bond, the principal is primarily liable to the obligee, and the surety is answerable in case of a default; the surety does not expect losses, and often takes safeguards against them, such as collateral and indemnity agreements and joint control arrangements; and the surety can reduce its net losses through subrogation *against its principal*. An insurer, on the other hand, is primarily responsible to its insured; it expects some losses; and it usually cannot subrogate against its insured (although subrogation against third parties may significantly reduce the net losses incurred by insurers).

General Types of Surety Bonds

Surety bonds are used for a variety of specific purposes, but they will be divided into five broad categories for purposes of this analysis: (1) contract bonds, (2) federal surety bonds, (3) license and permit bonds, (4) public official bonds, and (5) judicial bonds.

Contract bonds, in general, are those that guarantee the performance of certain public or private contracts. Within this category are bid, performance, payment, and maintenance bonds.

Federal surety bonds are those that guarantee compliance with federal laws or regulations, such as those concerning tobacco, alcohol, imports, and income tax.

License and permit bonds are those required by federal, state, or municipal governments as prerequisites to engaging in certain business activities. Among those who may need such bonds are contractors who work on public streets, plumbers, electricians, and real estate agents.

Public official bonds guarantee the honesty and faithful performance of those who are elected or appointed to positions in government.

Judicial bonds are those prescribed by statute and filed in either probate courts or in courts of equity. Probate courts deal with matters such as settlement of estates and appointment of guardians. Courts of equity are concerned with disputes involving specific performance, or other equitable remedies, rather than money damages.

Another category is that of miscellaneous bonds—those that do not fit into any of the other classes. Miscellaneous bonds fulfill a variety of special needs.

CONTRACT BONDS

Many of those who are involved in some form of contractual relationship involving work or service to be performed by others, require bonds as a means of obtaining additional assurance that the undertaking will be performed as specified. Contract bonds are used in these circumstances, since they generally guarantee the fulfillment of certain obligations required under contracts. As a class, these bonds guarantee both public and private contracts, with the former being the more prevalent because bonds guaranteeing public contracts usually are required by law.

Contract bonds may be classified into bid, performance and payment, and maintenance bonds. Contract bonds are not confined to construction operations. For example, contract bonds would also be required by the municipality that advertises for bids from firms which may be interested in handling its trash collections. It is understandable, however, that contract bonds are frequently confused with construction contract bonds, since contract bonds are predominantly used for construction purposes and generate the most premium volume of sureties.

Nature of Construction Contract Bonds

Contract bonds used for construction purposes include bid bonds, performance and payment bonds, and maintenance bonds. The nature of these contract bonds is summarized in Table 13-1.

Nature of Miscellaneous Contract and Indemnity Bonds

Bonds that guarantee contracts of a miscellaneous nature probably comprise the largest group in terms of numbers and variety. The purposes for which such bonds may be written include: the rental of mechanical equipment with or without operators; the transportation of school children; the removal of snow, garbage, and the cleaning of streets; patent infringements; the guarantee of students' tuitions and

Table 13-1

Contract Bond Comparison*

Bid Bond	Performance Bond	Payment Bond	Maintenance Bond
Obligee (Insured)			
The owner or party who is calling for the bid	The owner of the property or the person who is having the work done	Same as performance bond	Same as performance bond
Principal (Persons-Bonded)			
The bidder	The contractor	The contractor	The contractor
What Is Guaranteed			
That the bidder will enter into the contract and post a performance bond if the bid is accepted	That the work will be completed by the contractor according to plans and specifications	That the project will be free of liens—that is, all bills for labor and materials will be paid	That the work will be free from defects in materials and workmanship for a certain specified period
When Required			
Public work projects; a certified check is commonly substituted for the bond on private work	Pubic work projects	Public work projects	Usually private and nonfederal jobs
Underwriting Considerations			
The character, capacity, capital, and experience of the contractor; also information on work under bid	The qualifications of the contractor, i.e., character, capacity, capital, and experience, as well as copy of work specifications	Same as performance bond	Same as performance bond; also, term of bond

*Adapted from *FC &S Bulletins,* Casualty/Surety (Cincinnati: National Underwriter Company, October 1973), pp. Bonds Con-1, 2.

other fees for college; and the retention of workers' compensation loss exposures. Also in the miscellaneous category are supply bonds and subdivision bonds.

A *supply bond* generally is required when a supplier, dealer, or manufacturer is under an obligation to supply certain materials, commodities, or equipment at an agreed upon price and time. A supplier that fails to perform as required is usually liable for the difference between the bid price and the price of the materials which are accepted as a replacement.

A *subdivision bond* is generally required by the municipality when a developer of land desires to subdivide property into tracts for purposes of constructing houses or other structures. The basis of the bond agreement is that the developer promises to pay and complete all improvements such as streets, lighting, sidewalks, sewers, water, and other utilities.

General Underwriting Criteria

Since the surety is trying to select principals who will not default, the surety issuing a contract bond will carefully consider the ability of the principal to meet the terms of the contract. An understanding of the underwriting criteria involved will enable the reader to better comprehend the nature of the surety agreement. Understanding surety underwriting is important, not only to surety bond underwriters, but also to risk managers and other business managers whose firms may be obligees, or who may need to qualify as principals for a surety bond.

Construction contract bonds require the most in-depth underwriting scrutiny of any contract bonds. There are several reasons for this. First, construction firms are service-oriented. If for any reason the services they provide are interrupted, the income of that construction firm stops. From a financial stability standpoint, this does not favorably compare with manufacturers that may be able to utilize their inventories in the event of a work interruption of some type. Second, most contractors—with the possible exception of the larger firms—do not have the working capital required to withstand any long delay in completing work. Third, most construction work takes a long time to complete, and the longer the time period involved, the greater the chance that something unforeseen may adversely affect the project and the contractor. Finally, the construction industry, by its very nature, is especially vulnerable to economic, political, and social changes.

"The purpose of a contract bond is not to qualify a principal, but to assert and affirm that such person or entity is in fact qualified."[6] The fact that a bond is ultimately issued by a surety does not necessarily mean that the work will be completed free of any problems or losses. What it does mean is that, based upon the underwriting capabilities of the surety, the principal appears to have the qualities that are necessary to meet its commitments.

Unfortunately, losses arise in spite of stringent underwriting controls because there are many conditions which cannot be reasonably foreseen by underwriters. Any number of examples can be cited to illustrate this point—economic conditions, such as inflation, may cause material and labor costs to exceed expectations of a contractor; work may have to be delayed or terminated with the death or disability of a key person; a bank may decide not to extend credit in spite of its commitment to do so; extra costs may be incurred because of malicious interference or strikes, or because of delays, negligence, or changes by architects; a subcontractor may default in its commitments; or the obligee may fail to pay the principal for work that has been completed.

As is evident, losses sometimes occur under conditions which are not predictable. The purpose of underwriting is not to eliminate any chance of loss. That would be virtually impossible. The purpose, instead, is to reduce the surety's chances of loss or default to all but unforeseen conditions. In other words, *if the qualifications of a contractor are determined to be such that performance can be satisfactorily completed under normal or ordinary conditions, the chance of a contractor's loss is then reduced, hopefully, to those conditions which are unforeseeable or unpredictable.*[7] Even here a surety can often avoid the assumption of losses through proper underwriting safeguards.

The underwriting procedures and safeguards tend to be rather involved, but perhaps no more so than those required in underwriting certain other types of insurance coverage. In fact, the procedures normally followed in determining whether an applicant is acceptable, and under what conditions, are generally the same, whether the subject of coverage is a contract bond or an insurance policy.[8]

The underwriter, first of all, will have to collect as much information as possible about the applicant. Some of this information comes from the application and some comes from the producer in other forms. However, outside sources also will be sought. The surety, for example, may contact the applicant's bank, accountant, and the previous surety, if there was one. In addition, information may be sought from the credit bureaus, and even from architects or engineers who may have been involved with the applicant on a previous job, or who are involved with the contractor on the present job. (The type of specific information which generally is required is discussed later in these pages.)

Once all of the necessary information has been gathered and organized, the underwriter should be in a position to determine whether the contract bond applicant is fully qualified for the undertaking. If the applicant's credentials are questionable, the underwriter may utilize certain other safeguards, such as additional collateral or the use of another person's promise to indemnify the surety if the bond applicant becomes unable to do so.

The underwriter may even wish to have a conference with the applicant and the producer. This is not at all unusual with contract bonds. The purpose is to obtain a meeting of the minds and establish a rapport between the applicant and the surety. It is here, too, that the underwriter may inform the applicant as to the course of action which will be followed in issuing the necessary bonds.

The underwriting criteria behind all contract bonds are generally the same. The bond underwriter must determine (1) the nature of the underlying contractual obligations; (2) the extent of the surety's obligations; and (3) the qualifications of the principal—the principal's character, capacity, and capital—to determine the principal's ability to fulfill the obligation as bonded.

Nature of the Underlying Obligations Before a construction contract bond is issued signifying that the principal appears qualified to perform whatever is required by the obligee, the surety must consider the nature and the extent of all underlying obligations. Such obligations include, but are not limited to, the following: the terms of the contract— whether they are required by law, that is, whether the work is statutory as opposed to nonstatutory or private in nature; the type of work to be performed; whether any portion of the work will be subcontracted; the commencement and completion dates; the cost of the work and terms of payment; the rights and duties of the parties to the contract; the type and length of any maintenance guarantees which may be required; and whether the terms of the contract contain any penalties or liquidated damages.

Statutory Requirements. Ordinances, regulations, and statutes frequently dictate the specifications, conditions, and bond coverages that are required under a construction project. In such cases, the construction contract bond is a statutory one, since the law actually controls the terms of performance by the parties to the contract.

In spite of the fact that the statutory provisions will vary by jurisdiction, they usually do not present any problems to the bond underwriter because the scope and any peculiarities of such laws are determined by the Surety Association of America, or by the legal staff of sureties.[9]

Nonstatutory Contracts. When the performance of work is not controlled by law (nonstatutory), whether a construction contract bond is to be required is at the discretion of the obligee. The owner of property or other obligee will sometimes forgo the use of bonds and instead require some form of collateral from the contractor. On other occasions, the owner will require the use of bonds that follow the contractual provisions as drawn. This is an area that requires cautious underwriting because the contractual provisions may be contrary to the customary guarantees by the surety. In other words, the contractual provisions may subject the contractor to certain agreements which are virtually impossible for the surety to underwrite. More frequently, however, nonstatutory bonds are handled under bond forms prepared by the American Institute of Architects (AIA).[10]

The AIA is a national organization of architects which supports and encourages the use of contract bonds in private construction work. With the cooperation of the Surety Association of America, the AIA was able to develop standard bid, performance, and payment bonds. In addition they have developed general conditions of contracts that define the rights and responsibilities of all participants before, during, and after work is completed. A standardized certificate of insurance also is available, along with a checklist of coverages that may be needed by architects, owners, and contractors.

The advantages of standardized bonds for all users throughout the construction industry may be compared with the advantages of standardized insurance forms, discussed many times previously in this course. Moreover, the services offered by AIA are widely recognized and trusted.

Other Terms of the Contract. The terms of the contract relating to the type of work, commencement and termination dates, price, terms, and methods of payment by the obligee, and penalties are of vital importance to the bond underwriter. Certainly, the more complex the undertaking, the better the contractor must be qualified in terms of experience and financial capability.

The underwriter will want a complete description of the type of work involved under the contract to see whether it is within the scope of the contractor's expertise. Furthermore, the accessibility of the job site is important, since a geographic isolation may increase the likelihood of delays and other hardships. This consideration can be particularly important when the contract specifies certain penalties for noncompletion within a certain specified period. Time of completion must also be carefully considered, particularly if the contractor has other work in progress.

The underwriter must determine whether the bid price is sufficient—in relation to other bids—to cover all of the costs and still leave a margin for profit. Price is also important in the surety's exposure in the event the contractor is unable to fulfill the specified commitment.

Also worthy of consideration are the terms of payment by the owner. The underwriter must determine what portion of the contract price is to be retained by the owner pending final completion and acceptance of work. The higher the amount retained by the owner, the more working capital the contractor must have to discharge debts when they are due.

Extent of Surety's Obligations upon Default The second important underwriting consideration is a determination of the extent of the surety's obligations in the event of breach or default. Generally, the surety's obligations are dictated by the contract and the specifications, whether the work is of a private nature or required by law.

It is important for the surety to determine whether there is a specific time frame for completion of the work, whether penalties can be imposed in the event of default, and whether liquidated damages, a sum stipulated in the contract, can be assessed in the event work is not completed according to schedule. Terms and amounts of penalties or damages must be determined. This is especially important when an owner disclaims any liability under a written agreement as to delays the owner may cause the general contractor. Sometimes such disclaimers are unreasonable and unenforceable, but other times they are not. This same situation can be viewed from the standpoint of a subcontractor, because there are times when it can be assessed damages for delay which is caused by the general contractor. In other words, the general contractor may be so late in its performance that the subcontractor is unable to begin its work on time and, hence, will be drawn in on the damages along with the general contractor. The surety, therefore, will be interested in knowing about the contract provisions of its principal.

The principal almost always is obligated to remedy any work that is damaged or to pay others for claims stemming from its negligent acts or omissions. If proper liability insurance is not available, this may create a financial burden and, quite possibly, a default. The underwriter, therefore, will want to make sure that the principal has proper insurance coverage for sufficient limits of liability.

Additionally, the underwriter will want to determine whether and to what extent any indemnity agreements or exculpatory agreements may be required of the principal. Again, if there is an exposure, the underwriter will want to be certain that proper contractual liability insurance is purchased by the principal.

Qualifications of the Principal After having determined the nature of the obligations that will be imposed upon the principal, including the possible extent of the surety's obligation in the event of default or other problem, it is then necessary for the underwriter to determine whether the principal has the necessary qualifications. Such qualifications are dealt with in terms of *character*, *capacity*, and *capital*.

Character. In terms of character, the bond applicant—whether an individual, partnership, joint venture, or a corporation—must possess the traits of integrity and reliability, and must possess the leadership or drive that is necessary to accomplish goals, in spite of difficulties. The reasons are obvious. When a contractor does not deal properly with others, such as the obligee, the subcontractors, and the suppliers of material, problems most certainly will arise.

Many court cases have been instituted by suppliers of materials who were not paid. Another source of frequent argument arises when a contractor takes shortcuts which result in defective work. In the end, correcting the situation may cost more than the contractor can afford. And, finally, there are cases involving contractors who are just unreliable. They may, for example, possess certain habits which keep them away from their work for long periods, or they may not possess the stamina which is necessary in coping with problems and pressures that frequently occur in construction work.

The problems of underwriting a contractor's character have aptly been summarized as follows:

> Unfortunately, the only real test of character remains performance in adversity. Until actual proof is received under such circumstances, the underwriter's judgment of character is largely based upon (a) his own subjective reaction to personal contacts (this is why a contractor should know the company underwriter who passes on his bonds as well as the bonding agent), (b) the testimony of others who have had such contracts, and (c) the accumulated insights into character which come to one engaged in a business which guarantees that others will "well and truly perform" all of their agreements.[11]

Capacity. Another important factor which must be considered by surety underwriters is the capacity of the principal. In this context, "capacity" refers to the principal's technical or professional ability to meet commitments underlying work to be performed. To assess openly the principal's capacity, the surety must consider a number of points:

1. *The surety must consider the type of work to be done, and whether it is in line with the principal's expertise.* A contractor that has been previously engaged in the construction of dwellings may be suspect if the job sought involves the construction of a large commercial building. The reason should be obvious. The work, for one thing, may require additional and expensive labor and expertise. The contractor also may lack the experience that is required in estimating all costs of labor and materials for complex jobs. Too, some of the work will probably have to be subcontracted, and whether the principal is knowledgeable and experienced in subcontracting is something that should not be ignored.

2. *The surety must consider the type of equipment and tools that are owned or may be required.* An important task here is to determine whether the equipment is in good shape and properly maintained, and whether such equipment and tools are sufficient to handle a given job. If the equipment is poorly maintained, this gives some indication of the contractor's work habits. Moreover, if the equipment is old or in need of repair, or otherwise inadequate for the specific work to be performed, this may indicate the need by the contractor for some future additional outlay in replacing it, which may be further complicated if the contractor is still paying for old equipment and the additional payments for new or rented equipment are more than the contractor can handle financially.

3. *The surety must consider the amount of work in progress.* The surety will want to know what jobs the contractor may have in progress, whether the contractor's bonds are for each of them, and the extent of the other obligations. It is not at all unusual for a contractor to encounter difficulties by taking on too many jobs at the same time.

4. *The surety must consider the administrative abilities of the contractor.* This may overlap with various character traits. Nevertheless, the contractor's ability to administer and to perform a job properly to the point of satisfactory completion may be thought of as part of his or her capacity.

Capital. By far the single most important measure of a principal's qualifications is that of capital—financial resources, financial strength, and credit standing. Unless the principal has sufficient capital, the surety will not issue the bond. This stands to reason, since the contract bond is a financial guarantee. A surety that grants such a bond indicates that the principal is qualified in a number of ways—including financially—to meet certain obligations. And, if the principal should default on that obligation, the surety will fulfill such guarantee as may be required.

The balance sheet indicates to the indemnitor the financial standing of the business at any given point in time. The profit and loss statement or income and expense statement shows the results of operations for the accounting period. Both financial reports provide an indication whether the contractor is conducting a profitable business and, when compared with reports of previous years, whether the contractor is progressively growing. This result also will give the surety some indication of the amount of work that a contractor can safely assume.

Many other tools are available to the surety in determining the financial stability of contractors. But the point for verifying all avenues dealing with the finances of a contractor is to determine whether the contractor is financially competent to undertake a certain venture, and whether the principal can satisfy any debt that may unexpectedly occur.

Types of Contract Bonds

Contract bonds, as previously noted, are used and frequently required for two basic purposes. First, such bonds signify that the principal appears to the surety to be qualified to fulfill the terms of the contract. Second, the surety guarantees the performance of the obligations of the contract even if the principal defaults. Since most contract bonds are used in public construction work, the following description involves construction contract bonds.

Bid Bond A bid bond is furnished to an owner (obligee) of a project. It promises that the contractor or construction firm (principal) bidding for a contract will, if the bid is accepted, enter into a contract and furnish the other necessary contract bonds. If the bid is accepted and the contractor fails to provide such bonds or refuses to perform the work, the obligee is entitled to be paid the difference between the amount of that contractor's bid and the bid that is finally accepted by the owner.

Bids for public work are normally solicited through public advertisements. The terms of such advertisements, the bonds themselves, and the job specifications are controlled by statute. While some statutes allow the alternative of furnishing either a certified check or a bid bond for a certain percentage of the bid amount, bid bonds are more commonly used. Also, public work is usually awarded to the lowest bidder. On private work, the use of bid bonds or certified checks is purely a matter of discretion with the owner. Also, when private work is involved, the owner is under no legal obligation to accept the lowest bidder.

Potential Problems. Generally, the problems with a bid bond begin when, after being awarded the contract by the obligee, a contractor refuses to enter into a contract of performance and to supply the required bonds. The contractor usually refuses for one of two reasons. Either the contractor discovers that a mistake was made in the preparation of the bid so that performance is virtually impossible at the quoted price, or the owner or the architect changes the specifications or causes a delay in awarding the contracts and economic conditions increase the cost of performing the work and make the bid price inadequate. Of these two reasons, the first—mistake in bid preparation—seems to be the more common.

CLERICAL VERSUS JUDGMENT MISTAKES. It is not unusual for contractors to make mistakes. Some are purely clerical errors, while others are the result of poor judgment. However, it is often stated that neither reason for such mistakes should be condoned. To permit a contractor to withdraw a bid without penalty, after it is opened, defeats the purpose of sealed bids. Furthermore, granting such relief may invite intentional "mistakes" in order to gain unfair advantage, or it may create the opportunity for collusion among two or more contractors.

Generally, errors of judgment, such as the failure to consider and to include certain costs of a project, are indefensible in the courts. But miscalculations of costs, or mistakes in arithmetic or in the transfer of figures, are sometimes considered excusable by the courts. The problem is that it can be difficult to distinguish between an error in judgment and an error in arithmetic. Of course, when an error has been made, the burden of proof is on the contractor.

A court case that hinged on the type of error involved is Osberg Construction Co. v. The City of Dallas, 300 Fed. Supp. 442. On the day that the bids were to be opened, the contractor discovered that the cost of a portion of the work amounting to $125,000 had not been taken into consideration. The contract specifications stipulated that bids could be withdrawn at any time prior to the opening, but once opened the bids could not be withdrawn for thirty days. The contractor tried to modify the bid by using a telegram, but the telegram arrived too late.

Four days later the contractor wrote a letter requesting that the bid be amended or withdrawn. On the day the letter was written, the city awarded the job to that same contractor for the price of $499,975. The court contest arose when the contractor refused to enter into the contract and the city claimed that the bid bond penalty of $24,998.75 was forfeited. The courts ultimately held the contractor to its promise because the mistake committed by the contractor was anything other than one of judgment.

CRITERIA FOR AVOIDING LIABILITY. There are occasions when the courts grant relief to contractors. Certain criteria, of course, must be met.

First, the mistake must be of a serious nature, and to require performance would be unconscionable. This means that the mistake is so large that if performance were required, it inevitably would result in an undue hardship for the contractor.

Second, the error or mistake must not be the result of gross negligence. Gross negligence can be difficult to prove, because simple mistakes are also caused by negligence. Gross negligence concerns a complete lack of good faith in preparing a bid, and involves a decision which, though erroneous, is intended by the contractor. Conversely, an error which is generally excusable is one that involves ordinary negligence, such as those involving arithmetic calculations or the transfers of figures. However, even here, all requisites must be met before an error is considered excusable.

Third, the owner must not sustain a substantial hardship if the bidder is granted relief. This refers to damages sustained by the owner which are other than those damages stemming from loss of an especially low price. For example, if the next lower bidder's estimate is still less than what the owner anticipated the work would cost, it would be difficult for the owner to argue that a hardship will exist if the lowest bidder is permitted to withdraw from performance of the contract.

Fourth, the contractor must give the owner of the project timely notice of error and notice of intention to withdraw— before the award is made. Timely notice, however, is sometimes difficult to define. Moreover, contract specifications concerning withdrawals and the procedure to follow vary by jurisdiction. Some provide that bids may be withdrawn anytime before this opening if the withdrawal is made in some form of written communication. But once the bids are opened, they cannot be withdrawn for a certain specified period, usually ranging from thirty to ninety days.

One case that permitted nonperformance even when all criteria were met is Boise Junior College v. Mattefs Construction Co., 450 Pac. (2nd.) 604. This case is unusual because both the lowest bidder ($134,896) and the next lowest bidder ($141,048) refused to enter into the contract. The school district estimated that the work would cost $150,000. The work was awarded to the third lowest bidder for $149,000. The second contractor to withdraw was then sued for the difference between the bid that was submitted ($141,048) and the one finally selected, about $9,000. Following the criteria previously mentioned, the court decided to permit the contractor to withdraw without penalty. It stated that, except for loss of bargain, the school district would suffer no substantial hardship. In fact, the school district would still realize a savings of $1,000 on its estimate.

The fact that some courts allow contractors relief after weighing certain criteria should not be taken to mean that these procedures for granting relief are always followed. Even if they were, there is always the chance that a contractor will not meet all such criteria. Moreover, some courts have ruled that no mistakes are excusable. Therefore, contractors must exercise the utmost care in estimating costs and in checking figures. This is the best way to avoid expensive court costs and loss of additional valuable assets.

Bid Prices Affected by Changes in Specifications or Delays

Work specifications must occasionally be amended after a contractor's bid has been accepted. Whether this adversely affects the contractor really depends upon who is requiring the changes and whether additional costs are involved. If the owner of a project decides that changes are necessary, or if the architect requires certain amendments on behalf of the owner, the contractor generally is compensated for additions that require more cash outlays. However, when the contractor draws up the specifications and then decides that changes are necessary, the additional costs ordinarily must be assumed by the contractor. Whether this latter circumstance will present any difficulties to the contractor depends upon the amount of such additional costs and the contractor's financial ability to assume them.

Delays stemming from the postponement of bid openings or delays in the bidding process of public work contracts usually do not present any additional burdens for contractors. There are certain provisions dealing with the postponement of bid openings under public work projects which usually stipulate that if any postponement is necessary, the contracting officer will issue notices by mail or telegram as early as possible. If any emergency makes a bid opening impractical, an opening may be postponed without prior notice to prospective bidders. However, any such delays are usually taken into consideration for the benefit of the bidding contractors. Delays under private contracts normally are also adjusted so as to avoid any undue hardships.

An area which can present a potential problem to those who must submit bids concerns the time span between that period when a bid is submitted and that period when a contractor who wins the bid can begin working on the project. This time span can amount to four or five months—which is not at all unusual, considering the fact that the whole bidding process usually takes at least two months. This means that costs of certain materials, especially those such as steel and copper that fluctuate in price within relatively short periods, can adversely affect a contractor's estimate. To avoid any financial hardships, therefore, it behooves contractors to have some type of understanding with their suppliers on price estimates over long periods, regardless of how susceptible the materials may be to price fluctuations.

Performance and Payment Bonds When a bid is accepted, the contractor who is awarded the work not only must enter into a contract with the owner, but also must furnish the other bonds that may be required for completion of work. These usually include a performance bond and a payment bond, although the two are sometimes combined under one bond form. A maintenance bond may also be required as a guarantee that the completed work is free from defects for a certain period. Like the payment bond, the guarantee of the maintenance bond may also be included within the conditions of the performance bond.

Nature of Performance Bond Guarantee. The performance bond guarantees that the owner will be indemnified for any loss stemming from the failure of the contractor to perform the work according to the contract, plans, and specifications—which may or may not be subject to statutory provisions.

If a contractor defaults under a performance bond, or is in an impending stage of default, a surety has a number of options it can exercise. It can (1) complete the contract using the existing contractor, (2) complete the contract using a replacement contractor, (3) provide the existing contractor with financial assistance sufficient to avert loss, or (4) have the owner for whom work is being done make arrangements for completion of work with any losses payable by the surety up to the penalty amount.

A surety *may* elect to complete a contractual obligation, using the existing contractor or a replacement contractor. However, it is not compelled to do so, since the usual form of performance bond does not guarantee the completion of work *by the surety*. Confusion regarding a surety's obligation to complete an existing agreement of its principal probably stems from the popular use, many years ago, of completion or lender's bonds. The primary characteristic of such bonds was the "naked and unrestricted promise" of the surety to complete the contract should the principal be unable to do so. For all practical purposes, completion bonds are unavailable today, although many practitioners still seem to confuse performance bonds with completion bonds.[12]

Frequently a surety exercises its second option and completes the contract, using either the existing contractor or a replacement contractor. A surety sometimes uses the existing contractor when the reason for a problem is something other than the contractor's incompetence. Some circumstances of hardships that have led sureties to use existing contractors include: a bank's refusal to grant any additional extension of credit; an improper and an insufficient estimate of contract costs; delay brought about by modification of the contract; delay in receiving necessary equipment; and delays because of bad weather or labor disputes. On the other hand, a number of circumstances have caused sureties to use other contractors to finish work. These reasons include incompetence, bankruptcy, suicide, or disappearance of the principal.[13]

Sureties have provided financial help in order to avert additional hardships and possible defaults caused by forces of nature, overcommitments, or lack of liquid assets. Sureties have assisted their principals on many such occasions.[14]

Financial assistance by the surety will not always solve a performance problem. Sometimes, too, a surety will decide not to have the contract completed. It is then up to the owner or governmental body to proceed with the completion of the project. Whether a surety may become obligated for any damages depends upon the outcome of the completed work in terms of total, final costs. If the balance of funds retained by the obligee (that amount representing the unpaid balance which would have been paid to the original contractor had the work been completed) is sufficient to cover all costs of completion by others, there can be no claim against the surety under the performance bond. But, if the costs of completion exceed those originally estimated by the defaulting contractor, the excess represents the owner's loss, and is payable by the surety subject to the penalty amount of the bond.[15]

Any court costs assumed by the surety, however, are in excess of the penalty amount. Whatever the outcome in the event of default, the surety always has the right to seek reimbursement from the principal. The surety can collect from the principal (1) by an assignment of the obligee's rights to the surety, (2) by reason of the written indemnity agreement (typically included in the bond application), and (3) through the equitable right of subrogation.[16]

Since a performance bond guarantees the completion of work according to specifications, this also means that such work, when completed, will be free of any liens. This latter guarantee is especially important to owners of projects, because suppliers of labor and materials who go uncompensated usually can apply a mechanic's lien to the property. A mechanic's lien is a right granted by statute and is available to those who seek to secure the value of their work or services which have gone into the form of additions on real estate.[17] When a lien is placed on such property, the owner does not have clear title to it until all debts are settled. In fact, property has been sold in order to settle debts which have been secured by mechanic's liens.

From the owner's standpoint, therefore, the performance bond serves a dual purpose. It guarantees the completion of work as specified, and it guarantees that the work will be free of any liens. However, a performance bond does not provide total protection for suppliers of labor and materials, for the following reasons: First, a performance bond that guarantees the completion of work free of liens—without mention of any guarantee for the payment of labor and materials supplied by others—usually provides coverage only for claims that are properly liened. This sometimes means that suppliers who fail to file liens within the time period and other specifications of such mechanic's lien laws will have no protection.[18] Second, owners of projects have first claim to funds under the performance bond, while the claims of laborers and suppliers who have liens on such property have a secondary interest. In other words, the owner under a performance bond is entitled to be fully satisfied before claims of others are handled. This means that claims of others may be delayed, and there still is no guarantee that all such claims will be paid. Third, the mechanic's lien statute does not protect all suppliers. For example, the statutes sometimes limit the privilege to particular classes of workers such as plasterers or bricklayers. Furthermore, certain criteria must be met before a lien becomes effective. Finally, a mechanic's lien usually cannot be filed upon public property or public work.[19] So, if suppliers of labor and materials were to rely solely upon the performance bond of an owner for their only recourse, they could very well go without compensation for their services.

Nature of Payment Bond Guarantee. To avoid the utilization of mechanic's liens by suppliers, where such liens are permissible, and to provide a method whereby unpaid bills of creditors can be secured where mechanic's liens cannot be filed, owners of projects frequently request a payment bond in addition to the performance bond. A payment bond— often referred to as a labor and materials bond—guarantees that bills incurred by a contractor for labor and materials will be fully paid at the completion of the project.

Actually, a payment bond is often required for governmental work, whether the work is on a federal, state, or local level. Such a bond also is often suggested with private work when bond forms of the American Institute of Architects are used.

MILLER ACT. The Miller Act is a federal statute, enacted by the U. S. Congress in 1935, that governs contracts for the construction, alteration or repair of any public buildings, or public work for the federal government. This act states that when construction contracts exceed $2,000, a contractor must furnish a performance bond for the protection of the government and a payment bond for the protection of persons who supply labor and materials for the required work. The Miller Act does not provide for total payment to all creditors. Basically, there are two general categories of creditors who are protected under the payment bond of this act, provided, of course, the penalty of the bond is sufficient. The first category consists of material suppliers, laborers, and subcontractors who deal directly with the prime contractor. The second group comprises those who have a direct relationship with a subcontractor, but who do not have a contractual relationship, expressed or implied, with the prime contractor who furnishes the payment bond. Creditors in the latter category have a right of action under the bond which is conditioned upon the filing of written notice to the prime contractor within ninety days from the date on which such persons last performed labor, or last furnished material for which claim is to be made under the bond. The written notice condition serves two purposes. It enables the prime contractor to be informed of all liabilities incurred by its subcontractors, and it enables the prime contractor to withhold funds of subcontractors in order to satisfy the claims of those suppliers who have dealt directly with such subcontractors.[20] The mistaken notion that every creditor on a federal job is protected by the Miller Act is a cause of many disputes. Many of the problems deal with creditors who come within the second category—those who do not have a direct relationship with the prime contractor. While it is difficult to classify all such problems, the following illustrate questions often raised by creditors under the payment bond:

1. *Does a firm that sells materials to a supplier of a subcontractor have any right of recourse under the bond if the supplier does not pay for that material?* As noted previously, the Miller Act stipulates that a supplier must at least have a direct relationship with the subcontractor in order to have protection. Thus, it has been held that a firm which merely sells materials to a subcontractor's supplier is too remote from the prime contractor to have a right of recourse.[21]

2. *If the supplier, in the above situation, is deemed to be a subcontractor, would the firm then have a right of recourse?* The answer to this question depends upon the meaning of the term "subcontractor." This, in turn, depends upon court interpretations which are far from uniform.[22]

3. *What does the term "labor and materials" include?* Unfortunately, the courts are not consistent in the decision as to what specific equipment is included within that definition.

4. *When does the ninety-day period for giving notice by creditors begin? Is a supplier granted an extension if material is subsequently substituted?* In the case of Airthern Mfg. Co. v. Continental Casualty Co., 162 S.E. (2nd.) 752, the supplier was denied protection because notice was filed after the materials were actually installed, rather than within ninety days of the date when the material was last furnished. Another supplier was denied protection in State Electric Supply Co. v. McBride, 444 Pac. (2nd.) 978, when notice was given more than ninety days after material was furnished. The supplier thought that an extension of time was warranted because certain equipment had to be substituted.

There are a number of federal and state statutes, other than the Miller Act, which also affect contract bond work. Even though these various statutes differ in many respects, they also affect one another. It is not unusual for a court to utilize a Miller Act decision in deciding a case involving a state statute, nor is it unusual for a court to rely on a state statutory case in deciding a problem involving a municipal ordinance. In addition, both federal and state court decisions involving statutes often are employed as matters of guidance to the courts on cases involving private work contracts.[23]

The point worth stressing here is that there are countless ways in which laborers, suppliers, and subcontractors, among others, can find themselves without adequate compensation after having extended credit to others. The payment bond is no panacea, but when there is no satisfaction under the payment bond, creditors will seek out other means for compensation, even though other avenues, such as the performance bond, seem remote. For example, creditors of laborers provided to prime contractors under the Miller Act have been permitted recoveries as "implied obligees" under performance bonds.[24]

Maintenance Bonds Many jurisdictions have statutes, ordinances, or covenants which require that a certain degree of care be exercised in the construction of property. In addition, construction contracts often specify that contractors must remedy any work which is unsatisfactory due to faulty work or defective materials. To comply with these laws and specifications, contractors must usually provide obligees with a maintenance bond which guarantees that faulty work will be corrected or defective materials will be replaced.

Generally, a performance bond includes this maintenance guarantee, for a period of one year after completion of performance, without additional premium. Even when a separate maintenance bond is required along with a performance bond, there usually is no additional charge by the surety for the maintenance bond. But when a contractor does not have to furnish a performance bond, but still has to produce a maintenance bond, or when the contractor must guarantee certain work and materials for periods longer than one year, the maintenance bond requires an additional charge.

Sureties often are understandably reluctant to provide maintenance guarantees for periods over one year. First of all, the longer the guarantee, the greater the chance that a latent defect in materials or a faulty job will become apparent. It also becomes more difficult, after a lapse of time, to determine the cause of any defects. They could be caused by the contractor, by faulty specifications, by abnormal usage of property by the owner, or by some combination of reasons. And, finally, the reluctance of sureties to extend lengthy guarantees can be attributed in no small way to an apparent increase in contractors' vulnerability to claims after the work is completed. Part of this vulnerability is no doubt justified by a poor quality of construction workmanship and materials. The other part stems from a documentable tendency of the courts to award judgments holding contractors liable to owners on the basis of a variety of legal theories, including negligence, express and implied warranties of fitness, and strict liability in tort.[25]

There are a number of ways by which contractors can become implicated in suits involving faulty work. They may perform work which is done properly only to find out later that certain materials which had been used had latent defects. For example, green lumber can eventually warp or split, bricks of improper mix can retain moisture, and concrete products can fail to meet specifications relating to strength.

Plans and specifications prepared by the contractor or by others, such as architects, may be misleading or improper for the type of work that is being done. There may be times, too, when contractors are brought into suit because of the faulty work of subcontractors, especially when the latter are not asked to supply performance and maintenance bonds. Or, contractors may be implicated by accepting certain responsibilities under exculpatory or hold harmless agreements. And there are many situations when contractors clearly are negligent in the way in which they perform their work.

The fact that there is no relationship with products and completed operations insurance needs to be clearly stated. If the contractor is found to be responsible for defective work which is the subject of a maintenance bond, the work must be remedied at the contractor's own expense. Many contractors are not aware that faulty work is uninsurable, judging from the number of disputes and court decisions involving completed operations liability insurance claims. Nevertheless, most liability insurance policies, whether they are standard or nonstandard, exclude claims for property damage *to* work performed or *to* materials that are used in that work. Most such work is therefore done at a loss, since there is usually no insurance whatever available to treat this exposure. As a result, sureties are careful to bond only contractors that are financially capable of replacing defective work or materials, since they are in fact attesting to that capability by issuing maintenance bonds.

Miscellaneous Contract Bonds In addition to the bid bond, performance bond, payment bond, and maintenance bond mentioned above, there are a variety of types of "miscellaneous contract bonds." Complete analysis of all such bonds is beyond the scope of this course. However, an analysis of two of the more common types of miscellaneous contract bonds—subdivision bonds and supply bonds—will illustrate their intent and scope.

Subdivision Bonds. Developers of land and real estate firms often desire to subdivide large tracts of property for housing developments. Developers must not only build suitable homes, but also handle all improvements—such as streets, sidewalks, and streetlights. They also must provide proper sewage disposal systems, a water supply, and other utilities. Before such construction can begin, developers are usually required to obtain permits and to provide subdivision bonds to the local governmental authority.

EXTENT OF GUARANTEE. The subdivision bond is considered a financial guarantee because the developer (principal) promises the municipality (obligee) that the housing development will be completed properly, along with all of its improvements. If not, the principal is responsible for the payment of any damages sustained by the obligee.

Note that there is a marked difference between a subdivision bond and a performance bond that is used for construction work. Under a performance bond, the contractor (principal) enters into a written agreement with the owner (obligee) promising to complete the work as specified, free of any liens. The obligee, of course, promises to pay the principal for services rendered as work progresses. The relationship is different when a subdivision bond is involved. The principal, here, promises to complete the project as planned, but the obligee promises nothing in return.

Only when the property has been developed and sold does the developer begin to receive a return on its investments. Suppose, however, that the costs of building materials and labor far exceed expectations and, as a result, the land is not fully developed. Or, suppose the demand for such housing is not as great as anticipated because of the style of construction or the price range. Cyclical downturns of the economy may also have adverse effects on prospective homeowners. Any of these circumstances can create a hardship for the developer, who may face financial difficulties or even bankruptcy as a result. If bills cannot be paid so as to permit full completion of the project, or if damages ultimately assessed against the developer by the municipality cannot be paid, the surety becomes answerable under the guarantee of its bond.

Largely because of such hazards, a subdivision bond is difficult for developers to procure unless they can provide the type of qualifying credentials required by the surety.

QUALIFICATIONS OF APPLICANT. While the principal's character is important, capacity and capital are the most crucial factors in underwriting subdivision bonds. The capacity of a developer relates to an ability to meet the commitments underlying the work to be performed. The factors considered, therefore, are no different from those which are viewed when a construction contractor desires performance and payment bonds. The surety must determine whether the principal is qualified to perform the type of work involved, has the equipment and tools to do the work, and has the overall capabilities of completing the work as planned.

It is important in connection with subdivision bonds to learn whether the real estate firm or developer has ever handled projects of this nature before, and whether the developer has the expertise that is required in constructing houses on a large scale. When the developer neither has the knowledge nor experience for this kind of business venture, sureties certainly will not be interested in providing subdivision bonds. In such cases, satisfactory character and capital of the developer are not enough.

In cases where a developer intends to subcontract most or all of the work to another contractor who has the capacity to perform, many of the obstacles to qualifying for a subdivision bond can be overcome, particularly if the developer requires performance and payment bonds from a subcontractor which name the developer as the obligee.

The developer can still be confronted with difficulties. Nevertheless, the developer, in this type of arrangement, at least has a buffer— someone to look to for results—whether it is the contractor or the contractor's surety. Contract bonds are not total guarantees for all difficulties that may arise. There may be circumstances when the subject of any disagreement between the developer and the contractor is not within the scope of either the performance or payment bond. Should something like this arise, the burden is then shifted from the contractor to the developer and, perhaps to the developer's surety under the subdivision bond, if the developer is unable to meet the guarantees given to the municipality.

Capital or financial status of the real estate developer is also of extreme importance under subdivision bonds, whether the developer intends to complete the work itself or to subcontract all work. Some obligations of the developer cannot be transferred to the contractor, such as the guarantee to pay taxes and assessments on property. And, as previously mentioned, there may be occasions when the contractor is not under any obligation to the developer.

Since sureties view most subdivision bonds as precarious undertakings, sureties generally require that the developer provide collateral in the form of cash, in an amount sufficient to cover all costs of the entire project, including all costs of improvements when these are the subject of the contract, too. In lieu of cash collateral, some sureties may accept an escrow account so that money is available to pay for any costs of improvements and to pay suppliers of labor and materials.

Supply Contract Bonds. A supply contract is one that involves an agreement for furnishing and delivering materials or supplies at an agreed upon price, usually without any obligation to install whatever is to be delivered. Most such contracts are between private enterprise and federal, state, or local governmental bodies. A supply contract bond is one which is required by those governmental bodies (obligees) from their suppliers (principals) guaranteeing the performance of those supply contracts. Since, for the most part, these bonds are required by the government, they are statutory in form.[26]

EXTENT OF GUARANTEE.   Those who wish to obtain supply contracts, whether they are manufacturers, wholesalers, or dealers, must submit bids, a situation like that of contractors who wish to obtain public work contracts. Typically, the lowest bidder must be selected. When a bidder fails to furnish whatever is required according to the contract specifications, the supplier is liable for the difference between the bid price of the supplier originally selected and the cost of buying those materials or supplies on the open market.[27]

Occasions may arise when the property covered by a supply contract is not readily available on the open market. Equipment made to order by a manufacturer is an example. Unless the commitment to supply the equipment can be met, the manufacturer may be subject to extraordinary damages, including costs for the delay involved in having some other firm complete the contract.

QUALIFICATIONS OF THE APPLICANT.   Although character of the suppliers, that is reputability and responsibility, is important, the capacity (ability of suppliers to meet their commitments) and their capital (financial status) are by far more important. From the standpoint of capacity, sureties must determine whether suppliers have equipment with which to fulfill the contract, as well as sufficient sources from which materials or supplies are to be obtained. Depending upon the material or commodity in question, it is also important for the surety to determine whether the supplier has a fixed price contract from the ultimate source. The price of steel and copper, for example, fluctuates from week to week, and a supplier without a fixed price contract may be confronted with financial hardship if the price for supplying that material eventually exceeds the price for which the supplier has agreed to sell it. In other words, conditions may arise whereby a supplier may have to fulfill a contract at a loss. How much a supplier can withstand in terms of losses thus becomes an important point for the surety to consider.

FEDERAL SURETY BONDS

There are many taxes, duties, and sources of revenue for the federal government. Manufacturers, wholesalers, warehouses, carriers, and others are subject to income tax and other revenue-producing devices. Federal surety bonds guarantee to the federal government that business transactions involving commerce will be conducted as specified, and that businesses will faithfully pay taxes, fees, and penalties.

The forms for federal surety bonds are supplied by the government, and the terms of the bonds are prescribed by statute. Though the bonds are usually written on a continuous basis, they can be used for single transactions. In either case, most such bonds are noncancelable.

Major Types of Federal Surety Bonds

There are three major types of federal surety bonds; namely, customs bonds, internal revenue bonds, and immigrant bonds.

Customs Bonds   Any business which is directly or indirectly involved in importing or exporting goods must provide the federal government with a customs bond guaranteeing the payment of duties or taxes prescribed by law. The government is vitally interested in seeing to it that businesses abide by the laws or regulations dealing with customs, since, among other things, substantial revenues are derived from this type of operation.

Included among those who may be required to give customs bonds are carriers of merchandise, such as truckers, airlines, water carriers, railroads, warehouses that store merchandise subject to federal regulation, and brokers.

Internal Revenue Bonds   Those involved in the manufacture of tobacco products or in the production of alcohol and alcoholic beverages are required to furnish bonds guaranteeing to the federal government that taxes on these products will be paid when due. Those involved in the tobacco business are required to furnish tobacco bonds, while those involved with alcohol must obtain industrial alcohol bonds or alcoholic beverages bonds. Included in the latter category are manufacturers, distillers, brewers, dealers, and carriers of such products.

Since tremendous amounts of money may be held for future payment to the government as tax on these products, the surety must be certain that the principal has character, the capacity to handle such funds wisely, and the capital or financial strength to cope with any problems which may arise through mismanagement of funds or unforeseen circumstances (for example, an energy crisis).

Sometimes businesses can encounter problems involving taxes. The business may claim that the assessed taxes are unreasonable or unnecessary, and should be reduced or removed. In another case, a business may request a time extension or other temporary relief from the payment of taxes due. In either instance, an income tax bond may be required by the government pending final outcome of the request. In the case of a tax dispute, the bond guarantees the payment of those taxes, plus interest, if the principal loses the dispute with the government. If the principal is granted an extension, the bond guarantees that the taxes and any penalties will be paid at the expiration of a certain future date. These bonds, by their very nature, are extremely hazardous to sureties and require the surety to *obtain full collateral* as one of the prerequisites to furnishing such bonds.

Immigrant Bonds When persons of foreign birth enter the United States on either a temporary or a permanent basis, they may be required to furnish an immigrant bond. Depending on the circumstances of the case, the bond may guarantee that the alien will leave the country, or that the alien will not become a public charge.

LICENSE AND PERMIT BONDS

A good many enterprises that exist today need licenses to operate. Licenses provide special privileges entitling their holders to do something which they would not otherwise be entitled to do.[28] Licenses are required by states, counties, cities, and political subdivisions, for two primary reasons. First, they are a source of revenue, and second, they may help in the regulation of license holders through statutes, regulations, or ordinances which exist for the safety and general welfare of the community. Among those who must obtain licenses are auctioneers, automobile dealers, barbers, owners or operators of laundromats, commission merchants, electricians, plumbers, demolition contractors, fumigators, owners of gas stations, vendors of alcoholic beverages, grocery store proprietors, operators of parking lots, photographers, ticket brokers, and warehousemen.

Permits are somewhat like licenses. They, too, must be obtained from political subdivisions. They also serve as a means of regulation and as sources of revenue. However, they often are needed as prerequisites to performing special functions that are incidental to business operations. A licensed business, for example, may need a permit before it can use public property to park customers' automobiles. Permits are required when signs or canopies overhang public property, as well as for sidewalk elevators (invariably for freight handling) on public walkways. Truckers with oversize loads often need permits before they can legally use public roadways. Contractors who work on streets, sidewalks, and public sewer systems also need permits, as do individuals and firms who make structural alterations or improvements to their properties. Whatever the type, licenses or permits normally are not issued until those who are in need of them furnish license or permit bonds to the appropriate public bodies.

Purposes of License and Permit Bonds

License and permit bonds, though required for a variety of specific reasons, can be categorized into two general groups, according to their underlying purpose.

Under the first group are bonds which serve the purpose of holding public bodies harmless for any damages resulting from the failure of licensees to comply with statutes, regulations, ordinances, or codes that control their activities. Principals required to furnish this type not only are subject to revocations of their special privileges (licenses or permits), but also are subject to any damages and fines that may accrue as the result of their noncompliance with such laws. (The bond penalties are the maximum obligations of sureties.) What sets bonds in this group apart from the other group of bonds is that these bonds directly benefit public bodies. Members of the public do not have a direct claim under bonds per se. An example of a bond in this category is one required of merchants who agree to pay sales taxes collected on goods that are sold.

The second group of bonds serves essentially the same purpose, but also serves to provide members of the public, as third parties, with direct rights of action against the bondholders. For this reason, these are commonly referred to as indemnity bonds. In this category is the bond required of contractors who work on public sidewalks. Such bonds agree to protect and indemnify the public for any injuries or damages stemming from failure to complete the principal's obligations under the law requiring the bond.

License and permit bonds are usually written for one year, although they can terminate sooner, depending upon the reasons for their use. Since the bonds are statutory in nature, the laws are read into these bonds. This means, among other things, that whether these bonds may be cancelable depends upon the law for which they are issued. Many laws do permit cancellations.

Types of Guarantees—Examples

To achieve one or both of their general purposes, license and permit bonds may provide a number of guarantees. The guarantees can be grouped into five categories: (1) compliance guarantees, (2) good faith guarantees, (3) credit guarantees, (4) financial guarantees, and (5) indemnity guarantees.

Compliance Guarantees Consistent with their statutory nature, all license and permit bonds begin with the basic guarantee that principals will comply with those laws that affect them. Some bonds confine their guarantees to compliance with applicable laws. Among these are bonds which guarantee that principals who are to perform certain work must comply with building codes that may affect them. Licensed electricians and plumbers, for example, are required to adhere to certain specifications when installing wiring, electrical units, piping, and other fixtures. Public inspectors usually check all such work to determine whether, in fact, such work meets the required specifications.

Other bonds more specifically guarantee that principals will conduct their businesses in compliance with specified laws or codes. Vendors of alcoholic beverages, for example, must strictly adhere to alcoholic beverage control acts, or dram shop acts, which generally prohibit the sale or gift of beverages to a minor, a drunkard, or an intoxicated person. They also regulate the hours of sale, and sometimes the type of products that must be served. Others may prohibit carryout service, or entertainment, unless special permits are purchased in addition to the license to operate. Noncompliance with these laws can result in revocation of licenses and penalties.

Whether these bonds benefit only a public body in the event of default or also give third parties a right of action is sometimes difficult to determine. While the answers to many questions of this nature lie with the statutes or alcoholic beverage control acts that prescribe the obligations of these dealers or vendors of alcoholic beverages, many are questions of fact for the courts to decide.

Good Faith Guarantees Some license and permit bonds, in addition to guaranteeing compliance with the law, also carry the guarantee that principals will perform in good faith, and thus protect the public against any harm through unfair business practices.

For example, statutes in many jurisdictions require that used car dealers obtain licenses and furnish bonds. These bonds cover not only the actual sale or exchange of used automobiles, but also other details in connection with that business. These bonds benefit persons who sustain losses, and cover any unlawful act of dealers, whether criminal in nature or merely a tort. Because they can improve the reputation of the trade, these guarantees of good faith also can benefit other dealers.[29]

As another example, real estate agents and brokers bonds also come within this good faith category in most cases. The purpose of statutes requiring license and permit bonds, here, is to protect the public against fraud in real estate transactions. These bonds have been held to cover a broker's failure to convey property or to return the purchase price, damages for the conversion of funds, and vicarious liability of subordinates.[30]

Credit Guarantees Principals required to furnish bonds providing credit guarantees essentially promise to conduct properly their business affairs in the best interests of others, and to provide honest accountings of all funds in their possession. Auctioneers and dealers in agricultural products are among those who must obtain bonds with guarantees of this nature.

Commission merchants or factors also are required to provide the credit type of guarantee. These individuals or firms are employed to receive goods from others and to sell them for a commission. In that role, commission merchants are both bailees and sales agents for the owners of such goods. Therefore, they must be loyal to the interests of others, and they must comply with the instructions concerning time, place, and terms of sale. Generally, commission merchants who disregard or otherwise violate instructions concerning the sale of goods are held accountable for all damages specified by law. Whether this liability will present any financial hardships upon these merchants depends upon their financial status.[31]

Financial Guarantees Manufacturers, wholesalers, and retailers of goods, as well as firms which provide services, are almost always required to collect taxes on those goods and services at the time of sale. These can include amusement and sales taxes required under the laws of municipalities and/or tobacco and gasoline taxes as imposed by federal, state, and local laws.

Without a doubt, the responsibility for collecting and recording those taxes requires some additional bookkeeping expense for businesses. Some of the additional expense can be overcome through the profitable use of tax money until it is due. However, this is where much of the cause for concern lies. If the business uses tax money—which may involve many thousands of dollars—for the unsuccessful expansion of business, or if a business is confronted with financial difficulties, it may be unable to pay those taxes when due. In any case, the bonds required of those businesses guarantee the payment of those taxes, and when they cannot be paid, it becomes the obligation of the surety to pay them.

Since license and permit bonds are ordinarily written for high penalties, it becomes extremely important for sureties to determine the qualifications of their principals in terms of their capacity (their ability to meet commitments), character (reputability and responsibility), and their capital (financial standing or solvency).

Indemnity Guarantees Bonds which provide indemnity guarantees are distinguishable in one important respect from those which do not. Bonds limited to good faith guarantees, such as those dealing with automobile dealers and real estate agents and brokers, and bonds limited to financial guarantees, such as those given by merchants under various tax obligations, solely benefit public bodies. On the other hand, bonds that provide indemnity guarantees benefit not only public bodies but also third parties. Third parties, in other words, are given a right of action against principals of those bonds if the third parties sustain injuries or damages to their property through the acts or omissions of the bond principals.

Bonds with indemnity guarantees are usually required of those who must obtain permits from public bodies before commencing certain activities or before using public property. Among those who must obtain permits and bonds with indemnity agreements are contractors who work on public streets, walkways, and utility systems; contractors who must perform structural alterations, improvements, demolition or blasting work in areas of public exposure; truckers conveying wide loads or excessive loads on public roadways, including house movers; merchants who attach to their buildings signs or awnings that overhang public thoroughfares; those who construct billboards on public property; and, those businesses which utilize sidewalk freight elevators.

Bonds providing indemnity guarantees should not be confused with liability insurance policies, despite the apparent similarities. If a surety is required to indemnify a third party, it will later seek to recover from the principal. Liability insurance, in contrast, promises to pay on behalf of (or sometimes to indemnify) *the insured.* Sureties usually require verification that satisfactory liability insurance is in force before they will issue a bond providing indemnity guarantees.

If, in a given circumstance involving a third-party suit, it is determined that the claim is excluded under some form of liability insurance, it then is up to the bondholder to assume the financial consequences to the extent imposed under the law governing the permit in question. An example might be the demolition contractor who does not purchase optional collapse coverage under a general liability policy, and whose negligence results in collapse damage to adjoining property. Whether the bondholder can handle any such financial burdens depends upon the nature of the claim and the extent of the damages. If the damages are so extensive as to force the contractor into insolvency, the surety may ultimately become answerable for those damages.

PUBLIC OFFICIAL BONDS

Individuals who are appointed or elected to positions of public office have the obligation to faithfully discharge their duties to the best of their abilities for the purpose of protecting public interests. What those duties may encompass, and what liabilities personally may be charged against public officials varies with their position in government and with laws that control each situation. It can be said, however, that most such persons are obligated to act in good faith. When they hold public funds, they also have the duty of accounting for, and turning over such funds to their successors in office. With few exceptions, laws generally hold public officials personally accountable for losses, shortages or damage to public property. Some officials are even held responsible for the acts and the omissions of their subordinates.

All such obligations are placed upon public officials by their oaths of office, which are one condition precedent to acting in their official capacities. The other requirement is that these individuals furnish public official bonds guaranteeing the public or governmental agency that the officials will uphold their promises to faithfully and honestly perform official duties. Any public official who fails to fulfill those promises must then make restitution to the extent of his or her liability. If the official is unable to do so, the surety then becomes answerable up to the bond penalty for any damages. Interest on any judgments incurred is payable by the surety, in addition to the bond penalty.

Public official bonds are generally noncancelable. They continue in force throughout an official's term of office, and they terminate only when successors are appointed or elected and qualify for those positions. Sometimes there is a time gap between the expiration of one official's term of office and the beginning of the succeeding official's term. This period during the gap is considered to be part of the retiring official's term of office and is covered under that person's bond. In any case, the succeeding official should see to it that the necessary arrangements are made for the transfer of office—including the full accounting of all transactions, funds and other property. When a new public official takes office, an independent audit of the predecessor's office is often advisable. This prevents the new official from being held responsible for acts of a predecessor.

When an official is reappointed or reelected, a new bond is required for the new term of office. Sometimes individuals hold an office for an indefinite period. In these cases, bonds are written without expiration, but subject to annual premiums.

Public Official Bonds Versus Fidelity Bonds

The fact that honesty of an official is guaranteed by the public official bonds leads some persons to believe that the bond is more in the nature of a fidelity bond than a contract of suretyship. However, there are at least two points that distinguish public official bonds from fidelity bonds.

First, public official bonds generally guarantee both the honesty and the *faithful performance* of their principals. A fidelity bond, on the other hand, deals solely with the honesty of its principals. Second, the principal under a public official bond has an expressed contractual obligation to the obligee (public), provided under oath, and to the obligor (surety) that provides the bonds. The employee under a fidelity bond generally has no expressed contractual obligation with the employer concerning honesty and certainly no contractual relationship, expressed or implied, with the surety.

Required by Law

Since the duties of an office are usually prescribed by statute, the public official bond and its terms are likewise prescribed by statute. The applicable law is virtually read into the bond provisions, as is the case with other statutory bonds. It therefore behooves all public servants to know and understand the provisions of the law that apply to them, not only because ignorance of the law is no defense, but also because their potential liability may extend well beyond the penalty of the bond furnished.

It has been noted that most public official bonds are required by statute, ordinance or regulation, and that their provisions are prescribed by such laws. However, there are other bonds which, although mandatory under law, contain provisions which are drawn up by those authorities who require them. Then, too, some bonds are not mandatory, but their provisions track with those of statutory bonds. Finally, some bonds are both voluntary and nonstatutory—these are commonly referred to as common-law bonds, since their provisions are guided by whatever is decided upon by the contract of employment, and common-law rather than statute applies in the event of any dispute.

Some nonstatutory bonds guarantee only the honesty of officeholders, while others guarantee both honesty and faithful performance. Most also permit cutoff dates as to future liability, and they often contain provisions for cancellation. Statutory bonds are much more stringent, and all encompassing, and they are more truly contracts of adhesion, since the principal has no opportunity to change the bond provisions but merely adheres to the statutory provisions.

Those Who Must Be Bonded

It would be nearly impossible to list all the kinds of public officials who must be bonded by virtue of their functions within state, county, and city governments, as well as within political subdivisions. However, representative of those who frequently must be bonded are: agricultural commission treasurers; alcoholic beverage commissioners; attorneys general; conservation commissioners; constables; county assessors, auditors, clerks, commissioners, judges, treasurers, and sheriffs; insurance commissioners; justices of the peace; municipal court judges; notaries public; public service commissioners; state administrative officers, auditors, tax commissioners, treasurers; supreme court clerks; and township officials.

These public officials encompass members of three broad groups: (1) those whose primary duties require them to handle public funds—such as tax collectors and treasurers; (2) those whose primary functions are administrative in nature—such as assessors, insurance commissioners, and judges; and (3) those whose duties involve direct exposure to members of the public—such as constables and sheriffs.

Those whose primary duties involve the collecting, disbursing, and safekeeping of public funds have the responsibility of accounting for all such funds and the obligation to relinquish them whenever their successors take office. To these ends, such persons are charged with honesty of purpose, and with faithfully discharging their duties as specified by law.

Laws governing officials who handle public funds tend to be stringent (and rightly so, since the potential losses to taxpayers can be enormous and because—apart from losses per se—taxpayers and other voters have a right to *know* whether tax funds are being spent efficiently and properly). Yet, losses occur. Probably most losses are caused by misappropriations, which have proved to be rather difficult to prevent. Internal controls and regular audits by competent outside personnel help to reduce both the frequency and the severity of losses, but even the best run controls will not entirely prevent all losses.

Even when officeholders are honest, they may still be held accountable for loss of funds. This liability can arise through the failure of any bank where funds are deposited, unless the official is in strict compliance with the banking procedures, or unless the official is specifically exempt from liability in these situations. More important, perhaps, is the fact that public officials usually are held accountable for any defaults which are caused by their subordinates. While some officials sometimes may be relieved of that type of liability, the best way to treat that contingent responsibility is to require bonds of subordinates. In fact, this is a common practice.[32]

Under the terms of laws governing these public officials, the mere fact that a loss was caused by theft or some other crime usually does not relieve the public official from personal liability for the loss. Those whose duties do not involve the handling of public funds may be less susceptible than those who are held accountable for public funds. Nevertheless, city and county clerks, clerks of courts and other administrative personnel often cause problems through errors in judgment or in procedures, such as improperly filing a mechanic's lien with resulting hardship for others. Problems also may result when such persons make otherwise authorized expenditures but they complete them through improper procedures.

People dealing directly with the public, such as sheriffs and other law enforcement officers, are frequently confronted with arguments instituted by the public. Among those offenses which commonly lead these officials and their sureties to the courts are claims of liability for false arrest, assault and battery, malicious prosecution; failure to permit prompt medical treatment; making improper attachments or losing property once it is attached; permitting unauthorized use of public equipment; conversion of property; failure to serve summonses; and liability for acts or omissions of subordinates.

Qualifications of the Principal

Whether a public official bond is to guarantee only honesty or both honesty and faithful performance, it is not enough, for underwriting purposes, that an individual is elected or appointed to an office and accepts the oath of office. It is also important for the surety to consider that person's character, capacity, and capital.

Character Some of the more important qualities a surety underwriter looks for concerning a public official's character are honesty, integrity, reliability, and general good standing in the community. It therefore stands to reason that a surety will not give a bond that guarantees honesty unless the available evidence suggests that the principal is, in fact, basically honest and reliable.

Capacity The more important qualities of a public official's capacity to perform the duties involved with the office include experience and competence. For example, a high school dropout who has worked for the past five years as a used car salesman would not seem to have the capacity to perform the requisite duties of most public offices.

On the other hand, a senior member of the local bar association will likely have the capacity to serve as a judge.

Capital The primary point to consider concerning a public official's capital is whether that person will be financially able to make restitution for any loss or damage sustained by the public. This can be a problem because it is difficult, if not impossible, to estimate what a potential loss can be.

JUDICIAL BONDS

It has been noted that judicial bonds are prescribed by statute and are filed in either probate courts or in courts of equity. Judicial bonds are thus involved with a variety of types of court actions. Generally, a judicial bond guarantees that a person or firm will fulfill certain obligations—such as faithfully performing certain duties prescribed by law or by a court, or showing financial responsibility for the benefit of another until the final outcome of a court's decision. If the principal fails to do this, the surety guarantees to answer for damages.

These surety bonds are tripartite in nature, are usually noncancelable and, therefore, are continuous contracts. They are prescribed by statute and are filed in probate or in courts of equity. A probate court (or a surrogate's court, as it is sometimes called) deals with settlements of estates, appointments of guardians for minors and incompetents, and so forth. Each county has a probate court which administers the transactions which are domiciled in that county. A court of equity, on the other hand, is primarily concerned with arguments involving specific performance or other situations in which money damages would not provide an adequate remedy. For example, a court of equity is used when someone seeks an injunction against another or when someone seeks to regain possession of property which is in the hands of another.

Types of Judicial Bonds

There are two general classes of judicial bonds: court bonds and fiduciary bonds. These will be analyzed specifically following a brief introduction to each of the two types of judicial bonds.

A *court bond* generally deals with an action in equity—as opposed to an action in a court of law for money damages or an action in probate court concerning faithful disposition of property of others. The primary purpose of a court bond is to permit someone to seek a remedy in a court of equity and, at the same time, to protect the other party against whom claim is made for any damages sustained in the event the person seeking the remedy is unsuccessful. The person seeking a remedy is the principal under a court bond, and the person against whom action is made is the obligee. If the court decides in favor of the principal, the matter is settled and the bond terminates. But if the court decides that the principal does not have the rights or interests as claimed, the bond guarantees the obligee that the principal will pay any damages, including court costs. This bond, therefore, is principally one that is concerned with a person's financial responsibility. This will become clearer over the next several pages when specific court bonds are discussed and examples are given.

A *fiduciary bond* is required of a person who is selected by a probate court to administer the property or interests of others according to the specifications laid down by the court. It also is used in equity proceedings involving receivers and liquidators of property, among others. This bond guarantees that a fiduciary will faithfully perform as specified by the court, account for all property received, and make good any deficiency for which the court holds the fiduciary liable. When the matter is settled according to the specifications of the court, the fiduciary bond terminates. Otherwise, the bond remains in force until any deficiencies are settled.

Court Bonds Court bonds can be categorized into the following general groups: (1) bonds in civil proceedings (plaintiffs' and defendants' bonds), (2) bonds in admiralty proceedings (involving maritime questions), and (3) bonds for release of persons in criminal or civil proceedings (such as bonds used for bail).

Plaintiffs' and Defendants' Bonds. A person who commences an action against another in order to obtain some type of equitable remedy—be it the performance of a certain act, the repossession of certain property, or the fulfillment of some monetary obligation—needs a plaintiff's bond before the court will proceed with the action. This bond guarantees that if it is ultimately determined that such action was wrongfully taken, the plaintiff will pay the defendant for any damages that may have been sustained as the result of such action. If the defendant desires to continue the performance of a certain act or wishes to retain the property in question during the court proceedings, such person must give a defendant's bond. If the court decides in favor of the plaintiff, the defendant must then refrain from performing the act in question, return the property sought, or pay damages that are sustained by the plaintiff.

NATURE OF PLAINTIFFS' AND DEFENDANTS' BONDS. Bonds for actions in equity involving plaintiffs and defendants are statutory in nature, have open or fixed penalties, are noncancelable and continuous, and deal with financial guarantees. With at least one exception, explained below, each type of plaintiffs' bond has a sort of matching defendants' bond. The following paragraphs describe some of the more common bonds that are required of both parties to an action.

Before a court will attach property (take it by legal authority) at the request of another for some reason (for example, because the property is about to be removed from the state without leaving enough to satisfy the plaintiff's claim, or there is reason to suspect that the property is about to be wrongfully sold), the complainant or plaintiff must give the court an *attachment bond*. This bond guarantees that if the court decides against the plaintiff, the defendant will be paid any damages as the result of having such property attached. But, if the court decides in the plaintiff's favor, the bond automatically terminates.

However, after property of a defendant is attached, it can be released to the defendant pending final outcome of the court's decision, if he or she gives the court a *release of attachment bond*. This bond guarantees that the defendant will return the property in question and pay any damages and court costs if the court should decide in the plaintiff's favor (that is, if the court rules that the attachment was proper). The defendant is *required* to furnish a release of attachment bond only if the defendant desires to maintain possession of the property until the dispute is settled. To secure the bond, the defendant must satisfy the surety that he or she is financially responsible.

Disputes involving the attachment of property—particularly property such as merchandise of a going business or perishable commodities—can be particularly troublesome, especially when the defendant does not or cannot furnish a release of attachment bond. For example, the plaintiff may be liable in damages for any business interruption resulting from the attachment of merchandise, or the plaintiff may be liable for any decrease in value of perishables attached. Such problems are avoided when a release of attachment bond is secured, because the defendant retains possession of such goods.

Replevin is a form of action instituted by the alleged owner of personal property to recover possession of specific personal property which he or she alleges to have been unlawfully taken or unlawfully withheld. A *replevin bond* is somewhat similar to an attachment bond. With a replevin bond, the plaintiff takes immediate possession of the property allegedly belonging to the plaintiff, pending the final outcome of the court's decision. The bond guarantees the plaintiff will return property if ordered to do so, as well as pay any costs and damages.

A *counter replevin bond* is issued in a replevin procedure, and it has an effect similar to that of a release of attachment bond. When the bond is issued, the defendant regains possession of the specific personal property in question pending outcome of the court case. If the defendant should lose, the counter replevin bond guarantees that the defendant will return the property to the plaintiff.

Disputes in replevin cases sometimes involve the sale of merchandise, either with the use of a conditional sales contract or on an installment basis without a formal contract. Department stores are often involved. A conditional sales contract, when filed in the court of record where goods are sold, usually provides sufficient evidence for a seller to regain possession of personal property when a buyer fails to make payments. When such conditional sales contract is not so filed, or when a sale is made on an installment basis without a formal contract, and the buyer either fails to remit payments or sells the goods to a third person, the original seller must then institute a suit in replevin in order to secure such goods. It becomes particularly troublesome when a manufacturer sells goods to a dealer for resale and does not retain title to such goods. Most businesses should have little difficulty in establishing financial responsibility in order to purchase a replevin or counter replevin bond. But many individuals find it difficult to purchase a counter replevin bond, unless they can show that they are financially capable to pay any damages that may accrue as the result of a dispute.

When a plaintiff desires someone to perform or to refrain from performing some act or function (such as continuing a business, discontinuing a patent infringement, or removing trees from land where ownership is in dispute) a court injunction can sometimes be secured upholding the wishes of that plaintiff. Before an injunction is issued, however, the plaintiff must post an *injunction bond* guaranteeing to reimburse the defendant for any damages suffered if the court later refuses to uphold the injunction against the defendant.

The defendant in such a suit may have the injunction set aside until the dispute is settled merely by posting a *dissolve injunction bond*. This guarantees the plaintiff payment of any damages should a permanent injunction be granted in favor of the plaintiff.

An *appeal bond* is required of a plaintiff who did not obtain the remedy that was sought and desires to appeal an adverse decision to a higher court. Such bond, when posted, guarantees the payment of all court costs on the appeal. If, on the other hand, a lower court were to grant the defendant affirmative relief—instead of merely denying the plaintiff the remedy sought—then the plaintiff must post a *stay of execution bond* when the judgment is to be appealed. What the court does, in effect, is to halt execution of the lower court's decision pending outcome of the higher court's decision. The bond guarantees payment of any judgment and costs that may be awarded to the defendant by the higher court.

When the defendant desires to appeal a case to a higher court, an *appeal for defendant bond* or a *supersedeas bond*, as it is sometimes called, is required. It guarantees the plaintiff that the defendant will pay the entire judgment, plus court costs and interest, should a higher court sustain the initial judgment in favor of the plaintiff.

Some court bonds do not come in pairs, in the sense that there is no corollary bond available to one of the parties in an equity action. One of these is a *bond to discharge a mechanic's lien*. As was previously mentioned, it is often possible for suppliers of labor and materials to file a lien against property of an owner in the amount of debt outstanding. When a mechanic's lien is filed against property, it can be discharged by the property owner by filing a bond to discharge a mechanic's lien. This bond guarantees those who file such lien that the owner will pay the lien, if it is considered to be valid by the court.

QUALIFICATIONS OF THE PRINCIPAL. Court bonds are viewed as contracts of financial responsibility, particularly when these bonds guarantee the payment of any judgment and other costs that may be assessed by a court. Hence, it is usually considered important for the surety to have as much financial data about its principal as possible.

From the viewpoint of the surety, the furnishing of plaintiffs' bonds is generally less hazardous than the furnishing of defendants' bonds. First, plaintiffs usually are creditors who are seeking the return of property which is rightfully theirs. Vendors of goods sold on an installment basis are examples. Creditors do not ordinarily institute actions unless they have good reasons for doing so. Second, plaintiffs' bonds usually guarantee to reimburse defendants if courts determine that plaintiffs are not entitled to the remedy sought by them. However, a separate cause of action must be instituted by the defendants in order to establish the amount of damages which such plaintiffs may owe as the result of the inconvenience of such actions to defendants. Thus, the liability under a plaintiff's bond, unlike that of the defendant's bond, does not include judgment awards.

When a business desires a plaintiff's bond, a credit check may be all that is necessary to establish its financial responsibility. But when an individual desires such bond, the surety may make some in-depth inquiries in order to establish that an individual's financial condition is satisfactory.

Injunction bonds, unlike other plaintiffs' bonds, generally are written by a surety only with some reluctance. As mentioned earlier, the problem with these bonds is that the ultimate outcome of the dispute is usually uncertain even when the plaintiff feels strongly that an injunction is in fact warranted. This uncertainty, along with the uncertainty as to what damages may be assessed by a court, makes these bonds somewhat hazardous undertakings from a surety's standpoint. Although plaintiffs seeking injunction bonds must show the same qualifications as those under other plaintiffs' bonds, sureties usually may require other safeguards, such as collateral.

Defendants' bonds are almost always considered hazardous by sureties for the same reasons that plaintiffs' bonds are generally regarded as safe. With the exception of cases involving injunctions, defendants are those who possess certain property of others under questionable circumstances or conditions. Doubt is raised because another party (the plaintiff) usually institutes an action for repossession only for some good reason. Also, defendants' bonds guarantee upon the decision of the court the immediate return of property in question, along with the payment of damages for loss of use or for the amount of any judgment and other costs. Unlike the defendant, the plaintiff is not required to institute a separate cause of action in determining the amount of damages. For this reason, the amount of damages the defendant must pay may be uncertain until finally declared by the court.

Defendants, therefore, must have such qualifications as honesty and financial responsibility. In fact, sureties usually will not issue defendants' bonds unless they receive some type of acceptable collateral security, such as cash, certified checks, bank certificates of deposit, assigned savings accounts, assignments of cash values under life insurance, United States government bonds and treasury notes, or other assets which are readily converted into cash (not assets which are susceptible to wide fluctuations in value, such as common stocks). The security is required even though the bond applicant shows the ability to pay court costs, interest, or damages should a court render an adverse decision against that person. Legal suits are expensive. By the time a dispute between the plaintiff and the defendant is finally settled, the defendant may be unable to pay any damages. If this happens, the surety is required to pay, because the bond guarantees the defendant's promise to perform or to pay according to the ruling of the court. Whereas collateral security is often required from defendants, because of their vulnerable positions in such suits, plaintiffs ordinarily must produce such security only when their financial status is somewhat questionable.

Fiduciary Bonds The word *fiduciary* is a generic term which refers to persons or legal entities, such as administrators, guardians, and trustees who are appointed by a court under a will or a trust for purposes of managing, controlling, or disposing of property of others. Like court bonds, fiduciary bonds are a type of judicial bond used for a variety of purposes, and they are governed by statutes or by directives of probate and equity courts. Fiduciary bonds can be categorized into the following groups.

Bonds in Probate. Bonds in this class are written for administrators and executors who handle the estates of deceased persons (or persons who are presumed to have died); guardians who are appointed to administer the estates of minors; conservators, committees, and custodians who are appointed to handle the estates of incompetents; and trustees of trust estates.

Bonds in Equity. Included in this class are bonds for equity receivers, liquidators, trustees, and others appointed by a court to manage or to liquidate property. Also within this group are assignees, liquidators, trustees, and others, who are appointed by insolvent debtors to liquidate and to distribute property for the benefit of creditors.

Bonds in Bankruptcy Proceedings of Federal Courts. These bonds are written, usually on a petition of creditors, for receivers who commonly are appointed in bankruptcy to collect and to protect assets of an alleged bankrupt.

Miscellaneous Bonds. These bonds are required of receivers, trustees, and conservators of financial institutions and insurance companies. Fiduciaries are appointed by state or federal courts, depending upon the type of proceeding.

Nature of Fiduciary Bonds. Bonds written for fiduciaries generally guarantee that such persons who are entrusted with the care of property belonging to others, will exercise their duties faithfully, account for all property received, and make good any deficiency for which the courts—probate or equity—may hold such fiduciaries liable. Fiduciary bonds usually hold the principals and the sureties jointly and severally liable to obligees for the faithful performance of specified duties. They are continuous instruments which require no renewal, although premiums are charged annually, and they are noncancelable— usually running until the proceedings are completed and the sureties and the fiduciaries are released from further obligation.

Examples of Fiduciaries Bonded. Both individuals and corporations often are selected to act as fiduciaries. Guardians, administrators and executors, and receivers and trustees in bankruptcy proceedings are among those fiduciaries frequently bonded, as described in the following paragraphs.

GUARDIANS. Generally, a guardian is anyone who legally has the care of a person and/or a person's property because of the inability of that person to manage his or her own affairs. A guardian is often nominated in a will and appointed by a probate court to look after the affairs of a minor or other person suffering a legal disability (ward of the court). The one appointed to act as guardian can be a parent, a relative, or some other competent person. It usually is the responsibility of the guardian to see to it that the ward is properly supported, clothed, and educated. A *curator* is a guardian who controls property of a ward. Thus, it is possible for a ward to have a guardian and a curator, although an individual guardian can fill both roles. A *conservator* or a *committee* is a guardian selected by a court to manage the affairs of an incompetent.

All jurisdictions have statutes which safeguard the rights and interests of minors and others deemed legally incompetent. One of the provisions of those statutes is that a guardian give a bond before assuming the role of a fiduciary for such minor or incompetent. That bond guarantees that the fiduciary will faithfully perform all duties, observe all directives of the court, and provide an accounting of all money and other property when required by the court to do so. Failing this, the fiduciary is liable to the court for all damages. The surety is secondarily liable, but only up to the penalty of the bond. However, a surety can be required to pay, in excess of the bond penalty, any court costs and interest that has accrued from the time any judgment is rendered against the fiduciary.

Sometimes a surety will not write a fiduciary bond unless it is given joint control over the assets of an estate. This means that the estate monies are deposited in a joint bank account of the fiduciary and the surety, and they are disbursed only with the surety's approval. The primary purpose of joint control is to protect heirs of an estate against loss through some act of the fiduciary. This arrangement is particularly important when a large estate is involved and the fiduciary is not experienced in handling assets of that magnitude. A corporate trust company or a bank, of course, would be usually excepted from this arrangement, since such firms normally have the expertise and other qualifications that are required in handling such estates.

Just as a surety will prequalify its principal for the bond, a probate court may do likewise. The court will also consider the principal's character, capital, and capacity. Generally, if a person can take care of his or her own affairs in an efficient manner, then he or she is qualified to assume the responsibilities of a fiduciary. There have been occasions when a probate court has rejected a fiduciary nominated in a will and, instead, has used a substitute who is judged more capable of managing the affairs of a minor or incompetent. In any event, once the fiduciary posts a bond, it continues in force until it terminates at some time in the future as specified by the court. Generally, the bond for an estate of a minor terminates when that person reaches majority, although the bond for an estate of a person who is otherwise an incompetent may stay open until the court determines that a guardian or a conservator is no longer necessary.

There are times when a bond terminates prematurely because of the incompetence or the neglect of the fiduciary. In those cases, both the fiduciary and the surety are liable to the court for any damages. There have also been occasions when courts have permitted a surety to be relieved of liability for any future acts of its principal because the principal has been guilty of misconduct or breach of duties in handling the estate.

ADMINISTRATORS AND EXECUTORS. An *executor* (male) or *executrix* (female) is one named in a will to administer an estate. When a person dies intestate (without leaving a will), a court will appoint an *administrator* or an *administratrix* to settle the estate of the decedent. The duties and obligations of administrators and executors are generally the same, but there are distinctions. For example, administrators settle estates according to the directives of the courts, while executors settle estates as specified in the wills, subject to approval of the courts. The duties and responsibilities of these fiduciaries include collecting all assets of the estate and preserving them from loss, paying all debts which may have been incurred by the decedent, and providing the court with an accounting of all transactions. Upon the court's approval of such accounting, the fiduciary is obligated to distribute the remaining assets as specified in the will or by the statute in question. Upon satisfactorily completing these duties, the fiduciary is discharged by the court.

When a court requires an administrator or an executor to post a bond (the latter may be excused from doing so, if the will so specifies), the bond guarantees the fiduciary's faithful performance as dictated by law or by the court. The surety also may require, as a prerequisite to giving a bond, that it be given joint control, along with the fiduciary, over the disbursement of certain assets.

A bond that is furnished for an executor or an administrator of an estate has the same characteristics and guarantees as a bond which is furnished for a guardian or a conservator. It is noncancelable and terminates with the court's acknowledgement that all duties required of the fiduciary have been properly discharged. Also, the fiduciary is liable to the full extent of any losses, while, in the event of default, the surety must answer only to the extent of the bond penalty—and beyond the penalty for any court costs and any interest that may accrue on any judgment that is rendered against its principal.

Although this bond is noncancelable, it may be terminated prematurely with the death, resignation or discharge of the administrator or executor. If an administrator should die, resign or be discharged before the estate is settled, the person appointed by the court to succeed is referred to as an "administrator *de bonis non*." The person so appointed is to complete that which was not finished by the preceding administrator.

When a person is judged incompetent or is unwilling to accept the duties of an executor, or when there is a will which does not name an executor, the person subsequently appointed by the court is referred to as an "administrator *cum testamento annexo* (with will annexed)." This administrator assumes the duties of completing the whole estate, rather than only that portion which is unfinished.

If an executor dies, resigns, or is discharged before the administration is complete, the person appointed to succeed is referred to as an "administrator *de bonis non cum testamento annexo.*" As with an administrator *de bonis non,* the succeeding fiduciary is only held accountable for any liability on that which remains to be done to settle the estate. However, before a fiduciary is bonded under either of these circumstances, the surety normally requires a full accounting of all transactions that were made by the preceding fiduciary.

Finally, when either an administrator or an executor must sell realty of the estate, a special bond must be purchased and the fiduciary is referred to as an "adminstrator to sell real estate." Appropriate bonds are available for all these situations.

RECEIVERS AND TRUSTEES IN BANKRUPTCY PROCEEDINGS. In situations involving bankruptcies or insolvencies, two types of fiduciaries usually require bonds. One is the *receiver* who is appointed by the court or by the *referee* (an impartial person selected by the parties or appointed by the courts). It is the receiver's responsibility to assemble and to preserve all assets of a debtor until a *trustee* is elected from among the creditors or is appointed by the court. The trustee is the second fiduciary whose duties are to reduce any assets to cash, and to determine the priority of payment among the creditors for the final distribution of those assets.

Bonds written for receivers and trustees guarantee faithful performance of duties as directed by the court in bankruptcy. The trustee works closely with the referee, since the latter is an intermediary of the court. In fact, the referee must consent to the withdrawal of any funds by the trustee, in an arrangement similar to that of an administrator under a joint control arrangement with the surety.

Common Causes of Loss. In spite of the fact that courts usually exercise care in selecting guardians, administrators, and other fiduciaries, and even though sureties also try to ascertain the qualifications of the same people, losses nonetheless occur. Most problems involving bonds of fiduciaries and their sureties deal with administrators of estates and with guardians of minors and incompetents. Some of these claims involving administrators range from allegations of simple failure to perform to charges of mismanagement of estates' affairs because of ignorance, negligence, or dishonesty.

Adminstrators and executors are under an obligation to exercise reasonable care in notifying all heirs of an impending probate proceeding. This is not always done, and estates are sometimes settled without notification of all heirs. Courts have held administrators and their sureties accountable in cases when all heirs could have been determined if reasonable care had been exercised by the administrators.

Administrators and executors are also obligated to give public notice of the estate proceedings for a certain period, usually six weeks, in order to give creditors of the estate an opportunity to file claims against the estate. Problems often arise when fiduciaries begin to close the estate before the expiration of this period. Related to this are cases where fiduciaries do not make payments to secured creditors and general (unsecured) creditors in order of priority.

Finally, adminstrators who are direct heirs sometimes conceal funds or other property of the estate, so that they are not involved in the distribution among other heirs, and fiduciaries sometimes do not make a proper accounting for tax purposes and are subsequently involved in suits by the government.

Guardians of minors and conservators of incompetents who are bonded incur difficulties for a number of reasons, including the following:

1. Expenditures are improperly made by guardians under conditions when joint control arrangements are not required by sureties, or when certain expenditures are made by guardians without court orders.
2. Funds are misappropriated. Some fiduciaries who never before manifested dishonesty may nevertheless steal assets of an estate when an opportunity arises. Others commit dishonest acts because they are entangled in personal financial hardships of their own. Fiduciaries are tempted to recover from financial adversity of their own, such as gambling or conditions beyond their control. Whatever the reason, losses by dishonest acts of fiduciaries are extremely difficult to prevent.
3. Funds or property are mismanaged. Administrators and executors are only human and are therefore not infallible. They can make costly mistakes. For example, they may fail to collect all assets due the estate, or they may use assets or carry on the decedents' businesses without authorization. They may also delegate their duties to others for whose acts they will be held liable, or they may make improper investments. Whatever the reason—incompetence, negligence, or flagrant disregard of duties—these fiduciaries are usually held personally accountable to the estate for any losses. In any event, proper underwriting should screen out bond applicants who are inept or irresponsible,

so that losses are restricted to those caused by other types of errors.

4. Records are inadequate. Accountings of all transactions—which are required of the courts as conditions precedent to settling estates and to releasing guardians—are sometimes improperly prepared, and records are sometimes lacking in a number of ways. Courts or personal representatives of estates usually discover irregularities of fiduciaries because of the final accounting. However, there are times when misappropriations or other irregularities are not discovered until guardians have been released by the courts under apparently satisfactory conditions. However, sureties may still be held accountable for any losses, if guardians are unable to make restitution.

SURETY BOND GUARANTEE PROGRAM FOR SMALL CONTRACTORS

There are many small contracting firms (or individuals) that, although able to fulfill job contracts, lack a certain amount of the capital or capacity necessary to meet sureties' underwriting requirements for bid, performance, and payment bonds. To many such small firms, assistance is available through the Small Business Administration (SBA) under its Surety Bond Guarantee Program. The purpose of the program is to give small, experienced contracting firms the opportunity to be bonded so that they can compete for jobs. Having this opportunity, they can then prove themselves by performing work to specifications. A history of successful performance may in turn enable such firms to secure future surety bonds based upon their own reputation and financial ability.

Nature of the Program

The SBA program is intended only for individuals or firms that are required to obtain bid, performance, and payment bonds for work including, but not limited to, construction, repair, maintenance, service, supply, and janitorial services. Only work which requires a contract bond is within the scope of the program, although work requiring another type of bond is sometimes permissible if written in conjunction with a contract bond. For example, a license and permit bond that is required of a construction contractor working on a public highway may be included under this program, since it is considered to be incidental to a contract bond.

Eligibility The fact that the Surety Bond Guarantee Program is intended for small contracting firms that may be unable to secure financial assistance elsewhere does not mean *all* such firms automatically qualify for assistance. Actually, the program is not intended for blatantly unqualified contractors, but only for those that are considered borderline by normal underwriting standards. In fact, the program requires that sureties are not to lower their underwriting standards in determining contractors eligible under this program.

In order to evaluate an applicant under this program, the information sought by the surety corresponds with that required to underwrite a contractor under normal procedures. Among the data required are a financial statement no more than two months old and an annual financial statement. Furthermore, since the surety is interested in the management of the business, it will want background information on the character of the individual or on the principals of the firm.

A description of the job involved is always required. The surety, of course, requires a copy of the bid proposal, information concerning whether the applicant is required to bid for a job, and details concerning the financing of the job.

An explanation is required as to the applicant's expertise with the type of job being sought. As to previous experience, a surety needs to know about the types and amounts of contracts outstanding, and whether the applicant has ever previously served as a prime contractor or a subcontractor.

On some occasions applicants for this program are declined because they are unable to supply required financial data. However, there are other reasons for declination, such as insufficient capital and lack of technical expertise. When the reason is easily correctable, the SBA may try to assist the contracting firm in overcoming its deficiencies. Otherwise, the case is considered closed.

Even when a contracting firm is considered to be borderline, it must be one whose annual gross volume does not exceed an amount established by the SBA in order to be eligible for the program. One million is the maximum contract amount that may currently be bonded in the program. However, there is no limit to the number of bonds that may be guaranteed for a contractor, provided each separate contract does not exceed $1 million. For example, if an otherwise qualified contractor desires to perform two separate but related jobs and each requires a separate performance bond, the contractor may be able to secure guarantees for both, provided each contract does not exceed $1 million. On the other hand, a firm that needs a bid bond for 5 percent of a $2 million contract cannot receive an SBA guarantee even though the bond amount is $50,000.

Extent of Guarantees   The SBA is not a surety. Nor does it issue surety bonds. It merely guarantees a participating surety—which itself must be on the Treasury Department's list of approved sureties—up to 90 percent of any loss that is sustained under any bond of less than $250,000 and 80 percent on contracts between $250,000 and $1 million. The term "loss" in that guarantee encompasses all liability, damages, court costs, legal fees, charges, and expenses of any kind that the surety may sustain as the result of writing a bond under the SBA program.

In addition to issuing the required bond or bonds, the surety must pay the SBA a fee for guaranteeing the bonds that are written. This fee amounts to 10 percent of the bond premium, including a like percentage on any additional premiums which later may develop.

Effect of Breach   In the event that any contract is breached by a contractor bonded under the program and any claim or suit is brought against the surety, the SBA must be notified within a reasonable time. Even though the SBA requires notification of any breach, it is still the surety's responsibility to handle all phases of the claim. This usually includes determining the extent of the contractor's liability and taking whatever action is considered necessary in minimizing the loss, defending the contractor, and offering any settlements.

The Surety Bond Guarantee Program is a reimbursement program. This means that *after* the surety sustains losses it is reimbursed for those losses up to the 80 or 90 percent guarantee. However, the SBA reimburses the surety on a calendar quarterly basis, and it makes adjustments on a pro rata basis when the surety receives any recoveries through salvage or subrogation.

MUNICIPAL BOND ISSUES
OF GOVERNMENTAL ENTITIES

Nature of Bond Issues

State and political subdivisions, faced with large scale financial demands brought upon them by unprecedented population growth and the corresponding needs in their communities, often issue bonds (debt instruments) as sources of additional funds. These funds may be required to meet the demanding costs of current operation, to meet existing long-term debts, or to make possible capital improvements in housing, education, public utilities, streets, or similar areas.

These special issues, commonly referred to as municipal or revenue bonds when issued by political subdivisions, are often necessary when it is no longer possible to obtain sufficient financing through property tax, income tax, or sales tax. Most such municipality bonds are tax-exempt to holders. Historically, they have been considered as *safe*, long-term investments by those who purchase them. However, there have been occasions when municipalities have defaulted on their bond issues and have been faced with the possibility of bankruptcy, and the incidence of such default may well increase.

In any event, these municipal bonds are not surety bonds, since there is no third party who promises to be held accountable for the debt or default of those issues. Usually, there only are two parties involved: the state or municipality that offers such bond issue and promises to meet payments on principal and interest, and the investor who purchases those bonds.

Some municipal bond issues are difficult to sell, particularly those of the smaller municipalities which must compete on the open market with larger borrowers of funds. These smaller municipalities experience difficulties when they are not credit rated or carry inferior credit ratings. Certainly no investor can be expected to undertake such offerings without some extraordinary inducement, such as high interest rates.

Small *borrowers* of funds nevertheless can sometimes provide the reassurance that potential investors seek in these bond issues by purchasing what is referred to as municipal bond insurance, a special form of coverage designed specially for these types of small borrowers.

Municipal Bond Insurance

When municipal bond insurance is purchased—it is only offered by a couple of specialty companies—it guarantees payment of the borrower's principal and interest; that is, the insurer agrees to pay an investor that part of any principal or interest which a municipality is unable to pay when the debt becomes payable. In this instance, municipal bond insurance can be viewed as a form of suretyship because the insurer of that coverage is a third party that promises to be answerable for the debt or default of another.

Regardless of the arrangement used in issuing municipality bonds, borrowers must be able to show a financial ability to meet their debts when they become due and payable. Unless municipalities take special precautions to avoid problems—just as any enterprise must do if it intends to remain solvent— municipalities will find it extremely difficult to use bond issues as additional sources for obtaining funds in the future.

Chapter Notes

1. Henry Campbell Black, *Black's Law Dictionary*, 4th ed. (St. Paul: West Publishing Co., 1968), p. 1611.
2. Herbert S. Denenberg et al., *Risk and Insurance* (Englewood Cliffs, NJ: Prentice-Hall, 1974), pp. 152-53.
3. *Insurance Facts* (New York: Insurance Information Institute, 1977), p. 20.
4. G. W. Crist, Jr., *Corporate Suretyship* (New York: McGraw-Hill Book Co., 1950), pp. 4-5.
5. Ronald C. Horn, *Subrogation in Insurance Theory and Practice* (Homewood, IL: Richard D. Irwin, 1964), p. 227.
6. "Caesar was Ambitious," *United States Review*, 21 November 1959 as cited by Thomas E. Conlon, Jr., "Heads They Win—Tails We Lose," *The Annals*, Fall 1964, p. 233.
7. Luther E. Mackall, *The Principles of Surety Underwriting*, 5th ed. (Philadelphia: Chilton Co., 1940), p. 219.
8. For further information on the underwriting process in general, see J. J. Launie, J. Finley Lee, and Norman A. Baglini, *Principles of Property and Liability Underwriting* (Malvern, PA: Insurance Institute of America, 1976).
9. The Surety Association of America membership comprises both stock and mutual insurance companies which are engaged in the business of suretyship. It is the function of that organization to make classifications and manual rates; prepare bond forms, riders, and provisions; secure statistical data; make filings on behalf of its members and subscribers; and to provide a forum for the discussion of problems which may be of common interest to the members and subscribers.
10. The American Institute of Architects should not be confused with the American Insurance Association (also AIA), a trade and service organization of the property and casualty insurance industry.
11. Albert H. Walker, "Surety and the Contractor," *Inspection News*, November-December 1967, pp. 13-14.
12. Donald H. Rodimer, "Use of Bonds in Private Construction," *The Forum*, Vol. 7, No. 4, July 1972, p. 242.
13. *Contract Bonds: The Unseen Services of a Surety* (New York: The Surety Association of America, 1973), pp. 41-56.
14. Ibid., pp. 15-20.
15. Luther E. Mackall, *Surety Underwriting Manual* (Indianapolis: The Rough Notes Co., 1972), p. 103.
16. Ronald C. Horn, *Subrogation in Insurance Theory and Practice*, p. 228.
17. 53 *Am. Jur.* (2d) Sec. 1, p. 512.
18. George J. Couch, *Couch on Insurance*, 2nd ed. (Rochester, NY: The Lawyers Co-Operative Publishing Co., 1965), Vol. 13, Sec. 47:289, p. 441.
19. Frederick A. Collatz, "Claims for Equipment Use Under Public Contract

Bonds," *A.B.A. Section of Insurance, Negligence, and Compensation Law, 1969 Proceedings* (Chicago: American Bar Association), p. 60.

20. Robert Ward, "Timely Notice and Timely Suit Under the Miller Act: Current Developments," *A.B.A. Section of Insurance, Negligence, and Compensation Law, 1969 Proceedings* (Chicago: American Bar Association), p. 74.

21. John Hayes, "Suppliers to Materialmen and Others Too Remote for Coverage Under the Miller Act and State Statutory Bonds: What Is a Subcontractor?" *A.B.A. Section of Insurance, Negligence, and Compensation Law, 1969 Proceedings* (Chicago: American Bar Association), p. 31.

22. Ibid., p. 34.

23. Robert R. Hume and Roger A. Goodnaugh, "Fidelity and Surety Law," *Insurance Counsel Journal*, Vol. 40, No. 2, April 1973 (Chicago: International Association of Insurance Counsel), p. 303.

24. Richard P. McManus, "The Miller Act Performance Bond: An Additional Payment Bond," *Insurance Law Journal*, November 1968, pp. 882-83.

25. 25 *A.L.R.* 3d 383.

26. Luther E. Mackall, *The Principles of Surety Underwriting*, p. 253.

27. Donald Dickinson Jenne, *Jenne's Suretymaster* (St. Paul: Suretymaster of America), p. 38.

28. 51 *Am. Jur.* 2d, Sec. 1, p. 89.

29. George J. Couch, *Couch on Insurance*, 2nd ed., Vol. 13, Sec. 48, pp. 143-46.

30. Ibid., Sec. 48, p. 98.

31. 3 *A.L.R.* 3d, pp. 815-16.

32. Luther E. Mackall, *Surety Underwriting Manual* (Indianapolis: The Rough Notes Co., 1972), p. 58.

CHAPTER 14

Survey Cases

INTRODUCTION

Chapters 14 and 15 are the last two chapters in the CPCU curriculum dealing specifically with commercial risk management and insurance. The survey cases in these two chapters are intended to bring together and apply both the risk management process analyzed in CPCU 1 and the knowledge of commercial property and liability risk management and insurance which students have developed through a study of CPCU 3 and 4. Whereas previous chapters have been devoted primarily to individual analysis of various types of exposures and methods for treating those exposures, the survey cases will remove individual exposures from isolation.

These two chapters contain information regarding the exposures of four hypothetical firms. In each case, a description of operations is followed by a list of exposures that can be readily identified and a suggested risk management program for treating those exposures.

The examples used here involve purely hypothetical firms; any resemblance to actual firms is purely coincidental. The cases have been designed specifically for the CPCU program. However, the case studies here have several limitations common to most academic case studies. First, the information provided in describing each firm's exposures is no doubt less complete than that which would be available in a real risk management situation where insurance surveys, flow charts, physical inspections, personal interviews, additional financial statements, product brochures, and other data would provide much more complete information. Since it might take a week or more to study all the information necessary to a thorough analysis of a firm similar to those described

405

here, a summary of key information is deemed appropriate for review purposes.

It will become apparent that a number of assumptions have been made in developing illustrative risk management programs for these survey cases. It is readily acknowledged that hard fact should be substituted for assumption in real-world situations. However, the use of a few reasonable assumptions has also done a great deal to expedite the progression of these chapters and to reduce the amount of detail which otherwise would have been necessary.

Perhaps the biggest limitation in a review of this type lies in the fact that it is practical to present here only one suggested risk management program for each of the survey cases. Because of the insurance orientation of the CPCU program, emphasis here is on insurance as a primary risk management tool. It should be recognized that many different risk management programs could be developed for these firms, and that other risk management programs may be as good as or better than those illustrated here. The old adage, "There is more than one way to skin a cat," is as appropriate to risk management as it is to taxidermy.

ABC MANUFACTURING COMPANY

Description of Operations

ABC Manufacturing Company is a manufacturer of fine furniture designed to resemble the furniture used in various historical periods. The company's furniture is sold by approximately fifty dealers throughout the United States and in several foreign countries. Dealers are carefully selected by ABC to be sure they maintain the high quality image that ABC has established in its 100-year history of making fine furniture. Most dealers sell only ABC's furniture, but a few also sell noncompeting lines of similar quality. Dealers who sell only ABC's furniture are franchised to do business under ABC's trade name and would appear to the public to be branch stores rather than independent businesses.

ABC's factory is a three-story building of heavy timber (mill) construction located in a New England town of 2,500 population. The first floor is used for warehousing and office space, and the two upper floors house the production facilities. The building is seventy-five years old and has been occupied by ABC since its construction. The local fire department is above average for towns of this size, but its water supply system does not have adequate reserve capacity to maintain pressure for fighting a major fire over a period of several hours.

Adjacent to the factory building is a large frame structure used by ABC to store seasoned lumber for its furniture. Lumber is first air dried in the yard adjoining the shed, with the exact drying period depending on the kind of wood involved. The air-dried wood is then kiln dried in ABC's own kiln, after which it is stored in the frame storage building until needed. ABC's power plant is located in a brick building about fifty feet from the main plant. It furnishes heat and steam for all operations. Water for the steam boilers is drawn from a large river adjacent to the power plant. Electricity is purchased from a public utility.

Due to the length of the seasoning period, ABC usually has on the premises a supply of lumber adequate for four months of operations. Much of the lumber is purchased within a 200-mile radius of the factory, but substantial amounts are purchased from more distant sections of the United States or from foreign countries. For example, mahogany lumber, which is used in almost half of ABC's products, is imported by ABC from Latin America and Africa. Most of the lumber arrives at ABC's yard by railroad and is shipped FOB point of origin. The imported lumber is shipped by water to the nearest port, approximately 100 miles from ABC's factory, and then by train to the factory. Some locally produced lumber is delivered to ABC by truck, FOB ABC's yard.

Workers in ABC's factory use some small power tools, such as saws, planers, lathes, and similar equipment. However, the production process is primarily manual. Highly skilled craftsmen build the company's products, using many of the same techniques that were used two centuries ago. Furniture finishing is done by hand, and most of the stains, varnishes, and other finishing materials are compounded by ABC's employees according to the company's proprietary formulas. ABC's labor force is very stable because each craftsman undergoes a lengthy apprenticeship in the plant and because ABC pays wages that are relatively high by the standards of the community. Management considers the high wages to be necessary because of the time and expense required to hire and train a replacement for a craftsman who leaves the firm.

Some finished furniture is shipped by railroad, but most of it is shipped by contract carrier trucks. The contract with the trucker does not include any provision relative to liability for damage to goods in transit. Export shipments are transported by truck to the nearest port and by water to the country of destination. All shipments are made FOB purchaser's warehouse.

All sales, including export sales, are made on open account and only to ABC's established dealers. Export accounts usually are denominated in and payable in the currency of the importer's country. Accounts receivable, on the average, are equal to about one-eighth of annual sales. Accounts receivable records are kept on ABC's computer in the office section of the first floor of the factory building. The computer is also used for inventory and production control, payroll management, and other accounting functions. The computer equipment is owned by ABC. The office is cut off from the warehouse section of the first floor by a wood partition, and the computer room is cut off from the balance of the office by a similar partition. The office and computer room are air conditioned, but the remainder of the building is not. Duplicate computer tapes, updated weekly, are stored in a well-protected vault in another part of the city. A monthly fee is paid for the tape storage.

ABC owns several small trucks that are used to move lumber about its own premises and for local pickup and delivery. The trucks are kept in the lumber storage shed when they are not in use. Several lift trucks are used for moving lumber and other heavy items in and around the factory and lumber storage area.

A freight elevator moves materials, finished furniture, lift trucks, and other equipment between floors in the factory. Automatic grillwork gates have been installed to prevent workers from falling into the elevator shaft. There is no passenger elevator. Workers use either the freight elevator or the open stairwells when moving between floors. Steel fire escapes have been installed on the exterior of the building to facilitate evacuation of the upper floors in case of fire or other catastrophe.

ABC Manufacturing Company is wholly owned by its president, Mr. Carpenter, who is the grandson of the company's founder. Mr. Carpenter is considered wealthy by local standards. However, his fortune consists almost entirely of the stock of ABC Manufacturing Company, and he is dependent on his salary and company dividends for his livelihood. Nearly all of ABC's operating profit has been paid in dividends in recent years. Consequently, the company has only a modest cushion of liquid assets in excess of its operating needs. Profits have been consistent, but they have been relatively low because of the inefficiency of the present factory facilities. Although the dollar amount of ABC's sales has increased steadily because of price increases, the physical volume of sales has remained almost constant over the past several years. The lack of growth has resulted primarily from two factors. First, the present plant cannot accommodate greater production because of space limitations, and there is no available land adjacent to the plant to permit expansion. Second, the long training period required for new employees prevents rapid expansion of production. Mr. Carpenter has considered building a new factory at another location in the same town. However, such a move is not financially feasible unless the present plant can be sold, and no prospective purchasers have been

Table 14-1

ABC Company Building Values

Building	Actual Cash Value	Replacement Cost
Factory	$1,500,000	$2,500,000
Lumber shed	150,000	200,000
Power plant	230,000	300,000
Kiln	270,000	320,000

found. A move to any location outside its present hometown would not be practical because of the company's dependence on its well-trained craftsmen. The sales manager estimates that both the dealer network and sales could be increased by 30 percent over the next five years if production facilities could be provided.

The cost to rebuild the present factory building in its present form would be $2.5 million. However, Mr. Carpenter has indicated that he would not build a new mill-type building to replace the current structure because of the high cost of the thick brick walls and heavy timber interior construction. A new, one-story, noncombustible masonry and steel building of comparable floor area would cost approximately $2 million to build and would be more efficient for ABC's purpose. The actual cash value of the present factory building is estimated to be $1.5 million, and ABC has insured it for that amount against fire and the extended coverage perils. The lumber storage shed, power plant, table and lumber kiln are also insured for their actual cash values. Table 14-1 shows the actual cash value and replacement cost for each of the structures.

ABC's annual premium for fire and extended coverage insurance is $136,000, including the coverage for contents of the buildings and for lumber stored in the yard. There have been no fire or extended coverage losses during the past five years and only minor losses prior to that time. The company's estimated annual workers' compensation premium is $165,000. Loss experience has been fairly consistent from year to year. Based on past experience, with adjustments for inflation and current benefit levels, normal losses of $104,000 can be expected.

The most frequent claims have been small and have resulted from such minor injuries as splinters in hands, several minor dermatitis cases, and sawdust or metal particles in the eyes. The more serious injuries have included back strains and loss of fingers in power saws and other power tools. ABC now has a 15 percent debit under the workers' compensation experience rating plan. (That is, they are paying a rate 15 percent greater than manual rates.)

Identification of Loss Exposures

The direct property loss exposures to which ABC is subject are:

1. loss or damage to buildings and contents by fire, the extended coverage perils, steam boiler explosion, flood, and other perils;
2. loss or damage to lumber stored in the open from perils listed in 1;
3. loss or damage to motor vehicles by fire, theft, collision or other perils;
4. loss or damage to goods in transit from many perils;
5. loss of money or other property due to criminal acts of employees or others;
6. credit losses due to insolvency of open account customers; and
7. foreign exchange losses resulting from devaluation or blocking of foreign currencies.

Indirect property loss exposures to which ABC is subject are:

1. loss of earnings because of interruption of production following damage to property by various perils;
2. inability to collect accounts receivable because of destruction of accounts receivable records;
3. loss of use of vehicles following loss or damage to them;
4. loss of profits on finished goods resulting from loss or damage to such goods; and
5. cost to reconstruct data stored on destroyed data processing media.

Liability exposures to which ABC is subject are:

1. liability for injuries to workers arising out of and in the course of their employment;
2. liability to others arising from:
   a. ownership, maintenance, or use of motor vehicles, including nonowned vehicles;
   b. ownership, maintenance, or use of the premises, and operations at the premises;
   c. defective products; and
   d. vicarious liability for actions of dealers.

Suggested Risk Management Program

The low profit level of the company, Mr. Carpenter's dependence on company dividends, and the relatively small cushion of liquid assets all indicate that ABC probably cannot afford to retain any major loss exposures. Consequently, the risk management program outlined below will stress insurance and loss control, rather than retention.

1. The buildings, their contents, and lumber stored in the open should be insured at least against fire and the extended coverage perils. The cost of broader coverage should be carefully weighed against the probabilities of loss, particularly for the finished goods, which are susceptible to various types of damage. Finished goods should be insured for their selling price to protect ABC against loss of profits on such goods. The main factory building should be insured on an agreed amount basis, since ABC's maximum potential loss is greater than the actual cash value but less than replacement cost. The other buildings should be insured for replacement cost to avoid any uninsured loss caused by depreciation. From the information given, there is nothing that would indicate drastic fluctuations in value and suggest the use of a reporting form or a peak season endorsement. However, because of the way materials move around from one spot to another on ABC's premises, blanket insurance on contents would seem desirable.

   Serious consideration should be given to several loss control measures relative to the buildings and contents. First, the elevator shaft and stairwells should be enclosed in a manner consistent with the internal construction of the building in order to delay the vertical spread of fire between floors. Consideration should also be given to installing an automatic sprinkler system in the factory building. In view of the deficiency in the town's water system, it would probably also be necessary to install a storage tank to provide adequate water pressure for the sprinkler system. Of course, the cost of such a system would need to be weighed against its benefits. The relatively high cost of fire insurance for ABC indicates a probability that a sprinkler system would be economically feasible, but tax and financial considerations also need to be evaluated, particularly in light of the age and obsolescence of the building. It appears that finishing materials are manufactured and stored in the factory building. Since the solvents used in varnishes and stains typically create a fire hazard, the manufacturing and storage of such materials should be moved out of the main building, preferably to a separate small building. Likewise, wood stored in the open yard should be separated from buildings by as much open space as possible, to reduce the probable maximum loss in any fire.

2. Because of the proximity of the river, flood coverage should be obtained for buildings, contents, and lumber stored in the open, either under a difference-in-conditions policy or under the federal flood insurance program.

3. Boiler coverage should be purchased on a replacement cost basis for the steam boilers in the power plant and on steam pipes in all of the buildings, since the extended coverage endorsement specifically excludes loss from explosion of steam boilers and steam pipes. The boiler policy would cover such explosions (as well as other property losses caused by an accident) as defined in the policy. No details are given as to the size of the compressor in the air conditioning system, but it seems likely that the potential loss from that source could be retained by ABC. Together with the insurance coverage, the insurer will also provide valuable inspection and loss control services.

4. The computer equipment is covered under the contents fire and extended coverage policy. However, it may be desirable to insure it separately under a special electronic data processing policy because of the broader, "all-risks" coverage provided by such policies. Data processing media can also be insured under the data processing policy.

5. The company's owned trucks are small, so it seems likely that ABC can retain the collision exposure on them, or at least partially retain the losses through relatively large deductibles. Comprehensive coverage—or at least fire and combined additional coverage—should be obtained because of the possibility of several trucks being destroyed in a fire, windstorm, or flood which would also damage other property. The lift trucks would be covered under the previously described contents policy. However, broader coverage, including coverage against the peril of collision, could be purchased under an inland marine floater.

6. Two policies would be necessary to insure against loss to goods in transit. Shipments by rail or truck can be insured under an inland marine transit policy, either on a named-perils or "all-risks" basis. The policy should cover at least collision or upset of a conveyance, fire, theft, wind, and flood.

   Shipments by sea should be covered under an ocean marine open cargo policy. It can be written either "all-risks" or for the more common named perils of fire and the perils of the sea. The warehouse-to-warehouse clause should be included, since ABC ships FOB destination.

ABC should try to renegotiate its contract with the contract trucker to include a provision imposing liability upon the trucker for damage to goods in transit. Such a provision should reduce ABC's transit insurance costs. In the absence of such a provision, the carrier is liable only if the damage results from its negligence.

7. ABC's potential losses from criminal acts of employees can be insured under a blanket fidelity bond, either the commercial blanket bond or the blanket position bond. Other potential crime loss exposures appear to be small enough for ABC to retain.

8. Loss due to insolvency of U.S. open account debtors can be insured under credit insurance contracts available from several insurers. Loss due to insolvency of debtors in other countries can be insured under an export credit insurance contract available from the Foreign Credit Insurance Association. The latter contract would also cover losses resulting from devaluation of foreign currencies or adoption of rules by foreign countries prohibiting their citizens from paying ABC's accounts.

9. ABC's loss of earnings exposure should be insured under a gross earnings business interruption policy. Perils insured should include at least fire and the extended coverage perils. Flood should be included, if possible. Because of the company's dependence on its staff of craftsmen, no payroll exclusion would seem appropriate. The policy should be written blanket over the factory, power plant, lumber storage shed, lumber drying kiln, and lumber stored in the open yard. It would seem that a fire in any one of those areas could cause an interruption throughout the company's operations. The amount of insurance needed and the optimal coinsurance percentage cannot be determined from the facts given. However, factors to be considered in arriving at them are (1) the time required to rebuild and re-equip the factory, power plant, and kiln, (2) the time required to obtain, season, and dry a new supply of lumber, and (3) the seasonal variation, if any, in ABC's business. Off-premises power interruption coverage may also be needed in view of ABC's dependence on a public utility for electricity.

Business interruption coverage also should be purchased under ABC's boiler and machinery policy.

10. It seems likely that ABC could retain the exposure of the inability to collect accounts receivable following destruction of records. There are only about fifty customers involved, so reconstruction of accounts receivable records should be rela-

tively simple, especially since duplicate computer tapes are stored at a separate location and updated weekly.

11. The exposure arising out of loss of use of damaged vehicles also seems small enough to be retained by ABC.

12. Loss of profits on finished goods can be insured by endorsing the contents policy to cover such goods for their selling price rather than for actual cash value. (This coverage is necessary because the business interruption form for manufacturers covers only loss of production and not loss of sales.) Goods should then be valued at their selling price when the value of contents is determined for the purchase of insurance.

13. The cost of reconstructing data on computer tapes would seem to be relatively small, since duplicate tapes are stored at a separate location and are updated weekly. It seems likely that this loss exposure can be retained by ABC.

14. ABC's exposure to liability for injury to employees should be insured under a workers' compensation and employers' liability policy. The premium size and concentration of employees at one location would ordinarily enable ABC to give serious consideration to retaining this exposure (with some excess coverage for catastrophic loss). However, the company's need for stable profit, and therefore stable expenses, would seem to favor the guaranteed cost of insurance under present financial circumstances.

    The several eye injury and dermatitis cases indicate that ABC may not have an active or successful loss control program. The fact that ABC's workers' compensation premium is subject to a 15 percent experience debit tends to confirm this. A loss control program, including emphasis on both accident prevention and industrial hygiene, should be instituted and should receive rigorous support from Mr. Carpenter and other top management personnel. ABC probably is not large enough to justify a full-time loss control engineer, but the loss control program should be a major responsibility of some management person with the interest and the expertise to administer it.

15. Most of ABC's liability exposures can be adequately insured under a comprehensive general automobile liability policy (or a CGL and business auto policy). This should be written to cover the company's liability for (1) the ownership, maintenance, or use of owned, nonowned, or hired motor vehicles, (2) premises and operations, and (3) defective products. It would probably be advantageous to purchase the broad form CGL endorsement which, in addition to personal injury coverage, extends the comprehensive general liability coverage to include contractual

liability, medical payments, host liquor liability, fire legal liability, broad form property damage, incidental malpractice, nonowned watercraft, and other coverage extensions.

Because vendors appear to the public to be branch stores, there is a possibility that ABC will incur a claim because of the acts of one of its dealers. This vicarious liability exposure would be covered by the CGL policy, but the liabilities of ABC and its franchisees should be spelled out in the franchise agreement. Any liability of vendors assumed by contract should be covered with contractual liability insurance. ABC's CGL policy could also be endorsed to provide vendors' liability protection for the products exposure if the circumstances make this desirable.

A commercial umbrella liability policy may be needed to obtain adequate liability limits. An umbrella would also cover some exposures that are not usually covered under primary liability policies, but ABC does not seem to be especially subject to any of those unusual exposures.

Given the river location, the use of river water in the boiler, and the use of solvents in the manufacturing process, there is a chance that ABC could be held responsible for pollution of the river or of the air. The CGL would protect against sudden and accidental pollution losses. Loss control measures should be taken to prevent any other pollution occurrence.

BITE-O-BURGER COMPANY

Description of Operations

The Bite-O-Burger Company is a publicly held corporation. It owns and operates 843 fast-food restaurants located in eleven states. The restaurants feature a limited menu consisting of hamburgers, french fried potatoes, fried chicken, chili, related food items, and nonalcoholic beverages. The restaurants vary in size, but each is located in a free-standing building and surrounded by customer parking areas. All of the buildings were built to Bite-O-Burger's plans and specifications and share enough architectural characteristics to make them easily recognized as units of the chain. All have forced air heat and are air conditioned.

At current prices, the average replacement cost of the restaurants is estimated at $125,000 per unit for the building and $100,000 for the equipment. Because of differences in size, the replacement cost, including building and equipment, ranges from $175,000 for the smallest restaurant to $300,000 for the largest. The average actual cash value is $205,000 for building and equipment combined. The restaurants vary in age from a few days to approximately twenty years. All of them are owned by Bite-O-Burger, but the newer ones are subject to substantial mortgages.

The home office of the company is located in leased space in a building in the business district of a midwestern city. Bite-O-Burger occupies the upper three floors of the thirty-story building. The company's data processing center is located on the top floor. All of the computer equipment is leased from the manufacturer.

Bite-O-Burger also occupies a leased warehouse near the home office. It is used for storage and distribution of supplies (paper cups, wrapping materials, etc.) and nonperishable food items. Perishable food items are purchased from local suppliers near the restaurants in which they will be used, and they are delivered directly to the restaurants by the suppliers. There is no refrigeration equipment at the warehouse, but each restaurant has a large, walk-in refrigerator. Items from the company warehouse are distributed to the individual restaurants by a fleet of thirty owned tractor-trailer units. The same units also transport goods from the suppliers to the central warehouse when truck-load quantities are purchased. Smaller lots are shipped by common carrier FOB point of shipment.

The values of the contents at the warehouse and home office are $15,750,000 and $3,200,000, respectively. Values at both locations are relatively constant throughout the year.

Bite-O-Burger advertises extensively in newspapers in the cities in which it has several restaurants. Many of its advertisements feature endorsements of its products by prominent athletes and theater personalities. Some advertisements feature pictures of local people and their favorable comments on the company's food and service. The company also sponsors softball and bowling teams in some cities as a part of its public relations program.

Bite-O-Burger's profit and loss statement and an abbreviated balance sheet for last year are shown in Figures 14-1 and 14-2. The company's operating results for last year were typical of past years, but sales and assets have been growing at a rate of approximately 20 percent per year.

Bite-O-Burger's fire and extended coverage losses for the past five years are shown in Table 14-2.

The quotations shown in Table 14-3 have been obtained for fire and extended coverage protection—blanket on buildings and contents on an actual cash value basis. Bite-O-Burger is well aware of the fire exposures associated with restaurants. Extensive fire control equipment

Figure 14-1

Bite-O-Burger Company Profit and Loss Statement

Profit and Loss Statement		
Sales		$345,630,000
Cost of materials and supplies	$102,049,359	
Wages and salaries		
Officers and key employees	$ 13,306,755	
Other employees	107,663,740	120,970,495
Utilities		8,641,258
Maintenance and repairs		9,506,873
Taxes (other than income taxes)		6,920,101
Insurance		4,320,376
Advertising		14,368,897
Depreciation		10,176,438
Miscellaneous		3,974,744
		280,928,541
Net profit before taxes		$ 64,701,459
Income taxes		38,458,674
Net profit after taxes		$ 26,242,785

has been installed in the kitchens of all units, and especially in the range hoods and in the cooking areas.

Identification of Loss Exposures

The direct property loss exposures to which Bite-O-Burger is subject are:

1. damage by fire, wind, or other perils to the buildings and contents at the restaurants and to the contents at the home office and warehouse;
2. loss of money or other property by criminal acts of employees or others;
3. loss caused by mechanical breakdown of refrigeration or air conditioning equipment at the restaurants;
4. physical damage to owned motor vehicles by fire, collision, or other peril;
5. loss or damage by various perils to goods in transit either by company truck or by common carrier.

Indirect property loss exposures to which Bite-O-Burger is subject are:

Figure 14-2
Bite-O-Burger Company Balance Sheet

Balance Sheet

Assets

Cash	$12,357,821
Inventory†	10,879,643
Buildings†	73,730,466
Land	39,269,469
Furniture, fixtures and equipment†	54,757,469
Motor vehicles†	896,010
Miscellaneous assets	412,210
Total assets	$192,303,088

Liabilities

Accounts payable	$20,269,847	
Short-term bank loans	21,764,169	
Salaries and wages payable	2,419,410	
Mortgages on real estate	66,327,883	
Miscellaneous liabilities	831,779	
Total liabilities		$111,613,088

Capital and Surplus

Common stock	$20,000,000	
8% preferred stock	30,000,000	
Paid-in surplus	10,000,000	
Earned surplus	20,630,000	
Total capital and surplus		$ 80,690,000
Total liabilities, capital, and surplus		$192,303,088

†After deduction for depreciation.

Table 14-2

Bite-O-Burger Company Fire and Extended Coverage Loss History

Year	Number of Losses	Total Amount	Largest Loss
1 (most recent)	20	$ 17,860	$ 8,843
2	15	11,760	6,981
3	17	256,549	247,317
4	12	9,336	2,178
5	11	18,393	11,423
		$313,898	$276,742

Table 14-3

Bite-O-Burger Company Fire and Extended
Coverage Insurance Quotations

Deductible Amount	Annual Premium
$100 per occurrence	$769,000
$5,000 per occurrence	630,500
$10,000 per occurrence	545,900
$25,000 per occurrence	439,330
$100,000 per occurrence	357,600
$100,000 annual aggregate	461,000
$250,000 annual aggregate	243,000

1. loss of earnings following physical damage to restaurants;
2. extra expenses incurred to maintain normal operations following physical damage to the home office or warehouse;
3. cost to reconstruct the data stored on data processing media if the media are destroyed;
4. extra expenses to provide data processing services following damage to or breakdown of the leased computers.

The liability exposures to which Bite-O-Burger is subject are:

1. liability for bodily injuries to persons or damage to the property of others arising from the ownership or use of premises, defective products, construction of new buildings, ownership or operation of motor vehicles, sponsorship of athletic teams, or other causes;

2. liability for defamation, false arrest, false imprisonment, or other nonbodily injuries, including advertiser's liability;
3. liability for injuries to employees in the course of their employment, either under common law or under workers' compensation;
4. possible bailee liability for damage to leased data processing equipment, depending on the terms of the lease contract;
5. possible liability for damage to the leased office or warehouse, depending on the terms of the leases;
6. liability to stockholders or others for negligent errors or omissions by directors or officers in the discharge of their duties.

Suggested Risk Management Program

One suggested risk management program for Bite-O-Burger is outlined in the following paragraphs. Other programs could be designed, depending upon the attitude of management toward the financial uncertainty resulting from loss exposures.

Bite-O-Burger is in an unusual situation with respect to the exposure to loss of buildings and contents. It has 843 restaurants. Any one of them constitutes a small part of the total value, and they are widely spread geographically. Consequently, there is only an extremely low probability of a catastrophe loss involving more than one of the restaurants. In view of the relatively high cost of property insurance, Bite-O-Burger probably should retain the exposure to the property damage of restaurant buildings and contents. A funded retention program for losses could be established over time by setting aside all or a part of the funds that would otherwise be used as premiums for commercial insurance. However, it will probably be just as satisfactory to absorb such property losses as normal operating expenses since the maximum likely loss in any one year would be only a small percentage of the company's current assets or annual profits. (This recommendation assumes that the mortgage agreements do not require Bite-O-Burger to carry insurance.)

Insurance should be carried on the contents of the home office and warehouse because the amount subject to loss at those locations exceeds the amount of loss Bite-O-Burger can comfortably bear. Perils insured against should include at least fire and the extended coverage perils, and "all-risks" coverage may be considered if the additional cost is proportional to the exposure. A substantial deductible would be desirable if available rate credits are adequate to compensate for the additional exposure.

Most of the crime exposures could also be retained by Bite-O-

Burger. The one exception is the employee dishonesty exposure, from which very large losses could arise. The employee dishonesty exposure should be insured under a commercial blanket bond covering all employees and combined with excess coverage on key employees who are in a position to cause substantial dishonesty losses. Examples of the latter would include restaurant managers, the treasurer, and other persons who handle or control substantial amounts of money or property. Alternatively, a position schedule bond could be purchased for employees in this latter group and the exposure from other employees could be retained.

The potential direct loss from breakdown of air conditioning and refrigeration equipment at the restaurants is sufficiently small for Bite-O-Burger to bear as a normal operating expense. It appears that such losses at the warehouse and home office would be borne by the landlord.

No values are given for the tractor-trailer units, but it appears that even a total loss to a single unit would be within the amount that Bite-O-Burger could afford to bear. If several of the units are parked in the same building or the same storage lot at night, fire and combined additional coverage insurance may be desirable because of the wind-storm and vandalism exposures.

No values are given for goods in transit. However, if values of individual shipments are substantial, transit coverage should be purchased. This coverage is especially desirable for goods shipped on owned vehicles because damage to goods will probably be accompanied by damage to the carrying vehicle, and retention of the vehicle damage losses has already been suggested. If large values are not involved, the transit exposure might be retained. In view of the large number of locations and the relatively small contribution of each to the total company profit, the business interruption exposure at the restaurants should be retained by Bite-O-Burger. Most of the employees at the restaurants are unskilled and easily replaceable, and many of them probably are part-time employees. The small number of key employees results in a minimum of necessarily continuing expenses and, consequently, a relatively low business interruption exposure. In addition, it appears the restaurants could be quickly reconstructed following any loss, particularly since Bite-O-Burger has the architectural plans.

It appears that Bite-O-Burger might need to incur substantial extra expenses to continue normal operations after severe damage to the warehouse or home office. Extra expense coverage should be purchased in an amount adequate to cover this exposure. The perils insured against should include at least fire and the extended coverage perils. "All-risks" coverage should probably be purchased if the cost is commensurate with the exposure.

The cost of reconstructing data stored on data processing media may be substantial. Bite-O-Burger can reduce the potential loss substantially by keeping duplicate tapes at a separate location (such as the warehouse) and by updating the duplicates at frequent intervals. If the remaining exposure is still large, insurance should be purchased, especially since damage to media will frequently be accompanied by damage to other property. The exposure can be insured on an "all-risks" basis under a special electronic data processing (EDP) policy or under a valuable papers policy. The contents fire policy would pay for the cost of new blank materials but not for the cost of transcribing or reconstructing data.

The exposure to extra expenses for data processing following breakdown of or damage to Bite-O-Burger's computer may be handled most effectively by arranging a reciprocal agreement with a nearby user of similar computer equipment. Under such an agreement, each participant would make its equipment available to the other in emergencies, usually without charge. If such an agreement cannot be arranged, "all-risks" extra expense coverage is available under special EDP policies.

Most of Bite-O-Burger's liability exposures can and should be insured under a comprehensive general automobile liability (CGAL) policy. It would include premises and operations liability, products liability, liability arising from the operations of independent contractors involved in construction of restaurants, and liability arising from the ownership or use of motor vehicles, including the use of nonowned vehicles. Blanket contractual coverage and personal injury liability converage should be added. Advertisers' liability coverage is also needed. These additional coverages may be obtained with the broad form CGL endorsement.

Bite-O-Burger's liability for damage to leased computer equipment and leased premises could best be handled by amending the leases to eliminate such liability. However, the lessors may not be willing to accept such an amendment. Another approach would be to buy an inland marine bailee liability policy on the computer equipment and fire legal liability coverage for the leased premises, under the CGAL, the broad form CGL endorsement, or as a separate fire and allied lines policy.

Liability for injuries to employees should be insured under a workers' compensation insurance policy. It may be possible for Bite-O-Burger to qualify as a "self-insurer" under the various state laws involved, and thus to retain this exposure in most states, but it is doubtful whether retention would be economical because of the geographical spread of employees. The dispersion of employees would result in complexity in the handling of claims and in considerable expense in meeting state requirements to qualify as a "self-insurer."

The exposure to liability for errors of officers and directors can be insured under a directors' and officers' liability policy. It can cover the liability of (1) the company, (2) the directors and officers, or (3) both.

CHAPTER 15

Survey Cases, Continued

EARTHMOVERS INCORPORATED

Description of Operations

Earthmovers Incorporated is a general contracting company primarily engaged in building and paving roads. The company's home office is located in the southeast United States, and it operates in its home state and approximately ten nearby states, as jobs are available. Its main office and supply area are near a river where materials can be unloaded from barges docked at two wooden piers owned by the company. The two piers have a total actual cash value of $150,000. The materials consist primarily of sand, gravel, and asphalt. The sand and gravel are stored in piles on an open lot, and the asphalt is stored in bins. Floods have occurred in the area every thirty or forty years, but Earthmovers did not suffer any loss in the one flood that occurred after it moved to its present location.

The main location includes three structures. These structures are (1) the main office, which houses the corporate officers and their support staff; (2) a garage and paint shop; and (3) the firm's computer facility. The three buildings have a total actual cash value of $1 million and an estimated replacement cost of $1.5 million.

The main office contains most of the firm's records, some furniture, and office equipment worth $150,000, including a valuable oil painting worth $100,000. The office is also the collection point for all revenue. However, no more than $5,000 cash is on hand at any one time. All payroll is paid by check as are all other major expenditures. The office structure is quite old and, while it has been remodeled, it does not meet

425

present building code standards. A city ordinance requires damaged structures to be demolished and rebuilt according to the current code if loss is greater than 50 percent. Except for the reconstruction of the firm's records and engineering papers, the main office activities could be immediately moved and made operational within a day or two at one of several nearby locations if loss occurred. However, management expects to rebuild at the present location if such a loss occurs. Company officers estimate that sixty days' time and expenditures of approximately $100,000 would be required to reconstruct company records.

The garage and paint shop is used for equipment repair and maintenance. If it should be destroyed, it could be rebuilt in six months. The firm could operate without it in the meantime, but cost would increase since outside firms would have to be used to make repairs and to perform maintenance on the firm's automobiles and mobile equipment. The additional expense for the six-month period is estimated at $80,000. There is $160,000 worth of personal property in the shop.

All the firm's accounts receivable and payroll records are maintained at the computer facility, as are its inventory records. Over $1 million of owned computer hardware is also located there. Because the data processing operations of the company do not utilize all of the computer time available, the firm does the data processing work for several business concerns in its locality. This outside work produces $100,000 in revenue each year. The cost to reproduce the data stored on computer media is estimated at $175,000 for Earthmovers' own records and $50,000 for the other firms for which Earthmovers provides data processing services.

In addition to the three buildings at the main location, the firm also has several large fuel tanks for storage of solvents—including kerosene, naphtha and gasoline—and for fuel and diesel oils. In January the value of the tanks and fuel is at a low of $150,000, and a high value of $800,000 is reached in May.

Besides the property at the main office, the firm owns a lake cottage used to entertain customers. It is valued at $50,000 and contains $5,000 worth of contents. Employees often leave some of their personal property at the cottage, as do guests of the firm. The firm also owns a 140 horsepower inboard-outboard motorboat that is kept at the lake cottage site. The boat is valued at $10,000.

Since Earthmovers is in the contracting business, it has a large amount of automotive equipment. It has approximately 300 cars and trucks with a total value of $1.5 million, the maximum value of any one vehicle being $60,000. Besides this automobile exposure, the firm has $4 million of mobile equipment that is used to pave and build roads including a portable hot mix plant valued at $400,000 and an excavator valued at $500,000. Most of the cars, trucks, and construction equipment are located at job sites during the prime construction season. An open lot adjacent to the main office is used for storage of equipment not currently needed on jobs. Supplies and materials valued at approximately $500,000 are located at the various work sites at any one time during the prime construction season. These values are considerably less in the winter.

In its dealing with other firms, Earthmovers sometimes enters into hold harmless agreements under which it agrees to indemnify governmental bodies or other contractors for property damage or bodily injury liability arising from construction operations. Also, during peak periods the firm leases additional equipment and storage space. The storage space is usually near a major construction site and not at the home office. A company-owned airplane is used by company executives to travel to bid openings and job sites and to rush equipment repair parts and mechanics to job sites. The airplane is valued at $87,000. The firm often uses subcontractors to perform specialty work at a job site.

Earthmovers has shown steady growth of about 5 percent per year in the recent past. A satisfactory profit has been earned in most years. However, a very large loss was sustained last year because of severe cost overruns on a large job that Earthmovers had undertaken on a fixed-price basis. The surety company refused to continue to provide contract bonds for the firm unless the six stockholders put additional funds into the company. The stockholders were able to provide the required capital, but the additional investment imposed some hardship on three of the stockholders.

Identification of Exposures

The direct property loss exposures to which Earthmovers is subject are:

1. loss or damage by fire, wind, flood, or other perils to the buildings and contents at the home office location;
2. loss or damage by fire, wind, flood, or other perils to the asphalt storage bins and asphalt stored therein, and to tanks and their contents;
3. loss or damage to materials stored in the open;
4. loss or damage to piers by vessel collision, fire, flood, or other perils;
5. loss or damage by various perils to the lake cottage and its contents;
6. loss or damage to the motorboat by various perils;

7. loss or damage to automotive equipment by collision, fire, theft, flood, or other perils;
8. loss or damage to construction equipment by various perils;
9. loss or damage to supplies and materials stored at job sites;
10. loss or damage to airplanes by various perils either in flight or on the ground; and
11. loss or damage to money or other property by criminal acts of employees or others.

The indirect or consequential loss exposures to which Earthmovers is subject are:

1. extra expenses incurred to maintain normal operations following a loss to buildings, contents, or materials at the home office location;
2. extra expenses incurred to provide data processing services following damage to computer equipment;
3. loss of income from data processing services to others following damage to the computer system;
4. extra expense of bringing materials to home office location following damage to or destruction of piers;
5. loss from inability to collect accounts receivable or expenses to reconstruct accounts receivable records resulting from destruction of the records;
6. expenses to reconstruct engineering records and data stored on computer media following the destruction of such records or media;
7. extra expenses to rent automotive or construction equipment following damage to or destruction of owned equipment; and
8. extra expense incurred for the rush transportation of officers, mechanics, and repair parts following damage to or destruction of the company airplane.

The liability loss exposures to which Earthmovers is subject are:

1. liability, either at common law or under workers' compensation acts, for injuries to employees arising out of and in the course of their employment;
2. liability for bodily injuries to others or damage to property arising from the ownership, maintenance, or use of the home office location or other premises, or from construction operations or other operations necessary or incidental to the company's business;
3. liability for bodily injury and property damage arising from defective or hazardous conditions in jobs completed by the company;

4. bodily injury and property damage liability assumed by Earthmovers under contract;
5. liability for bodily injury and property damage arising from the operations of independent contractors employed by Earthmovers;
6. liability for libel, slander, false arrest, false imprisonment, invasion of privacy, and similar injuries;
7. liability for errors and omissions in performing data processing services for other firms;
8. liability for bodily injury and property damage arising from the ownership, maintenance, or use of owned or nonowned automotive equipment;
9. liability for damage to automotive or construction equipment rented by or leased to Earthmovers;
10. liability for bodily injury and property damage arising from the ownership, maintenance, or use of the boat; and
11. liability for bodily injury and property damage arising from the ownership, maintenance, of use of the airplane.

In addition to the aforementioned exposures, the ability to obtain contract bonds is essential to remaining in the contracting business; if for any reason Earthmovers is unable to obtain bonds, it could be forced out of business.

Suggested Risk Management Program

Because of the recent financial reverses of the company and the fact that at least some of the stockholders are apparently dependent on the company for their livelihood, it does not appear that Earthmovers is in a position to absorb large fortuitous losses if insurance is available at reasonable costs to cover the exposures. In addition, since the ability to supply surety bonds is essential in Earthmovers' business, it is important that they regain a financial position in which sureties will not question their capital when underwriting a contract bond. Sureties are better satisfied with a contractor's capacity when it is evident that all significant loss exposures have been treated with insurance. Consequently, the risk management program suggested below stresses insurance and loss control and provides for loss retention only through modest deductibles or for those exposures for which insurance is not likely to be available.

The property risk management program recommended for Earthmovers is as follows:

1. The buildings and their contents at the home office location and the lake cottage building should be insured for replacement cost against at least fire and the extended coverage perils. Since the home office building does not comply with current building codes, the fire insurance policy should be endorsed to cover [1] the possible increase in the loss resulting from the building code requirement that a severely damaged building be torn down, [2] the cost of demolishing that part of the building not destroyed by an insured peril, and [3] the increased cost of building a new building to comply with current building codes. Insurance against flood should be purchased if it can obtained at a reasonable cost either under the federal flood insurance program or under a difference in conditions policy. A relatively modest deductible, perhaps $5,000 or less per occurrence, should be provided under the foregoing policies if available at commensurate premium reductions.

2. Collision insurance should be provided only for the more expensive automotive units, perhaps those with an actual cash value of $5,000 or more. Coverage for fire, wind, theft, and flood should be provided on all vehicles because a substantial number of them may be stored on the open lot adjacent to the home office or at a job site, creating the possibility of damage to more than one vehicle in a single occurrence. Comprehensive coverage will provide protection against all of the foregoing perils. A deductible of $500 per loss could apply to collision coverage, but perhaps a smaller deductible should apply to the other physical damage perils because of the possibility that one occurrence may damage several vehicles.

3. Coverage for physical damage to construction equipment can be provided under a contractors' equipment floater—an inland marine policy. The policy may be written either on a named peril or "all-risks" basis, but it should cover at least the perils of fire, wind, flood, collapse of bridges and culverts, theft, and collision or overturning of conveyances on which the equipment is being transported. The deductible under this contract should be modest, perhaps $250 or $500 per loss, because of the possibility of damage arising from a single occurrence, such as damage to several pieces of equipment and perhaps to other property as well.

4. The piers should be insured against at least the perils of fire, wind, and, if possible, flood. Additional perils coverage should be considered if the cost is reasonable. Only a small deductible should be provided because of the likelihood of other damage

concurrent with damage to the piers, especially from wind or flood.

5. The valuable painting would be covered under the contents policy. However, an inland marine fine arts floater is more desirable for two reasons. First, it provides "all-risks" coverage, which is more appropriate for fine arts items. Second, coverage under the fine arts floater is on a valued basis, thus eliminating disagreements over value at the time of loss.

6. Crime loss to the valuable painting would be covered under the fine arts floater recommended above. Theft coverage for automotive and mobile equipment has already been recommended. Earthmovers' other crime exposures, except for employee dishonesty losses, are small enough to be retained without insurance. Management should review the practice of keeping $5,000 in cash on hand to see if that amount exceeds the company's needs. It seems rather large for petty cash needs. A safe, and other appropriate security measures, should be used to safeguard money. The employee dishonesty exposure should be insured under a commercial blanket bond. The bond should provide coverage for all employees and excess coverage for employees who have ready access to money or other valuable property or to employees who control purchases or contracts. The amounts of excess coverage would vary by position, and additional information would be necessary to determine amounts of bonds to suggest.

7. Physical damage coverage on the motorboat can be provided under a yacht policy—an ocean marine policy—since the motor size indicates that it is a relatively large boat.

8. Physical damage coverage on the airplane should be for "all-risks" and should cover the airplane while in flight and on the ground.

9. Insurance coverage on the construction materials presents something of a problem. The asphalt and storage bins probably can be insured against the usual fire, extended coverage (and possibly flood) perils. The sand and gravel are not subject to loss by most perils, but they might be carried away by flood waters. It is doubtful that insurance for such loss can be obtained, so Earthmovers may have to retain the exposure. Perhaps dikes could be constructed to prevent or minimize loss. Construction materials at the job site are vulnerable to small theft losses. This exposure could be retained.

10. The computer equipment would be covered under the contents coverage. However, it is usually more desirable to specifically insure such equipment on an "all-risks" basis under a data

processing policy designed for that purpose. If the computer equipment is now on the ground floor, Earthmovers should consider moving it to a higher floor, if possible, or provide some other protection against flood damage.

The suggested risk management program for indirect loss exposures is as follows:

1. Extra expense insurance for fire, the extended coverage perils, and flood, if possible, should be purchased to cover the additional expenses necessary to maintain normal operations following damage to the home office building, repair shop, or computer building. More information would be needed to determine the amount of coverage needed and the maximum percentages to be payable for various time periods. No substantial deductible should be provided in this policy, since loss under it would be concurrent with direct loss. A deductible for direct loss was suggested above.

2. Coverage for extra expenses incurred to maintain data processing services following damage to or breakdown of the computer equipment is available on an "all-risks" basis under special data processing policies. However, a better risk management measure would be an agreement with one or more nearby users of similar equipment to permit Earthmovers to use available time on their computer systems in such emergencies. Of course, Earthmovers would be expected to provide the same backup services to other firms. If such agreements to include arrangements for handling the data Earthmovers is processing for others can be made, Earthmovers would not need indirect loss coverage on the computer system.

3. Although there is no standard policy form to cover the extra expenses required to maintain normal operations following damage to the piers, it seems likely that such a form could be obtained from specialty insurers if the potential loss is of sufficient magnitude to justify the expense of insurance. This depends on the availability of alternative piers, material delivery systems, and similar factors. Otherwise, Earthmovers will have to retain the exposure.

4. Coverage for loss resulting from destruction of accounts receivable records is available on an "all-risks" basis under the accounts receivable policy. However, it seems unlikely that a road contractor would have a large number of accounts receivable, as do many other types of businesses. Chances are that any destroyed records could be reconstructed with the assistance of customers' accounting departments. As an addi-

tional safeguard, duplication of the records, with the duplicates stored at a location different from that of the originals, would seem to be a more effective and less expensive method of risk management than the purchase of insurance.

5. Duplication would also appear to be the best method of coping with the valuable papers exposure. However, "all-risks" coverage is available under the valuable papers policy if desired.

6. The exposure to loss of use of most automotive and construction equipment and aircraft would seem to be within the ability of Earthmovers to retain, assuming backup equipment is available. However, it is likely that damage or destruction of the portable hot mix plant or the excavator would cause a significant interruption, and coverage should be obtained under an inland marine form.

7. If the company airplane is damaged or destroyed, it would be necessary for Earthmovers to rent a substitute airplane or to utilize public or private air services. Although some extra expense and delay would be involved, it does not appear that the exposure would be too great to retain. Some cost studies should be done to verify this assumption.

The recommended liability risk management program for Earthmovers is as follows:

1. As to the workers' compensation exposure, the relatively large number of states in which Earthmovers does business and the necessity for filing numerous certificates of insurance on construction projects make retention unattractive. Since Earthmovers needs to keep its future costs relatively predictable, it seems that the best method for meeting this exposure is a guaranteed-cost workers' compensation and employers' liability policy.

2. Earthmovers can cover most of its liability exposures under a comprehensive general-automobile liability (CGAL) policy (or a CGL combined with a business auto policy written by the same insurer). This policy should include coverage for:
   a. premises and operations liability (including liability arising from the use of mobile equipment);
   b. completed operations liability;
   c. blanket contractual liability;
   d. owners' and contractors' protective liability;
   e. personal injury liability;
   f. automobile liability, including nonowned and hired cars; and
   g. broad form property damage, including completed operations.

The broad form CGL endorsement would provide coverage for items c, e, and g, as well as providing several additional fringe coverages.

It is possible that coverage for liability arising from the boat could be provided by deleting or amending the watercraft exclusion in this policy, but another policy is suggested below for this exposure.

3. A commercial umbrella liability policy may be purchased by Earthmovers to (1) provide higher limits above the comprehensive general-automobile liability policy and (2) cover (subject to a large deductible or retention) some exposures which are not covered by the CGAL policy.

4. Coverage for data processing errors and omissions liability should be obtained under a specialized data processing policy.

5. Perhaps the best solution to the exposure to liability for damage *to* rented or leased equipment is to include in the lease a provision exempting Earthmovers from such liability, provided, of course, that the lessor will agree to such a provision. If an exemption cannot be obtained, there are two possible methods of treating the exposure. First, an inland marine bailee liability policy could be purchased. Second, if insurance is unavailable or overly expensive, the exposure must be retained.

6. Liability arising from the ownership or operation of the airplane is excluded from coverage under the CGAL policy and probably also under the commercial umbrella. High limits of aircraft liability coverage should be provided for (1) liability to passengers and (2) liability to others under an aircraft liability policy.

7. The best way to provide liability coverage for the boat is through the yacht policy (already recommended) which includes some liability coverage through the running down clause of the hull coverage, as well as protection and indemnity coverage.

Some loss control measures have been suggested above in the discussion of specific exposures. However, other loss control measures should be instituted to the extent that they are practical and have not been undertaken already. For example, Earthmovers might consider the installation of a Halon fire control system in the data processing facility and automatic sprinklers in the other buildings. Dikes or other flood control measures might be considered, such as moving damageable property to upper floors.

Safety programs should be instituted in all of the company's operations if they are not already provided. Loss control programs are sometimes reduced when a firm experiences financial problems.

However, they are especially important at that time because they reduce both insurance costs and uninsured losses.

In addition to the insurance and loss control measures discussed above, it is recommended that Earthmovers carefully review their procedures used in estimating costs for contract bids and improve the procedures, if necessary, so as to minimize the chance of error. Also, if fixed-price contracts can be negotiated with suppliers and labor unions, this may prevent recurrence of the problems that recently developed.

PANACEA PHARMACEUTICAL COMPANY

Description of Operations

The Panacea Pharmaceutical Company is a publicly owned corporation. Its common stock is traded on a major stock exchange. The company is engaged in the manufacture and distribution of both ethical drugs (sold only by prescription) and patent medicines sold over the counter by drug stores and other outlets. Some of the ethical pharmaceuticals contain narcotics, and substantial amounts of narcotics are stored in the manufacturing plant for use in the preparation of such products.

Although Panacea makes and sells over 100 different drug products, approximately 30 percent of sales and a slightly higher percentage of profits are derived from one product, an ulcer remedy. There are other similar ulcer remedies on the market, and management concedes that some of them are equally effective. However, Panacea's product was the first on the market and has acquired a large following among doctors, who usually prescribe it by Panacea's brand name.

Management is concerned that any prolonged absence of their ulcer medicine from the market would cause doctors to prescribe another brand and they might not return to Panacea's brand when it becomes available again. The manufacturing process for the product is relatively simple. Only stock machinery is needed. Replacement machinery would be available immediately, and several buildings suitable for the purpose are also readily available. The manufacture of the product (and all other company products) could be subcontracted to other pharmaceutical manufacturers who specialize in making such products on a contract basis. However, about thirty days would be required to negotiate contracts, obtain packaging materials, and make other necessary arrangements to farm out production.

The formula for the ulcer medicine includes one chemical compound that is manufactured in only one chemical plant in the world. The reason for its limited production is lack of demand. Panacea uses about one-half of the amount produced. The compound is not difficult to produce and is not protected by patents. Panacea's production manager estimates that Panacea could install the necessary equipment, obtain necessary materials, and begin producing the compound themselves in about sixty days. However, they would prefer to continue purchasing it from the present supplier if possible. All other materials used in Panacea products are readily available from several sources.

Panacea's sales are growing at a rate of about 20 percent per year, mostly as the result of the introduction of new products. The company has extensive research facilities and has developed and introduced an average of five new products per year over the last six years. Many other potential products are developed and tested but are not introduced because they prove to be ineffective, dangerous, or both. The testing process for some products is long and complex. Some products may involve several years of testing on dogs, primates, or other relatively long-lived animals, possibly followed by testing on human volunteers. Voluminous records are accumulated during such tests. The records must be retained for many years for use in licensing applications and defense of products liability claims, for use in future research projects, and for other purposes.

The research records are kept in fire-resistive filing cabinets in the records room of Panacea's research center. The center also houses research laboratories, offices for research personnel, and cages for experimental animals. It is located in a sprinklered, fire-resistive building adjacent to Panacea's factory.

The factory building also is fire resistive and is sprinklered in all areas except the clean room. The clean room is used for manufacturing and packaging processes that require complete sterility. It has its own air conditioning system with special filtering equipment to eliminate dust or other potential contaminants. Other equipment is also provided to maintain the sterile atmosphere. Even very slight contamination of the clean room would require that production be discontinued for several days until sterility could be reestablished. All workers in the clean room must wear special sterile uniforms and surgical masks.

Both the factory and the research center are five years old. They are surrounded by a carefully maintained lawn, and are separated from the nearest building by a distance of 200 feet. They are located in a medium-sized city with excellent public fire protection and water supply.

Panacea's products are marketed through company branches. Each branch consists of an office and a warehouse. There are twenty-three branches in the United States and eighteen branches in Canada, Europe, and Latin America. Each branch has several sales representatives who call on doctors, hospitals, pharmacists, and other retailers of drug products. The sales representatives at the foreign locations are citizens of the countries in which the branches are located. However, most of the branch managers, assistant branch managers, and branch sales managers are U.S. citizens. The company's products are offered for sale in approximately 40,000 retail establishments here and abroad.

The branches are located in leased quarters, but the office and warehouse equipment and drug inventory total about $350,000 at each location. Most shipments to domestic branch locations, as well as incoming shipments of materials, are made by common carrier trucks and railroads. Foreign shipments usually go by ship. However, air freight shipments, both domestic and foreign, are sometimes made if great speed is necessary. The only motor vehicles owned by Panacea are twelve private passenger cars used by executives and messengers and three light trucks used for local pickup and delivery. All of them are at the home office. Branch office officials and sales representatives use their personal automobiles for business-related travel. Panacea does not own any boats or aircraft, but small airplanes, with crew, are sometimes chartered for executive transportation. The sales vice president, a licensed pilot, sometimes uses his personal airplane on company business.

Panacea's products are advertised extensively. Ethical pharmaceuticals are advertised primarily by direct mail to doctors and in medical journals. These advertisements tend to be technical and medical in nature. Advertisements for patent medicines appear on radio and television and in consumer magazines and newspapers. Such advertisements are nontechnical and are designed to appeal to consumers. Endorsements by prominent persons are sometimes used.

Panacea is in an exceptionally strong financial condition. Profits have been very satisfactory and have been quite stable over the past ten years. The company is accumulating a fund from retained earnings to expand its production facilities. The fund, which now stands at $10 million, is invested in liquid securities. The securities that are nonnegotiable are kept in a safe in the office section of the factory building. Management estimates that present production facilities are adequate for the next five years and that the fund will be adequate by the end of that period to pay for the needed expansion. Panacea does not have any long-term debt, and its only short-term debt consists of accounts payable to suppliers.

The present manufacturing vice president who has occupied that position for five years has been more aware than his predecessor of the importance of loss control. The safety and industrial hygiene programs he has initiated have been very successful in reducing employee injuries. The company's workers' compensation premiums, losses, and experience rating modifications for the last five years are shown in Table 15-1.

The experience rating modification for the current year is a credit

Table 15-1

Panacea Pharmaceutical Workers' Compensation History

Year	Premium	Losses Number	Losses Amount	Experience Debit (+) or Credit (−)
1	$110,000	57	$87,000	+ 30%
2	120,000	48	73,000	+ 23%
3	125,000	46	75,000	+ 18%
4	125,000	47	71,000	+ 12%
5†	127,000	43	66,000	+ 3%

†Most recent completed year.

Table 15-2

Panacea Pharmaceutical Estimated
Cost of Workers' Compensation
Retention Program

Losses	$52,000
Excess insurance	9,200
Self-insurer bond	1,900
Taxes	600
Service fee	10,200
Total	$73,900

of 2 percent. The increasing premium reflects increases in manual rates and payrolls, which have more than offset the improved experience modification. The factory, research center, and home office payrolls account for about 75 percent of the workers' compensation premium. Panacea has been considering the feasibility of retaining the workers' compensation exposure for all employees in its home state. Commercial insurance would be continued for all other employees because of the expense and inconvenience of qualifying as a "self-insurer" in all states. A risk management consultant has prepared an estimate of the annual cost of a retention program for Panacea's home state employees, as shown in Table 15-2.

The estimated annual workers' compensation premium for the same part of Panacea's payrolls is $96,000. The excess insurance premium would provide coverage for $2 million in excess of aggregate losses of $125,000 in one year. The self-insurer bond is required by the state to guarantee the payment of benefits, and the taxes are for the support of the state workers' compensation board. The service fee would be paid to a service company for loss adjustment, loss control, and administrative services furnished by that firm. The service company's staff is capable of providing those services on the same level now provided by the insurance company. Panacea does not have any employees qualified to provide claims service. It has only one safety engineer on its staff.

Identification of Exposures

The direct property loss exposures to which Panacea Pharmaceutical Company is subject are:

1. loss to the factory and research center buildings and contents and to contents at branches by fire, the extended coverage perils, and other perils. The factory and research center are also subject to loss by sprinkler leakage;
2. physical damage to automotive equipment by collision, fire, theft, and other perils;
3. damage to or destruction of goods in transit;
4. loss of money, narcotics, or other property by criminal acts of employees or others;
5. loss of experimental animals; and
6. loss or destruction of securities.

The indirect property loss exposures to which Pancea is subject are:

1. loss of earnings due to loss of production during the time required to establish new facilities or to farm out production following direct loss;
2. loss of earnings due to inability to produce the ulcer medicine if the key chemical compound becomes unavailable;
3. extra expenses incurred to establish new production facilities or farm out production operations following damage to factory;
4. loss of earnings because of inability to introduce new products if research facility is damaged;
5. research expenses incurred to reconstruct research records if they are destroyed;
6. extra expenses to decontaminate clean room, and loss of production during decontamination process; and
7. extra expense to repeat research if test animals die or are killed before experiments are completed.

The liability loss exposures to which Panacea is subject are:

1. liability, either by statute or at common law, for job-related injuries to employees;
2. liability for injuries to others or damage to their property resulting from:
    a. ownership, operation, or use of automobiles, either owned or nonowned;
    b. use of nonowned aircraft;
    c. premises and operations;
    d. defective products;
    e. libel, slander, or other similar personal injuries;
    f. violation of copyright, or similar injuries for advertising operations.
3. liability for damage to leased premises by fire or other perils;
4. liability for injuries to human volunteers used for testing drugs;
5. liability arising out of activities of directors or officers of the corporation.

Suggested Risk Management Program

Panacea Pharmaceutical's strong financial position and substantial and stable profits permit the consideration of retention programs in the firm's risk management plan. Management is already aware of the value of loss control, so only a few additional loss control measures will be discussed in this suggested risk management program. Of course, loss control measures already undertaken should be continued.

The factory and research buildings should be insured for at least fire, the extended coverage perils, and sprinkler leakage. Coverage against earthquake and other perils, and possibly "all-risks" coverage, should be considered if the cost is commensurate with the exposure. The coverage should be written for replacement cost, since the buildings are now five years old and have incurred modest depreciation.

Contents of the two owned buildings and the branches should be insured for the same perils indicated for the buildings, except that sprinkler leakage may not be needed at the branch locations, since there is no indication that they are sprinklered.

If there are substantial fluctuations in the total value of inventory, contents should be insured on a reporting form. In such case, the multiple location forms should be used in order to qualify for rate credits for dispersion of values and favorable loss experience. Finished goods should be insured for their selling price, since the manufacturing form of business interruption insurance does not cover loss of profits on finished goods. Foreign branches should be insured under the same policy to the extent permitted by the law of the country in which they are located. Insuring foreign branches under the U.S. policy with losses payable in dollars reduces or eliminates the perils of currency devaluation, blocked currencies, and similar problems. Local insurance practices should be carefully studied to prevent unforeseen problems overseas.

A substantial deductible, applicable separately to each occurrence, should be provided for in the policy on buildings and contents. A deductible of $100,000 would not be excessive for Panacea, but the exact amount of the deductible should be determined on the basis of more complete data.

The property insurance on contents normally would not include coverage for securities or for the experimental animals. Coverage for these items will be discussed later.

The automobile physical damage exposure is relatively small, since Panacea owns only a few private passenger cars and light trucks. Although physical damage losses might occur concurrently with a fire, wind, or other loss to buildings and contents, the total would be within Panacea's financial ability to retain.

The value of goods in transit is not given. However, the nature of Panacea's products would seem to indicate that large individual shipments are likely and would be a target for theft losses. Land or air shipments by common carrier should therefore be insured under an inland marine transit policy on an "all-risks" basis. Waterborne shipments should be insured under an ocean marine open cargo policy with a warehouse-to-warehouse clause. "All-risks" coverage should be obtained if the premium is reasonable. Substantial deductibles should be provided under both policies if appropriate premium credits are granted for them. Shipments by owned vehicles should not be insured, because Panacea owns only light trucks and the cargo carried on them would not have sufficient value to require insurance.

One major crime exposure to which Panacea is subject is the exposure to dishonest acts of employees. This exposure can be insured under a blanket fidelity bond, either the commercial blanket bond or the blanket position bond. Excess coverage may be needed for key employees, such as the treasurer. The presence of substantial amounts of narcotics on the premises increases the exposure to burglary or robbery as well as the chance of a fidelity loss. Presumably the narcotics are stored in a safe or vault until needed for production purposes. If so, safe burglary and inside robbery coverages, along with the fidelity coverage, could provide the necessary protection.

Since the securities are not negotiable, the maximum loss is likely to be the cost of lost securities bonds required to obtain new certificates, and other minor costs of obtaining such certificates. Such loss seems within Panacea's ability to retain. Of course, "all-risks" coverage for the securities could be provided under money and securities broad form insurance if desired.

No values are given for experimental animals in the research center. However, it seems likely that some form of insurance protection is needed for two reasons. First, a large number of animals might be killed concurrently with damage to the buildings and other contents by fire, wind, explosion, or other peril. Second, if animals were killed in the middle of a long testing program, it probably would be necessary to repeat several years of experiments. While animal mortality insurance, similar to human life insurance, is sometimes written, it probably would be either unavailable or prohibitively expensive in this case. A more desirable alternative would be an inland marine policy covering accidental death either from named perils or from all external perils not specifically excluded. A special valuation clause would be needed to cover the increasing value of experimental animals, as the experiments progress; or perhaps a monthly report of values could be required.

A major loss to Panacea's production facilities would result in an interruption of production for up to one month while alternative production arrangements are negotiated and prepared. This exposure should be insured under a gross earnings business interruption policy for at least fire and the extended coverage perils. The policy should not include a deductible, since loss under it would be concurrent with a direct loss to property for which a substantial deductible has already been recommended.

Management of Panacea would be anxious to resume production as soon as possible in order to avoid losing its market position, especially that of ulcer medicine. Other production arrangements can be made in a relatively short period of time, either by farming out production or by establishing a temporary production facility at other premises. However, it seems likely that substantial additional expenses would result. The business interruption policy would cover such extra expenses but only to the extent that they resulted in a reduction of the business interruption loss. If that coverage is not adequate, it can be supplemented by an extra expense policy. Damage to the research center could reduce future profits by preventing the introduction of new products. There is no standard insurance form to protect against such a loss. It may be possible to negotiate a special form of coverage. If not, Panacea will have to retain the exposure.

The contingent loss from inability to obtain the key chemical compound for the ulcer medicine can be insured under a contingent business interruption policy. However, insurance is not the best solution to the problem, for two reasons. First, it would cover only if the inability to obtain the chemical was the result of damage by an insured peril to the supplier's facilities. It would not, for example, cover strike or a mere decision by the supplier to discontinue production. Second, insurance payments would not enable Panacea to maintain production, and would not protect its market position with regard to that drug. As an alternative, Panacea should establish a policy of keeping at least a sixty-day supply of the chemical on hand at all times. They could then maintain normal production of the ulcer medicine until they could establish their own production facility for the key chemical compound.

The cost of research to reconstruct destroyed research records could be insured under a valuable papers policy. However, a better solution would be to duplicate the records on microfilm and store the duplicates at a separate location, such as in a bank vault. It would be necessary to update the microfilms periodically.

Business interruption resulting from contamination of the clean room would not be covered under a standard business interruption policy unless the contamination resulted from an insured peril. It may be possible that a special policy could be negotiated to cover contamination itself as a named peril. If not, Panacea will have to retain the exposure.

Panacea's liability for injuries to its U.S. employees should be insured under a workers' compensation and employers' liability policy with the broad form all-states endorsement. It may also be desirable to provide foreign voluntary workers' compensation, in accordance with the statute of its home state, for U.S. citizens employed abroad. Foreign citizens employed in their home countries should be insured for workers' compensation according to the laws of their own countries.

The retention plan recommended by the service company is a possible alternative to workers' compensation insurance for Panacea's home state employees. However, it seems unattractive for two reasons. First, the recommended aggregate excess policy has a limit of $2 million for all losses in one year. Losses could go well in excess of that amount if several employees were permanently disabled in a single accident or a series of accidents. Second, large compensation losses could occur concurrently with large property losses for which a large deductible has already been suggested. The relatively small saving of $22,000 does not seem to justify the uncertainty involved.

An advertisers' legal liability policy is needed to cover Panacea's potential liability for libel, slander, violation of copyright, invasion of privacy, or other injuries resulting from its advertising operations. This is a specialty line of coverage available from a limited number of insurers. Panacea's other liability exposures, with the possible exception of liability for testing drugs on human volunteers, could be covered under a comprehensive general-automobile liability (CGAL) policy. Such a policy would automatically cover automobile liability (for both owned and nonowned cars), as well as premises and operations and products liability (unless excluded); but several endorsements and modifications would be needed. Nonstandard products liability coverage could be sought to provide coverage worldwide or at least in all countries in which Panacea has branches. It should cover suits brought in those countries and not be limited to suits brought in the United States or Canada, since Panacea has substantial assets abroad that could be seized to satisfy judgments handed down by foreign courts.

Personal injury liability coverage should be added for coverage against libel, slander, invasion of privacy, false arrest, and similar injuries. This endorsement would not cover personal injuries resulting from advertising covered under the advertisers' liability policy already mentioned.

Insurance is also needed to cover Panacea's liability for the use of nonowned aircraft. This coverage is available under an aircraft liability policy from insurers that specialize in that line.

The CGAL should also be endorsed to cover Panacea's liability for accidental damage to leased premises. The usual method of providing such coverage is by adding a fire legal liability endorsement which may cover liability for explosion damage as well as fire damage. A less common way, and one that provides broader coverage, would be to delete or modify the care, custody, or control exclusion so that it does not exclude liability for damage to leased premises. An even more desirable form of protection would be to renegotiate the lease contracts to provide that Panacea is not liable for accidental damage to the leased premises. However, such renegotiation is not always possible.

Panacea probably should have the CGAL policy endorsed to clarify the coverage for testing of drugs on human patients or to seek to obtain specific coverage elsewhere for that exposure.

Finally, Panacea should acquire an umbrella liability policy to:

1. provide higher limits for employers' liability, advertisers' liability, and the exposures insured under the CGAL policy; and
2. provide coverage in excess of a large retained limit for some exposures not insured under the policies listed.

If the umbrella insurer is willing and the deductible is not too large, Panacea may want to dispense with primary coverage for advertisers' liability and fire legal liability. It would then retain the first layer of losses under the umbrella and rely on the umbrella for excess coverage.

Bibliography

"A Trend Toward Coalescence of Trespass and Nuisance: Remedy for Invasion of Particulates." *Washington University Law Quarterly*, Vol. 1, 1961, p. 64.

"Accident Cost Control." *Bureau of Labor Standards Bulletin*, 1965. Cited in *RM 55 Practices in Risk Management, Selected Readings*. Malvern, PA: Insurance Institute of America, 1977, p. 170.

Accident Facts. Chicago: National Safety Council, 1977.

Alt, Susan. "Product Liability Costs Force Machine Builder to Liquidate Company." *Business Insurance*, 25 Oct. 1975, pp. 1-2.

6 *Am. Jur.* 2d, "Pollution Control," 142. Rochester, NY: The Lawyers Co-operative Publishing Co., and San Francisco, CA: Bancroft-Whitney Co., 1973.

22 *Am. Jur.* 2d, "Damages," 241 et seq. Rochester, NY: The Lawyers Co-operative Publishing Co., and San Francisco, CA: Bancroft-Whitney Co., 1973.

61 *Am. Jur.* 2d, "Pollution Control," 43, 141, 168 and "Trespass," 143, 149. Rochester, NY: The Lawyers Co-operative Publishing Co., and San Francisco, CA: Bancroft-Whitney Co., 1973.

American Law Reports Annotated. Rochester, NY: Lawyers Co-operative Publishing Co.

Baglini, Norman A. *Risk Management in International Corporations*. New York: Risk Studies Foundation, 1976.

Ballantine and Sterling California Corporation Laws. 4th ed. Ed. R. Bradbury Clark. New York: Matthew Bender, 1978.

Ballantine's Law Dictionary with Pronunciations. 3rd ed. Ed. William S. Anderson. Rochester, NY: Lawyers Co-operative Publishing Co., 1969.

Black, Harry Campbell. *Black's Law Dictionary*. 4th ed. St. Paul: West Publishing Co., 1968.

Brainard, Calvin H. *Automobile Insurance*. Homewood, IL: Richard D. Irwin, 1961.

Brockmeier, Warren G. "Status of D & O Liability Coverage." *Risk Management*, Vol. 24, No. 1, January 1977, p. 20.

Brown, Samuel P. "Criteria for Judging Preventative Programs—the View of One Outside Director." *Preventing Directors' Liability Under the Securities Laws.* New York: Practicing Law Institute, 1976.

Buell, Robert R. "Product Withdrawal Expense Insurance." *Products Liability: Practical Defense Problems II.* Milwaukee, WI: Defense Research Institute Monograph, 1976, p. 41.

Burton, Francis X., Jr. "Historical, Liability and Insurance Aspects of Pollution Claims." *A.B.A. Section of Insurance, Negligence, and Compensation Law, 1971 Proceedings,* p. 305.

Businessmen's Attitudes Toward Commercial Insurance. A Sentry Insurance national opinion study conducted by Louis Harris and Associates and the Department of Insurance, The Wharton School, University of Pennsylvania, 1974.

"Caesar Was Ambitious." *United States Review,* 21 Nov. 1959 as cited by Thomas E. Conlon, Jr. "Heads They Win: Tails We Lose." *CPCU Annals,* Vol. 17, No. 3, Fall 1964, p. 233.

Calamari, John D. and Perillo, Joseph M. *Law of Contracts.* St. Paul: West Publishing Co., 1971.

Campbell, David C. and Vargo, John F. "The Flammable Fabrics Act and Strict Liability in Tort." *Ind. L. Rev.,* Vol. 9, 1976, p. 395.

Catherwood, Robert H. *E.D.P. Risks, The Management of Insurable Risks Incident to the Use of Electronic Data Processing Equipment.* Toronto: Canadian Underwriting Magazine, 1963, p. 5.

Clapp, Wallace L., Jr. *Specialty Coverage Market Reports.* Indianapolis: Rough Notes Co., October 1976.

Collatz, Frederick A. "Claims for Equipment Use Under Public Contract Bonds." *A.B.A. Section of Insurance, Negligence, and Compensation Law, 1969 Proceedings.* Chicago: American Bar Association.

Contract Bonds: The Unseen Services of a Surety. New York: The Surety Association of America, 1973.

Corbin, Arthur Linton. *Corbin on Contracts.* St. Paul: West Publishing Co., 1962.

Corpus Juris Secundum, Vol. 168, *Partnership.* Brooklyn: American Law Book Co., and St. Paul: West Publishing Co., 1946.

Couch, George J. *Couch on Insurance.* 2nd ed. Rochester, NY: The Lawyers Cooperative Publishing Co., 1971.

"Criminal Responsibility of Corporate Officials for Pollution of the Environment." *Albany Law Review,* Vol. 37, 1972-1973, pp. 84-88.

Crist, G. W., Jr. *Corporate Suretyship.* New York: McGraw-Hill Book Co., 1950.

Daenzer, Bernard J. "Market Availability of Products Liability." *Excess and Surplus Lines Manual,* March 1976, pp. 8-10.

Davids, Lewis E. *Dictionary of Insurance.* Totowa, NJ: Littlefield, Adams & Co., 1970.

Donaldson, James H. *Casualty Claim Practice.* 3rd ed. Homewood, IL: Richard D. Irwin, 1976.

Drake, Norbert A. "Adjusting and Defending Claims Under Architects' and Engineers' Professional Liability Policies." *Adjusters Reference Guide.* Insurance Field Co., Liability 23.

Esposito, John C. "Air and Water Law Pollution: What to Do While Waiting for

Washington." *Harvard Civil Rights—Civil Liberties Review*. Vol. 5, 1970, p. 37.

F.C.&S. Bulletins. Cincinnati: The National Underwriter Co., 1974.

Feuer, Morton and Johnston, Joseph E. *Personal Liabilities of Corporate Officers & Directors*. 2nd ed. Englewood Cliffs, NJ: Prentice-Hall, 1974.

Fisk, George and Chandran, Rajan. "How to Trace and Recall Products." *Harvard Business Review*, November-December 1975, p. 91.

Folk, Ernest L. "Civil Liabilities Under the Federal Securities Acts: The BarChris Case." *Virginia Law Review*, Vol. 55, 1969, p. 1.

Frumer, Louis R. and Friedman, Melvin I. *Products Liability*, Vol. 3, New York: Matthew Bender Co., 1973.

Gamlin, Joanne. "Profit Sharing Plans Stand to Suffer Significant Lawsuits Under ERISA." *Business Insurance*, 3 Nov. 1975, p. 4.

——————. "Record D & O Settlement in Mattel Case." *Business Insurance*, 17 Nov. 1975, p. 1.

Geisel, Jerry. "ERISA Wrecks Some, But Not All, Pensions." *Business Insurance*, 20 March 1978, p. 1.

——————. "Work Comp Costs Climb; Self-Insuring Pools Grow." *Business Insurance*, 12 Dec. 1977, p. 69.

Georgia Chapter CPCU. *The Hold Harmless Agreement*. Cincinnati: The National Underwriter Co., 1973.

Glass, Joseph E. "Fleet Evaluation and Loss Control." *The National Insurance Buyer*, March 1968. Quoted in *RM 54—Principles of Risk Management Additional Supplemental Readings*. Malvern: Insurance Institute of America, 1969.

Gosnell, Maurice E. "Omnibus Clauses in Automobile Insurance Policies." *Insurance Law Journal*, April 1950, p. 237.

Grad, Frank P. *Environmental Law*. New York: Matthew Bender, 1973.

Gregory, Charles A. and Kalven, Harry, Jr. *Cases and Materials on Torts*. 2nd ed. Little, Brown & Co., 1969, p. 23.

Hayes, John. "Suppliers to Materialmen and Others too Remote for Coverage Under the Miller Act and State Statutory Bonds: What is a Subcontractor?" *A.B.A. Section of Insurance, Negligence, and Compensation Law, 1969 Proceedings*. Chicago: American Bar Association.

Hill, J. L. "How Strict is Strict?" *Texas Bar J.*, Vol. 32, November 1969, p. 759.

Hoffman, Norman. "How to Face Your Company's Many Ecology Exposures." *Business Insurance*, 14 Feb. 1972, p. 25.

——————. "Record Keeping to Reduce the Product Liability Risk." *Business Insurance*, 25 Oct. 1971, p. 33.

Hogue, Michael E. and Olson, Douglas G. *Business Attitudes Toward Risk Management, Insurance and Related Social Issues*. Philadelphia, PA: The Wharton School, University of Pennsylvania Press, 1976, p. 76.

Horn, Ronald C. *Subrogation in Insurance Theory and Practice*. Homewood, IL: Richard D. Irwin, 1964.

Hume, Robert R. and Goodnaugh, Roger A. "Fidelity and Surety Law." *Insurance Counsel Journal*, Vol. 40, No. 2, April 1973. Chicago: International Association of Insurance Counsel.

"Indemnification of the Corporate Insider: Directors and Officers Liability Insurance." *Minn. L. Rev.*, Vol. 54, 1970, p. 667.

Insurance Facts. New York: Insurance Information Institute, 1977.

"Insurer Would Pay Half of Gulf Directors' Settlement." *Business Insurance*, 4 Oct. 1976, p. 1.

Jenne, Donald Dickinson. *Jenne's Suretymaster.* St. Paul: Suretymaster of America.

Johnston, Joseph E. "Practical Considerations in Developing an Officers' and Directors' Protection Program." *Protecting the Corporate Officer and Director from Liability.* New York: Practicing Law Institute, 1976.

Jorling, Thomas. "The Federal Law of Air Pollution Control." *Federal Environmental Law.* Environmental Law Institute. St. Paul, MN: West Publishing Co., 1974.

Juergensmeyer, Julian Conrad. "Control of Air Pollution Through the Assertion of Private Rights." *Duke L. J.*, 1967.

Knepper, William E. "Indemnification and Liability Insurance—An Update, Officers and Directors." *Business Law*, Vol. 30, 1975, p. 951.

——————. *Liabilities of Corporate Officers and Directors.* 2nd ed. Indianapolis: Allen Smith Co., 1973.

Lake, William. "Noise Emerging Federal Control." *Federal Environmental Law.* Environmental Law Institute. St. Paul, MN: West Publishing Co., 1974.

Launie, J. J.; Lee, Finley J.; and Baglini, Norman A. *Principles of Property and Liability Underwriting.* Malvern, PA: Insurance Institute of America, 1976.

LeRoux, Margaret. "California Cities Face $1 Million Retention." *Business Insurance*, 31 Oct. 1977, p. 38.

——————"Self-Insurance of Work Comp Heats Up Market for Administrative Services." *Business Insurance*, 11 Nov. 1974, p. 78.

Lettow, Charles F. "The Control of Marine Pollution." *Federal Environmental Law.* Environmental Law Institute. St. Paul, MN: West Publishing Co., 1974.

Life Insurance Fact Book, '77. Washington, D.C.: American Council of Life Insurance.

Long, Rowland H. *Law of Liability Insurance.* New York: Matthew Bender Co., 1976.

Loss, Louis. *Securities Regulations.* 2nd ed. Boston, MA: Little, Brown & Co., 1961.

Loss, Louis and Cowett, Edward M. *Blue Sky Law.* Boston, MA: Little, Brown & Co., 1958.

Lowenfeld, Andreas F. "The United States and the Warsaw Convention." *Harv. L. Rev.*, Vol. 80, No. 3, 1967, p. 497.

Maatman, Gerald L. "Interpret Product Safety as Profit, Bonus." *Business Insurance*, 8 Dec. 1969, pp. 26, 34.

Mackall, Luther E. *The Principles of Surety Underwriting.* 5th ed. Philadelphia: Chilton Co., 1940.

——————. *Surety Underwriting Manual.* Indianapolis: The Rough Notes Co., 1972.

"Malpractice in Focus." *Journal of the American Medical Association*, August 1975, p. 12.

McManus, Richard P. "The Miller Act Performance Bond: An Additional Payment Bond." *Insurance Law Journal*, No. 550, November 1968, p. 875.

Merrion, Paul R. "No Nationwide Product Crisis, Reports Task Force." *Business Insurance*, 27 Dec. 1976, p. 1.

Meyers, Robert J. "The Viability of Common Law Actions for Pollution Caused Injuries and Proof of Facts." *New York Law Forum*, Vol. 18, 1972-1973, pp. 948-949.

Mosk, C. J. Stanley. "Finding a Direction for Our Environment." *Barrister*, Vol. 3, No. 2, 1977, p. 16.

1975 Motor Truck Facts. Detroit: Motor Vehicle Manufacturers Association, 1975, pp. 10 and 56.

Nachman, Norman. *Products Liability Insurance*. New York: Insurance Services Office, 1972.

Nash, Ralph C., Jr. and Linden, Susan. "Federal Procurement and the Environment." *Federal Environmental Law Institute*. St. Paul, MN: West Publishing Co., 1974.

Nelson, Paul C. "Manufacturing Irregularities Often Crux of Product Cases: Attorney." *Business Insurance*, 30 June 1975, p. 3.

"No Easy Way Out for OSHA." *Business Insurance*, 8 July 1974, p. 16.

Pfenningstorf, Werner. "Government Risk Management in Public Policy and Legislation: Problems and Options." *American Bar Foundation*, 1977, pp. 257-265.

Phipps, David L. "When Does a 'Service' Become a 'Sale'?" *Products Liability: Practical Defense Problems*. Defense Research Institute Monograph, 1972, pp. 23, 31.

Practical Risk Management. San Francisco: Warren, McVeigh, Griffin and Huntington.

"Product Safety Hearing Examines Seals, Advertising Claims." *Business Insurance*, 17 March 1969, p. 12.

Products Liability Loss Prevention Manual. Chicago: Alliance of American Insurers (formerly American Mutual Insurance Alliance), August 1976.

Products Liability Reports. Chicago: Commerce Clearing House, p. 4733.

Professional Corporations and the Alternatives. Illinois Institute for Continuing Legal Education, 1976.

Property and Liability Insurance Handbook. Eds. John D. Long and David W. Gregg. Homewood, IL: Richard D. Irwin, 1965.

Prosser, William L. *Handbook of the Law of Torts*. 4th ed. St. Paul: West Publishing Co., 1971.

Prunty, Bert S., Jr. "The Shareholder's Derivative Suit: Notes on Its Derivation." *N.Y.U.L. Review*, Vol. 32, 1957, p. 980.

Ramp, David L. "The Impact of Recall Campaigns on Products Liability." *Insurance Counsel Journal*, January 1977, pp. 83-96.

"Recordkeeping Key to Product Recall Program." *Business Insurance*, 30 June 1975, p. 3.

Restatement of Agency. St. Paul, MN: American Law Institute, 1958.

Restatement of Torts. 2nd ed. St. Paul, MN: American Law Institute, 1965.

Rheingold, Paul D. "The Expanding Liability of the Product Supplier, A Primer." *Hofstra L. Rev.*, Vol. 2, 1974, pp. 521, 525-6.

450—Bibliography

Roberts, Kathryn McIntyre. "Retentions Key to Excess for Municipalities." *Business Insurance*, 19 Sept. 1977.

Rodimer, Donald H. "Use of Bonds in Private Construction." *The Forum*, Vol. 7, No. 4, July 1974, p. 236.

Rottman, Dick L. "Analysis of the Lawyer Malpractice Problem." *CPCU Annals*, March 1971, p. 66.

Rough Notes Policy, Form and Manual Analyses (P.F.&M.). Indianapolis: Rough Notes Co.

Sheehan, Thomas F. "Beware of the Broad Form Excess or Umbrella Excess Policies." *CPCU Annals*, Vol. 22, No. 2, June 1969, pp. 165-174.

Stearns, Arthur Adelbert. *The Law of Suretyship*. Cincinnati: W. H. Anderson Co., 1951.

Topical Law Reports. Vol. 2. *Pollution Control Guide.* Sec. 6203. New York: Commerce Clearing House, 1976.

"Tort Liability of Independent Testing Agencies." *Rutgers L. Rev.*, Vol. 22, 1968, p. 299.

Very, Donald L. "The Pennsylvania Unfair Insurance Practices Act: The Sleeping Giant." *CPCU Annals*, Vol. 28, No. 2, June 1975, p. 109.

Walker, Albert H. "Surety and the Contractor." *Inspection News*, November-December 1967, pp. 11-14.

Wander, Herbert S. "Protecting Directors Against Securities Liability." *Preventing Directors' Liability Under the Securities Laws.* New York: Practicing Law Institute, 1976.

Ward, Robert. "Timely Notice and Timely Suit Under the Miller Act: Current Developments." *Section of Insurance, Negligence, and Compensation Law, 1969 Proceedings*, pp. 74-88.

Washington, George T. and Bishop, J. W., Jr. *Indemnifying the Corporate Executive: Business, Legal and Tax Aspects of Reimbursement for Personal Liability.* New York: The Ronald Press Co., 1963.

Wilder, Brooks. "Mobilizing the Use of the Board's Talents." *Preventing Directors' Liability Under the Securities Laws.* New York: Practicing Law Institute, 1976.

Williams, C. Arthur, Jr. and Heins, Richard M. *Risk Management and Insurance.* 2nd and 3rd eds. New York: McGraw-Hill, 1971 and 1976.

Williston, Samuel. *A Treatise on the Law of Contracts.* 3rd ed. Ed. Walter H. E. Jaeger. Mount Kisco, NY: Baker, Voorhees & Co., 1972.

Wolff, Herbert E. "OSHA Not Enough, Loss Control Also Needed." *The National Underwriter* (Property/Casualty), 15 Aug. 1975, p. 28.

The Wyatt Company. "Directors and Officers Liability and Fiduciary Liability Survey." *Summary Report*, 1975, p. 1.

Yannacone, Victor J. and Cohen, Bernard S. *Environmental Rights and Remedies.* Vol. 1, Sec. 4:6. New York: The Lawyers Co-operative Publishing Co., and San Francisco, CA: Bancroft-Whitney Co., 1972.

Zeldin, Marvin. *The Campaign for Cleaner Air.* New York: Public Affairs Pamphlet, 1973.

Index

451

D

E

F

M

N

U

V

W